HUMAN RIGHTS AND SOCIAL POLICY IN THE 21ST CENTURY

A history of the idea of human rights and comparison of the United Nations Universal Declaration of Human Rights with United States federal and state constitutions

Revised Edition

With a Collection of Essays Toward the
Creation of a Human Rights Culture

Joseph Wronka

Foreword by
David Gil

University Press of America,® Inc.
Lanham • New York • Oxford

Copyright © 1998 by
University Press of America,® Inc.
4720 Boston Way
Lanham, Maryland 20706

12 Hid's Copse Rd.
Cummor Hill, Oxford OX2 9JJ

Library of Congress Cataloging-in-Publication Data

Wronka, Joseph.
Human rights and social policy in the 21st century : a history of the
idea of human rights and comparison of the United Nations
Universal Declaration of Human Rights with the United States
federal and state constitutions / Joseph Wronka. —Rev. ed.
p.   cm.
Includes bibliographical references and index.
1. Human rights—History. 2. United Nations. General Assembly.
Universal Declaration of Human Rights. 3. Constitutional law—
United States. I. Title.
JC571.W96   1998   323'.09 —DC21   97-46436 CIP

ISBN 0-7618-1010-2 (cloth: alk. ppr.)
ISBN 0-7618-1011-0 (pbk: alk. ppr.)

♾™ The paper used in this publication meets the minimum
requirements of American National Standard for information
Sciences—Permanence of Paper for Printed Library Materials,
ANSI Z39.48—1984

To the memory of my father,
whose values are still alive
in this work

Experience should teach us to be most on our guard to protect liberty when the government's purposes are beneficent. Men born to freedom are naturally alert to repel invasion of their liberty by evil-minded rulers. The greatest dangers to liberty lurk in insidious encroachment by men of zeal, well-meaning but without understanding.

* Supreme Court Justice Louis Brandeis

CONTENTS

PART I

The Historical-Philosophical Context: A History of the Idea of Human Rights

CHAPTER ONE

INTRODUCTION - 1

CHAPTER TWO

A HISTORY OF THE IDEA OF HUMAN RIGHTS - 23

CHAPTER THREE

THE UNITED NATIONS AND BEYOND - 89

PART TWO

A Human Rights Analysis: Implications for Social Policy

CHAPTER FOUR

COMPARISON OF THE UNITED STATES CONSTITUTION
WITH THE UNIVERSAL DECLARATION OF
HUMAN RIGHTS - 133

CHAPTER EIGHT

SOCIAL ACTION IN THE STRUGGLE FOR HUMAN DIGNITY - 253

LIST OF TABLES

FOREWORD

By David G. Gil

Human needs are rooted in nature. they are products of biological evolution, and they affect, and are affected by, social and cultural evolution. Human needs are universal attributes of all people, regardless of time, place, age, sex, and race. the expression of human needs changes, however, over time, as a result of social and cultural processes.

Human rights, on the other hand, are not products of nature, but of social and cultural processes. Rights may be understood though, as related to nature, since they evolved over time as social responses to, and acknowledgments of, nature-based human needs of individuals and groups or classes of people.

Because of their different origins, human needs and human rights do not share the same history. While nature-based human needs are essentially constant and universal over time, socially constructed human rights, as abstract ideas and as concrete human experiences, have continuously changed within and among different human groups.

Dr. Wronka's book traces the history of the idea and practice of human rights from ancient times until the present. It identifies major sources and stages of this quest, which has culminated in this century in the unopposed adoption, by the United Nations, of a *Universal Declaration of Human Rights*. This Declaration is gradually being perceived as *customary international law* and as a standard by which the policies and practices of different societies ought to be guided and judged.

An important aspect of Dr. Wronka's study is a comparison of human rights as defined by the Universal Declaration on the one hand, and by the Constitutions of the United States and its fifty states on the other. Not surprisingly, this comparison reveals significant gaps between the standards of the Universal Declaration and those of our Constitutions, and the policies and practices based on them.

Troubled by the gaps in the standards of human rights revealed by his study, Dr. Wronka has recently initiated an action-research project aimed at:

a. expanding people's awareness of the Universal Declaration of Human Rights; and

b. using the Declaration as a frame of reference to assess progress toward the realization of internationally acknowledged human rights, draw attention to significant violations, and suggest avenues to overcome such violations.

Because of my involvement in Dr. Wronka's study of human rights, and in his subsequent action-research project, it is my hope, that this book will not only enrich readers intellectually, but will also motivate them to join local and global movements to promote human rights as defined by the Universal Declaration.

January 10, 1992

• Dr. David Gil is Professor of Social Policy and Director, Center for Social Change at the Heeler Graduate School, Brandeis University. He is also author of numerous articles and books on social policy, including *Unraveling Social Policy* and *Violence Against Children.*

PREFACE TO THE REVISED EDITION

It is perhaps fitting that a revised edition of *Human rights and social policy in the 21st century* should come out on the 50th anniversary of the Universal Declaration of Human Rights, a document of increasing moral and legal significance not only in the United States, but throughout the world. That document, increasingly referred to as *customary international law*, which countries ought to abide or risk international approbation, asserts with clarity and simplicity that every human, regardless of race, color, creed, class, or any "other status," has rights, not just to expression or religion, more commonly understood as rights, at least in the United States, but to shelter, security in old age, employment, and health care among others, which are generally less understood as rights.

In this International Decade for Human Rights Education (1995-2004), the Universal Declaration ought to be taught not only in college and graduate level courses, but also, in primary and secondary schools, thereby fulfilling the dreams of the Chairperson of the Drafting Committee of that document, an American, Eleanor Roosevelt that it be known among schoolchildren as much as the Declaration of Independence or the Bill of Rights. Its rights, which go beyond the U.S. Constitution's Bill of Rights, a beautiful, but, limited interpretation of human rights, need to be embedded in one's consciousness, until they are "lived". Only nonviolent and non-coercive means, however, will make these rights living realities, as research has consistently demonstrated that for values to endure, they must be chosen. Once chosen, values are difficult to change. In this regard, I see education as they key. At some point, these values "crystallize" into rights and become inserted in a community's legal codes, hopefully their constitutions, which can be the final arbiters of social policies.

As of the writing of this preface, the United States remains the only country in the world that has not ratified the Convention on the Rights of the

Child. That Convention, which reflects "timeless values," to quote Pope John Paul II and "the long train of declarations and covenants" as that Pope also put it, that followed the Universal Declaration, such as the Conventions on Civil and Political Rights (ratified by the United States in 1992), the Elimination of All Forms of Racial Discrimination (ratified in 1994) Against Torture (ratified in 1994), the Convention on the Elimination of Discrimination Against Women, and the Convention on Economic, Social, and Cultural Rights (both not ratified) also need to be part of the equation. These conventions, having the status of treaty, for instance, once ratified, according to the U.S. Federal Constitution in Article 6 "shall be the Supreme law of the land and the judges in every state shall be bound thereby." The UN Charter, also ratified by the United States in 1945, is considered a treaty. It asserts, for example, that the UN shall promote "higher standards of living, full employment, and conditions of economic and social progress and development (Article 55)."

While I do not doubt the importance of these treaties, the Universal Declaration, like the Declaration of Independence, which asserts "life, liberty, and equality," ought to become goals that we aspire in our struggle for social justice. To emphasize, its principles ought to become "lived," a phrase also used often by the internationalist and peace activist, Jane Addams. Once public sentiment is in accordance with the Universal Declaration, then its principles may attain the status of rights in our legal structure. For the sake of brevity, however, I must draw the line somewhere, having chosen in this book, therefore, to emphasize the Universal Declaration and the notion of customary international law, which, nevertheless, some scholars have asserted has a "loftier position" than the covenants. As the reader will see, issues are complex. Yet, I invite the reader's critical attitude. The basic point is merely that we need what can be called a "human rights culture" where rights in human rights instruments, particularly the Universal Declaration of Human Rights, the authoritative definition of human rights standards, are realities, thereby fulfilling human need.

Changes in this Revised Edition

This second edition, continues in the humanistic-phenomenological tradition, straying away as far as possible from "elitist language," as Eleanor Roosevelt had urged us decades ago, to language that an "educated lay person" could understand. Furthermore, I chose in this edition to limit my comparison of the Universal Declaration with state constitutions to only select ones, thereby, being able to include additional essays written over the years, and, for a lack of a better way of saying it, to "keep the price of the book down." I have been told on at least one occasion that I shouldn't "hark back" to the Universal Declaration and that "amendments to the U.S. Constitution" are too difficult.

If that is so, why did a recent editorial in the *Boston Globe* (November 23, 1997) speak about that "venerable document [the U.S. Constitution] ticketed for change," given a present "upsurge in proposed amendments" and an article in the *New York Times,* "Constitutions are the New Writer's Market" (November 30, 1997) which speaks of "the new era of constitution-writing" (November 30, 1997). Why not, therefore, have an amendment to the U.S. or state constitutions guaranteeing "special protections for children" or "security in old age," asserted in the Universal Declaration, thereby keeping with our promises of 1948.

Apart from the changes just mentioned, the first six chapters I essentially kept them the same as the historical and theoretic bases and implications of human rights for social policy (parts one and two) are "ageless". That is, one can never speak about contemporary human rights discussions, and attendant social policy implications in a historical and philosophical vacuum, which I had written about in the first edition. I did, however, add a section about the Native American influence, which despite my sympathies, I had previously "blindly" left out. I also updated recent regional developments, as well as, more recent developments, making note in particular of the Vienna Declaration and the new office of the UN High Commission of Human Rights, which appears very promising, especially given Ms. Mary Robinson's proclivities for economic, social, cultural, and solidarity rights..

The third part, a collection of essays toward the creation of a human rights culture is entirely new. These essays, of course, like any others are always in danger of merely being a "bunch of words," if they do not lead to social action in this struggle for human dignity, also the title of a course that I teach on policy implementation. Briefly, these essays' purposes, are to discuss ways to create a human rights culture, so that the social construct of "human rights" exists, not merely in the mind, but in the spirit (or heart), and body (or behavior), which is also consistent with the Humanics tradition of Springfield College.

To be sure, there was so much more that I wanted to include in this book, such as more on social action strategies, like the report on U.S. compliance on the economic and social rights of the Universal Declaration, which I had worked on with the commitment and enthusiasm of my students; actual experiential exercises which can assist in having human rights "lived"; an Action Alert to repeal the so-called Personal Responsibility and Work Opportunity Reconciliation Act of 1996 and a compendium perhaps of what others are doing to realize economic and social rights. But I suppose that is for another book and another time. To quote the "good book," to every thing there is a season.

Celebrating the Universal Declaration - A Flood of Hypocrisy?

To borrow a term from Noam Chomsky, I am afraid, however, that a "flood of hypocrisy" will arise as the world celebrates the birth of the Universal Declaration. While the United States might criticize the massacres of Tianamen square, certainly an event of horrendous proportion, what is this country to say about the longevity rate of 43 for African-American men in its inner cities, or its approximately 25% of children living in poverty? Was all the publicity surrounding Tiananmen square, nevertheless, an event of horrendous proportion, the final coup to denigrate an economic system that was generally cooperative and collective and replace it with the idea of a "free market"? Is the market free after all? At a recent conference in November, 1997, *Economic Security for the 21st Century: Building a Campaign for United Action* sponsored by a coalition of groups working for human rights and social justice at Northeastern University, it was asserted that 20 years ago, there were 6 billionaires in the United States; today there are approximately 200. Eighty percent of Americans also have a sense of insecurity not only in their everyday lives, just to make ends meet, but also in regards to their old age, and the future of their children. I ask you...is that justice?

While I do not pretend to answer all these questions, I hope that this revised edition, will at least provide some information for the reader's critical evaluation and possibly action. I am reminded here of the words of President Clinton inscribed on the walls of the entrance to the Holocaust Museum: "humility"... "not arrogance" will advance the cause of human rights.

On Waging Peace

It was also a U.S. President, John F. Kennedy, who once said that once a society glorified the peace maker as much as the warrior, then a society of peace might be possible. Perhaps, slowly, but surely, society is moving in this direction as, for example, Nobel Prize winners, like Jody Williams, who campaigned against Land Mines or Filipem Ximenes Belo and Jose Ramos-Horta of East Timor and, the recently deceased and beloved Mother Theresa of Calcutta known for her unending devotion to the "least of these" and, perhaps even Princess Diana, as some would argue, was also known in part for her good works, get front page press.

At the dawn of the 21st century, it is perfectably acceptable then to wage peace, which William James referred to as the moral equivalent of war. If people wish to engage in creating a human rights culture, the thrust of this revised edition, then, it is quite possible that such peace makers may "get some respect" in these troubled times. However, the task ahead and the challenges are great, as the global mal distribution of wealth is ever growing with its attendant complications: violence, genocide, extreme poverty, and environmental degradation.

Perhaps the time has also come to speak about world citizenship and world government. There are so many of us referring to ourselves as world citizens. What does this mean? What can we do? While world government, which would still be able to maintain a sense of cultural identity, may seem to many as "pipe dreaming," I am reminded first of the ancient injunction to cast one's net into deep waters. Why not? Who would have thought that Europe would be moving toward a single currency, the euro, and equity among European nations. Also, there is talk and rightly so, considering centuries of acknowledged European domination of Africa, about including at least some northern African countries, like Tunisia and Algeria in the equation. Once unthinkable the former Soviet Union and the United States, now allies, have the potential to truly create a new social and international order, which the Universal Declaration, asserts in Article 28 as a necessity to realize human rights for all. International distributive justice can become a reality. With the invention of gunpowder, who would have thought that in the Second World War one bomb would destroy an entire city in a flash and that in 1997 one submarine would carry more firepower than was released during World War II? Many had such dreams, which became horrible realities. Often state governments, insisting that the lines separating their nations from others remain in tact, spend billions in arms to maintain a so called "balance of power," a moving, but faulty, metaphor indeed. Instead why not spend resources on human need? Are we still so socialized into believing in the inevitability of war that we fail to wage peace?

Some Acknowledgments

Finally, I want to acknowledge in this second edition all my students in the School of Social Work at Springfield College who have challenged my thinking and continued to teach me. Their struggles, juggling family life, studies, and often full-time work are just a few evidences of their commitment. I would like to thank in particular Vaughn Harding, Jennifer Markens, Sandra Lemlin, Celeste Mattingly, Neal O'Kefe, Anita Minkin, William Kuehn, and Wendy Wilcoxen for assisting me in some of my human rights work. I know there were and continue to be other students who are silently waging peace and doing other things to create a human rights culture. While in my weakness I may have not mentioned you, please know that, while weak words, I appreciate your commitment, which I have often found exhilarating.

Dr. Francine Vecchiolla, Dean of this School of Social Work deserves mention not only for her commitment and administrative skills, but for her support during the arduous tenure process. To Dr.'s Joan Grannucci-Lesser,

Ann Roy, and Lirio Negroni, I also must say thank you for your support. Dr. Mulugetta Agonafer of the School of Human Services has further taught me about the ravages of international distributive injustice. Dr. Malvina Rau, Vice-President of the college also merits praise for her support not only for some of my human rights work, but for her commitment to social justice in general. I also want to thank Dr. William Sullivan and the Graduate Research Council for some of their early monetary support. I mustn't also forget our library staff, in particular Sherry Sochrin, William Kudlay and William Stetson who have been most gracious not only in helping my students, but also doing their best to order human rights materials. I must also thank Noam Chomsky for offering to give helpful criticism to some of my work. Dr. Antonin Wagner of the University of Zurich, School of Social Work, also deserves mention for his support and insights. Garry Davis, President of the World Citizen Foundation, also deserves mention, not only for his commitment, but also for his continued enthusiasm and hard work to promote the idea of world citizenship, despite what appears insurmountable odds. It goes without saying that I wish to acknowledge once again Dr. David Gil of Brandeis, "sounding board" for my thesis and now for his continuing inspiration and commitment, and support of my efforts. I also do not wish to forget the other members of my thesis committee: Dr.'s Jack Backman, Gordon Fellman, and James Callahan as well as Philip Alston, a human rights scholar and activist of international stature, whom I studied with nearly ten years ago. I was most fortunate to have worked and studied with "the best".

Family, of course, however one defines it, is what makes all things possible. In addition to my mother, brother, John and my sister, Joan, who have always "been there," my wife, my friend and partner, Barbara, whom I have told knows and lives the secret and true meaning of life, continues to be with me as I am often "lost" in a lot of pies and despite what can I say, but my "many flaws" to borrow a self-descriptive term from Nelson Mandela, who, over the years, has served as a model of commitment for me. Then, in the middle of it all, while she too must juggle work and family, nevertheless, will often find time to help, when as often occurs some, if not many, of these pies get lost. Her intellectual insights continue to be sources of inspiration and encouragement. Watching our children, Brendan, Christopher, and Carolyn grow and, among other things, observing their antics with the newest addition to our family, a golden retriever, whom my six year old affectionately calls "The Boo" continue to give my work and my life, which are really one and the same, unfathomable meaning.

Joseph Wronka

December 1, 1997

PREFACE

A few years ago, while traveling on my snowmobile in the Alaskan Arctic, I noticed that in the dead of winter the Chukchi sea was melting. this thawing occurred in not one, but two consecutive winters, due perhaps to increasing global industrial pollution. An Inupiaq Eskimo friend told me that warming trends in the middle of winter were a rare occurrence, rarer still to occur in two consecutive winters. Other friends told me that in the 1950s and 1960s they had become "radioactive" because they ate caribou, which feasted on lichen contaminated by radioactive fallout from Atomic tests. Dentists, according to one person, had merely to place a non-exposed film in front of a person's teeth to visualize an x-ray!

At the turn of the twentieth century, surely something is wrong. today, for instance, in the United States, which has the world's largest per capita prison population, one in four children is born into poverty, 3 million people are homeless, and 35 million citizens lack any type of health insurance (Nelson-Pallmeyer, 1992). Worldwide, the maldistribution of wealth between the developed and developing countries has accelerated.

On the positive side, the recent celebration of the 200th anniversary of the United States Constitution's Bill of Rights, witnessed a renewed commitment to many civil and political rights which Americans basically enjoy, like freedoms of religion, the press, and speech. The Commonwealth of Independent States, previously the Soviet Union, released, by most accounts, thousands of political prisoners from its Gulag.

A fortuitous occurrence in the United States was the *Filartiga v. Pena* (1980) decision which ruled against a Paraguayan official for the torture and death of a seventeen-year old boy, Joelita Filartiga. This hideous act occurred, not in the United States, but Paraguay. The judges declared that the United States had jurisdiction to try that case, ruling that the prohibition against torture is a violation of customary international law, "as evidenced and defined by the Universal Declaration of Human Rights" (630 F.2d 884-885).

The United Nations (1985) has referred to the Universal Declaration as the "authoritative definition" of human rights standards. World leaders, like Pope John Paul II (1979) have praised that document, declaring it, for example, as a "milestone on the long and difficult path of the human race." Using the Universal Declaration of Human Rights, which the United States signed and the UN General Assembly endorsed with no dissenting vote on December 10, 1948, as the standard of comparison therefore, this book compares all United States' federal and state constitutions with its principles. Because human rights discussions cannot take place in an historical philosophical vacuum, it also examines the history of the idea of human rights. Finally, it looks at the implications of this analysis for social policy.

This book suggests that, in the twenty-first century the Universal Declaration of Human Rights should be the primary ethical and legal gauge of human rights standards. Human rights standards throughout the world ought to be expanded throughout the world to include not only civil and political rights, but also economic, social, and cultural guarantees, such as rights to health care, employment, education, and shelter. they also include the "new" solidarity rights which emphasize duties to the community and intergovernmental cooperation, indispensable to such basic human rights as peace and a clean environment.

In addition, social policies, often equated with social welfare programs, need to be expanded to include effective ways to match human needs with all resources that can be made available. Human needs must be transformed into legally mandated rights in order for society to effectively distribute these resources.

Should the reader read only this Preface and the Universal Declaration of Human Rights found at the end of Chapter One and the inform others about the existence of this document as the universal expression of human rights, then I would be satisfied. Should the reader desire further knowledge about the origins and debates leading up to the adoption of the Declaration and how the Federal Constitution and his or her state measure up[to that document, then he or she may wish to read further. While I have concentrated upon the United States, I hope that individuals will compare constitutional documents of other countries with the Universal Declaration. Then, working together we may be able to effect positive social change in ways that create a more humane and socially just world.

Joseph Wronka

January 20, 1992
Arlington, Massachusetts

ACKNOWLEDGMENTS

I want to first acknowledge David Gil, whose insights for the creation of a just society, have inspired me throughout my career at the Heller School. I would like also to recognize the members of my dissertation committee, Jack Backman, Director of the Backman Center for Social Justice at the University of Massachusetts and formerly Massachusetts State Senator and Chair of the Senate Committee on Human Services and Elderly Affairs; James Callahan, Acting Dean of the Heller School; and Gordon Fellman, Professor of Sociology at Brandeis for their meticulous reading of my dissertation and constructive suggestions which have assisted in the completion of this book. I am especially thankful for Jack Backman's gracious contribution of his legal expertise.

Appreciation must also go to Philip Alston, presently Professor of Law and Director, Centre for Advanced Legal Studies at Australian National University and formerly Assistant Professor of International Law at Tufts University. While in the Boston area, he was most generous with his time and willingness to entertain my questions about human rights. Noteworthy also is Richard Parker, Professor of Constitutional Law at Harvard University, who was more than helpful in assisting me in my understanding of constitutional law.

Other individuals have also contributed by graciously consenting to answer more specific questions regarding many of the issues related to human rights and social policy. Ms. Stamatapoulou, Director of the Liaison Office for the Commission of Human Rights at the U.N. offices in New York City immediately comes to mind. She always found time from an extremely busy schedule to discuss via telephone some of my concerns and send relevant materials. Other persons, particularly Jonathan Fine, Executive Director of Physicians for Human Rights; Detlev Vagts, Professor of International Law at Harvard and Associate Reporter for the *Restatement (Third);* Jordan Paust, Professor of Law, University of Houston; Lance Leibman, Professor of Law and Social Policy at Harvard; Professors of Social Policy, Deborah Stone, Janet Giele, and Norman Kurtz of the Heller School at Brandeis; Rolf Von Eckartsberg, Professor of Phenomenology at Duquesne University; Andreas Teuber, Professor of Philosophy at Brandeis; Peter Galie, Professor of Constitutional Law at Canisius College; Howard Zinn, author of *A People's History of the United States*; Philip Harvey, author of *Securing the Right to Employment;* Eric Berney, Professor of Constitutional Law at Boston College; Professors Henry Steiner, Chair of the Human Rights Program and Jack Tobin, Professor International Human Rights Law, at Harvard; Laurie Wiseberg, Editor of the *Human Rights Internet Reporter* at the University of Ottawa; and Richard Caputo, Professor of Social Policy at the University of Pennsylvania were also more than accommodating in their willingness to volunteer much needed information to assist in the completion of this research project.

In addition, I would like to commend the staff at Brandeis University's Library. Ralph Szymczak and Virginia Massey-Burzio were particularly helpful in assisting me through a maze of legal, international, and policy documents. Mary Del Grosso is also noteworthy for literally, working overtime while graciously aiding me in rather complicated computer searches. Karen Walz, the secretary for Harvard's Human Rights Program, was also most considerate in directing me to available resources.

I also want to comment upon the concern and patience that the Production Editor for University Press of America, Ms. Helen Hudson, has shown in producing this book. I was most fortunate to work with someone who shares my enthusiasm for the advancement of human rights.

I would like to also acknowledge all my teachers, as well as, students, too many to mention, whose insights have augmented my interests for a just society based on the fulfillment of basic human needs and human rights. The commitment of all my friends and colleagues in the 29th PhD Class at the Heller School also deserves mention. I am also appreciative of my friends in the Fairbanks Chapter of Amnesty International for their tireless dedication to human rights, a "cause that knows no frontiers." They have also taught me that, although human rights is a serious undertaking, common commitments can make such a project exciting and lively at the same time.

Writing this work was not without its obstacles. Individuals, for instance, commented that only a sophisticated knowledge of certain disciplines like ethics, political philosophy, law, or history could tackle human rights issues. While I have some sympathy with those who advocate the priority of a specific discipline to deal with a particular social issue, I think that all specialties may have limitations which can obscure basic phenomenon. The purpose of human rights advocacy, for example, is to advance the fulfillment of human needs. Legal scholars, political scientists, sociologists, psychologists, and other professions can all provide valuable contributions. No field should have a monopoly on human rights work.

There were also those who commented that social policy should deal with only specific groups, like children, the elderly, or the disabled. I think that the only criteria to provide for others' needs is their "humanity." Certainly, some individuals like children may have "more"needs than others, requiring, therefore, special protections. Yet, while working toward the fulfillment of children's needs, society can still choose to concomitantly work for the satisfaction of other basic human wants, specific to other populations, like the disabled or various disenfranchised minority groups. Without this commitment to *all human beings*, society may rob Peter to pay Paul, which may result in the endowment of one group at the expense of another.

My family, including, my mother; brother, John; and sister, Joan have also provided much encouragement to complete what I felt was a formidable, yet worthwhile task. I also want to acknowledge Barbara, my wife, companion, and intellectual partner, not only for her love, but also for her invaluable comments throughout the development of this book. Then, there are our children, Brendan, Christopher, and Carolyn who have given this work an unfathomable significance.

Finally, I want once again to acknowledge my father to whom I have dedicated this work. As a child, I can remember him commenting upon the injustices he perceived in the world, including the imprisonment of some of our relatives in concentration camps during World War II. His concern for the plight of all the unfortunate instilled in me a concern that continues to this day. It is my hope that I can impart a similar concern in my children.

PART ONE

THE HISTORICAL-PHILOSOPHICAL CONTEXT

A HISTORY OF THE IDEA OF

HUMAN RIGHTS

CHAPTER ONE

▥▥▥▥▥▥▥▥▥▥▥▥▥▥▥▥▥▥▥▥▥▥▥▥▥▥▥

INTRODUCTION

The objectives of this book are to analyze the extent of human rights principles, as defined by the United Nations Universal Declaration of Human Rights, in United States' federal and state constitutions and to identify the implications of this analysis for social policy in the twenty-first century.

Because human rights discussions cannot take place in a philosophical vacuum, a subsidiary purpose is to examine the history of the idea of human rights. Although human rights traditions are often unarticulated, all human rights standards have historical and philosophical underpinnings. Because the Universal Declaration is a philosophical and political compromise, a knowledge of the historical-philosophical dimension is necessary to illuminate many of the traditions which it reflects. This study, therefore, will trace the origin and evolution of the idea of human rights from antiquity to contemporary times.

Whereas this book is basically an "intelligent layperson's" reading (i.e. a "people's reading") of the United States Constitution and all state constitutions in comparison with the Universal Declaration, it also considers United States

Supreme Court interpretations of two phrases: "to promote the general welfare" and "to establish justice." I chose those two principles because they seem to speak to the welfare of *all*, rather than the rights and liberties of the individual, which appear to be the fundamental rights asserted in the Federal Constitution. To me, the words "general welfare," conjure up images of adequate health care, housing, and employment opportunities. When I think of "justice," furthermore, I imagine social and economic justice where there is a fair distribution of wealth and people have the of the Court in *Filartiga*, moreover, seemed hopeful that other internationally opportunity to lead decent lives. My concerns here, however, are how the Supreme Court has interpreted these two phrases.

Because rights in state constitutions must be consistent with decisions of the United States Supreme Court, this investigation will also include Supreme Court rulings which have guaranteed rights stated in the Universal Declaration and generally embraced by American jurisprudence. Such rights include, for example, the right to travel (*Shapiro v. Thompson*, 1969) and the right to mrry (*Loving v. Virginia*, 1967). Although the Federal Constitution does not explicitly state these rights, the Supreme Court has chosen to guarantee these fundamental freedoms. I think that it would be beyond the scope of this book, however, to consider state supreme court decisions of rights not established by the United States Supreme Court, although such an investigation might be a viable future study.

Even though this research project deals in part, therefore, with legal analysis, it is essentially an interdisciplinary approach to the phenomenon of human rights integrating insights from history, philosophy, religion, and the social sciences. As human rights scholar Philip Alston (1985) states, discussions of human rights do not necessitate thorough legal analyses: "We should never assume that talking about human rights requires us at all times to get into deeply legalistic analyses. Voluntary acceptance of such a positivistic strait-jacket will cause us all too often to find ourselves at the mercy of the vagaries of legal interpretation" (p. 512).

Consequently, this study departs from more traditional methods of studying human rights which have primarily embraced a legal perspective (Pritchard, 1989). It also departs from a more conventional way of studying constitutional law which, following the lead in *Marbury v. Madison*, tends to emphasize the importance of Supreme Court interpretations. While I do not discount the importance of these approaches, my aim is essentially to study the phenomenon of human rights as a multifaceted phenomenon (i.e. having historical-philosophical foundations and amenable to other than legal interpretations), rather than from the viewpoint of any particular discipline.

My concern, therefore, is primarily to identify constitutional rights that have good "face validity," that is, can be recognized by a general consensus of people. The Universal Declaration was written to be simple, clear, and easily understood by all laypeople. In like manner, I think that United States' constitutions ought to state succinctly a person's fundamental rights. A reading, for example, of Article 25 of the Universal Declaration reveals: "Everyone has the right to a standard of living adequate for the health and well-being of himself and his family, including food, clothing, housing and medical care." This statement definitively asserts, for example, health care as a human right. The question that this book will pose is whether there are rights in United States' constitutions which correspond to rights as described in the Universal Declaration.

Rights that can be read by every person in United States' constitutions would seem to create a more definite sense of an individual's entitlements. Clearly stated rights should also facilitate the banding together of individuals to collectively assert their rights definitively and forcefully. That way, the "will of the people" can indeed be the basis of governmental social policy. The rubric of human rights can thus help achieve a match between human needs and available resources (Gil, 1990a) a basic criterion of good social policy.

RELEVANCE OF THIS RESEARCH PROJECT

I chose the United Nations Universal Declaration of Human Rights as the standard of comparison because it is considered customary international law (Humphrey, 1976; *Filartiga v. Pena*, 1980; Vasak, 1982; Buergenthal, 1988; Rosensweig, 1988; Kiss, 1988; Lillich, 1989, 1990; Reismam, 1990). John Humphrey, for example, first director of the U.N. Human Rights division stated:

> The Declaration is now part of the customary law of nations and therefore is binding all states. The Declaration has become what some nations wished it to be in 1948: the universally accepted interpretation and definition of the human rights left undefined by the Charter. (p. 529)

Human rights scholars Thomas Buergenthal and W. Michael Reisman have also respectively asserted: "Today, few international lawyers would deny that the Declaration is a normative instrument that creates legal obligations for the member states of the U.N." (p. 29) and "The Universal Declaration of Human Rights, a document then describing itself as 'a common standard of achievement'...[is] now accepted as declaratory of customary international law" (p. 867).

In *Filartiga v. Pena,* furthermore, a United States court ruled against Pena, a military commander, for torturing and murdering a high school student,

Joelita Filartiga in Paraguay! The court composed of Federal Chief Justice Feinberg of the Second Circuit and Circuit Judges Kaufman and Kearse, reached the following conclusion:

> Official torture is now prohibited by the law of nations. This prohibition is clear and unambiguous and admits no distinction between treatment of aliens and citizens....This prohibition has become part of customary international law, as evidenced and defined by the Universal Declaration of Human Rights. (630 F.2d 884-885)

Since that ground breaking decision, other suits based on the "Filartiga principle," as it has become known, have been applied to government officials allegedly participating in acts of torture from Chile, Ethiopia, Guatemala, and the Philippines. Most recently, a Massachusetts court declared General Hector Gramajo, a former Minister of Defense in Guatemala, in default in two Filartiga suits against him (Rohter, 1991).

In addition to the prohibition against torture in *Filartiga v. Pena*, other human rights have also achieved customary international law status as stated in the *Restatement (Third) of the Foreign Relations Law of the United States*[1]. At present, genocide, slavery, murder, the causing of disappearances, prolonged arbitrary detention, systematic racial discrimination, and consistent patterns of gross violations of internationally recognized human rights are now identified as violations of customary international law. These rights emanate not only from the Universal Declaration, but also from human rights treaties signed by the United States which pertain to slavery, the political rights of women, the law of war and refugees, and genocide (Lillich, 1989). The Universal Declaration, however, is the first all inclusive statement on human rights which has, in part, attained legal status in United States courts. It appears only a matter of time before other human rights recognized in the Universal Declaration become part of customary international law. The opinion accepted human rights may be forthcoming in United States jurisprudence: "International law confers fundamental rights upon all people vis-a-vis their own governments...the ultimate scope of those rights will be subject for continuing refinement and elaboration" (630 F.2d 884-885).

Human rights scholar and President of the Procedural Aspects of International Law Institute, Richard Lillich (1990) in the *Harvard Human Rights Journal* has also declared: "Arguments that other human rights now are part of customary international law can be expected to be made with increasing frequency" (p. 73), adding that "Numerous litigants and judges already have invoked the Declaration" (p. 77). He perceives the Universal Declaration as significantly impacting the United States legal system indirectly, by assisting

U.S. courts in the establishment of rules of customary international human rights law.[2]

Assuming that eventually the entire Universal Declaration becomes customary international law, therefore, this investigation will point out discrepancies between that document and United States' constitutions in order to suggest that these constitutions concur with increasingly accepted international standards. Should none of United States' constitutions assert, for example, the right to security in old age (as in Article 25 of the Universal Declaration), a recommendation would be to incorporate this right in these constitutions.

Incorporation of universally accepted standards of human rights as expressed in the Universal Declaration in United States' constitutions may also have important implications for social policy development. For instance, one study by Braddock, Hemp, Fujiura, Bachelder, & Mitchell (1989) states that the most significant variable relevant to social policies in connection with public expenditures for mental retardation and developmental disabilities was "civil rights innovativeness" which included the modification of constitutional and other legal documents. Innovative states, for example, which were "early adopter[s] of civil rights statutes in public accommodations, fair housing and fair employment" (p. 28), exhibited statistically significant differences in expenditures for mental retardation and developmental disabilities, than non-innovative states.

Writing about states that have an equal rights amendment (ERA) in their constitutions, another investigation by MacManus and Van Hightower (1989) acknowledges that states with ERA amendments in their constitutions do not appear any more progressive in implementation of statutes protecting women's rights than non-ERA states. They cited judges, local law enforcement officers, certain prosecuting attorneys and specific social service agency personnel as impediments to the implementation of constitutional and statutory law. Despite these difficulties, however, the authors concede that good laws are a "first step" (p. 273).

There are also some constitutions, such as in Sweden and Cuba which emphasize certain economic and social rights, including the rights to work, to shelter, to education, and to health care. In those countries health care, for example, is paid for by taxes and available to everyone. In the United States, which does not contain this right in its Federal Constitution, approximately 30 million people do not have health insurance. In Sweden, furthermore, the literacy rate is "virtually 100%" and in Cuba the rate is "96%." In the United States where the Federal Constitution does not guarantee the right to education, "adult 'functional' literacy may not exceed 85%" (*Britannica World Data Annual*, 1991, p. 728).

Recently, furthermore, the Supreme Courts of Montana, Kentucky, and Texas (Suro, 1990) struck down their states' school financing systems, citing "unconstitutional disparities" in what is spent for rich and poor districts. The State Supreme Court of New Jersey has also insisted that New Jersey "provide enough aid to poor districts to allow them to provide a 'thorough and efficient' education as guaranteed by the State Constitution" ("Spend Fairly," 1990). Partly because state courts are often influenced by rulings in other states, presently poorer districts in New York, citing unconstitutional disparities, are challenging state educational aid as unequal (Verhovek, 1991).

In addition, Rosenbaum (1989, pp. 119-20)) has documented a case, *Boehm II v. Superior Court* (178 Cal. App. 3d 496, 1986), which sidestepped California's state constitution in championing economic rights in American jurisprudence. In Boehm, the plaintiffs contended that welfare relief payments for food and shelter did not adequately "relieve and support" that county's indigent population as required by state law. The court agreed that the grant reduction was arbitrary and capricious. The judge's opinion referred specifically to Article 25 of the Universal Declaration of Human Rights in stating that "it defies common sense and all notions of human dignity" to exclude clothing, transportation, and medical care from the minimum subsistence allowance.

The above examples attest, therefore, to the leverage that constitutions, even the Universal Declaration itself, have upon social policy. Today, the idea of human rights is also widely accepted among the general populace (Henkin, 1978; Drinan, 1987; "A Movement for Humanity," 1990; "Trials and Error," 1991). A recent editorial in *The Boston Globe* has stated, for example: "Today's anniversary of the 1948 Universal Declaration of Human Rights, observed as International Human Rights Day, celebrates the gains that have been made and serves as an occasion to renew dedication to a cause that knows no frontiers ("A Movement for Humanity," 1990).

Along with this concern for human rights, there is also a resurgence of interest in state constitutions among governmental bodies and people in general in order to secure a person's fundamental freedoms (Brennan, 1977; Collins, 1985; Friedelbaum, 1988; Galie, 1988; Marks & Cooper, 1988; Hennessey, 1990; Murphy, 1991). According to former Supreme Court Justice William Brennan (1977), for example:

> Numerous state courts...have already extended to their citizens, via
> state constitutions, greater protections than the Supreme Court has
> held are applicable under the federal Bill of Rights....More state
> courts are construing state constitutional counterparts of provisions
> of the Bill of Rights as guaranteeing citizens of their states even
> more protection than the federal provisions....This is surely an

important and highly significant development for our constitutional
jurisprudence....It would be most unwise these days not...to
raise...state constitutional questions....Every believer in our concept
of federalism, and I am a devout believer, must salute this development in our state courts. (pp. 489-501)

This book, therefore, should have relevance not only because the rubric of
human rights appears important to the development of socially just policies, but
also because it is consistent with contemporary concerns for both human rights
and states' rights. The results of this study may be able to help harness the
public's present enthusiasm for these two concerns in ways that may effectively
modify constitutions to address present needs. There are, for example,
approximately three million homeless people in the United States. Perhaps this
is the time that public sentiment can provide the thrust to modify constitutions
in order that they clearly state that people have the right to housing (as in
Article 25 of the Universal Declaration). First, it may be necessary, however,
to point out which constitutions do not contain this right. Providing for this
right may eventually lead to decent housing for all.

PERSONAL MOTIVATIONS IN THIS RESEARCH PROJECT

Probably the most important influence in pursuing this topic is my
acculturation in the Christian faith. I was baptized and raised Catholic.
Although I have largely abandoned the numerous rituals and church
obligations of Catholicism, its essences are still very much alive for me. Such
essences include the performance of good works for the "least of these
brethren" and the fundamental injunction to "love one another, lest we die."
During my adolescence I frequented *The Catholic Worker* in the Bowery
section of New York City. My attendance at their Friday night meetings and
association with various members of that community reinforced my beliefs in
the real essence of Catholicism. Rather than stressing the need to attend Mass
or to receive sacraments, individuals there were intent upon organizing against
military expenditures in Vietnam which they perceived were at the expense of
economic and social rights, such as the rights to health care, education, and
housing.

To this day, I remember my interview with David Miller, one of the first
draft card burners in the 1960s, who was then apparently in hiding from the
FBI at *The Catholic Worker*. Because the interview was "too controversial,"
my high school refused to print it in the school newspaper. Nevertheless,
Miller's belief that his act of civil disobedience was in strict accordance with his
conscience and Catholic principles had a tremendous impact on me. In short,
my experiences at *The Catholic Worker* strongly reinforced my beliefs in the

essences of Catholicism. At present, I find that the concept of human rights speaks directly to the religion of my childhood.

Another reason for pursuing a research project on human rights and its relation to social policy is my background in existential-phenomenological psychology. The basic point of this approach is to question assumptions of methods within disciplines or the discipline itself in order to be open to a phenomenon, thereby transcending the encapsulation of a particular approach. In many psychology experiments, for example, the experimenter must first operationalize variables. Then, by manipulation and control of these variables, he or she attempts to predict behavior. The phenomenologist feels, however, that the phenomenon is dropped for manipulation and control. He or she may also question why it is important to predict behavior in the first place. Quantifying human phenomena, furthermore, such as friendship, love or happiness may distort the richness of lived experience. While existential-phenomenological psychology does not deny that quantification of human phenomena may have some validity, as an alternative it proposes more qualitative approaches such as description and reflection which appear more fruitful in understanding the structure of a phenomenon.

Similarly, in this work I am questioning some of the basic assumptions of research in human rights and constitutional law which seem to emphasize judicial interpretations and a legal perspective. I do not deny the validity of these approaches, yet I think that there are other ways to study the structure of this multifaceted phenomenon of human rights. An interrogation into the evolution of the idea of human rights and an "intelligent" reading of constitutions should provide a viable alternative.

Experiences in Europe and Alaska

From 1974 to 1975 I lived in Nice, France where I worked on a doctorate. Largely, because of a sudden death in my family, I was unable to continue my studies. My everyday encounters in France, however, enhanced my burgeoning interest in human rights.

I remember vividly viewing Stanley Kubrick's *Paths of Glory*, apparently forbidden to be shown in France for over a decade, yet finally released in 1975. In one scene, the French soldiers were advancing toward the enemy, crawling under barbed wire surrounded by bombs and fusillade. The audience was shocked. Nearly everyone was speaking loudly: *"Incroyable!* (Unbelievable!)....*Tu peux imaginer!* (Can you believe that!)....*Jamais! Jamais!* (Never, never again!). In a documentary on World War II, when a picture of Hitler appeared on the screen, the audience burst into loud hisses, boos, and curses such as I had never heard in the United States. Also, a German friend, upon learning about my Polish ancestry recounted rather angrily how Hitler's invaded the lesser armed and poorer country Poland. Teary-eyed, she recounted how Hitler's tanks fought Polish soldiers horseback, when they crossed the Polish border precipitating World War II.

With the Vietnam War still raging, I expressed my utter disappointment and shame that the United States continued with this war. But, to my astonishment, my French friends told me that Vietnam was nothing compared to the atrocities committed by their government! They then described the numerous accounts of government sponsored torture during the Algerian War and their early involvement in Vietnam, and other forms of structural violence, such as excessive taxes in the French colonies, which contributed to the poverty and misery of millions of people. They were as ashamed as I.

When the Vietnam War ended in the Spring of 1975, I noticed numerous signs throughout Nice which read typically "Victory for the Communist Party" or "American Imperialism Smashed." While I was opposed to the War, I felt, nevertheless, that Solzhenitsyn's *Gulag* was an accurate depiction of a totalitarian and corrupt communist system. If Vietnam were a victory for communism, surely it was a defeat for very basic freedoms of speech, of the press, and free expression in general. Yet, I thought, if the United States had "won" that war, would Vietnam then have the gross mal distributions of wealth and the sprawling urban ghettos which existed in the United States?

My purpose in relating these few accounts is not to overburden the reader with unnecessary travelogues of a distant land. Rather, it is to point out that the consciousness of the people in Europe, at least as I experienced it, concerning war and human rights in general, seemed so different from what I was accustomed to in the United States. It elicited in me numerous questions.

Why did France, the home of Voltaire, Montesquieu, and Rousseau, proud defenders of free speech and inquiry, censor a film which was primarily about certain abuses in the French military? How did France and the United States in the wake of the atrocities of World War II, escape international disapproval of such horrors as torture? What is more important, the right to express oneself freely or the right to work and to be free from poverty? Finally, considering the devastating effects not only of war, but also of structurally violent social policies which violate the human rights of millions, how can these destructive policies be prevented? This book, it is my hope, may provide some answers to these questions.

One final reason for choosing this project on human rights derives from my experience with Native Americans when I lived in Alaska from 1981 to 1987. I held a number of positions there, one of which was to develop a paraprofessional counselor training program in the northwest arctic region of Alaska which has a predominantly Inupiaq Eskimo population.

As I became increasingly involved with the development of that program, I realized more and more the intrusion of my Western values upon the self-determination of these and other Native Americans. One-to-one counseling, for example, though applicable for a white middle class professional, seemed unacceptable to a culture that believed in more traditional and communal ways of healing.

I felt, furthermore, that the many fragmented social programs which existed supposedly for the benefit of the Eskimo actually eroded his/her sense of human dignity. While western foods were purchased with food stamps, for example, the Eskimo was slowly abandoning a cultural tradition that emphasized a subsistence lifestyle of hunting and fishing. As some Native American students woefully remarked: "They make life too easy for us now."

Overall, I sensed that western culture was depriving the Inupiaq Eskimo of their human rights. While a barrage of social service providers and social policy analysts streamed into Rural Alaska in the last thirty years, the alcoholism, suicide, domestic violence, and rape rates remained constant. The suicide rate, for example, among Native Americans through at least 1983 was approximately ten times the average for white Americans (Schaeffer, 1983).

My experiences in Alaska, in addition to my academic background in phenomenology, forced me to evaluate the faulty application of well-intentioned social policies. This critical appraisal led me to believe that the denial of the Eskimos' solidarity rights, including the right to self-determination, (i.e. self and group empowerment) slowed the advancement of the quality of life among indigenous peoples. By at least bringing the issues of solidarity to light in this book, I believe that social policies affecting indigenous peoples might be more humane and, in the long run, more self-empowering.

After moving from the Arctic, I settled in Fairbanks. There, I volunteered as Group Coordinator for the Fairbanks Chapter of Amnesty International. Whereas I understood the importance of Amnesty International's mandate to work exclusively for the release of political prisoners and for the humane treatment of the accused, I became increasingly aware that the scope of its work was extremely limiting. At one meeting of state group coordinators, I suggested that the United States adopt a more humble approach in regard to "shaming" the Soviet Union to release its political prisoners. I thought that we could, for example, acknowledge poverty and violence in our ghettos and urge that we both work together to advance human rights for all. I was told in no uncertain terms to "keep the United States problems out of this."

Moreover, the many letters which I had written to heads of state on behalf of the release of these political prisoners, for example, referred to their incarceration as a violation of the Universal Declaration of Human Rights. When I read that document, I could not understand why Amnesty International did not also investigate the abrogation of other rights also described, such as the rights to housing, health care, education, and favorable conditions of work.

While I acknowledged the importance of Amnesty's work, the constricted approach of this major human rights organization, nevertheless, troubled me. This work is an attempt to extend my concerns for human rights beyond the range of a major human rights organization.

REVIEW OF THE LITERATURE

A major impetus for this study is the dearth of literature which compares the Universal Declaration of Human Rights with United States' constitutions. Concerning rights in the United States Constitution, I think that it is already widely recognized that this document emphasizes civil and political rights, such as freedom of speech, the press, and religion. The question this book will pose is to what extent the Constitution conforms not only to the civil and political guarantees as described in the Universal Declaration, but to all of the rights described therein. While researching the literature, therefore, I found general statements about the exemplary character of the United States Constitution in regards to civil and political rights (e.g. Goldstein, 1987), but no actual comparison with the Universal Declaration.

The only analysis which compares explicit statements on rights in state constitutions with the Universal Declaration is Galie (1988a). He states that New York has the right to the care and support of the needy; Florida, Montana, New Jersey and New York have the right to bargain collectively; Georgia, North Dakota, and South Dakota have the right to work; Montana and Rhode Island have environmental rights; and a number of states have provisions for free education and protection of the handicapped. Galie acknowledges that this list is illustrative and not exhaustive (personal communication, April 23, 1990).

Other resources, although not referring specifically to the Universal Declaration, list rights mentioned in state constitutions. Collins (1985) analyzes a select core of rights in state constitutions: equality of treatment, gender discrimination, religion, freedom of speech and the press, self-incrimination, sentencing and treatment of arrested or confined persons, administration of justice, imprisonment for debt, right to possess arms, and right to private property.

Collins compares various models of statements of these rights in state constitutions. Concerning private property, for example, the author notes four models which express this right: Model 1 -"No part of a man's property shall be taken from him, or applied to public uses, without his own consent, or that of the representative body of the people (NH, Part First, Art. 12); Model 2 - "The property of no person shall be taken for public use without just compensation therefor (WIS, Art. I, S13); Model 3 - "Private property shall not be taken for private use unless by consent of the owner, except for private ways of necessity, and except for reservoirs, drains, flumes or ditches on or across the lands of others, for agricultural, mining, milling, domestic or sanitary purposes (CO, Art. II,S14) and Model 4 - "Private property shall not be taken or damaged for public use without just compensation as provided by law. Such compensation shall be determined by a jury as provided by law (II, Art I, S15).

He then lists states which contain the models in their constitutions for all of the rights stated above. Thus, for example, only Delaware, Kentucky and New Hampshire ascribe to Model 1. The author admits, moreover, that his inventory of rights is selective and not conclusive of all the rights in state constitutions.

The most extensive listing of rights is Sachs's (1980) *50-State Index. The author offers an alphabetical listing of all of the rights Constitutions of the United States: National and State - Fundamental Liberties and Rights*, in all of the state constitutions from "Accused, Rights of" to "Writ of Habeas Corpus."

Whereas this list is extensive and not illustrative like Galie and Collins, I find it limiting first because it is dated. Furthermore, it does not include many of the statements in the Universal Declaration which are not easily amenable to a strict classification. Article 29(1) of the Universal Declaration states, for example: "Everyone has duties to the community in which alone the free and full development of his personality is possible." Sachs's survey of rights does not answer the question of the extent of duties in state constitutions. How might one also list Article 28 of the Universal Declaration: "Everyone is entitled to a social and international order in which the rights and freedoms set forth in the Declaration can be fully realized"?

In addition, journal articles seem to refer only in general terms to rights in state constitutions. The *Harvard Law Review* (1982) states, for example: "State constitutions typically encompass a far broader range of concerns in far greater detail than does the lean Federal Constitution....Most state constitutional texts indicate an intent to limit the ability of government to interfere with property rights" (pp. 1355, 1482).

Authors such as Abrahamson (1987) also note some general historical and contemporary developments in state constitutions intimating certain rights in state constitutions. He states, for instance, that constitutions in the 1800's reflected problems with banking, corporations, local government and education. In the early to mid 1900s changes in state constitutions reflected reforms in labor and woman's suffrage. By the 1980s state constitutions reflected such concerns as race, gender discrimination, invasion of privacy, water and air pollution, and gambling.

It appears, therefore, that only a reading of *all* the most recent state constitutions in comparison with the Universal Declaration of Human Rights will compensate for the selectivity, limitations, and general statements which appear to comprise previous research in regard to rights elucidated in state constitutions.

There are numerous authors who address the history of the idea of human rights. I will incorporate many of their thoughts in the next section, A History of the Idea of Human Rights. These authors, however, seem to emphasize the historical development of civil and political rights. As Alston (1990) notes, "The literature on economic, social and cultural rights in US publications is meager at best....Given the paucity of serious scholarly analysis...of the issues pertaining to economic, social and cultural rights, a good starting point would be to encourage more sophisticated and sustained research in this regard" (p. 392). The only authors who devote some time to economic and social rights are Mower (1985) and Trubek (1985) commenting briefly, for example, upon Old Testament sayings and constitutions, such as in the Soviet Union which include these rights. Nevertheless, the main focus of their works is upon current day legal human rights developments. They do not systematically examine the evolution of these rights.

There does not appear as yet, therefore, an all inclusive study of the evolution of the idea of human rights which utilizes crucial notions of *all* human rights as expressed by the Universal Declaration.

My research on literature pertaining to the two clauses "to promote the general welfare" and "to establish justice," has revealed only Adler and Gorman (1975). Briefly, these authors mention two cases, *Steward Machine Co. v. Davis* (1937) and *Helvering v. Davis* (1937) which referred to the general welfare clause. In the former case, the Supreme Court used that clause to bolster a decision to provide for unemployment compensation; in the latter one it supported a decision to provide for old age pensions. At present, however, it appears that no research has analyzed in depth Supreme Court interpretations of these two clauses.

Now that I have related this book's objectives, the relevance of this work, my personal motivations, and the paucity of literature which approaches the idea of human rights from the perspectives of this book, it is necessary to first examine the history of the idea of human rights. After this inquiry, I will compare United States' constitutions with the Universal Declaration. Following this comparison, I will examine the implications of this analysis for social policy into the next century.

Although the Universal Declaration of Human Rights is often placed in the Appendix, for the sake of convenience and because of the pivotal importance of that document in this work, I have chosen to include it at the end of this Introduction. A reading of that document, at this point, should provide a fuller understanding of the subsequent historical-philosophical piece and comparison with select United States' constitutions.

THE UNIVERSAL DECLARATION OF HUMAN RIGHTS

Preamble

Whereas recognition of the inherent dignity and of the equal and inalienable rights of all members of the human family is the foundation of freedom, justice and peace in the world,

Whereas disregard and contempt for human rights have resulted in barbarous acts which have outraged the conscience of mankind, and the advent of a world in which human beings shall enjoy freedom of speech and belief and freedom from fear and want has been proclaimed as the highest aspiration of the common people,

Whereas it is essential, if man is not to be compelled to have recourse, as a last resort, to rebellion against tyranny and oppression, that human rights should be protected by the rule of law,

Whereas it is essential to promote the development of friendly relations between nations,

Whereas the peoples of the United Nations have in the Charter reaffirmed their faith in fundamental human rights, in the dignity and worth of human person and in the equal rights of men and women and have determined to promote social progress and better standards of life in larger freedom,

Whereas Member States have pledged themselves to achieve, in cooperation with the United Nations, the promotion of universal respect for the observance of human rights and fundamental freedoms,

Whereas a common understanding of these rights and freedoms is of the greatest importance for the full realization of this pledge,

Now, Therefore, The General Assembly Proclaims
This Universal Declaration of Human Rights

as a common standard of achievement for all peoples and all nations, to the end that every individual and every organ of society, keeping this Declaration constantly in mind, shall strive by teaching and education to promote respect for these rights and freedoms and by progressive measures, national and international, to secure their universal and effective recognition and observance, both among the peoples of Member States themselves and among the peoples of territories under their jurisdiction.

Article 1

All human beings are born free and equal in dignity and rights. They are endowed with reason and conscience and should act towards one another in a spirit of brotherhood.

Article 2

Everyone is entitled to all the rights and freedoms set forth in this Declaration, without distinction of any kind, such as race, color, sex, language, religion, political or other opinion, national or social origin, property, birth or other status.

Furthermore, no distinction shall be made on the basis of the political, jurisdictional or international status of the country or territory to which a person belongs, whether it be independent, trust, non-selfgoverning or under any other limitation of sovereignty.

Article 3

Everyone has the right to life, liberty and security of person.

Article 4

No one shall be held in slavery or servitude; slavery and the slave trade shall be prohibited in all their forms.

Article 5

No one shall be subjected to torture or to cruel, inhuman or degrading treatment or punishment.

Article 6

Everyone has the right to recognition everywhere as a person before the law.

Article 7

All are equal before the law and are entitled without any discrimination to equal protection of the law. All are entitled to equal protection against any discrimination in violation of this Declaration and against any incitement to such discrimination.

Article 8

Everyone has the right to an effective remedy by the competent national tribunals for acts violating the fundamental rights granted him by the constitution or by law.

Article 9

No one shall be subjected to arbitrary arrest, detention or exile.

Article 10

Everyone is entitled in full equality to a fair and public hearing by an independent and impartial tribunal, in the determination of his rights and obligations and of any criminal charge against him.

Article 11

(1) Everyone charged with a penal offence has the right to be presumed innocent until proved guilty according to law in a public trial at which he has had all the guarantees necessary for his defence.

(2) No one shall be held guilty of any penal offence on account of any act or omission which did not constitute a penal offence, under national or international law, at the time when it was committed. Nor shall a heavier penalty be imposed than the one that was applicable at the time the penal offence was committed.

Article 12

No one shall be subjected to arbitrary interference with his privacy, family, home or correspondence, nor to attacks upon his honor and reputation. Everyone has the right to the protection of the law against such interference or attacks.

Article 13

(1) Everyone has the right to freedom of movement and residence within te borders of each State.

(2) Everyone has the right to leave any country, including his own, and to return to his country.

Article 14

(1) Everyone has the right to seek and to enjoy in other countries asylum from persecution.

(2) This right may not be invoked in the case of prosecutions genuinely arising from non-political crimes or from acts contrary to the purposes and principles of the United Nations.

Article 15

(1) Everyone has the right to a nationality.

(2) No one shall be arbitrarily deprived of his nationality nor denied the rig ht to change his nationality.

Article 16

(1) Men and women of full age, without any limitation due to race, nationality or religion, have the right to marry and to found a family. They are entitled to equal rights as to marriage, during marriage and at its dissolution.

(2) Marriage shall be entered into only with the free and full consent of the intending spouses.

(3) The family is the natural and fundamental group unit of society and is entitled to protection by society and the State.

Article 17

(1) Everyone has the right to own property alone as well as in association with others.

(2) No one shall be arbitrarily deprived of his property.

Article 18

Everyone has the right to freedom of thought, conscience and religion; this right includes freedom to change his religion or belief, and freedom, either alone or in community with others and in public or private, to manifest his religion or belief in teaching, practice, worship and observance.

Article 19

Everyone has the right to freedom of opinion and expression; this right includes freedom to hold opinions without interference and to seek, receive and impart information and ideas through any media and regardless of frontiers.

Article 20

(1) Everyone has the right to freedom or peaceful assembly and association.
(2) No one may be compelled to belong to an association.

Article 21

(1) Everyone has the right to take part in the government of his country, directly or through freely chosen representatives.
(2) Everyone has the right of equal access to public service in his country.

Article 22

Everyone as a member of society has the right to social security and is entitled to realization, through national effort and international co-operation and in accordance with the organization and resources of each State, of the economic, social and cultural rights indispensable for his dignity and the free development of his personality.

Article 23

(1) Everyone has the right to work, to free choice of employment, to just and favorable conditions of work and to protection against unemployment.
(2) Everyone, without any discrimination, has the right to equal pay for equal work.
(3) Everyone who works has the right to just and favorable remuneration ensuring for himself and his family an existence worthy of human dignity, and supplemented, if necessary, by other means of social protection.
(4) Everyone has the right to form and to join trade unions for the protection of his interests.

Article 24

Everyone has the right to rest and leisure, including reasonable limitation of working hours and periodic holidays with pay.

Article 25

(1) Everyone has the right to a standard of living adequate for the health and well-being of himself and his family, including food, clothing, housing and medical care and necessary social services, and the right to security in the event of unemployment, sickness, disability, widowhood, old age or other lack of livelihood in circumstances beyond his control.

(2) Motherhood and childhood are entitled to special care and assistance. All children, whether born in or out of wedlock, shall enjoy the same social protection.

Article 26

(1) Everyone has the right to education. Education shall be free, at least in the elementary and fundamental stages. Elementary education shall be compulsory. Technical and professional education shall be made generally available and higher education shall be equally accessible to all on the basis of merit.

(2) Education shall be directed to the full development of the human personality and to the strengthening of respect for human rights and fundamental freedoms. It shall promote understanding, tolerance and friendship among all nations, racial or religious groups, and shall further the activities of the United Nations for the maintenance of peace.

(3) Parents have a prior right to choose the kind of education that shall be given to their children.

Article 27

(1) Everyone has the right freely to participate in the cultural life of the community, to enjoy the arts and to share in scientific advancement and its benefits.

(2) Everyone has the right to the protection of the moral and material interests resulting from any scientific, literary or artistic production of which he is the author.

Article 28

Everyone is entitled to a social and international order in which the rights and freedoms set forth in this Declaration can be fully realized.

Article 29

(1) Everyone has duties to the community in which alone the free and full development of his personality is possible.

(2) In the exercise of his rights and freedoms, everyone shall be subject only to such limitations as are determined by law solely for the purpose of securing due recognition and respect for the rights and freedoms of others and of meeting the just requirements of morality, public order and the general welfare in a democratic society.

(3) These rights and freedoms may in no case be exercised contrary to the purposes and principles of the United Nations.

Article 30

Nothing in this Declaration may be interpreted as implying for any State, group or persons any right to engage in any activity or to perform any act aimed at the destruction of any of the rights and freedoms set forth herein.

Notes - Chapter One

[1] Although the *Restatement (Third)* is not an official government document, the American law community generally considers it a reliable statement of current law (D. Vagts, Professor of International Law, Harvard University and Associate Reporter for the *Restatement (Third)*, personal communication, June 12, 1991).

[2] The Supreme Court ruled that corporal punishment in the schools was not a violation of the Bill of Rights. Although the major United Nations human rights covenants, the International Covenant on Civil and Political Rights and Optional Protocol and the International Covenant on Economic, Social, and Political Rights were submitted to Congress for ratification, they were submitted with the stipulation that they be "non self-executing," that is, unenforceable in the United States. Ratification, therefore, would have symbolic and not legal significance. The 1994 ratification of the United Nations Convention Against Torture and Other Forms of Cruel, Inhuman or Degrading Treatment or Punishment was stipulated to be non-self-executing consistent with the Senate resolution on October 27, 1990 in part so as not to invalidate the Supreme Court decision of *Ingraham v. Wright* (1977) which Eighth Amendment of the Bill of Rights ("Human Rights Treaty Update," 1991). In that case, the student had to be hospitalized (Cohen, 1995)! The burgeoning status of the Universal Declaration as customary international law may be more appropriate, therefore, than the Covenants as the standard of comparison. (See also Ismail (1991) and Meron (1989) who speak of the "loftier position" and "enhanced status" of customary rights and norms, as opposed to treaty rights and norms.) Yet, I do not deny the importance of the Covenants. Symbols, of course, throughout history have "moved" people (Gil, 1992).

Rights liberties, privileges, the wheels and checks of a system, depend not on arbitrary notions of individual leaders, but on the scars of experience left on the body politic by the period of its most radical testing.

- *Eugene Rosenstock-Heussy*, Out of Revolution: The Autobiography of Western Man

CHAPTER TWO

A HISTORY OF THE IDEA OF HUMAN RIGHTS

This chapter will trace the evolution of the idea of human rights from antiquity until the events immediately preceding the inception of the United Nations Universal Declaration of Human Rights.

METHOD

The method, which I have chosen in this section, is compatible with Babbie's (1986) comments on methodology for historical/comparative research:

> There are no easily listed steps to follow in the analysis of historical data...[yet] the historical/comparative researcher must find patterns among the voluminous details describing the subject matter of study...[representing] data from a variety of sources and...different points of view. (pp. 294-295)

Although my discussion is not an objective representative sample of sources from the birth to the development of the idea of human rights, it is, nevertheless, consonant with the approach advocated by historian Howard Zinn (1970) who states, that "To be objective in writing history...is as pointless as trying to draw a map which shows everything-or even samples of everything-on a piece of terrain" (p. 10). He also ponders that "Even if it were possible to list *all* the events of a given historical period, would this really capture the human reality of this period?" (p. 24). He acknowledges, in addition, that in a world where justice is maldistributed, both historically and at present, there is no such thing as a neutral or representative recapitulation of the facts.

As an alternative approach, he recommends that the researcher approach historical data with a deliberate purpose to further certain fundamental values in the present. Such an examination would make the researcher not engage in his or her analysis as a dispassionate outsider, but rather as someone committed to a cause.This history of the idea of human rights, therefore, is not *the* history of the idea, for a *definitive* statement about the evolution of an idea is not possible. Rather, this historical analysis is *a* history of the idea of human rights.

My primary focus in this historical analysis, therefore, is to illuminate the predominant historical-philosophical foundations which have culminated in contemporary understandings of human rights, with particular emphasis upon understanding the Universal Declaration of Human Rights as a document of customary international law. My point is not to trace in linear fashion the development of all the rights in the Universal Declaration, an undertaking, human rights scholars such as Henkin (1978) view as questionable.

Rather, it is to illustrate likely correspondences between historical and later conceptions suggesting in the final analysis, as Jacques Maritain (1947) states, "No declaration of rights can ever be exhaustive and final [but is an]...expression of the moral conscience of civilization at a given moment in history" (p. 673).
This understanding could also hopefully further some of the principles found in that document in domestic contexts, in this case, the United States and become an effective vehicle for social change.

THE NATURE OF RIGHTS

In order to adequately understand this history of the idea of human rights, it is first necessary to discern the nature of rights. The idea of human rights, therefore, is a social construct which reflects social acknowledgements of individual and communal basic and perceived needs in a particular historical period. In short, human rights are statements of human needs.

The Vulnerability of the Human Condition

Of all the species of the animal kingdom, humans (i.e. *homo sapiens*) appear the most vulnerable. The susceptibility of humans to succumb to illness and misfortune is a prime reason that the social construct "human rights" is necessary. This concept can help ensure the satisfaction of basic human needs.

Of all species of both the plant and animal kingdoms, the human species appears the least suited for survival unless it creates its own viable systems. It is also the least genetically programmed to create these life supporting patterns of survival (Gil, 1990a). As a substitute for this lack of specificity of genetic programming, humans must create social policies (i.e. ways of life to ensure their survival).

These policies, however, can be either socially just or unjust. Just policies would adequately distribute obligations (e.g. work) and the benefits to the community that these obligations create, such as health care, housing, and recreational facilities. Unjust policies would distribute these duties and benefits inadequately, that is, in ways that satisfy the needs of a few, rather than everyone. It is common knowledge, for example, that today in the United States young children constitute the nation's poorest age group. The social policies which created this situation are not genetically programmed but rather the product of human choices.

Constitutions are one example of social policies which serve as guides necessary for the human species to endure. Rights often contained in these constitutions are human designs. Whether they are explicitly recognized in such documents, or implicitly understood as in some cultures, they are, nevertheless, human creations. The challenge is to assert constitutional rights which can fulfill rather than deny human needs.

Because of the vulnerability of the human condition, therefore, which includes the lack of specificity of genetic programming in the human species, it is an existential imperative to create life enhancing social policies. This imperative is reflected throughout history in the common struggle of humans to survive in an indifferent world.

By focusing upon the notion of human rights, which is only one aspect of this common struggle for survival, this book will relate in part the playing out of this existential imperative from antiquity to the present time.

The Relation Between Needs and Rights

For the purposes of this project on human rights and their implications for policy, I have chosen to define needs in accordance with David Gil's (1990a) most recent statements of needs in *Unravelling Social Policy*. He views them as dynamic sources of social life and social policies. Whereas these needs are intrinsic, (i.e. basic to human survival), such as the need for food or shelter, they are, to some extent, culturally elaborated and conditioned.

Over time, for example, an individual's need to eat takes the form of the need to eat certain foods which are consistent with his/her cultural upbringing.

Some Native Americans, for example, accustomed to a subsistence lifestyle would take delight in moose, caribou meat, or seal oil. A slice of white bread would cause indigestion. To a person accustomed to a more modern and urban environment, drinking seal oil, rather than eating white bread, would cause indigestion.

A recent report by the United Nations Commission on Human Rights also emphasizes the importance of the cultural elaboration of a need:

> Food is a basic need for all human beings. Everyone requires access to food which is a) sufficient, balanced and safe to satisfy nutritional requirements, b) *culturally acceptable* [italics added] and c) accessible in a manner which does not destroy one's dignity as human beings. (Eide, 1987, p. 12)

A problem may arise, however, if certain needs are culturally conditioned in such a way that they are at odds with more intrinsic needs. For example, the need to become a productive member of society (i.e. to work) can become thwarted if the cultural elaboration of this need becomes the need to work at a job which, although unfulfilling, is monetarily profitable. Rather than a satisfying job, therefore, a person might say that he or she "needs" money. Yet, the satisfaction of this need through a job that gives no self-fulfillment would thwart the basic need to be a productive member of society or to self-actualize.

It is one matter, therefore, to desire food that is culturally acceptable. It is another thing to crave something in itself like money which can be at odds with intrinsic needs. In both instances culture is at work. Yet, the former instance seems to enhance intrinsic needs; the latter seems to deny them. My concerns are with cultural elaborations that enhance rather than deny basic human needs.

Knowledge concerning human needs is imperfect. However, the following interrelated basic needs appear necessary for human growth and development. They are: *biological-material, social-psychological, productive-creative, security, self-actualization,* and *spiritual* (Gil, 1990a). The rights to food, clothing, housing and medical care as stated in Article 25 of the Universal Declaration, for example, are social acknowledgements of biological-material needs. The right to marry and found a family in Article 16 is an acknowledgement of social-psychological needs. The right to work in Article 23 recognizes a person's productive-creative needs. The right to privacy in Article 12 speaks to a person's security needs. The right to self-actualization can be recognized in Article 26 which states in part that education should be directed to the full development of the human personality. Finally, spiritual needs are recognized in part by the right to freedom of thought, conscience and religion as in Article 18. While these needs are just examples, all of the rights in the Universal Declaration could roughly correspond to the list of needs as described above.

Table 1 on the following page summarizes primary correspondences between the rights listed in the Universal Declaration and Gil's list of human needs. This table also makes note of the three generations of rights and the interdependency and indivisibility of rights discussed below.

In addition to the immutability of basic human needs and the cultural conditioning of needs, basic needs are often invoked into consciousness in times of crisis. As a person appreciates air at the moment of suffocation (Von Eckartsberg, 1972) so too, do individuals recognize needs in hard times. The need to participate in the processes of government (a civil and political right) becomes apparent if that government levies taxes without representation; the human need to work, to become a productive member of a community (a social and economic right) is evident when economic and other societal forces result in unemployment; and the need for a clean environment (a solidarity right) is apparent when contaminated air and drinking water is an increasing everyday phenomenon.

These needs then, which are evoked into consciousness in times of crises, can become translated into rights in legislative documents for all people in a society or for specified groups. Thus, for example, there is: "The right of the people peaceably to assemble, and to petition the government for a redress of grievances" (The United States Constitution [1791], Amendment I); "The right to labor...including the right to choice of occupation, type of employment and work" (The Soviet Constitution [1977], Article 40); and "The right to clean air and water, freedom from excessive and unnecessary noise, and the natural, scenic, historic and aesthetic qualities of their environment " (Massachusetts Commonwealth Constitution [1984], Article XCVII).

The Three Generations of Rights

Weston (1989), building upon French jurist Karel Vasak's notion of these three generations, speaks of these generations as roughly corresponding to the categories of rights in the Universal Declaration and to the three normative themes of the French Revolution.

The first generation is civil and political rights (*liberté*) which derives primarily from the seventeenth-and eighteenth century reformist theories which were associated with the English, American, and French revolutions.

Table 1.
Relation Between Needs and Rights in the Universal Declaration

RIGHTS		NEEDS					
Gener-tation	Art-icle	Bio-logic.	Soc.-Psych	Prod. Creat.	Sec-urity	Self-Act.	Spirit-ual
1st.	1		x			x	
Gen.	2					x	x
	3	x			x	x	x
c	4			x	x	x	
I	5	x			x		
v	6		x		x		
I	7		x		x		
l	8		x		x		
and	9		x		x		
p	10		x		x		
o	11		x		x		
l	12		x		x		
I	13		x		x		
t	14		x		x		
I	15		x		x		
c	16		x		x		
a	17		x		x		
l	18		x		x	x	x
	19		x	x	x	x	
	20		x				
	21		x	x	x	x	
2nd	22	x	x	x	x	x	
Gen.,	23	x	x	x	x	x	x
eco.,	24	x	x	x	x	x	
soc.,	25	x	x		x	x	
cult	26		x	x		x	
	27			x	x	x	
3rd.	28	x	x	x	x	x	
Gen.	29		x	x	x	x	x
solida.	30				x		

Note: "x's" indicate primary correspondences, yet rights are interdependent.

Belonging to this first generation are such claimed rights as set forth in 2-21 of the Universal Declaration of Human Rights. These are also referred to as "negative" freedoms (i.e. freedom *from* government intervention in the quest for human dignity). Such rights include, for example, freedom from arbitrary arrest, the right to a fair and public trial, and freedom from interference in privacy. The second generation of economic, social and cultural rights (*egalité*) has its origins in early nineteenth century France. It has become reemphasized by socialist and various welfare movements and revolutionary struggles ever since. Belonging to this generation are the rights as set forth in Articles 22-27 of the Universal Declaration of Human Rights. These rights are also referred to as "positive" freedoms (i.e. rights *to* just governmental intervention in the quest for human dignity). Such rights include the right to work, the right to a standard of living adequate for the health and well-being of self and family, the right to education, and the right to protection of one's scientific, literary and artistic productions.

Undoubtedly, not all the rights in the above articles fit neatly into the above categories of negative and positive rights. Nevertheless, most of the first generation rights necessitate the abstention of political authority in human affairs; most of the second generation require the intervention of political authority.

The third generation of solidarity rights (*fraternité*), still in the process of conceptual elaboration, appears best understood as a product of both the rise and, most recently, the consolidation of nation-states in the last half of the twentieth century in such arrangements as, for example, the North Atlantic Treaty Organization, the Organization of American States and the European Common Market.

The United Nations General Assembly (1990) has recently adopted a resolution to formally deliberate upon the precise meaning of these rights. This resolution reaffirms the importance of the Universal Declaration of Human Rights in alleviating the plight of individuals living in conditions of extreme poverty and calls for the strengthening of a common sense of human solidarity.

Despite these present conceptual difficulties, however, noted human rights advocates and scholars have stated some observations concerning these new rights. Stamatapolou (personal communication, April 14, 1990), Director of the Liaison Office for Human Rights at the United Nations in New York, states, for example, that implicit in this right is the right of all individuals to have their governments cooperate with other governments. The rights to self-determination, to economic and social development, to peace, to a clean environment, to participation in the "common heritage of mankind," (i.e. its cultural traditions, sites, and monuments) and to humanitarian disaster relief are seen also as solidarity rights by Weston (1989). These rights cannot be realized unless there is a worldwide effort to combat the forces which have led, for example, to a deteriorating environment and eroding cultural conditions. The global maldistribution of wealth and the rights claimed by the Third World countries and Fourth World nations (i.e. indigenous peoples) to the wealth of the richer nations and to self-determination are also often discussed in terms of solidarity rights.

These solidarity rights have been foreshadowed by Article 28 of the Universal Declaration of Human Rights which proclaims that "Everyone is entitled to a social and international order in which the rights set forth in this Declaration can be fully realized." Such a right also implies corresponding duties and obligations not only among governments, but also among individuals in order that human rights be realized (Vasak, 1977). These rights appear to be a resurrection of old wisdom concerning the interrelationship between rights and duties.

Each of these three generations of rights arose out of different historical periods which reflected the struggle of people against the absolutism and arbitrariness of tyrannical rulers (i.e. the first generation); socially structured poverty (i.e. the second generation); and the inadequacies of domestic sovereignty (i.e. the third generation).

This model of the three generations of rights is a simplified expression of an extremely complex historical record which is "not intended as a literal representation of life in which one generation gives birth to the next and then dies away" (Weston, 1989, p.17). Rather each generation has evolved and built upon the other generation in ways that have led to contemporary conceptions of human rights.

Kinds of Rights

There are three different "kinds" of human rights: rights as ideals, rights as enactments, and rights as exercised.

Declarations, assertions, and claims by individuals and groups are examples of human rights as *ideals*. They are goals that members of a society view as important in meeting individual and/or group needs. The United States Declaration of Independence and the Universal Declaration of Human Rights are examples of human rights as ideals. They assert, for example, goals such as equality and just and favorable conditions of work.

It is here that human rights scholar Maurice Cranston's (1983) criteria of rights are applicable. According to him, human rights must be: *universal, practicable*, and *of paramount importance.* Taking into consideration Cranston's first criterion, these rights would be based not on status, privilege, sex, occupation, race, class or any other accidental characteristic, but rather upon the essence of being human. That is, they would be universal. *All* members of the society would have them. Such a society should also have the economic and other means to provide for a right. That is, they would be practicable. The right to education, for example, would be meaningless if the society did not have the resources to provide for such a right. Finally, that right would have paramount importance. It would be necessary to the fulfillment of one's basic needs. The right to health care, for example, would be quite different than the right to a candy bar unless the candy bar were necessary for survival.

All of the rights in the Universal Declaration seem to meet Cranston's criteria. They are for everyone and of paramount importance. They are also practicable, that is "entitled to realization...in accordance with the organization and resources of each State" (Article 22). They are ideals. I know of no society that meets these ideals. One way to transform these ideals into reality is to codify them in documents, usually legal instruments such as constitutions or statutes. Human rights as *enactments*, therefore, are formal statements of ways to provide for human needs, which have the force of law behind them. In the United States Constitution, for example, it is a law that: "Congress shall make no law respecting an establishment of religion or prohibiting the free exercise thereof" (Amendment 1). In some societies, however, it is not necessary to codify these rights in written form. In many Native American cultures, for example, it appears understood that a hunter will share his game with the community.

Human rights as *exercised* are rights that are actually enjoyed. They are needs that are satisfied by individuals irregardless of the sources of these rights. They may be due to declarations (ideals), constitutions (enactments), or to none of these. In contemporary American society, for example, many economic, social and cultural rights are possessed by individuals engaged in gainful employment rather than by everyone. Basic rights to housing and medical care in the United States are primarily available to those who can afford rents, mortgages and insurance premiums. Most often wages, earned through work, pay for these rights. I know of no formal statement that says "Only people who work have the right to a house or health care." Yet, this situation is often the state of affairs.

On the other hand, it is obvious that if there weren't legislative documents that, for instance, allowed for the free expression of religion, there would be untold massacres of non-believers. The Reformation in Europe is one example among many which attest to this reality. Often elaborate enforcement mechanisms such as the courts or the police force exist to *implement* the rights proclaimed in legislative documents.

Certainly, implementation is the chief difficulty in the realization of human rights and, according to Brownlie (1971) "Many constitutions bear but an obscure relation to the actual state of affairs in political and legal life" (p. 1). Although I appreciate the difficulties of implementation, Brownlie's comment appears an exaggeration. Legislative documents are not always necessary to exercise one's rights, but why then did the barons struggle for a document against King John at Runnymede? Why did the early Americans see the need for a Bill of Rights?

History is replete with individuals clamoring to have their rights stated in clear and precise language in order to have these rights realized. The Universal Declaration is one such example, for member states wanted a document that was "short, simple, and easy to understand and expressive" ("International Bill," 1947).

Distinctions among rights as ideals, enactments and exercised are often blurred. The Universal Declaration of Human Rights, for example, was originally meant to be a mere assertion, an ideal that all nations should strive for. Yet, it now is perceived as having the force of customary international law. Thus, in the United States in 1991, no torturer is considered safe from prosecution.

The major thrust of this study, therefore, is to determine how the ideal, the Universal Declaration of Human Rights, compares with certain enactments of human rights as in the United States federal and state constitutions. It does not appear reasonable, however, to consider all the issues involved with implementation. Nevertheless, it will broach this issue by looking at certain situations which purport to manifest these ideals.

The Interdependence of Rights

Human rights are interdependent and indivisible (Stamatapolou, 1989; Weston, 1989). According to the UN Commission on Human Rights : "The indivisibility and interdependence of the two sets of human rights - civil and political rights on the one hand and economic, social and cultural rights on the other - is a fundamental tenet of the United Nations approach to human rights" (Eide, 1987, p. 10).

Lamenting the traditional dichotomy between civil and political and economic, social and cultural rights, Donnelly (1989) comments:

Similarities and linkages across the categories of the standard dichotomy arise because our lives do not fall into largely autonomous political and socioeconomic spheres. Economic and social rights usually are violated by or with the collusion of elite-controlled political mechanisms of exclusion and domination. Poverty in the midst of plenty is a political phenomenon as much as it is an economic one, and civil and political rights are often violated to protect economic privilege....Political power cannot be neatly separated from economic power. (pp. 36-37)

Other examples can also demonstrate the interdependence and indivisibility of rights. The social or cultural right to education is intimately connected with the civil or political rights to freedom of speech, belief, and opinion. The right to travel, (a civil and political right), furthermore, is possible only if one has worked (an economic and social right) and earned enough wages to afford the fare to move freely. Likewise, it is meaningless, to give a person the right to participate in government, if he/she is a person with disabilities and has no access to health care, lacks transportation, and is unable to take part in governmental decisions. Similarly, the right to vote is trivial if the voter lacks education, is illiterate, and/or uninformed.

The interdependency of human rights can also lead to a limitation of certain rights. The rights of any particular individual need at times to be restricted in order to secure comparable rights to others and for the general welfare. Article 29 of the Universal Declaration, for example, speaks of the need for limitations upon one's rights "for the purpose of securing due recognition and respect for the rights and freedoms of others." There is an interdependence, furthermore, between rights and responsibilities, obligations and duties. The right to food, for example, also implies corresponding duties to be productive and not to overconsume (Alston, 1989).

Given then, the interdependence and indivisibility of the three sets of rights (civil and political; economic, social and cultural; and the "new" solidarity rights), I feel that it, nevertheless, makes sense to trace the evolution of the idea of human rights by reference to these three categories. This sketching of major issues can only be accomplished by acknowledging that this model is a simplified expression of an extremely complex history (Weston, 1989). With the acknowledgement of the interrelatedness and indivisibility of rights, this model should, nevertheless, provide the necessary contours to understand the historical unfolding of this idea.

HUMAN RIGHTS IN ANTIQUITY

Whereas this historical analysis is essentially a chronological sketch of major issues, I have chosen not to subject this inquiry to the "tyranny of dates" (Ebenstein, 1960). That is, the following historical divisions, while largely arbitrary and often overlapping, provide only focal points to discuss major developments of the idea. Consequently, within each historical period, I will also draw correspondences, when appropriate, with later, if not contemporary, conceptions of the idea of human rights. In discussing Christianity, for example, whereas I emphasize original Biblical texts, I also make note of later encyclicals which are elaborations of ideas found in these ancient documents.

Throughout this historical analysis I have also chosen to identify "crucial" conceptions of rights in the Universal Declaration and to note correspondences with these notions and historical periods. These conceptions, furthermore, are not all inclusive, but are statements of basic notions in that document. They will provide focal points for sketching major developments in the history of the idea.

These basic notions are:

1) The equality, dignity and worth of each individual (as stated in Article 1);
2) The right of liberty to pursue this quest for human dignity against the abuse of political authority (as stated in Articles 2-21 also referred to as "negative" freedoms i.e. civil and political liberties as discussed above);
3) The right to basic necessities to ensure an existence worthy of human dignity (as stated in Articles 22-27 also referred to as "positive" freedoms i.e. economic, social and cultural rights as discussed above);
4) The obligations and responsibilities of individuals to God, others, and nature to ensure the rights specified in the Universal Declaration (as stated in Articles 28-30 also referred to in varying contexts as solidarity rights as discussed above).

Whereas these crucial notions are interdependent and overlapping they will, nevertheless, provide an adequate frame of reference to note any resemblances between them and religions, social theorists, historical documents, and contemporary ideas of human rights in general.

This account, furthermore, is a *sketch* of important issues. Consequently, it will only highlight major themes which are apparent in certain predominant authors and documents in historical periods. Although I will occasionally comment upon cultural conditions which may have inspired developments of the idea of human rights, the principal thrust of this chapter is to trace the evolution of this idea from antiquity to the present time.

Although my concerns in this section are primarily with original texts, which include scriptural passages, I will also make note of scholars' observations which could embellish the meanings of these original texts. I will also comment occasionally in general terms about a specific author's or document's apparent contributions to the development of the idea of human rights.

Concerning my discussion of Judaism, Christianity, and Islam[1], my purpose is *not* a comparative study of these religions' adherence to human rights standards. My aim rather is only to indicate correspondences between doctrinal texts and these crucial notions. These correspondences, furthermore, are meant to be illustrative rather than exhaustive. Undoubtedly, other major religions and traditions also illustrate correspondences with the Universal Declaration. Hinduism, for example, has its concept of *Dharma* or obligations ("Evolution of Human Rights," 1946); Confucianism taught that "The ethical man did not owe allegiance to a tyrannical government" (Palumbo, p. 20). Furthermore, distributive economic and social justice is an important principle in African culture (Legesse, 1980).

I chose, however, to narrow my considerations, first because time and space will not permit *all* religions, as well as, other traditions to be scrutinized. Secondly, I am interested in religions that have common traditions. Judaism, Christianity, and Islam emanate from the same heritage.

The idea of human rights initially began, therefore, when humans first existed. In order to foster the satisfaction of human needs in a finite world, it was necessary to develop certain rules of conduct, including obligations, in order to distribute rights to limited resources to satisfy these needs.

It is difficult to determine precisely when these rights to the distribution of resources first evolved. Authors, such as Palumbo (1983) state: "The Hebrews were among the first to put into practice a policy of respect for the dignity of every individual" (p.13).

Others, like Weston (1989), view human rights, as a replacement of the phrase "natural rights," the former being a relatively new term "having come into everyday parlance only since World War II and the founding of the United Nations in 1945" (p. 13). He states, "Most students of human rights trace the historical origins of the concept back to ancient Greece and Rome, where it was closely tied to the premodern natural law doctrines of Greek Stoicism" (p. 13).

The *United Nations Weekly Bulletin*, begins its discussion of the evolution of human rights with the Chinese emperor Mencius who "23 centuries ago" said "The individual is of infinite value, institutions and conventions come next, and the person of the ruler is of least significance" ("The Evolution of Human Rights, 1946").

Because the "origins and ancestry of ideas are rarely single or simple, or readily disentangled," (Henkin, 1978, p. 4), I have *arbitrarily* chosen, therefore, to begin this inquiry with religious precursors to contemporary conceptions of this idea.

Judaism

The equality, dignity and worth of the individual in the first notion (i.e. human dignity) is illustrated in Genesis 1:27 - "God created man in His image. In the image of God He created him. Male and female He created them."[2] Writing about human rights in Judaism, Abraham Kaplan (1980, p. 55) remarks that the creation of the human in the image of God embodies the "ultimate and supreme worth" of each individual. Rabbi Ben Azzai, an early Talmudic scholar, sees this passage as "the most important single verse in scripture" (Kaplan, p. 55).

These notions are also demonstrated in at least two other scriptural passages: Gen. 5:1-2 - "When God created man, He made him in the likeness of God. Male and female He created them, and He blessed them and called them Man when they were created."; Prov. 22:2 - Rich and poor have a common bond: the Lord is the maker of them all."

The rights of the individual against the abuse of political authority as suggested in the second notion (i.e. negative rights) above are portrayed, for example, in Lev. 24:22 - "You shall have but one rule for alien and native alike." Deut. 1:16-17 also states: "I charged your judges at that time: Listen to complaints among your kinsmen, and administer true justice to both parties even if one of them is an alien. In rendering judgment, do not consider who a person is; give ear to the lowly and to the great alike." Deut. 16: 19 states: "You shall not distort justice; you must be impartial. You shall not take a bribe; for a bribe blinds the eyes even of the wise and twists the words even of the just."

According to Judaic scholar, Rabbi Daniel Polish, and author of *Formation of Social Policy in the Catholic and Jewish Traditions*: "Equality under law was more than an abstract ideal; it was the concrete embodiment of basic tenets of the theology of the Jewish community" (1982, p. 43).

Regarding the right to basic necessities under the third notion (i.e. positive rights), Judaic scripture reveals, for example, in Deut. 24:14-15: "You shall not defraud a poor and needy hired servant....You shall pay him each day's wages before sundown on the day itself, since he is poor and looks forward to them."

Poverty, moreover, is not seen as a blessing or particular spiritual state, which is a rationalization that is foreign to Judaism. (Kaplan, 1980). "The rich man's wealth is his strong city, the ruination of the lowly is their poverty" (Prov. 10:15). Proverbs 25:21 also proclaims "If your enemy be hungry, give him food to eat, if he be thirsty, give him to drink."

Finally, in Job 29:12-17 scripture states: "I rescued the poor who cried out for help, the orphans, and the unassisted; the blessing of those in extremity came upon me and the heart of the widow I made joyful. I wore my honesty like a garment; justice was my robe and my turban. I was eyes to the blind, and feet to the lame was I; I was a father to the needy."

The notion of obligations as discussed in the fourth notion (i.e. duties and solidarity rights) appears throughout Judaic scripture. Lev. 19:18 states: "Thou shalt love thy neighbor as thyself." Deut. 6:5 asserts: "Thou shalt love the Lord thy God with all thine heart." This love is also meant for one's enemies: "When you come upon your enemy's ox or ass going astray, see to it that it is returned to him. When you notice the ass of one who hates you lying prostrate under its burden, by no means desert him; help him, rather, to raise it up" (Exodus 23:4-5). In Deut. 10:17-19 there is: "The Lord, your God...who has no favorites, accepts no bribes; who executes justice for the orphan and the widow, and befriends the alien, feeding and clothing him. So you too must befriend the alien, for you were once aliens yourselves in the land of Egypt."

The obligation to seek justice is also apparent in Isaiah 1:17: "Make justice your aim: redress the wronged, hear the orphan's plea, defend the widow." Also, in Prov. 21:3 scripture says: "To do what is right and just is more acceptable to the Lord than sacrifice." Also, "Refuse no one the good on which he has a claim when it is in your power to do it for him. Say not to your neighbor, 'Go and come again, tomorrow I will give,' when you can give it at once" (Prov. 4:27-28).

In Exodus 20:8-10 the obligations to work *and* to rest is also apparent: "Remember to keep holy the Sabbath day. Six days you may labor and do all your work, but the seventh day is the Sabbath of the Lord, your God." As the Jewish scholar Maimonides emphasizes, the highest form of charity is to make it possible for the recipient to provide for himself, by giving him work (Kaplan, 1980).

In Judaism, furthermore, the rights of the needy appear to take precedence over property rights (Polish, 1982). "When you knock down the fruit of your olive trees, you shall not go over the branches a second time; let what remains be for the alien, the orphan and the widow" (Deut 24:20).

There are also other scriptural references, as well as Jewish celebrations and sacred texts, such as the Talmud, which proclaim a standard of conduct which is compatible with respect for human rights. The above enumeration of scriptural texts while not exhaustive, nevertheless, testifies to concepts of human rights which are inherent in the Hebraic tradition and may have contributed to contemporary conceptions of this idea.

All humans, however, were not able to exercise all the rights espoused by Judaism. Non-Jewish prisoners of war, for example, were permitted to be enslaved. Although they were to be released after serving a period of six years, in their condition of slavery they were, nevertheless, subject to economic disabilities (Polish, 1982).

Christianity

The condemnations of injustice in the Old Testament and the absolute demand for justice which transcended sacrifices and prayers, have echoed throughout the Christian tradition (Henle, 1980). In the New Testament, the teachings of Jesus Christ and his disciples, seem to either reify or elaborate upon the teachings of the Old Testament.

Whereas Christianity spread the moral philosophy of Judaism over the Mediterranean world, the major difference between these two religions was the Christian claim to universality. Judaic teachings were primarily identified as a faith of the chosen people, the Hebrews. This new religion was for all peoples. (Palumbo, 1982).

Christians accept, therefore, the sanctity and dignity of the human person as proclaimed in Gen. 1:27 (Henle, 1980). John 1:1-4 also states: "In the beginning was the Word, and the Word was with God; He was in the beginning with God. All things were made through Him, and without Him was made nothing that has been made. In Him was life, and the life was the light of men." The Secretary of State for the Holy See, Reverend Casaroli, at the World Summit for Children at the United Nations on September 30, 1990 spoke of the dignity of the human person which derives from the creation of the individual in the image and likeness of God.

Concerning the protection of the individual against the abuse of political authority, in John 1:17, Christians also accept the "law given through Moses." The few quotes mentioned above from the Old Testament, which speak of impartiality of the law and equality before the law, are to be accepted by the Christian. And in John 8:51 it is asked: "Does our Law judge a man unless it first give him a hearing, and know what he does"?

In Mark 12:17 Jesus says "Render, therefore, to Caesar the things that are Caesar's and to God the things that are God's." This statement appears to acknowledge duties to the community and to God. It also suggests that governments can be accountable to another spiritual authority. Consequently, individuals, could refuse to yield to a governing authority should its mandates conflict with a "higher law," (i.e. God's law). Whereas I will discuss this idea more fully in the next section on the Middle Ages when it came to prominence, this notion of a higher law is often also referred to as "natural law." Despite its potential for abuse, it appears to have become a central concept in the development of the idea of human rights.

Numerous scriptural passages suggest entitlement to basic needs. Christ says to the rich man, for example, in Luke 18:22: "Sell all that thou hast, and give to the poor, and thou shalt have treasure in heaven; and come, follow me." The corporal works of mercy discussed below also attest to these entitlements in Christian scriptural texts.

As in Judaism, the notions of obligations and justice run throughout the New Testament. When asked what the greatest commandment in the Law was, Jesus Christ replied "Thou shalt love the Lord thy God with thy whole heart, and with thy whole soul, and with thy whole mind. This is the greatest and the first commandment. And the second is like it, Thou shalt love thy neighbor as thyself. On these two commandments depend the whole Law and the Prophets" (Matthew 22:36-40). Also, "Love your enemies, and do good, and lend, not hoping for any return, and your reward shall be great, and you shall be children of the Most High, for He is kind towards the ungrateful and evil. Be merciful, therefore, even as your Father is merciful" (Luke 6:35-36).

Everlasting life is also given to those who practice the corporal works of mercy as found in Matthew 25:34-46: to feed the hungry, to give drink to the thirsty, to visit the sick and the imprisoned, and to take in the stranger. "Amen, I say to you, as long as you did it for the least of these brethren, you did it for Me" (Matthew 25:40). Furthermore, in the Beatitudes (Luke 6:20-26) Christ blesses those who hunger and thirst for justice.

Christ's teachings must also be practiced: "But why do you call me, 'Lord, Lord,' and not practice the things that I say?" (Luke 7:46).

Since a complete doctrine of human rights in Christian teaching cannot be drawn from scripture or deduced from Christ's commandment to love one another (Henle, 1980), a mention of other Christian statements concerning human rights, such as papal encyclicals, appears necessary.

Pope Leo XIII's *Rerum Novarum* (*The Condition of Labor*) (1891) (Gibbons, 1963), for example, which inevitably drew upon scriptural writings, such as the corporal works of mercy, nevertheless, initiated a new phase in social and political thought in Christian teaching (Hollenbach, 1988). In this encyclical the Pope protests against an emerging industrial economy wherein "A small number of very rich men have been able to lay upon the teeming masses of the poor a yoke little better than slavery itself" (Gibbons, p. 2). He also specifies the "principles which truth and justice dictate" for dealing with the "misery and wretchedness" caused by these changes and attempts "to define the relative rights and mutual duties of the rich and the poor, of capital and labor" (Gibbons, pp. 1-2).

Pope Leo XIII's emphasis upon "positive duties to aid persons in need, to participate in the maintaining of the public good, and to share in efforts to create the kinds of institutions that promote genuine mutuality" (Hollenbach, p. 19) was a radical departure from more pervasive and traditional notions of negative rights at that time. Pope John XXIII in 1963 also emphasized these positive rights in *Pacem in Terris (Peace on Earth):*

> Every man has the right to life, to bodily integrity, and to the means which are necessary and suitable for the proper development of life; these are primarily food, clothing, shelter, rest, medical care, and finally the necessary social services. Therefore, a human being also has the right to security in cases of sickness, inability to work, widowhood, old age, [and] unemployment. (Gibbons, 1963, p. 291)

These notions of positive rights and duties, as well as human dignity, while having scriptural antecedents, appear consistently emphasized and further elaborated upon in later Christian moral discourse. Pius XI, for example, in *Divini Redemptoris (Atheistic Communism)* (1937) stresses that "Both justice and charity often dictate obligations" (Gibbons, p. 195). John Paul II in *Laborem Exercens (On Human Work)* (1981) emphasizes that work, a duty, is not simply "merchandise" to be bought and sold, but rather a way to realize one's humanity and to participate in the dignity of being human. All humans have dignity because God created them in his image. Finally, *Pacem in Terris* speaks of the "reciprocity of rights and duties between persons" (Gibbons, pp. 291, 295). Pope John XXIII speaks, for example, of "a social duty essentially inherent in the right of private property" (Gibbons, p. 293).

The 1971 Synod of Catholic Bishops stressed that the church's mission, based on the Gospel is action on behalf of justice and redemption and liberation of the human race from every oppressive situation. The Bishops also emphasized the current international socioeconomic situation, stressing the serious injustices building up around the world which are giving rise to increasing numbers of marginal persons, who are ill-fed, inhumanly housed, illiterate, and deprived of political power and the suitable means to acquire responsibility and moral dignity (Gremillion, 1981).

These papal and ecclesiastical pronouncements have led to the contemporary movement of liberation theology which is "first and foremost, a profoundly Christian protest against a world in which a pampered minority condemns the majority to a life sentence of misery and hopelessness, if not to death" (Higgins, 1990, p. 392).

Certainly, these pronouncements are similar to contemporary notions of solidarity rights as discussed earlier. But, more importantly, these encyclicals and bishops' statements attest to the continuing thrust of major conceptions of human rights originally found in ancient scriptural texts.

At varying times in the history of Christianity, clergy used scriptural texts to justify violations of the dignity of the human person. In St. Luke 17: 22 it is written: "And it came to pass that the poor man died and was borne away by the angels into Abraham's bosom." Throughout the Middle Ages, therefore, the poor were considered to be poor by God's will (Foreman, 1972).

During the Spanish Inquisition, furthermore, "God Himself" was seen as the first inquisitor. His expulsion of Adam and Eve from Eden was seen as the first "Act of Faith." This expulsion became a "proper precedent for the confiscation of the property of heretics" (Sabatini, 1924, p. 3). The numerous tortures that ensued during the Inquisition, many of these abuses "greatly favored by the Papacy" (Sabatini, p. 205), suggest once again that the rift between stated rights and rights as exercised is often a harsh reality.

The official sanction of anti-semitism in Christianity is also well known, although recently ecclesiastical authorities have repudiated anti-semitism as contrary to notions of human dignity found in scripture (Bishop, 1974).

Islam

Concerning the dignity and worth of the individual, Muslim religious scholar Riffat Hassan (1982), states: "The sanctity and absolute value of human life is upheld by the Qur'an" (p. 55). She notes (Sura 6:15).[3] "Take not life, which God/Hath made sacred, except/ By way of justice and law." In Sura 17:70 the Qur'an states also "Verily, we have honored every human being." According to Professor Nasr (1980), furthermore: "Humans are, according to the Islamic perspective, created in the image of God" (p. 95).

In the Qur'an "Tremendous emphasis is placed upon the right to seek justice" (Hassan, p. 56): "O ye who believe/Stand out firmly/For justice as witnesses/To God, even as against/Yourselves, or your parents,/Or your kind and whether/It be (against) rich or poor: /For God can best protect both/ Follow not the lusts/(Of your hearts), lest ye/Swerve, and if ye/Distort (justice) or decline/To do justice, verily/God is well-acquainted/With all that ye do" (Sura 4:135).

Hassan (1982) goes so far as to say "A large part of the Qur'an's concern is to free human beings from the chains which bind them: traditionalism, authoritarianism (religious, political, economic), tribalism, racism, sexism, and slavery" (p. 58). Whereas it is not within the scope of this discussion to note all the ways which Islam attempts to free the individual from the abuse of political authority, Hassan notes that numerous passages, such as Sura 9:60 encourage efforts toward the emancipation of slaves: "Alms are for the poor/And the needy, and those...in bondage/ And in debt; in the Cause/Of God; and for the wayfarer."

The right to entitlements to necessities is suggested in Sura 2:177: "It is righteousness/...To spend of your substance,/Out of love for Him,/For your kind,/For orphans,/For the needy,/For the wayfarer,/For those who ask./ For the ransom of slaves;/To be steadfast in prayer,/And practice regular charity;/To fulfill the contracts/Which ye have made;/And to be firm and patient,/In pain (or suffering)/And adversity." According to Hassan, "The Qur'an expresses deep sympathy for the downtrodden, oppressed, or weak classes of human beings (such as women, slaves, orphans, the poor, the infirm and minorities)" (p. 58).

Concerning the notion of duties in the Qur'an, A. Ali's commentary on Sura 2:177 is noteworthy:

> Practical deeds of charity are of value when they proceed from love,and from no other motive. In this respect, also our duties take various forms, which are shown in reasonable gradation: our kith and kin; orphans (including any persons who are without support or help); people who are in real need but who never ask (it is our duty to find them out, and they come before those who ask) *ie.* not merely lazy beggars, but those who seek our assistance in some form or another (it is our duty to respond to them); and the slaves (we must do all we can to give or buy their freedom). Slavery has many insidious forms, and all are included. (p. 43)

Amnesty International Reports of the 1970s and 1980s document that throughout much of the Islamic world, freedom of expression is nonexistent and torture of political prisoners is routine (Farhang, 1988). This suggests that certain ancient notions of Islam, such as human dignity, are often far removed from contemporary realities. Scriptural texts, then, in the Qur'an, as well as the Bible, suggest strong affinities with contemporary notions of human rights. In all religions there appear to be various inconsistencies between the affirmation of these notions and everyday realities. While it is not my purpose to compare religions, certainly not to desecrate them, these inconsistencies are noteworthy.

Although it is difficult to determine if these religious writings had a direct influence upon contemporary human rights notions, it is apparent that many important beliefs concerning rights in certain scriptural writings do exist in the Universal Declaration of Human Rights. Some authors, such as Drinan (1987), assert more emphatically that several key concepts in contemporary notions of human rights derive "more from the Judaic-Christian tradition than from other religions, and the religious origins of these concepts-for example, the notion of fraternity endorsed by the UN charter-are clear and undeniable" (p. 9). This accent upon that heritage appears due to the preponderance of American, northern and western European member states during the early years of the United Nations.

The Greeks

The literature of ancient Greece also attests to certain crucial notions in the Universal Declaration.

In Greek literature, Aristotle (384-322 B.C.) appears to be the most In important author concerning these important notions. He wrote extensively, for example, in *Nicomachean Ethics* on the notions of equality and justice:

> Since the unjust man is a man who is not content to have an equal share with others, and since the unjust thing is the unequal thing, it is obvious that there must be a mean between the greater and the less inequality...If then the unjust is the unequal, the just is the equal. (Thomson, 1953, p. 126)

Aristotle, furthermore, recognized that these notions overlap in meaning and are thus interdependent. (Von Leyden, 1985)In the *Politica* he was also aware of the possible abuses of government: "When the rich grow numerous or properties increase...or owing to carelessness, when disloyal persons are allowed to find their way into highest offices" (Ross and Jowett, 1961, p. 1303).

To protect the individual from such abuses he appears to advocate "political or social justice" which:

Is manifested between persons who share a common way of life which has for its object a state of affairs in which they will have all that they need for independent existence as free and equal members of the society. (Thomson, 1953, p. 136)

Concerning political justice, furthermore:

There are two forms of it, the natural and the conventional. It is natural when it has the same validity everywhere and is unaffected by any view we may take about the justice of it. It is conventional when there is no original reason why it should take one form rather than another and the rule it imposes is reached by agreement, after which it holds good. (Thomson, p. 137)

Aristotle, therefore, wanted citizens not to regard government as their enemy (Von Leyden, 1985).

In terms of positive freedoms, a "shortcoming of Aristotle's theory is that he has overlooked an important reason for regarding one's social class, or certain of its members, as more worthy of consideration than others, (i.e. [those in] need)" (Von Leyden, p. 57).

Whereas he does speak of the need for the rich to be generous to the poor he also speaks of those "who *ought* to be poor" (Thomson, p. 97). Giving to the poor does not appear to emanate from care and concern, but, rather from "a motive of patriotism" (Thomson, p. 99), a quality much admired in Greece. I would have to agree with Von Leyden (1985) who concludes: "He has nothing to say on hardship" (p. 57).

On the notion of duties, Aristotle states: "All virtue is summed up in dealing justly" (Thomson, p. 122). To him, to be virtuous is to be moderate and "observe the mean" in all things (Thomson, p. 52).

It is not within the scope of this work to examine in depth Aristotle's notions of equality, natural and conventional justice, virtue and moderation in all things. The point of the above quotes, indeed, there are many others, is to suggest that correspondences did exist with Aristotle's notions of equality and justice and key notions in the Universal Declaration.

My general impressions, however, are that Aristotle's notions of equality and justice seem to concern themselves primarily with civil and political rights, more specifically, equality before the law. Thus, all individuals should have equal opportunity to make laws. In violation of these laws, they, too, should be treated as equals.

Other Greeks also expounded upon ideas which seem to have affinity with many of Aristotle's notions. The statesman Pericles (490-429 BC) advocated democracy:

Our constitution...favors the many instead of the few; this is why it is called a democracy. If we look to the laws, they afford equal justice to all...advancement in public life falls to reputation for capacity, class considerations not being allowed to interfere with merit; nor again does poverty bar the way, if a man is able to serve the state, he is not hindered by the obscurity of his condition. (Kagan, 1965, pp. 124-125)

The playwright Sophocles (469-406 BC) in *Antigone* gave tribute to the virtues of civil disobedience to an unjust political authority. By burying her brother Polynices, Antigone disobeyed King Creon. Instead, she upheld the immutable laws of heaven and gave him the right to a burial (Palumbo, 1982). The Greek historian Herodotus also stressed *isonomia*, (i.e. equality before the law); *isotimia*, (i.e. equal respect for all) and *isogoria*, (i.e.freedom of speech) (Lauterpacht, 1950). The Stoics, founded by Zeno of Citium (c. 300 BC), also stressed equality, universality of all human beings, and moderation (Curtis, 1981).

In Greek mythology, notions of hospitality and benevolence to strangers and beggars are strong. "Strangers and beggars are under Zeus' care" (Lloyd-Jones, 1971, p. 30). He is their protector to such an extent that he and the other gods visit cities of mortals to observe their *hybris* (pride). Should they fail to respect them, they perish.

This concern for the poor and the unknown stands in stark contrast to Zeus' condemnation of Prometheus, who, in defiance of the Lord of Olympus, gave humans fire. Zeus punished him by tying him to a rock in the Caucus mountains and sending an eagle to gnaw at his liver (Oates and Murphy, 1944). The right to protection from political abuse in Greek mythology appears scant. If Aristotle and other Greek philosophers suggest advances in the idea of human rights, these advances appear in the realm, therefore, of civil and political rights.

Despite this Hellenistic emphasis upon equality, justice, and universality, women had very few rights. Slavery was widespread. There were probably more slaves than freemen in ancient Greece (Curtis, 1981). Even more troubling, however, than this rift between ideals and practice is, for instance, Aristotle's acceptance of individuals who "are by nature slaves, and it is better for them as for all inferiors that they should be under the rule of a master" (Ross and Jowett, 1961, p. 1254). "The slave...is a living tool, just as a tool is an inanimate object" (Thomson, 1953, p. 223).

Whereas I will discuss the concept of Natural Law in depth in the section on the Middle Ages, it appears that this concept owed much of its origin to Greek thought, due in large part to Aristotle's notion of slavery as a "natural" state. Owning slaves, therefore, was legal because it was natural. Similarly, Antigone's act of civil disobedience was in order to conform to natural law.

People, furthermore, often tend to view how they live as natural. In competitive societies, for example, selfishness is natural; in cooperative ones, sharing is natural. In both instances, these views are actually reflections of a dominant ideology, rather than statements of fact concerning human nature. Competition or cooperation are possibilities, not inevitabilities; they are human choices, not givens. As the notion that slaves as property can be used to justify the lifestyles of the privileged, so too, claims that humans are by nature selfish, can be used to rationalize the successes of the dominant classes. My point is that civil, political, economic, or social abuses of the human person, can easily be justified in the name of natural law. This concept appears to be a most distressing theme in the evolution of the idea of human rights.

The Romans

After Rome conquered Greece and most of the Mediterranean world, the Romans appeared to have incorporated and built upon much of Greek culture. Consequently, notions of equality, justice and virtue expounded upon by Aristotle and apparently adopted by the Stoics, continued to flourish. Stoicism became the religion of the educated classes (Staniforth, 1984).

The Stoics then placed much emphasis upon equality. The concept of the Brotherhood-of-Man became central to the thinking of later stoics (Higginbotham, 1967).   According to Cicero, a convert to Stoicism: "Nature...unites man with man and joins them in bonds of speech and common life" (Higginbotham, p. 43).

According to Cicero, furthermore, from nature flowed the concept of international law: "And not only nature, which may be defined as international law, but also the particular laws by which individual peoples are governed similarly ordain that no one is justified in harming another for his own advantage" (Higginbotham, p. 144).

Concerning the notion of negative freedoms the Romans had The Twelve Tables, which date from 449 BC and stress the necessity for a proper trial, the presentation of evidence and proof, and the illegality of bribery in judicial proceedings (Palumbo, 1982).   Certainly, these Tables have direct correspondences with the Universal Declaration's concern for just government.

The notion of positive rights, as in Greek thought, does not appear developed in Roman literature: "The necessities of life may be taken from an idle and useless member of the community provided that they are needed for a man of wisdom, goodness and courage, whose death would be a disaster to the community" (Higginbotham, p. 146).

Occasionally, however, there appears an emperor-philosopher such as Vespasian who wants to ensure that the working classes earn enough money to buy themselves food (Suetonius, 1957). My impressions are, however, that the notion of political authorities providing for basic needs is minimal.

Whereas Cicero says, "Justice...consists in preserving a fair relationship between men, giving each his due and keeping one's word" (Higginbotham, p. 44), the emphasis appears to be on negative freedoms. It is unjust, for example, to refuse "to prevent injustice being done to the innocent as far as one can" (Higginbotham, p. 47). The Twelve Tables, also speak to that emphasis in the Romans.

Another Stoic philosopher is the Emperor Marcus Aurelius, who stresses in his *Meditations*, duties to the community: "Let every action aim solely at the common good" (Staniforth, 1984, pp. 183) and "Put your whole heart into doing what is just, and speaking what is true;....know the joy of life by piling good deed on good deed until no rift or cranny appears between them" (p. 186); and "What need for guesswork when the way of duty lies there before your eyes?....To achieve justice is the summit of success, since it is herein that failure most often occurs" (p. 156). Concomitantly, notions of brotherhood are strong in this philosopher's writings: "Neither can I be angry with my brother or fall foul of him; for he and I were born to work together, like a man's two hands, feet, or eyelids, or like the upper and lower rows of his teeth. To obstruct each other is against nature's law" (p. 35).

Despite these lofty notions, however, the problem of slavery persisted in Rome. Whereas slavery in Rome was "non-ethnically" or "non-racially" based and was a "misfortune that could happen to anyone," (Watson, 1987, p. 10) slaves could work as doctors, business agents for their masters, artists, gladiators, or craftsmen. The problem, however, was that the slave was still a "thing" who "remained for the Roman...corporeal property whose value could be measured in monetary terms" (p. 46). At the time of The Twelve Tables, for example, the breaking of a slave's bone gave rise to a fixed penalty that was estimated at 50% of such an injury to a free person. Cleavages, therefore, between rights as ideals or enactments and rights as exercised in Roman society continued to exhibit marked contrasts.

Greek and Roman literature, in sum, suggest strong affinities with notions of equality, justice and the Brotherhood of Man as defined in the Universal Declaration. Although this literature is cognizant of the need to protect the individual from the abuse of political authority, it does not appear to seriously entertain the notion of providing for those in need. Cer-tainly, the circumstances of certain groups, such as slaves, stand in stark contrast to any of these lofty promises.

THE MIDDLE AGES

The Middle Ages began after the downfall of Rome in 476 BC. With the fall of this universal Roman empire, government control, as direct central government, was weak. Local government became the norm and the local lord was the important administrative figure (Curtis, 1981).

Historians such as Ebenstein (1960) attribute much of Rome's decline to its "unwillingness or inability to solve the social conflicts born of poverty, slavery and serfdom" (p. 167). The codes on positive rights and the justification of slavery on natural grounds during the Greco-Roman period, seem to have had a direct impact upon the fall of Rome.   This suggests a need for social acknowledgements of more humane notions of rights, such as stated in the Universal Declaration. Without such notions, a society can easily founder.

Natural Law

This concept of natural law appears central to the development of the idea of human rights in the Middle Ages. According to Lauterpacht (1950), during this period, there is a "striking continuity of thought between the Stoics and the most representative political literature of the Middle Ages in the affirmation of the principle of higher law - which is the law of nature - as the source of the rights of freedom and of government by consent" (p. 84).   This notion, however, of a higher law (i.e natural law) can be seen not only in the Stoics, as in Cicero's quote above in which "nature unites man with man", or Marcus Aurelius's appeal to brotherhood in the name of natural law, but also in Antigone's adherence to the "immutable written laws of heaven" and Christ's acknowledgement to "Render unto Caesar the things that are Caesar's and to God, the things that are God's" (Mark 12:17). This view, therefore, of a natural law that the ruler or government is subject to an authority higher than him/herself or itself is the principal feature of the Middle Ages (Lauterpacht, 1950).   Basically, the idea of natural law suggests a justice that is always fair and proceeds perhaps from God, the universe, or the inborn qualities of human nature (Weinreb, 1987).

I have previously mentioned that in Aristotelian thought it was natural for certain individuals to be slaves. Throughout the historical development of the idea of human rights, the appeal to natural law, "as a justification of legal and, subsequently, economic slavery is a frequent occurrence" (Lauterpacht, p. 104). The appeal to natural law was also the basis for the justification of slavery in the infamous Dred Scott Decision (1856) by the United States Supreme Court. Thus, it was a universal truth that "the right of property in a slave is distinctly and expressly affirmed" (Dred Scott v. Sandford, 1856).

On the other hand, Pope John XXIII writes: "By natural law every human being has the right to respect for his person, to his good reputation, the right to freedom in searching for truth and in expressing and communicating his opinions....[and] natural law also gives man the right to share in the benefits of culture and...the right to education" (Gibbons, pp. 291-292).

It seems, therefore, that this concept of natural law with its ancient origins and later prodding by Medieval thinkers, is an integral strand in more contemporary notions of human rights. As in the past, it has, at present, much potential for substantial misuse. If, for example, one of the laws of God and of Nature, as stated in the United States Declaration of Independence, is the inalienable right to liberty, how far can one exercise this right until it becomes a pretext for impinging upon another individual's apparent equally inalienable rights to privacy or to property? Stated simply, since both liberty and property are "natural," is a person justified in seizing another's assets?

It was necessary at this point to stress the notion of natural law because, as I have argued, this concept appears to have been a driving, if not, at times, unsettling influence behind the further development of the idea of human rights.

Social Theorists

Because of the general lack of central authority in the Middle Ages, I have chosen to divide this section into predominant social theorists and documents, that exhibit similarities with these crucial notions of human rights, instead of referring to specific groups such as the Greeks or the Romans. Certainly, these theorists and documents emerge from broad cultural identities. The Magna Carta (1215), for example, emanates from a society of scattered Anglo-Saxon and Danish tribes and territories, which were originally unconnected yet slowly united to eventually become the state of England (Mc Kechnie, 1914). Yet, it appears that the Magna Carta and other documents, rather than their specific

English or other identities, had a predominant influence in the development of the idea of human rights. Similarly, it was St. Thomas Aquinas's (1225-1274) influence, rather than his identity as an Italian that appears to have had a dominant sway in the development of the idea of human rights.

The notion of human dignity appears to have been entrenched during the Middle Ages. It seems that the inheritance of Stoic and early Christian ideas (D'Entreves, 1959), which stressed the dignity and equality of the human person, kept this idea operative in the social and political thinking of that time. Writing on the Middle Ages, Gierke (1951, p. 10) states: "Mankind is set before us as a single, universal Community...one mystical body...one single, and internally connected people or folk... called...the Commonwealth of the Human Race."

Certainly, the writings of John of Salisbury (1120-1180), considered the most typical medieval political writer before the thirteenth century (Ebenstein, 1960) mirrored Gierke's assertions. Using the human body as a metaphor, he compares humankind "to a body each organ, group, and class representing symbolically parts of the body" (Ebenstein, p. 191). Writing, in his *Policratus (Statesman's Book)* for example, on the State as an Organism, "The eyes, ears and tongue...claimed by judges... soldiers correspond to the hands...husbandmen correspond to the feet" (Ebenstein, p. 200). Whereas different individuals serve different functions, they are nevertheless, equally connected and part of the same body. To John of Salisbury, "The good of the community is assured by the virtue of all the individual members" (Hearnshaw, 1928, p. 61).

Other authors such as St. Augustine (354-430), who stood at the turning point between antiquity and the Middle Ages and Thomas of Aquinas, the most constructive and systematic thinker of the Middle Ages (D'Entreves, 1959), also espoused notions of equality and human dignity. Augustine acknowledges, for example, in his *City of God* that "Man...was made in His image" (Ebenstein, pp. 183-184).

Aquinas's contribution appears, however, more substantive than Augustine's mere reiteration of a basic Judaic-Christian principle. Whereas the "fundamental doctrine of St. Thomas... was that the individual alone has ultimate value" (Morris and Morris, 1924, p. 78), he also believed that "in natural law is expressed the dignity and power of man...which allows him, alone of created beings, to participate intellectually and actively in the rational order of the universe" (D'Entreves, p. 21).

Although he saw philosophy (i.e. reason) as the handmaiden of theology (i.e.faith), following St. Thomas reason triumphed over faith, which saw its rebirth in the classic humanism of the 14th and 15th centuries and seemed to pave the way for the social theorists of the Age of Enlightenment. Aquinas's position, thus, is an "enormous concession to rationalism" although "faith gives [reason] guidance and purpose" (Ebenstein, p. 215).

Aquinas's *Summa Theologica*, consequently contains numerous questions such as "Whether the Reason of Any Man Is Competent to Make Laws?" (Ebenstein, p. 232). He then quotes an authoritative source, usually a Biblical reference, in this case, Romans 2:14 "That when the Gentiles, who have not the law, do by nature those things that are of the law...are a law to themselves." He then reasons that "Anyone can make a law for himself" (Ebenstein, p. 232). My point of this discussion is to illustrate that Aquinas' process of reasoning which leads a person to know the "divine" nature of things (i.e. natural law) is to him, an indispensable expression of the dignity of the human person.

In regard to negative rights, John of Salisbury leaned heavily on the Old Testament with a strong bias against temporal rulers (Ebenstein, 1960). In the *Policraticus* (Ebenstein, p. 204), for example, he writes of the need to resist, yet, pardon tyrants "if they return into the way of righteousness." He then quotes I Kings 21:29: "Acab has humbled himself before my face; therefore will I not bring evil in his days."

Although he is best known for championing the supremacy of the ecclesiastical over worldly powers (Ebenstein, 1960), John of Salisbury never ceased to relentlessly expose the hypocrisies and abuses of both state and ecclesiastical authorities. Writing on the clergy for example, he states: "A poor man is seldom or never admitted to their number, and then rather as a result of his own vainglorious ambition than for the love of Christ" (Ebenstein, p. 205).

John Locke's later doctrines of resistance to tyrants, which influenced the framers of the American Declaration of Independence, strongly resembled the words of John of Salisbury's (Ebenstein, 1960).

St. Thomas Aquinas also believed that men had the right to disobey manmade legislation which violated eternal principles (Palumbo, 1982). To quote human rights scholar Lauterpacht (1950) on Aquinas:

> The justification of the state is in its service to the individual; a king who is unfaithful to his duty forfeits his claim to obedience. It is not rebellion to depose him, for he is himself a rebel; all political authority is derived from the people, and laws must be made by the people or their representatives. (p. 84)

Like Aristotle, Aquinas also recognized the legitimacy of slavery (Weston, 1989). This suggests once again that the appeal to natural law can lead to inhumane practices.

Another philosopher, Marsilius of Padua (1275 - 1343) used almost identical language as Aquinas concerning the need to thwart the abuses of political authority. It was he who stressed, for example, the will of the community, which anticipated the later doctrine of popular sovereignty (D'Entreves, 1959). To Marsilius, "The human authority to make laws belongs only to the whole body of the citizens or to the weightier part thereof" (Ebenstein, p. 271).

Whereas notions of the rights of the individual against the abuses of political authority seemed to gain popularity during the Middle Ages, the obligations of official authorities to provide for the needs of individuals appear less pronounced.

There were some social theorists, such as John of Salisbury, who spoke of the church as not compassionate to the suffering and misery of the afflicted. Speaking of the pope, he wrote: "He has built for himself palaces, and walks abroad not merely in purple but in gold. The palaces of priests dazzle the eye, and meanwhile in their hands the Church of Christ is defiled" (Ebenstein, p. 194).

St. Thomas Aquinas, however, did write extensively on almsgiving:

> Since love of one's neighbor is commanded us...it is essential...not merely to wish him well, but to act well towards him....[This] implies that we should succor him when he is in need, and this is done by almsgiving....It must be consonant with right reason....For a man must first provide for himself and those of whom he has the care, and can then succor such of the rest as are necessitous...For in this case the words of Ambrose become applicable: "Feed them that are dying of starvation, else shall you be held their murderer." Hence, it is a matter of precept to give almost to whosoever is in extreme necessity. But in other cases (namely, where the necessity is not extreme) almsgiving is simply a counsel, and not a command. (Jarrett, 1914, pp. 83-84)

Most striking is Aquinas's statements in which he quotes St. Basil and Ambrose respectively: "It is the clothes of the naked that hang locked in your wardrobe; it is the shoes of the barefooted that are ranged in your room" and "Whatever a man possesses above what is necessary for his sufficient comfort, he holds by violence." Noteworthy also is St. Augustine's statement: "When superfluities are retained, it is the property of others which is retained" (Jarrett, pp. 84-86).

Authors such as Jarret (1914) suggest that the theory which was in vogue during the whole of the Middle Ages was to give to the needy, what was superfluous to the giver, out of justice, not necessarily out of charity. Yet, this notion of positive action on behalf of the impoverished does not appear to be as compelling an argument, as the need to resist abusive political authorities, who are not accountable to the will of the people, in the social-political thought of the Middle Ages. The latter idea became even more pronounced during the Age of Enlightenment; the former idea began to flourish in the early nineteenth century.

The beginnings of an acknowledgement that an unjust social order can lead to indigence is apparent during the Middle Ages. The corollary here is Article 28 of the Universal Declaration which states the entitlement of everyone to a just "social and international order in which the rights and freedoms set forth in this Declaration can be fully realized."

Consequently, the notion of duties of the individual and the community is not merely to give to the needy out of charity. Rather, this notion takes on a broader meaning. It is the obligation to create a socially just world devoid of superfluities.

Historical Documents

Undeniably, the Magna Carta is a great landmark in the development of the idea of human rights. This document laid the groundwork for the many advances in human rights which were to come in England and then, throughout the world, in the following centuries. To this day, heads of state such as former Prime Minister Thatcher, referring to the changes in Eastern Europe, speak of the need for a "European Magna Carta which would entrench for the whole of Europe the rights, freedoms and rule of law which we in the west take for granted" (Whitney, 1990). At Runnymede, England in June 1215 scores of English nobility, bishops, and archbishops forced King John to sign this document which demanded an end to his abuses. It was significant because the nobility demanded peace with order and without revenge. Instead of violent insurrection, the traditional processes of the past, they chose to reach mutual understandings about each other's needs in this peace treaty (Stringham, 1966). It is not my purpose here to speculate why the nobility did not slaughter the king and his immediate entourage. In the final analysis, the king was practically alone and at the mercy of these men. Yet, he was allowed to continue his reign. With much humiliation and dishonor, he signed that document. He was in such disgrace that there was no King John the Second. That name died in British royalty. To this date, human rights activists often utilize the "mobilization of shame" (Joyce, 1978) as a political strategy against tyrannical governments.

The extraordinary legacy of this document suggests the efficacy of reconciliation without vengeance and savagery. Clause 62^4 clearly states: "And we have fully remitted and pardoned to all men, all the ill-will, rancor and resentments which have arisen between us and our subjects."

Considering the significance of the Magna Carta, this section will primarily deal with the relation of that document to the four identified crucial notions in the Universal Declaration. However, there are also other documents during the Middle Ages which seemed to pave the way to the Magna Carta.

William the Conqueror's Coronation Charter in 1066, for example, in which he pledged "to protect the holy churches of God and their governors, and to rule the whole nation subject to him with justice and kingly providence; to make and maintain just laws, and straightly to forbid every sort of rapine, violence and all unrighteous judgments" (Stringham, 1966, p. 110) is one such document. In 1100, furthermore, Henry I issued a charter which assured freedom of the church, promised the barons rights to inheritance and recognized some restraint on his power to dictate marriages of his barons' female relatives.

Under the Assizes of Jerusalem (1099), a document of government drafted by the Crusaders who captured that city from the Moslems, the power of the king was distinctly subordinate to the power exercised by the barons in council. Many English barons had participated in the Crusades and in the organization of Jerusalem's new government. It is quite possible that the spirit of the Magna Carta arose a century before Runnymede or was unrecognized until conditions demanded harsh leadership (Stringham, 1978).

The entire document of the Magna Carta, therefore, seems to be a statement of the dignity of the human person against the abuses of political authority. To the nobility of that time its merit was its articulation of definite and utilitarian measures to give relief from current wrongs (McKechnie, 1914). Although it was a very practical document, its list of demands to once again restore the dignity of the human person in the face of substantial mistreatment, became an ideal, a symbol standing for the need for humane constitutions. It eventually became a bill of rights, not only for the nobles, but for everybody. It became a universal document.

In the area of negative rights its contributions are substantial. The Magna Carta decreed the separation of church and state. Clause 63, for example states: "Wherefore our will is, and we firmly command that the church of England be free." Prior to this time, the church had sought control over the state and the state attempted to oversee religion. The church freedom of 1215 seems to have become the religious freedom of later centuries.

Numerous clauses, moreover, forbid the arbitrary taking of property such as Clause 30: "No person shall take the horses or carts of any free-man" or Clause 31 forbidding the seizure of "another man's wood... unless by the consent of him to whom the wood belongs." Certainly, there is an obvious correspondence between these clauses and Article 17 (2), of the Universal Declaration: "No one shall be arbitrarily deprived of his property."

Clauses such as 52 also prohibited land theft: "If any have been...dispossessed by us, without a legal verdict of their peers, of their lands, castles, liberties, or rights, we will immediately restore these things." This clause also speaks of the right to trial by jury.

Of significance also are clauses 45 and 40: "We will not make Justiciaries [judges]...excepting of such as know the laws of the land, and are well disposed to observe them" and "To none will we sell, to none will we deny, to none will we delay, right or justice." They suggest the importance of "fair hearings" by "independent and impartial tribunals" (Article 12 of the Universal Declaration).

Clause 12 forbids a "scutage [tax] or aid" to be imposed, "unless by common council." This clause speaks of the need for representative government. Certainly, it suggests strong correspondences with the rallying cry, "Taxation without representation is tyranny," during the American revolution.

Clause 41 expresses the right to travel: "All merchants shall have safety and security in coming into England, and going out of England and in staying and in travelling through England. Furthermore, Clause 42 states: "It shall be lawful to any person, for the future, to go out of our kingdom, and to return, safely and securely." Article 13 of the Universal Declaration expresses that right to travel.

The admonition against arbitrary arrest, detention or exile (Article 9 of the Universal Declaration) is evident in Clause 39: "No freeman shall be seized, or imprisoned, or dispossessed, or outlawed, or in any way destroyed...excepting by the legal judgment of his peers, or by the laws of the land."

In the area of economic, social, and cultural rights the most noteworthy contribution to the idea of human rights appears to be the protection and preservation of family life, one of the main goals of Magna Carta (Stringham, 1966).

In at least ten clauses of the Magna Carta, for example, the safety of families from abusive treatment was sought. King John, for example, as a feudal Lord often had control over marriage (Stringham, 1978). To end this abuse, "No widow shall be distrained to marry herself, while she is living without a husband" (Clause 8) Furthermore, "If anyone shall die indebted to the money lenders, his wife shall have her dower and shall pay nothing of that debt; and if children of the deceased shall remain who are under age, necessaries shall be provided for them, according to the tenement which belonged to the deceased" (Clause 11). Until the heir comes of age, a warden "shall keep up and maintain the houses, parks, warrens, ponds, milles and other things...and shall restore to the heir when he comes of full age, his whole estate, provided with ploughs and other implements of husbandry" (Clause 5). If, furthermore, a property owner failed to leave a will, under Clause 27 his holdings would be distributed for the benefit of the widow and children by "relatives and friends."

I have already discussed some of the many clauses protecting property rights such as Clause 15 preventing excessive taxation and Clause 30 forbidding arbitrary seizure of one's horse or wagon (i.e. a means of livelihood). In fact, twenty-one of the sixty-three clauses of the Magna Carta are concerned with property rights.

My observations suggest, however, that the nobles, who were ordinary men, fathers with wives and children, were most concerned with the dour economic and social consequences upon their families, while at the hands of a tyrannical ruler, in the event of their untimely deaths. Considering the recent Crusades, the onset of the Bubonic Plague, and the numerous other battles fought in service of the King, these concerns are understandable.

While crude, these clauses, nevertheless, were a beginning toward the amelioration of the often hard lots of women and children. It was not until the onset of industrialization in later centuries that the needs of women, children, *and* men became even more frustrated which, in turn, led to a more substantive cataloging of economic and social rights.

It appears, furthermore, that King John's right to govern depended upon his obligations to fulfill the pledges of the Magna Carta. While it was primarily directed against King John, the nobles and clergy knew that they were also bound by the promises of that document. In time it became common law which also bound justices, sheriffs, mayors and other public officials. (McIlwain, 1917a).

The above examples of rights, while not exhaustive, demonstrate, nevertheless, the overwhelming importance of the Magna Carta upon subsequent developments of the idea of human rights. Speaking of United States' constitutions, the Magna Carta's impact has led some authors such as Hazeltine (1917, p. 214) to state emphatically: "In the Bill of Rights, which forms a part of each of the written constitutions, both State and Federal, there is a persistence of those fundamental rights of Englishmen embodied in Magna Carta....The Bill of Rights of the State Constitutions traces its pedigree back to Magna Carta."

Jan Martenson (1988), Director-General of the United Nations Office at Geneva and Under-Secretary-General for Human Rights has remarked, furthermore that "The Universal Declaration of Human Rights...is nothing less than a monument to humankind, a veritable Magna Carta enumerating specific standards of achievement in the civil, political, economic, social and cultural fields that had never been attempted before and which are valid for all members of the human family" (p. 1).

THE RENAISSANCE

Generally speaking, the era from 1350 to 1600 includes most of the developments commonly dealt with under the heading "Renaissance." This period embraces, therefore, not only the Renaissance, (i.e. rebirth) in classical ideas, as espoused in Greek and Roman literature, but also the Reformation and Counter-Reformation. The Reformation represented a breakup of western Christendom in response to the failure of the official church Catholicism through greed and corruption to satisfy the spiritual needs of the community. The Counter-Reformation consisted primarily of the attempt to reform this official church within in order to thwart the further proliferation of the many Christian sects which arose at that time. These three movements, which occurred simultaneously with the birth and growth of the modern national state, are inextricably interwoven.

During that epoch, Gutenberg's invention of the printing press in 1450, the Ottoman conquest of Constantinople in 1453, the landing of Columbus in the Western Hemisphere in 1492, and the massacre of thousands of French Huguenots in Paris on St. Bartholomew's day in 1572 were some of many pivotal events which appear to have contributed to contemporary notions of human rights.

The settling of Europeans in the New World seemed to have necessitated ample justifications not only to claim these newly discovered lands as their own, but also to dominate its indigenous peoples. The right to property as a natural phenomenon appeared to have become increasingly stressed until the Age of Enlightenment when, in the writings of John Locke, it became an "unalienable truth."

With the Ottoman conquest, furthermore, scholars of the classics sought refuge in Italy, carrying with them vast knowledge of Greco-Roman literature. Consequently, the teachings of Aristotle continued to dominate the intellectual life of the Italian universities and philosophy in general (Cassirer, 1948). It is plausible, therefore, that Aristotle's notion of the slave as a natural state and as a tool, conformed nicely with this new conquista-tador's ethic of domination, the increasing expropriation of indigenous land and the subsequent bondage of Africans to develop this land. Thus, the right to own slaves to develop this new land, which "belonged" to the newly arrived settlers, was natural, if not God given.

The aims of very first settlers in the Americas were clear: slaves and gold (Zinn, 1980). As I have argued previously, natural law can be seen to proceed from something God given. Although Columbus did not use the term natural law, he wrote, nevertheless, that "in the name of the Holy Trinity" slaves could be subjugated and sold (Zinn, 1980, p. 4). Coming from this classical tradition, therefore, it seemed clear to Columbus and subsequent settlers, that it was natural law to own slaves and to expropriate lands. The printing press could spread these and other "natural truths" quickly to a growing literate population thereby gaining strong massive acceptance.

Whereas the Universal Declaration of Human Rights acknowledges rights to property (Article 17), it clearly rejects the idea of slavery (Article 4) and adds that rights shall be subject to limitations in order to secure respect for the rights of others (Article 29). That document attempts, consequently, to avert such an insensible outcry for liberties, as embraced by many European settlers, without regard for others' rights. The settling of the New World is one notable case in history in which the rhetoric of natural rights appears to mask exploitation.

During this period, there was also an anti-Protestant frenzy throughout much of Europe which came to a climax in the Massacre of St. Bartholomew in which thirty thousand Huguenots lost their lives. The Pope and thirty-three cardinals celebrated that massacre at a solemn Mass of Thanksgiving (Ebenstein, 1960).

Social Theorists

Although this epoch did not appear to produce philosophers of major importance, it seems, nevertheless, to have produced a few scholars who speak directly to the previously mentioned crucial notions of human rights.

Concerning the notion of human dignity, it is undeniable that the Renaissance emphasized the dignity of the human person. The numerous artistic masterpieces of that time, such as Michelangelo's David, his Creation of Adam in the Sistine Chapel, and Leonardo Da Vinci's Mona Lisa seem to reflect this *zeitgeist* which emphasized the beauty, value, and dignity of the human being.

The philosopher, Giovanni Pico, Count of Mirandola (1463-1494) author of *Discourse on the Dignity of Man* is one of the best examples of the Renaissance focus upon the dignity of the human person (Jones, 1952). In his *Oration on the Dignity of Man*, he writes:

> Man is the most fortunate of creatures and consequently worthy of all admiration....To [man] it is granted to have whatever he chooses, to be whatever he wills....When he came into life the Father conferred the seeds of all kinds and the germs of every way of life. Whatever seeds each man cultivates will grow to maturity and bear in him their own fruit. (Jones, 1952, pp. 565-566)

On the notion of negative freedoms, Martin Luther's (1483-1546) idea that religious belief is a matter of one's conscience, that faith is an expression of freedom and that it cannot be imposed by force is a substantial advancement over the concepts of theological and papal supremacy of the previous epoch.

Unfortunately, Luther also writes that a person should endure violence from his ruler, and obey not only the good but also the wicked lords (Waring, 1978). Such a statement is hardly indicative of human rights. Yet, I think that his call to freedom of conscience in religious matters, is a significant departure from the Middle Ages.

John Calvin (1509-1564), who also espoused Luther's notion of freedom of religious belief, differed substantially with him on the right of resistance to tyrannical rulers. To Calvin, considered a "nursing mother" of civil rights (Hearnshaw, 1949c), resistance was not the right of the people, but the right of magistrates and organized estates who were appointed for the protection of the people.

In his *Institutes of the Christian Religion*, Calvin also stresses the importance of conscience in religious belief writing that, "conscience is as a thousand witnesses," and quotes St. Paul (Romans 2:15) "Their conscience also bearing witness, and their thoughts accusing, or else excusing, one another" (Ebenstein, 1960, p. 317).

Addressing the notion of positive rights, the most important development in the Renaissance is an increasing concern for education, the arts, and development of the individual. The most outspoken social theorist in this regard is Desiderius Erasmus (1466-1536). In his *Institution of the Christian Prince* he emphasized the moral training of the individual, not only for the rulers of a state, but for everyone: "Precisely because the position of the ruler is so powerful, every effort must be directed toward providing him with a proper education" (Gilmore, 1952, pp. 129-130). He also writes:

> For I utterly dissent from those who are unwilling that the sacred Scriptures should be read by the unlearned and translated in their vulgar tongues....I long that the husbandman should sing portions of them to himself as he follows the plough, that the weaver should hum them to the tune of his shuttle. (Jones, 1952, p. 579)

His better known *Praise of Folly* attempted to expose the snobbishness, vanity and immorality of many of the scholastic theologians and monks of that time. Erasmus seemed to be one of the first who felt that education, which included learning the simple truths of the Judaic-Christian heritage of love and humility, was for everyone.

Other scholars such as Petrarch (1304-1374) held that education should have a "sober use," that is, education was a means to become a good and moral person. Without such a purpose, Petrarch felt that "learning inflates, it tears down....it is a glittering shackle, a toilsome pursuit and a resounding burden to the soul" (Jones, 1952, p. 564).

Erasmus and Petrarch were a few of a growing number of social theorists who revealed an increasing awareness of the expanding scope of governmental activity, which included an awareness of the duty to educate its citizens.

Considering the emphasis of this period upon the development of the personality, and education, including the arts and culture, it appears credible that notions of "the right to education...[which] shall be directed to the full development of the human personality and to the strengthening of respect for human rights and fundamental freedoms [which shall] promote understanding, tolerance and friendship" (Article 26 of the Universal Declaration), and "the right freely to participate in the cultural life of the community, to enjoy the arts" (Article 27) may have stemmed from this emulation of education during the Renaissance.

Jean Bodin (1530-1596), although a follower in Aristotle, in his *Books of the Six Commonwealth* clearly rejected the idea of slavery: "The cruelties one reads about are unbelievable" (Bodin, 1956, p. 17). Equally important, however, is his acknowledgement that excess wealth of the few can lead to the poverty of the many. His thinking emphasizes notions of egalitarian orders and distributive justice: "By justice I mean the proper distribution of rewards and punishments, and of those advantages due to each individual as a matter of right" (Bodin, pp. 204-205). Such language clearly reflects a newly developing doctrine of individual rights prior to the state.

Bodin, therefore, appears to build upon St. Augustine's notions of justice to create a just social order. Such an order can be accomplished not only as a responsibility of individuals but also as a duty of the state.

Historical Document

It appears that *The Vindiciae Contra Tyrannos (Defense of Liberty Against Tyrants)* is the only important document of this Renaissance period. Written under the pseudonym Stephen Junius Brutus in 1579, it consists of a mass of tracts published by many of the French Huguenots who, after the religious wars of the Reformation, were diminished to a small minority and forced to live in exile.

The purpose of the *Vindicae* is to inquire into the problem of obedience to the state. It underscores the importance of individual conscience rather than consent to the force of arbitrary state powers. It seems to stress the idea of popular sovereignty in its modern sense, emphasizing the importance of a people to freely express themselves and participate in the policies of their government (Reisman, 1990). The *Vindicae* also seems to anticipate John Locke in its accent upon one purpose of government which is to act as a third party to decide civil disputes about property.

Some correspondences with the *Vindicae* and the Universal Declaration are: Article 10, of the Universal Declaration, "Everyone is entitled to a fair and public hearing before an independent and impartial tribunal"; Article 17, "No one shall be arbitrarily deprived of his property"; and Article 21, "The will of the people shall be the basis of the authority of government."

The *Vindicae* seems to have had a powerful effect upon the Age of Enlightenment. Considered a dangerous book, it was burned publicly at Cambridge University in 1620 and later at Oxford in 1683. However, it continued to be widely read and seemed to inspire many liberation movements of the following epoch (Ebenstein, 1960).

The tenor of the *Vindicae* emphasizes, therefore, the notion of negative freedoms. The following excerpts are typical of this spirit:

> The people establish kings, puts the scepter into their hands, and
> who with their suffrages, approves the election. (Laski, 1925, p.
> 118)...The whole body of the people is above the king (p. 124)...
> Subjects are the king's brethren and not his slaves (p. 156)...A king
> may not lawfully take any honest man's estate from him, but by a
> manifest injustice (p. 160)... Justice requires that tyrants and
> destroyers of the commonwealth be compelled to reason. Charity
> challenges the right of relieving and restoring the oppressed. (p.
> 229)

It is undeniable that notions of human dignity run through the *Vindicae*. For example, "Life is a thing precious, and to be favored" (Laski, p. 153). Duties of rulers and everyone to treat others with charity is also a recurring theme.

On the notion of positive rights the *Vindicae* does mention the Judaic-Christian tradition which commands that "we ought to love our neighbor as ourselves" (Laski, p. 224). It makes note also of the importance of Christ's corporal works of mercy to feed the hungry, give drink to the thirsty, clothe the naked, lodge the stranger and visit the sick and imprisoned. It acknowledges also that the aims of justice are "first, that none be wronged; secondly, that good be done to all, if it be possible" (Laski, p. 225). Yet, these obligations to help the oppressed come toward the end of the *Vindicae*. It seems to relegate these positive rights to secondary importance to civil and political guarantees. These intellectual stirrings of the Renaissance, which seemed to emphasize, therefore, the dignity of the human person, the priority of conscience, the importance of education and culture, and the right to defend against tyrannical rulers, became the headwaters of the next epoch, the Age of Enlightenment.

THE AGE OF ENLIGHTENMENT

Although the Enlightenment is the most fully developed in eighteenth century France, it gradually evolved over several generations before becoming conscious of itself as a movement. Immanuel Kant's essay *An Answer to the Question: What is Enlightenment* seems to describe quite well this period with its emphasis upon human understanding: "Enlightenment is man's emergence from his self-imposed minority. This minority is the inability to use one's own understanding without the guidance of another....Thus the motto of the Enlightenment is 'Sapere aude'! Have the courage to use your own understanding!" (Goldmann, 1973, p. 3).

During this era, which I will roughly delineate as the 17th and 18th centuries, individuals questioned and often refuted numerous dogmas, religious, and other belief systems. In their place they substituted reason and understanding which would also discover objective answers and be valid eternally. The literature of this period suggests that overall the numerous religious wars of the previous era led to a disillusionment with religious doctrine. These creeds had often justified oppression by government or religious heads, or a collusion of both, with such notions as "in the name of the Holy Trinity" or "Divine Right." Totally breaking with this tradition, the following social theorists and historical documents represent attempts of this period to use reason and experience, as an antidote to the tyrannies emanating from religious tenets, to carve out a socially just world.

This belief in reason and experience, however, spurred by the numerous scientific breakthroughs of that period, such as Newton's law of gravity, may have proved elusive. If the central belief of the Enlightenment period were to prove that the evils of the world could be cured by the appropriate technology and science, rather than religious belief systems, then there would exist engineers of human souls and bodies (Berlin, 1956). It would be quite possible, therefore, for scientists, rather than the clergy of the previous era, to collude with government. It appears that, although reason may have triumphed over faith, the eternal truths that reason could objectively find might also have disastrous consequences. Therefore, as the philosophers of the Enlightenment such as John Locke were engineering human souls, by preaching "life, liberty and property," in lieu of more religious statements such as "God" or the "Holy Trinity," European settlers were continuing to import slaves and take the lives of countless indigenous peoples, depriving them of their liberty and their lands. influential in the field of international law (Curtis, 1981; Moynihan, 1990).

Doctrine of Humanitarian Intervention

The exiled Dutchman Hugo Grotius (1583-1645), extremely expounded upon this doctrine in 1625 in *De Jure Belli ac Pacis (On the Rights of War and Peace)* which:

> Recognized as lawful the use of force by one or more states to stop the maltreatment by a state of its own nationals when that conduct was so brutal and largescale as to shock the conscience of the community of nations. (Buergenthal, 1988, p. 3)

To Grotius, war could be started "for the enforcement of rights," but "only within the bounds of law and good faith." (Curtis, 1981a, pp. 303-304). He appeared to be one of the first to rely on experience and the senses, a basic tenet of the Age of Enlightenment rather than only faith to reach such an inalienable truth. He writes: "The principles of [natural law]...are in themselves manifest and clear, almost as evident as are those things which we perceive by the external senses; and the senses do not err" (Curtis, p. 324).

This doctrine seems to have become inextricably linked to the idea of human rights. In the name of human rights, countries have waged war and inspired revolutions. To illustrate, the French assisted the Americans in the Revolutionary War against the tyrannies of England; in the Civil War the North invaded the South in order to liberate the slaves; and, most recently, the United States fought Iraq to liberate the citizens of Kuwait from the asserted tyrannies of Saddam Hussein. My point is not to question the legality or morality of these interventions. Rather, it is to point out an apparent intimate connection between the idea of human rights and Grotius's doctrine of humanitarian intervention. This connection seems to persist today.

Although this doctrine was the first in the history of the idea of human rights to state that there are limits that apply to governments in the treatment of their own nationals, this doctrine was often misused and served as a pretext for the occupation or invasion of weaker states (Buergenthal, 1988). Irving Kristol also echoes this idea about human rights in general when he states: "Beneath the surface there is always a hidden agenda. An issue of 'human rights' today is all too likely to be an issue exploited in bad faith" (Laqueur and Rubin, 1990, p. 393).

Surely, however, the unconscionable silence of the world during Germany's pogroms of the 1930s and 40s and, more recently, the killing fields of Cambodia in the 1970s indicates the need for humanitarian intervention. The question, therefore, becomes the appropriateness of such intervention. Is it more appropriate, for example, to invade, which Grotius sees as humanitarian, or to confront the human rights violator with non-violent, but direct measures? Was the recent release of thousands of political prisoners in the Soviet Union due to the mass letter writing campaigns and the mobilization of shame in general over such an outrageous human rights situation? Would an invasion have had the same effect? *Glasnost* means not only "openness," but also "publicity." Did the former Soviets, through the policies of *Glasnost*, merely engage in a massive advertising campaign to compensate for an extremely tarnished image?

Undoubtedly, these questions are controversial. My purpose is not to answer them, but rather to emphasize that the doctrine of humanitarian intervention, which emerged during the Enlightenment period, is, like the doctrine of natural law, a troublesome, yet, nevertheless, important issue in the evolution of the idea of human rights which persists to this day. It has the potential to enhance as well as destroy life.

Social Theorists

The social theorists and historical documents of this era suggest a flowering of civil and political liberties (i.e. negative freedoms).

John Locke.

John Locke's (1632-1704) teachings appear extremely pervasive in the evolution of the idea of human rights. His primary contention is that there are certain rights which are self-evident. Chief among these rights are "rights to life, liberty, (freedom from arbitrary rule) and property." These rights existed "in a state of nature, before humankind entered into civil society." Upon entering into civil society, they formed a social contract in order to secure these "natural rights" (Weston, 1989, p. 14).

According to Locke, the people set up government as a "fiduciary trust" (Ebenstein, 1960), whose primary purpose is to be responsive to the needs of the people in order to secure these natural rights, that is, inalienable rights. If unresponsive to the people's needs, they had a right to a responsible revolution of the people.

Locke's triad of "life, liberty and property," or referred to at times as "life, liberty, and estates," became almost universally accepted doctrines in American prerevolutionary literature (Adler & Gorman, 1975). Nevertheless, Jefferson, in drawing up the Declaration of Independence, conspicuously dropped the final right, the right to property from that document, substituting "the pursuit of happiness." He also counseled his friend, Lafayette against the inclusion of the right to property (Adler & Gorman) in the French Bill of Rights. Jefferson, it appears did not deny that there was a right to property, but did not see it on the same fundamental level as the rights to life and liberty.

Locke, therefore, seemed to have a direct influence on the Declaration of Independence. Yet, Jefferson's substitution enabled that document to achieve a universality beyond Locke's original intentions. As Adler & Gorman (1975) state:

The means for the pursuit of happiness that societies and governments might subsequently discover in the ongoing historical effort to
provide human beings with the conditions *they need for their
well-being and welfare* [italics added]. The possession of property,
or its economic equivalents, is certainly only one of such conditions.
(p. 40)

Jefferson's contention with Locke's triad, therefore, seemed to pave the way
toward the theoretical development of economic and social rights (i.e. positive
freedoms) in the following century.

Although the "right to own property" is also recognized in Article 17 of the
Universal Declaration, in Article 3, "security of person" is substituted for the
phrase property in Locke's triad: "Everyone has the right to life, liberty and
security of person." Jefferson's concerns, therefore, seemed prevalent even up
to the drafting of the Universal Declaration.

It appears that the core of John Locke's argument is that humans do not
have to submit their lives, liberties, and estates to the arbitrariness of political
authority. The only way that they can divest themselves of their natural
liberties is by mutual consent to social compacts, such as constitutions and
laws, which would ensure the comfort and safety of all members.
Governments, which grow out of these social compacts, are at all times
amenable to the will of the people.

Notions that government should provide for individuals appear notoriously
absent from his philosophy. Although he does speak of the "good of mankind,"
he "regarded poverty not as a misfortune, but as a sign of moral failure.
Unemployment, Locke wrote, was due to 'the relaxation of discipline and the
corruption of manners' and the first step 'towards setting the poor on work'
should be the closing of 'unnecessary alehouses.'" Locke "also proposed
methods for 'taking away the pretence' that there was no work for the idle to
do" (Cranston, 1961, pp. 30-31).

Locke, furthermore, assisted Lord Ashley, one of the founders and chief
owners of the Carolinas, in drawing up the *Fundamental Constitutions of
Carolina* (1669). Although this constitution guaranteed religious toleration, it
accepted "Negro" slavery as a form of rightful property: "Every freeman... shall
have absolute power and authority over his negro slaves, of what opinion or
religion soever." To Locke, slavery was a state of war which existed between a
lawful conqueror and a captive (Lichteim, 1970).

Notions of negative freedoms, therefore, appear strong in Locke's philosophy; positive freedoms are barely negligible. This point is significant considering his enduring legacy upon subsequent theorists and the documents of this period which appear to emphasize civil and political freedoms. An apparent preponderance of negative rights in the Universal Declaration also seems to reflect Locke's influence.

The French Philosophers.

Another important thinker is Charles-Louis de Secondat, Baron de la Brede et de Montesquieu, (1689-1755), who was a great admirer of Locke.

Montesquieu, like Locke, made no effort to study the condition of the lower class and believed that government ought to protect the liberty and property of individuals. Because he was fearful that power corrupts, he strongly advocated moderate governments, comprised of checks to power. He was also a strong believer in the responsivity of laws to the needs of the people. Legislation should adapt itself to the customs, religion, and principle occupations of a country's inhabitants (Laqueur and Rubin, 1990). The writings of John Locke and Montesquieu appeared influential in the formation of British law; Voltaire and Rousseau seemed to provide a philosophical basis for the French Revolution.

Francois Marie Voltaire (1694-1778) was a strong proponent of freedom of person, the press, and religious thought. In his writings he stresses the need, for example:

> To be secure on lying down that you shall rise in possession of the same property with which you retired to rest: that you shall not be torn from the arms of your wife, and from your children, in the dead of night, to be thrown into a dungeon or buried in exile in a desert; that, when rising from the bed of sleep, you will have the power of publishing all your thoughts....Every private individual who persecutes a man, his brother, because he is not of the same opinion, is a monster. (Laqueur and Rubin, 1990, pp. 79-81)

Jean Jacques Rousseau (1712-1778) appears different from the philosophers of the Enlightenment just mentioned because he realizes that the purposes of government were not merely to protect individual liberty, but also to ensure equality among its citizens. It was he who seemed to add compassion for the lower classes to the philosophy of the Enlightenment.

Although he recognizes a right to property, he knew that it could easily become a source of inequality and a form of private domination which needed to be kept under control by the will of the people (Cobban, 1964). In a similar vein, Rousseau also concerns himself with distributive justice. In his *Social Contract* (1762) he writes that no citizen "shall ever be wealthy enough to buy another, and none poor enough to be forced to sell himself." Although he acknowledges that the ideal of equitable distribution of property is difficult to maintain in practice, it "is precisely because the force of circumstances tends continually to destroy equality that the force of legislation should always tend to its maintenance" (Ebenstein, 1960, p. 440).

A strong proponent of popular sovereignty, which he views as the social contract which creates government, is conceived among equals, not "between a superior and an inferior, but [as] an agreement of the body with each of its members... it can have no other object than the general welfare" (Laqueur and Rubin, 1990, p. 75).

The major historical significance of Rousseau is that he represented a complete break from John Locke's emphasis upon individualism (Cobban, 1964) and negative freedoms which seemed so characteristic of the Age of Enlightenment. It is quite possible that the opening words of the United States Constitution "We the People" and the phrase "the general welfare" have their origins in the writings and spirit of Jean Jacques Rousseau.

A lesser known, but important social theorist is Gracchus Babeuf (1760-1797) who, like Rousseau, also showed compassion for the lower classes. Babeuf and his followers, the Babouvists, proclaimed, for example, in his *Manifesto of Equals* that "We demand the communal enjoyments of the fruits of the earth: the fruits are for all." He was concerned about inequality and envisioned a society where "Everything will be appropriated and proportioned in terms of present and predicted needs and according to the probable growth, and ability, of the community." (Harrington, 1972, p. 24).

With Rousseau's emphasis upon equality, the General Will and the potential abuse of property, and Babeuf's concomitant concerns for equality, the community and human needs, there appeared to be stirrings for concerns for positive freedoms among these French social theorists. Clearly, however, the basic mood in France, as in John Locke's thinking, was in the direction of negative freedoms.

Other Social Theorists.

Thomas Paine's (1737-1809) influence upon the development of the idea of human rights is irrefutable. In his *Rights of Man*, he wrote passionately of the duty of government to provide for its citizens in order to prevent poverty. Paine's strategy was in large part progressive taxation, education for all, and full employment.

By following Paine's strategy:

> The hearts of the humane will not be shocked by ragged and hungry children, and persons of seventy or eighty years of age, begging for bread. The dying poor will not be dragged from place to place to breathe their last....Widows will have a maintenance for their children, and not be carted away, on the death of their husbands, like culprits and criminals...the haunts of the wretched will be known...and the number of petty crimes, the offspring of distress and poverty, will be lessened...and the cause and apprehension of riots and tumults will cease. (Fast, 1946, pp. 255-256)

Paine dedicated himself to do away with the Poor Laws which were first enacted in 1601, and endured well into the Industrial Revolution. These laws resulted in the establishment of poor houses, set up to care for the aged, the sick, and the insane (Katz, 1986). Thomas Paine's strategy by preventing poverty, therefore, would do away with these houses which he viewed as socially sanctioned torture.

It was Immanuel Kant (1724-1804) who radically went beyond the thinking of the Enlightenment by proposing a federation of nations dedicated to peace and human rights which might rally world opinion against human rights violators. He constantly emphasized the need for political action among reasonable people to thwart the spread of all social evils and inspired hopes to expunge hypocrisy from the practices of nations. According to Orwin and Pangle (1984), he provided a theoretical basis for the League of Nations.

In his *Fundamental Principles of the Metaphysic of Morals*, for example, Kant emphasizes a moral obligation to act: "The first proposition is: An action to have moral worth, must be done from duty" (Curtis, 1981b, p. 40). On the acknowledgement of the hypocrisy of nations he writes in his *Project for a Perpetual Peace:*

> The only difference between the savages of America and those of Europe, is, that the former have eaten up many a hostile tribe whereas the latter have known how to make a better use of their enemies; they preserve them to augment the number of their subjects, that is to say, of instruments destined to more extensive conquests. (Crocker, 1969, pp. 301-302)

He is also known for his criticism of Grotius "and other useless and impotent defenders of the rights of nations [who] have been constantly cited in justification of war" (Crocker, p. 302).

Yet, Kant appears hopeful that nations could secure their own safety, by agreeing to constitutions which should guarantee to all their human rights. Accordingly, in Kant there appears the beginning of a movement toward solidarity rights, that is the duty of governments which are representatives of the people to cooperate.

All of the above social theorists attest, therefore, that the predominant social philosophy of the Age of Enlightenment was the emphasis upon civil and political liberties. Yet, in varying degrees, Rousseau, Babeuf, and Paine began to go beyond these negative rights and to emphasize the duty of government to provide for its citizens. Kant went even further by acknowledging the hypocrisies of civilized nations and calling for the moral obligation of all nations to work together for perpetual peace and human rights.

Native American Influence.

According to   Native American scholar and member of the Choctaw Nation , Devon A. Mihesuah (1996, p. 55):

> American Founding Fathers...who drew up the U.S. Constitution were influenced not only by European writers such as Locke, Rousseau and Montesquieu, as well as ideas found in the Magna Carta and the Greek and Roman empires, but also by the powerful, well-organized Haudenosaunee (Iroquois) Kaianerekowa (Great Law of Peace). The Constitution framers therefore adopted certain aspects of the Iroquois Confederacy...such as impeachment, equal representation of nations (states), checks and balances, and the concepts of freedom, peace and democracy.

Certainly, it would appear that Thomas Paine, who had tremendous respect for the way of governance and sense of equality among the aboriginal people of North America (Paul, 1993), and   the European colonists, who largley conducted their "relations with Indians on an explicitly nation-to-nation basis involving formal treaties" (Churchill, 1994, p. 304), learned a lot about alternative ways of governing and community in general, which they may have incorporated in their writings and documents.   John Marshall, in fact, first Supreme Court Chief Justice recognized the Cherokee "as a people capable of maintaining the relations of peace and war....[therefore] bound by [the] numerous treaties made with them" (Churchill, p. 305).

To be sure, it is an understatement to say that the Americans, then indiscriminately violated these treaties, which, anyway they often "bribed, threatened, intoxicated or gulled" (Misuah, 1995, p. 30) the indigeneous people into signing.

At any rate, Chief Joseph Brant, the Iroquois Statesman (1742-1807?) (Britt, 1938, p. 67) states:

> It is not the quantity of lands claimed at this time, which alarms the Indians, but the principle upon which it is claimed, for it is opening a door for extending it over the whole of the Indian lands...and the highest degree of injustice....the disgust is spreading where no prejudice had before existed.... it may be well known that the personal interest prompts them to it, not the public good. (pp. 87-88)

These words of this statesman, a "gentleman to the end" (Britt, p. 92), who on his death bed lamented the fate of the "poor Indians," and asked to "endeavor to do them all the good you can" (Britt, p. 91) are perhaps exemplary of a general spirit of cooperation among indigenous people and concern for the public good or general welfare of all, a notion eventually to be found in the United States Constitution and United Nations human rights instruments.

Historical Documents

The Age of Enlightenment also saw a tremendous expansion of documents proclaiming rights and liberties.

Early Colonial Charters.

Many of the earlier charters and statements of liberties of the American colonies seem to have played a pivotal role in the establishment of rights in the more enduring documents of this period, such as the English Bill of Rights (1689), the United States Declaration of Independence (1776), the United States Constitution (1789) and its Bill of Rights (1791), and the French Declaration of the Rights of Man and Citizen (1789).

Such charters and statements include, for instance, the First Virginia Charter (1606), the Charter of Massachusetts Bay (1629), the Charter of Maryland (1632) and the Fundamental Orders of Connecticut (1639), the Charter of Rhode Island and Providence Plantations (1663), and the Concessions and Agreements of West New Jersey (1677).

Perry and Cooper (1959) note that the First Charter of Virginia was probably modeled on the charter of the East India Company, a corporation formed to establish colonies and carry on trade. By the beginning of the seventeenth century individual financing was inadequate to meet the tremendous expenses involved in exploring and colonizing the New World.

Because colonization was undertaken by companies organized for private profit, broad considerations of national policy also motivated the colonial movement which included incentives to spread Christianity, to establish England as a national power, and to relocate some of England's surplus population (Perry and Cooper, 1959).

There was also a strong corporate aspect to these colonial charters (Chafee, 1952b). These charters primarily served as a kind of corporate prospectus, designed in part to entice settlers to the New World. Initially, they were charters forming corporations. Eventually, they became charters for their settlements. All individuals in these charters were associated with each other to do business through the power conferred on them by the King. Therefore, they became a legal entity.

Consequently, the Massachussets Bay Company was something like the General Electric Company. Through these charters, companies could finance voyages to North America. Numerous people expected to make money out of these companies. The King was to get his cut in the form of a "Fifth Part of the Ore of Gold and Silver", which the settlers discovered. These charters also provided for such frequent problems as keeping order, defense against the Indians and possibly the French or Spanish, ownership of land, settlement of disputes, and coining of money (Chafee, 1952b).

These early charters, sanctioned by the King and the government, provided for a large measure of spiritual liberty. It appears, however, that this provision of religious toleration was included, not because of humanitarian concerns, but because officials felt that they could kill two birds with one stone by making useful colonists out of people who were a nuisance in England! During this time, the English were constantly punishing Presbyterians, Separatists, and Quakers. The granting of religious liberty to the colonists, however, would entice settlers to the New World thereby providing England with the necessary resources to develop the land and carry back gold and other riches to England. Although there would be a detestable diversity of faiths overseas, England would not have to worry about this diversity three thousand miles away (Chafee, 1952b).

These companies also used other devices to obtain desirable immigrants, such as the exempting of colonial settlers from feudal burdens, which included engaging in knight service as an obligation of a man to his lord; the lifting of excessive restrictions on travel to the new world; and the granting of the rights of Englishmen to the settlers and their children.

In the early seventeenth century, there existed no precise statement concerning the rights of Englishmen, although the Magna Carta constituted the primary source of the rights of the individual (Perry and Cooper, 1959). Yet, the guarantees of these charters eventually played an extremely important role in the struggles of the American colonists against the tyrannies of the English rulers.

These charters, therefore, designed in large part to entice settlers to the Americas, indicate that there indeed *may* be hidden agenda when speaking about human rights.

It is difficult to definitively state these charters' influence upon later documents. Surely, later English developments such as the Petition of Right had an influence upon subsequent colonial charters. Yet, irrespective of probable motivations behind the early charters, certain rights such as religious liberty, exemptions from certain feudal burdens, freedom to travel, and the assurance to the colonists of the rights of Englishmen, which stemmed from the pronouncements of the Magna Carta, seemed to usher in a new and important era in the declaration of human rights in constitutions and other documents.

The First Charter of Virginia (1606) therefore, appearing typical in tone and substance to other early colonial charters, states, for example, that the settlers have "power to mine gold and silver, yielding a fifth to the Crown [Article IX]....[and] power to transport supplies to colonies without customs for seven years [Article XIII]" (Chafee, 195la, Pam. 1, p. 47). In spite of its apparent tolerance for religion, the "Infidels and Savages, living in those parts," must be brought to "human Civility," by accepting the *Christian* religion (Perry, and Cooper, 1959, p. 40).

Developments in England.

England's Petition of Right (1628) appears the second great Charter of English Liberty next to the Magna Carta and a vital antecedent to the American Bill of Rights.

In response to the abuses of Charles I, under the Stuart theory of prerogative, this document established the following:

> The king was forbidden to imprison persons without showing cause, the quartering of soldiers and mariners in private homes was stopped, the trial of civilians by courts-martial was declared illegal, and the king's power to levy taxes with the consent of the peoples' representatives in Parliament was restricted. (Perry and Cooper, 1959, p. 72)

The third great Charter of English liberty was the English Bill of Rights (1689). Its purpose was to correct specific grievances which had arisen during the reigns of Charles II and James II. It reflected a deep need among seventeenth-century England for a clarification of many legal issues, and, considering the objections of the time, a logical time for such clarification. This document appears a direct ancestor to the bills of rights adopted by the states at the time of the American Revolution and to the first ten amendments of the Constitution of the United States (Perry and Cooper, 1959). It was also the culmination of the Glorious Revolution of 1688, often considered one of the least violent and the most beneficent of revolutions (Schwartz, 1980).

This document called for a number of restraints upon the abuses of the monarchy. Specifically, it stated that "Excessive bail ought not to be required, nor excessive fines imposed, nor cruel and unusual punishments inflicted." It also named the right to trial by jury which is similar to the United States Constitution's Eighth Amendment word for word with the exception of "shall" for "ought."

It declared in addition that "Election of members of Parliament ought to be free; that freedom of speech and debates in Parliament ought not to be questioned in any court or other place" and "Forfeitures of particular persons before conviction are illegal." Specifically condemning the abuses of prerogative by James II, it declared that "The pretended power or suspending of laws or the execution of laws by regal authority without consent of the parliament is illegal" (Schwartz, 1980a, p. 41).

Certainly, the above rights have strong correspondences with the Universal Declaration. Article 11, for example, states "The right to be proven innocent until proven guilty" and admonishes against unfair penalties; Article 5 states "No one shall be subjected...to cruel, inhuman or degrading treatment or punishment."

Further Developments in the United States.

Whereas Virginia provided the first colonial charter, this state was also the first to adopt guarantees of human rights, segregating these provisions in a Declaration of Rights (June 12, 1776). It also served as a model for other states and had a direct influence upon Madison's proposed amendments for the Bill of Rights thirteen years later (Chafee, 1952b).

What is most significant about this document, however, is that it was the first document in which a sovereign state desired to prevent its own legislature from infringing upon basic human rights. Prior to this time, the major documents limited the prerogatives of the monarchy.

This document appears, however, to be not only a reiteration of English principles which existed in the Magna Carta, the Petition of Right, the Commonwealth Parliament, and the Revolution of 1688, but also reflected in large measure the unofficial writings by individuals like John Locke and other social theorists of the eighteenth century (Chafee, 1952b). James Madison, for example, noted that English documents did not specify freedom of the press and the rights of conscience.

The following examples in the Virginia Declaration are illustrative of certain rights:

> Section I: All men[5] are by nature equally free and independent, and have certain inherent rights...namely the enjoyment of life and liberty, with the means of acquiring and possessing property, and pursuing and obtaining happiness and safety; Sec. 2: All power is vested in, and consequently derived from the people; magistrates are their trustees and servants, and at all times amenable to them; Sec. 13: The freedom of the press is one of the great bulwarks of liberty and can never be restrained but by despotic governments [and] Sec. 16: Religion, or the duty which we owe to our Creator, and the manner of discharging it, can be directed only by reason and conviction, not by force or violence. (Perry and Cooper, 1959, pp. 311-312)

Undoubtedly, state constitutions had an effect upon the development of the Universal Declaration. The United Nations *Yearbook on Human Rights* in 1946 contains, for example, all the provisions relating to human rights of every constitution in force in the world on December 31, 1946. Included is the United States Constitution, as well as, declarations of rights in state constitutions.

It is apparent, furthermore, that the Virginia Declaration of Rights influenced the drafting of the Declaration of Independence by Thomas Jefferson, a representative from Virginia. This document was an important development in the evolution of the idea of human rights. It did not appear to state anything new. Its significance, however, seems to lie in its *summarization* of many of the major principles of that era which included equality, the inalienable rights to life, liberty and the pursuit of happiness, governments deriving their powers from the consent of the governed, and the right to abolish unjust governments and the numerous abuses of the English King. Significant also was Congress's refusal to include in Jefferson's draft his condemnation of the slave trade (Perry and Cooper, 1959). Yet, while expounding upon the equality of all men, that document did refer to the "merciless Indian savages."

The final development in the United States during this time is the United States Constitution (1789) which now includes its Bill of Rights (1791). Like many other documents of this era, it appears to exhibit a preponderance of negative rights, such as in Amendment 1 which emphasizes freedom of religion, freedom of the press, the right to peaceably assemble, and to petition government for a redress of grievances. This stress upon negative rights seems due to the general tenor of that period, as reflected in major social theorists and documents which emphasized such rights. Furthermore, most of the members at the constitutional convention were wealthy slaveowners, landowners, and merchants. Not one member represented the small farming or mechanic classes (Beard, 1929). James Madison and Alexander Hamilton in the *Federalist Papers*, furthermore, appeared concerned about a possible insurrection by the poorer classes clamoring for an equal distribution of property, which these Founding Fathers viewed as wicked and improper (Zinn, 1990).

These apprehensions about the equal distribution of wealth suggest in part why the United States Constitution does not mention the word "equality," a pivotal concept in the Declaration of Independence. It appears that a growing class of merchants and land owners was beginning to exchange places with the unjust monarchies of previous decades. It remained for the following century to assert rights against these new factions.

Developments in France.

The most important development in France was the French Declaration of the Rights of Man and Citizen adopted by the National Assembly on August 26, 1789.

Many of the rights in the United States Bill of Rights are also in this Declaration, including no deprivation of liberty or property except by established processes, no excessive punishments, freedom of thought and religion, freedom to speak, write and print. This document, like the Bill of Rights, was greatly influenced by United States state constitutions, which were circulated throughout Paris as early as 1783 (Chafee, 1952b).

The following select phrases illustrate striking correspondences between the French Declaration and the Universal Declaration.

Article 1 of the French Declaration states in part: "Men are born and remain free and equal in respect of rights"; Article 1 of the Universal Declaration states in part: "All human beings are born free and equal in dignity and rights."

Article 4 of the French Declaration states:

Liberty consists in the power of doing whatever does not injure another. Accordingly, the exercise of the natural rights of every man has no other limits than those which are necessary to secure to every other man the free exercise of the same rights; and these limits are determinable only by the law;

Article 29 of the Universal Declaration asserts:

In the exercise of his rights and freedoms everyone shall be subject only to such limitations as are determined by law solely for the purpose of securing due recognition and respect for the rights and freedoms of others.

Article 6 of the French Declaration states: "The law is an expression of the common will. All citizens have a right to concur, either personally or by their representation in its formation"; in the Universal Declaration Article 21 reads: "The will of the people shall be the basis of the authority of government...[and] Everyone has the right to take part in the government of his country, directly or through freely chosen representatives."

Articles 8 and 9 of the French Declaration state:

No one ought to be punished but by virtue of a law promulgated before the offence, and legally applied;... Every man being counted innocent until he has been convicted... all vigor more than is necessary to secure his person ought to be provided against by law;

In the Universal Declaration, Article 11 reads:

No one shall be held guilty of any penal offence on account of any act or omission which did not constitute a penal offence, under national or international law, at the time when it was committed...[and] everyone charged with a penal offense has the right to be presumed innocent until proven guilty.

Finally, Article 10 of the French Declaration states: "No man is to be interfered with because of his opinions, not even because of religious opinions"; in the Universal Declaration Articles 18 and 19 state: "Everyone has the right to freedom of thought, conscience and religion...[and] Everyone has the right to freedom of opinion and expression: this right includes freedom to hold opinions without interference."

The preceding examples suggest that the French Declaration, along with other primary human rights documents of this era, emphasize negative freedoms and directly influenced the Universal Declaration.

The calls for equality, so essential to human dignity and the realization of positive freedoms, from such social theorists as Rousseau, Babeuf, and Paine were noted briefly, yet forcefully, in the Virginia Bill of Rights, the Declaration of Independence and the French Declaration.

Article 6 of the French Declaration of the Rights of Man and the Citizen states specifically furthermore:

> The law...should be the same for all, whether it protects or punishes; and all being equal in its sight, are equally eligible to all honors, places and *employments* [italics added] according to their different abilities, without any other distinction than that of their virtues and talents.

It appears that this declaration is the first to express the human need to work. In the following century this need, along with other positive freedoms, becomes more forcefully expressed.

A summary of the belief in reason in the Age of Enlightenment, the preeminence of civil and political liberties, and the beginnings of a concern for positive freedoms appears evident in a letter from Thomas Jefferson to the mayor of Washington D.C. Written on June 24, 1826 two weeks before his death, he had to decline an invitation to attend a fiftieth anniversary celebration of the Declaration of Independence because of ill health:

> May it [the Declaration of Independence] be to the world, what I believe it will be...the signal of arousing men to burst the chains under which monkish ignorance and superstition had persuaded them to bind themselves, and to assume the blessings and security of self-government. That form which we have substituted, restores the free right to the unbounded exercise of reason and freedom of opinion. All eyes are opened, or opening, to the rights of man. The general spread of the light of science has already laid open to every view the palpable truth, that the mass of mankind has not been born with saddles on their backs, nor a favored few booted and spurred, ready to ride them legitimately by the grace of God. (Commager, 1960, p. 19)

THE AGE OF INDUSTRIALIZATION

I have chosen to include in this era all social theorists and historical documents after the French Declaration until the events immediately preceding the formation of the United Nations at the San Francisco Conference in 1945. Characteristic of this time is a deepening of the division of labor and a marked increase in the production of industrial goods concomitant with the introduction of sophisticated machinery and the decline of domestic production. People could earn money to buy goods and services, not only by working, but by speculation with their capital. Replacing entirely the former feudal arrangements, capitalism became the new social and economic structure.

As a result of these changes brought about by industrialization, poverty became rampant. The social structures of the time necessitated that many individuals work at jobs which were a drudgery. Unemployment became synonymous with poverty and often led to deprivation of such basic needs as food and shelter. Stresses resulting from this difficult situation often included domestic violence, crime, drug addiction, and other social ills. In this newly industrialized world, wealth became increasingly maldistributed causing, for instance, shanty-towns and other makeshift dwellings to spring up next to luxurious urban developments.

In response to these newly developed conditions, the claim for human rights widened. Positive rights became emphasized and added to the list of the more common negative freedoms. It is likely that these negative freedoms with their emphasis upon individuality even legitimated, if not condoned, the abuses which arose during this period. The new oppression, however, resulted from an unjust social and economic order, rather than a tyrannical monarch as in the previous epoch necessitating, therefore, the enumeration of economic and social rights in order to have basic human needs realized. In fact, many of the national constitutions drawn up during this time began offering guarantees of full employment, unemployment insurance, old age and sickness benefits and the right to a free education (United Nations, Department of Public Information [Dept. of. Pub. Inf.], 1950).

Social Theorists

Karl Marx (1818-1883) appears the most predominant social theorist of this era. Of significance also are two of Marx's followers, Friedrich Engels (1820-1895), who collaborated with Marx on the *Communist Manifesto*, and

Vladimir Ilyich Ulyanov, (Lenin) (1870-1924), who, following Marx's famous dictum that the point of philosophy is not to interpret the world, but to *change* it, made Marxism a political reality in Russia. The encyclicals of Pope Leo XIII, *Rerum Novarum* (*On the Condition of Labor*) (1891) and Pope Pius XI *Quadragesimo Anno* (*Reconstructing the Social Order*) (1931) (Gibbons, 1963) also seem to have had a major impact upon the social and political thought of this era. Marx, who was extremely critical of the idea of natural law, launched a new direction for the struggles which began in the Age of Enlightenment. His critique of basic notions of rights as expressed during the Enlightenment is evident in his essay *On the Jewish Question* (1843). Here he reproaches in part some of the Bills of Rights of American state constitutions and the French Declaration of the Rights of Man and the Citizen stating that these rights exalted the ethic of individualism rather than the need to participate in community life: "These so-called rights of man...are simply the rights of...egoistic man, of man separated from other men and from the community" (Tucker, 1978, p. 42).

The following excerpt illustrates his criticisms of some of the rights which emerged in the Age of Enlightenment, more specifically, in the French Declaration:

> Article 6. Liberty is the power which man has to do everything which does not harm the rights of others.... It is a question of the liberty of man regarded as an isolated monad, withdrawn into himself... liberty as a right of man [therefore] is not founded upon the relations between man and man, but rather upon the separation of man from man.... Article 16. The right of *property* is that which belongs to every citizen of enjoying and disposing *as he will* of his goods and revenues, of the fruits of his work and industry. The right of property is, therefore, the right to enjoy one's fortune and to dispose of it as one will; without regard for other men and independently of society. It is the right of self-interest...it leads every man to see in other men, not the *realization*, but rather the *limitation* of his own liberty. (Tucker, p. 42)

To Marx, therefore, none of these "supposed" inalienable rights, go beyond the individual, that is "egoistic man." The individual is "separated from the community, withdrawn into himself, wholly preoccupied with his private interest...[and] private caprice" (Tucker, p. 43).

One of Marx's most famous sayings, furthermore, that men's social existence determines their consciousness is evident when he notes that therights of the Enlightenment are the rights of "man as a bourgeois and not man...who is considered the *true* and *authentic* man" (Tucker, p. 42). These rights, in fact, are "the recognition of the *frenzied* movement of the cultural and material elements which form the content of his life" (p. 45). One of Marx's most famous sayings, furthermore, that men's social existence determines their consciousness is evident when he notes that the

To Marx, therefore, class ideology seems to justify rights and behavior. As Kolakowski (1983) states emphatically,: "[To Marx] human rights, in other words, are simply the facade of the capitalist system" (p. 85). Marx criticizes, therefore, not the rights of the Enlightenment in themselves but rather their hidden agenda which legitimates, by proclaiming *individual* liberties, and condoning the rights of the "isolated monad...withdrawn into himself," the abuses of the industrial age, such as unemployment, poverty, and homelessness. It does not appear, however, that Marx wants to do away with individual civil and political rights. Rather, he wants to extend them. Therefore, he is a precursor of the notion of the interdependency of rights.

Lenin, in the following two excerpts, seems to express well this apparent sham of civil and political liberties and the need for another set of rights, economic and social liberties. In the *State and Revolution* (1917) he states:

> Freedom in capitalist society always remains just about the same as it was in the ancient Greek republics: freedom for the slave-owners. The modern wage slaves, owing to the conditions of capitalist exploitation, are so much crushed by want and poverty that democracy is nothing to them. (Laqueur and Rubin, 1990, p. 180)

In the *Report to the First Congress of the Third International* (1919) he writes, furthermore:

> Freedom of the press[!]....this freedom is a deception while the best printing-presses and the biggest stocks of paper are appropriated by the capitalists, and while capitalist rule over the press remains....The capitalists have always used the term "freedom" to mean freedom for the rich to get richer and for the workers to starve to death. In capitalist usage, freedom of the press means freedom of the rich to bribe the press, freedom to use their wealth to shape and fabricate so-called public opinion. (Laqueur and Rubin, p. 184)

Marx assumed that this exploitation of the working class (i.e. the proletariat) by the capitalists of the industrial era, would lead to communism and the abolition of classes and class struggle, thereby extirpating the roots of social conflict. The individual would identify with the values and aspirations of the whole community (Kolakowski, 1983) and not withdraw into himself, like an isolated nomad.

In the *Communist Manifesto* Marx and Engels speak of some measures which will engender such a classless society in which individuals can realize their human needs. Some examples are:

> Abolition of property in land and application of all rents of land to public purposes...A heavy progressive or graduated income tax...abolition of all rights of inheritance...centralization of credit in the hands of the state...equal obligation of all to work. Establishment of industrial armies, especially for agriculture...Free education for all children in public schools...Abolition of child factory labor in its present form...[and a] Combination of education with industrial production. (Ebenstein, 1960, pp. 702-703)

With his concern for the teeming masses of the poor who became so evident during this epoch, Marx seemed to revive the ancient wisdom of the Judaic-Christian tradition. To him it was necessary to question the inviolable truths of reason, science, and technology so characteristic of the previous era. Yet, whereas Marx, like Jefferson, refused to accept the monkish ignorance of the Middle Ages, which seems to have justified poverty as a natural state, Marx went beyond Jefferson by articulating more precisely some of the ways to achieve equality. Pope Leo XIII, like Marx, also concerned himself with social and economic justice. In response to the transformations of this era, *Rerum Novarum* stressed limits upon the accumulation of property but only if such ownership were harmful to the common good. Otherwise, property is natural and necessary for a person's development. A state cannot deprive a person of this property through excessive taxation.

Clearly, the emphasis of this encyclical is upon positive rights for "wage earners, who are, undoubtedly, among the weak and necessitous, should be especially cared for and protected by the commonwealth" (Gibbons, 1963, p. 18). Emphasizing the dignity of labor, he enunciates, for example, a number of workers' rights such as rights to form trade unions, to just wages and hours of work, and to rest from work. Challenging the rich to share their possessions with the poor, he concludes by accentuating the virtue of Charity. This is the "mistress and queen of virtues," a person's "surest antidote against worldly pride and immoderate love of self" (Gibbons, p. 30) and the fulfillment of the Gospel which demands the sacrifice of one's self for the sake of another.

On the fortieth anniversary of this encyclical, called the Magna Carta of the new social order by Pope Pius XI author of *Quadragesimo Anno*, many of the abuses of this era continued, if not worsened. Pope Pius XI saw the need for another encyclical to respond to these continuing developments of this capitalistic economic order. In *Quadragesimo Anno*, therefore, he emphasized that domination on an international level had replaced free competition. He acknowledged, for example, that since *Rerum Novarum* there have been some improvements for workers in the more developed states, but he expressed concern that on the international level the abuses of industrialization have "increased exceedingly."

Competition, therefore, must be brought under public authorities on domestic *and* international levels in order to regulate it in ways that conform to notions of Christian moderation and charity. One way to correct, for example, for the failure of workers to own the means of production and the ever increasing maldistribution of wealth worldwide was to provide for just wages. Employers and employees can agree to just wages, furthermore, only if there are equitable relations between them. Mediating state authorities may also be necessary to intervene but not if they themselves are slaves to human greed and blind to the needs of the common good.

In Pope Pius XI's thought, therefore, positive rights are emphasized as in *Rerum Novarum*. *Quadragesimo Anno* seems to go beyond Pope Leo XIII, however, by accentuating the need for a just international order (i.e. solidarity rights).

Historical Documents

Marx was an extremely important influence, in the development of revolutionary communism. The Russian Revolution of 1917 served as a catalyst for the development of positive rights extending ideas enunciated by Marx as well as some presocialist thinkers like Jean Jacques-Rousseau, Gracchus Babeuf, and Thomas Paine. Marx's thinking fit very well in a society which had never experienced the individualism of the Renaissance or the Enlightenment period and was dominated by an Orthodox Church which stressed communal rather than individualistic relationships (Lane, 1989). His thinking, furthermore, promised liberation for millions of people suffering from the most extreme forms of poverty of any European nation at that time.

An important document of this period is the Soviet Constitution of 1936 (Chafee, 1952a, Pam. 3, pp. 911-916). It was much more liberal than the first Soviet Constitution of 1923, providing a foundation for substantial development of Soviet life after the difficult early years following the revolution (Brownlie, 1971).

It had numerous references to civil and political rights, such as:

(Article 125) In conformity with the interests of the toilers, and in order to strengthen the socialist system, the citizens of the USSR are guaranteed: a) freedom of speech; b) freedom of the press; c) freedom of assembly and of holding mass meetings; d) freedom of street processions and demonstrations. These rights of the citizens are ensured by placing at the disposal of the toilers and their organizations printing presses, supplies of paper, public building, the streets, means of communication and other material requisite for the exercise of these rights... (Article 127) The citizens of the USSR are guaranteed inviolability of person. No person may be placed under arrest except by decision of a court or with the sanction of a State Attorney.

It also stressed economic and social rights, for example:

(Article 118) Citizens of the USSR have the right to work--the right to guaranteed employment and payment for their work in accordance with its quantity and quality....(Article 119) Citizens of the USSR have the right to rest and leisure. The right to rest and leisure is ensured by the reduction of the working day to seven hours for the overwhelming majority of the workers....(Article 120) Citizens of the USSR have the right to maintenance in old age and also in case of sickness or loss of capacity to work....(Article 121) Citizens of the USSR have the right to education....(Article 122) Women in the USSR are accorded equal rights with men in all spheres of economic, state, cultural, social and political life....(Article 123) The equality of the rights of citizens of the USSR irrespective of their nationality or race, in all spheres of economic, state, cultural, social and political life, is an immutable law.

It is also replete with notions of duties, such as:

Article 12: In the USSR work is the duty of every able bodied citizen, according to the principle: "He who does not work, neither shall he eat." In the USSR the principle of socialism is realized: "From each according to his ability, to each according to his work."... (Article 131) It is the duty of every citizen of the USSR to safeguard and fortify public, socialist property as the sacred and inviolable foundation of the Soviet system. (Chafee, 1952a)

Undoubtedly, this constitution may have helped the Soviet Union achieve some economic progress for it has numerous social programs, such as child-care, universal health care, free education, retirement benefits, and full employment (Zinn, 1990). These social programs, however, are slowly eroding during the latter years of the 1990s (Van Wormer, 1997). Yet, this constitution overlapped with the many crimes of the Stalinist era (1934-53) which included torture, imprisonment of dissidents and the collective murders of peasants. The Soviet *Gulag* also has an austere resemblance to the promises of that document.

The more recent document of the Soviet Union, drafted in the Congress of People's Deputies, on September 5, 1991, The Declaration of Human Rights and Freedoms, succinctly states in Article 1: "Every person possesses natural, inalienable and inviolable rights and freedoms. *They are sealed in laws that must correspond to the Universal Declaration of Human Rights* [italics added]." This new Declaration attests, therefore, not only to the importance of the Universal Declaration, but, in the wake of the revolutions in the Soviet empire to a continued commitment to basic human values. It appears that this document may also influence some of the laws of the newly formed Commonwealth of Independent States.[6]

Another important document is the Mexican Constitution of 1917 which is an outgrowth of the Soviet revolution and includes rights provisions which are the most elaborate in the world. This constitution reveals a concern for workers and the poor, reflecting Mexico's turbulent history, which is related in part to excessive foreign investment and the historically privileged position of the Catholic Church (Blaustein, Clark and Sigler, 1987). Some of its rights provisions are:

> (Article 4.2) The law shall protect the organization and development of the family....(Article 5.1)...No person can be prevented from engaging in the profession, industrial or commercial pursuit or occupation of his choice....(Article 8) Public officials and employees shall respect the exercise of the right of petition....(Article 24) Everyone is free to embrace the religion of his choice....(Article 27) The Nation shall at all times have the right to impose on private property such limitations as the public interest may demand, as well as the right to regulate the utilization of natural resources...in order to conserve them to ensure a more equitable distribution of public wealth. (Blaustein et. al., 1987)

Clearly, these social theorists and documents significantly contrast with the Age of Enlightenment with their emphasis upon positive freedoms.

THE LEAGUE OF NATIONS

A prominent development in this era was also the League of Nations. Formed in the wake of World War I, the League of Nations was established by the Treaty of Versailles in 1919.

The Covenant of the League reflected very limited international concern with human rights. In fact, the phrase "human rights" did not appear in it. The drafters of the Covenant seemed more preoccupied with the maintenance of security, the pacific settlement of disputes, the establishment of a mandates system for former German and Ottoman territories, and the protection of minorities in Central Europe. The systematic suppressions of human liberty in Communist Russia, Fascist Italy, and Nazi Germany went officially unnoticed by the League, even though member states recognized the implications of these and other countries' tyrannical acts (Asher, Kotschnig, Brown, Green & Sady, 1957).

A principle exception to the basic notion of the League, that the purpose of international law was to cover relations between states and not the relation of the citizen to the state, was the Minorities Protection System. After World War I, a series of treaties and declarations attempted to secure the rights of special groups. Provisions, for example, on the rights of minorities were included in the peace treaties with Austria, Bulgaria, Hungary, and Turkey. Furthermore, declarations to protect minorities were made before the League of Nations by Albania, Estonia, Finland, Iraq, and Lithuania and special provisions were included, for instance, in the convention concerning Upper Silesia by Germany and Poland.

These instruments guaranteed, for example, freedom of religious worship, equality before the law, free use of the mother tongue in private intercourse, commerce, and religion and a right equal to other nationals to maintain, but at their own expense, charitable, religious, social and educational institutions (Asher et. al., 1957). Despite these declarations, however, many violations of these rights surfaced in certain countries. States began filing complaints against other states concerning their treatment of minorities. Switzerland and France, for example, in the Minorities Section of the League Secretariat criticized Germany's application of anti-Semitic measures in German Upper Silesia, which restricted Jews in various occupations (Veatch, 1983). A resolution was passed reaffirming that the minorities treaties must be applied without exception to all classes of nationals of a State that differ from the majority of the population in race, language, or religion. Soon thereafter, on October 14, 1933, Germany withdrew from the League. Consequently, any opportunity to exert pressure on Germany through the League's implementation mechanisms came to an end. That resolution , needless to say, was not adopted (Veatch, 1983).

Prior to Germany's withdrawal, it had demanded full compliance with the minorities treaties, especially by Poland in its treatment of its German minority. Germany's action appears hypocritical. Although Germany's action was self-deceptive, other countries, which also appeared to have violations of the rights of minorities, also filed complaints against Poland's treatment of its German minorities. On September 13, 1934, the Polish Foreign Minister Joseph Beck announced - at a time when the usual large number of minorities' complaints against Poland was pending - that Poland would refuse any further cooperation with the League's minority protection system (Veatch, 1983).

Consequently, there were complaints. But, like the resolution against Germany, it appears that no formal statements of abuse were declared which resulted in no formal acknowledgement of the human rights abuses of that time. All the controversies of Grotius's doctrine of humanitarian intervention, therefore, seemed to have surfaced in the minorities protection system of the League. There was much controversy over alleged unfair treatment. Often it appeared that governments hoped to maintain cohesive and dissatisfied minorities and manipulated minorities' discontents as a basis for eventually regaining lost territories (Veatch, 1983).

Yet, this system, on a more informal level, produced many humanitarian achievements, such as some compensation for expropriated properties, withdrawal of restrictions on minority educational, religious and cultural activities, and punishments for some lower level officials responsible for some acts of violence (Veatch, 1983). Another major exception to the lack of human rights provisions in the Covenant of the League was the System of Mandates. Established by Article 22 of the Covenant, it proclaimed that to the German and Ottoman territories "There should be applied the principle that the well-being and development of such peoples form a sacred trust of civilization" (Asher et. al, 1957, p. 651). Although there was no provision hearing for petitioners,under this System of Mandates, provision was made for receipt and examination by the League of petitions from individuals and organizations regarding these territories. This procedure was different from the Minorities System in which petitions were handed over by governments to other governments allegedly abusing minorities. In the Mandates system, however, *individuals* and *groups*, not only governments, could petition the League for alleged human rights violations. This System of Mandates, therefore, represented a radical departure from more traditional notions that the concern of international bodies should only be between governments and not between individuals and their governments (Asher et. al., 1957).

Overall, however, procedures to deal with petitions, which included, for example, no hearing for petitioners, suggest a strong reluctance on the part of governments to deal with human rights abuses. This reluctance under the auspices of the United Nations seems to persist today.

In addition to establishing the League of Nations, the Treaty of Versailles also created the International Labor Organization (ILO). In 1946 it became a specialized agency in the United Nations. This was an important human rights development which over the years has concerned itself with such issues as full employment, employment discrimination, migrant labor, child labor, social security, equal pay for equal work, trade union rights, the right to collective bargaining, and the right to strike (Claude and Weston, 1989).

The League was also concerned with the welfare of children and endorsed the Geneva Declaration of the Rights of the Child, in 1925. Furthermore, it attempted to eliminate on the international level slavery, forced labor, the traffic in narcotics, and the traffic in women and children (Asher et. al., 1957).

The League of Nations did, therefore, touch upon some aspects of human rights especially in the areas of minorities, mandated territories, labor, and to a lesser extent, the welfare of children, slavery and traffic in narcotics. In general, however, it appears that the League upheld the long held conviction that individual human rights were strictly a concern of the national state.

The League also provided for the beginnings of a system of implementation mechanisms to implement human rights complaints rather than to define human rights standards explicitly. The United Nations, formed in the wake of the following World War, was to develop these standards and find more efficient ways to implement them.

Notes - Chapter Two

[1] Although Islam began during the Middle Ages, I chose to include it in this discussion of the Judaic-Christian heritage.

[2] Biblical quotes are from *The Holy Bible* (1961), New York, Enziger Bros.

[3] All quotes are from A.Y. Ali, *The Holy Qur'an*, Hyberbad, India, Husami Book Depot.

[4] Original authors did not number the clauses. Translators added numerals. All clauses in this section are from Richard Thomson's translation (1827) in Stringham (1966).

[5] It is an unfortunate legacy of documents preceding the Universal Declaration that they used the word "men" when in more contemporary times they might have referred to "persons." Although the Universal Declaration attempts to improve upon this tradition, by mentioning "all human beings" and "everyone," which would therefore include men *and* women, it nevertheless retained the masculine pronoun "he," suggesting that the sexism embedded in earlier documents surfaced to some extent in the wording of the Universal Declaration of Human Rights.

[6] As of the writing of this book, this Commonwealth includes the republics of Belarus, Kyrgyzstan, Moldova, Tajikistan, Turkmenistan, Russia, Ukraine, Kazakhstan, Armenia, Azerbaijan, and Uzbekistan.

Would you ou say then that the Universal Declaration of Human Rights is dangerous to governments? Yes.......Oh, yes.
  • *Eleanor Roosevelt, responding to Eric Sevareid,* The United Nations Today.

CHAPTER THREE

📖📖📖📖📖📖📖📖📖📖📖📖📖📖📖📖📖📖📖📖📖

THE UNITED NATIONS AND BEYOND

The Initial Phases

The creation of the UN at the San Francisco Conference in June 1945was the culmination of four years of concentrated preparation. Prior to that conference, the London Declaration (June, 12, 1941), the Atlantic Charter (August 14, 1941), the United Nations Declaration (January 1, 1942), the Moscow Declaration (October 30, 1943), the Dumbarton Oaks Conference (August 21-October 7, 1944), and the Yalta Conference (February, 1945) expressed concern over the failure of the League of Nations and the need to develop a "united nations," (coined at the United Nations Declaration) for the maintenance of international peace and security (World Encyclopedia of Nations, 1971).

On January 26, 1941, President Franklin D. Roosevelt in his address to Congress also enunciated "four freedoms": freedom of speech and expression, freedom of worship, freedom from want (i.e. economic security) and freedom from fear (i.e. international peace). In 1944 he asked Congress to explore the means for implementing an Economic Bill of Rights which included the rights to: a useful and remunerative job; earn enough money to provide for adequate food, clothing and recreation; a decent home; medical care; adequate protection in old age, sickness, accident and unemployment; and a good education (Laqueur and Rubin, 1990). These goals, especially in the wake of the atrocities of World War II, became perceived throughout the world community as goals mandating global cooperation.

Most significant of this time, however, is that, apart from Roosevelt's concerns, these earlier Charters and Declarations seemed to provide only brief references to the promotion of human rights. Proposals at the Dumbarton Oaks Conference, for example, contained only one reference to human rights. In Chapter XI, it called only for a new international organization that "should facilitate solutions of international, economic, social and other humanitarian problems and promote respect for human rights and fundamental freedoms" (UN Dept. of Pub. Inf., 1950, p. 3).

At the San Francisco Conference in 1945, furthermore, many governments were reluctant to include more detailed provisions concerning human rights. Many countries appeared eager to conceal human rights abuses of their own. The Soviet Union had its Gulag, the United States had its numerous racial problems, and the Europeans had their colonial empires (Buergenthal, 1988). It was certainly not in their interests to establish effective international mechanisms for the promotion and protection of human rights.

However, to San Francisco came a great many representatives of various non-governmental organizations (NGO's). Without official mandate of any kind, they convinced the official representatives of governments of the necessity of expanding the original provisions of the Dumbarton Oaks Proposals (UN Dept. of Pub. Inf., 1950).

According to John Humphrey, first Director of the Division of Human rights at the UN, were it not for the efforts of a few deeply committed delegates and the representatives of some forty-two private organizations brought in as consultants by the United States, human rights would have received "only a passing reference" (Farer, 1989, p. 195).

Upon the urging of these NGO's and *also* states such as some Latin American countries, the United Nations Charter adopted at San Francisco contains numerous references to human rights such as in Article 1(3) which states that one of the purposes of the UN is the promotion and encouragement of "respect for human rights and for fundamental freedoms for all without distinction as to race, sex, language, or religion." The Commission on Human Rights, furthermore, was specifically provided for in the UN Charter in Article 68 which states: "The Economic and Social Council shall set up commissions in economic and social fields and for the promotion of human rights." This Commission on Human Rights is the only commission mentioned in the Charter.[1]

In addition to the commitment of the NGO's, some Latin American states were eager to include more detailed statements of human rights in the Charter. Chile, for example, suggested that the Charter should include such rights as the right to live and to work, freedom of religion, profession, and the press. Cuba proposed that the Charter provide that member states conform to principles contained in a "Declaration of Rights and Duties of Nations" and "Declaration of the International Duties and Rights of the Individual" within the shortest possible time (Green, 1956).

Panama also suggested that a "Declaration of Essential Human Rights" be integrated into the Charter which would include such matters as "freedom from wrongful interference with person, home, reputation, privacy...and property; freedom from arbitrary detention...the right to a fair trial and the right to own property; the right to education; and the right to work" (Green, p. 17).

These Latin American proposals were rejected because they were too controversial (Farer, 1989) and, according to the official records, because of insufficient time: "The present conference, if only for lack of time, could not proceed to realize such a draft in an international contract" (UN Information Organization, 1945, p. 456).

In the first session of the General Assembly in 1946 Chile, Cuba, and Panama reintroduced proposals for the preparation of a bill of rights. As a result of the initiative by the United States, the General Assembly decided not to consider a draft of a "Declaration on Fundamental Human Rights and Freedoms," which these countries submitted. They chose rather to transmit that document to the Economic and Social Council for consideration by the Commission on Human Rights in its preparation of an international bill of rights (UN Dept. of Pub. Inf., 1950).

First Meetings of the Commission on Human Rights

Prior to the first meeting of the Commission on Human Rights, a nuclear commission met at Hunter College in New York City from April 29 to May 20, 1946. At that meeting it began a study of various drafts submitted by delegations of Panama, Chile, Cuba, the American Federation of Labor and private drafts by Dr. Lauterpacht of Cambridge University, Dr. Alvarez of the American Institute of International Law, Rev. Parsons of the Catholic Association of International Peace and the author, Horace G. Wells (*Yearbook of the UN*, 1948-49).

In 1940 the renowned writer H.G. Wells had drawn up a draft "World Declaration of the Rights of Man." Because of his unparalleled world prestige at that time, this draft was eventually translated into 10 languages and dropped by microfilm to the Resistance in occupied Europe and distributed worldwide to 300 editors in 48 countries. The final version of this World Declaration was undoubtedly a forerunner of the Universal Declaration of Human Rights. Briefly, Wells's list of rights included: the right to live, protection of minors, duty to the community, right to knowledge, freedom of thought and worship, right to work, right to personal property, freedom of movement, personal liberty, freedom from violence, right of law making (Dillow, 1986).

The Commission on Human Rights, held its first session in January-February 1947. It elected Mrs. Eleanor Roosevelt, president and Mr. René Cassin (France) vice-president. This 18 member commission, established by the Economic and Social Council, which coordinates the economic and social work of the United Nations, consisted additionally of representatives from Australia, Belgium, Byelorussian Soviet Socialist Republics (S.S.R.), Chile, Egypt, India, Iran, Panama, the Philippines, the Union of Soviet Socialist Republics (U.S.S.R.), the United Kingdom, Uruguay, and Yugoslavia.

A major item on its agenda was consideration of an "International Bill of Rights." At this time it appears that René Cassin drew a comparison of the human rights structure at the United Nations to a triptych of which one of the panels, the central panel, was the Declaration, while the two side panels could be said to be formed by the various conventions and the covenants on the one hand and the implementation measures on the other (Szabo, 1982).

The initial concerns of the commission became which section of the triptych to concentrate: a declaration or statement of rights that was non-legally binding, a treaty which would have the force of law or measures of implementation. The representatives soon recognized that it would be relatively easy to reach agreement on the text of a declaration, but that acceptance of a legally-binding treaty would prove much more difficult to obtain (Buergenthal, 1988).

Although some states like India pressed for implementation measures immediately, the USSR, who thought that any decision as to the legal form of the Bill was premature (UN Dept. of Pub. Inf., 1950) appeared more typical of the general consensus.

At the first session, different ideological convictions surfaced almost immediately. France wanted to emphasize one right which it thought was absolutely unconditional, namely the right to conscience. The Philippines proposed that such a bill should establish a balance between political and economic rights, which would create a system of government which truly expressed the will of the people.

Yugoslavia noted that modern times had developed a spirit of collectivity and solidarity of the popular masses, that true individual liberty could be reached only in perfect harmony between the individual and the collectivity. Speaking on the right to work, the Soviet representative stated that there could be no right to work without a corresponding duty to the community.

The United States suggested that the International Bill of Rights should consider personal rights, such as freedom of speech, information, religion, and rights of property; procedural rights, such as safeguards for persons accused of crime; social rights, such as the right to employment and social security and the right to enjoy minimum standards of economic, social, and cultural well-being; and political rights, such as the right to citizenship and the right of citizens to participate in their government.

As early as February 1947 the Secretariat already received hundreds of letters protesting alleged violations of human rights and appealing to the United Nations for assistance. At the first session of the Commission on Human Rights, this flood of appeals was perceived as only just beginning.

The Commission at this first session also recognized that it had no power to take any action regarding any complaints concerning human rights. It decided to deal with these complaints by requesting the Secretary-General to compile a confidential list of communications (i.e. complaints) received concerning human rights before each session of the Commission.

The Secretariat would then furnish this confidential list upon request to the members of the Commission without divulging the contents of these communications or the identity of their authors. The Secretariat was also directed to enable the members of the Commission to consult the originals of these communications if they requested. Finally, the Secretary-General was to inform the writers of all communications that their concerns would be brought to the attention of the Commission on Human rights.

This rather lengthy and bureaucratic procedure for handling communications suggests that in the initial phases the Commission appeared a rudimentary receptacle for human rights complaints (Farer, 1989). Whereas the relatively recent procedures and human rights committees suggest a more active role of the UN in promoting and *protecting* human rights, there appeared at the outset a resistance to act on the part of the UN.

Mr. Laugier, Assistant-Secretary General for Social Affairs, addressing the Commission at this first session made this point quite well when he said that he doubted whether the Commission had the competence to conduct enquiries or hold hearings on complaints from individuals, groups, or governments concerning violations of Human Rights. Still as we shall see, in 1998 and into the next century the major challenge will be to strengthen the implementation and enforcement mechanisms of human rights standards.

At the conclusion of this first session the Commission on Human Rights decided to petition the Secretariat, the administrative arm of the United Nations headed by the Secretary-General, to begin the collection of data to draw up an initial outline of a Bill of Rights.

The Draft of the Secretariat

Between the first and second sessions of the Commission, the Secretariat prepared a 408-page document which included excerpts from observations of members of the Commission; draft declarations sponsored by Chile, Cuba, India, Panama, and the United States; principal provisions from the constitutions and the laws of all member states; and a proposal put forward by the American Federation of Labor. The Secretariat, furthermore, made "every effort...to produce articles which were clear, concise and well worded" (UN Dept. of Pub. Inf., 1950, p. 8).

This draft reaffirmed such simple, elementary rights as the right to life, which many constitutions failed to mention. These rights also took into account existing laws and practices, but in many cases went beyond rules and customs which were generally already recognized.

The first article, for example, speaks of duties to the state, to international society, and to a "just share of responsibility for the performance of such social duties and his share of such common sacrifices as may contribute to the common good." Article 2 says: "In the exercise of his rights every one is limited by the rights of others and by the just requirement of the State and of the UN."

Articles 3 through 34 deal primarily with negative freedoms such as the right to emigration and expatriation, the right to resist oppression and tyranny, and the right to political asylum.Articles 35-44, concern themselves basically with positive freedoms, such as the right to medical care, the right to education, the right to socially useful work, the right to an equitable share of the national income as the need for one's work and the increment it makes to the common welfare may justify, and the right to good food, decent housing and to live in surroundings that are pleasant and healthy.

Articles 47-48 speak primarily of duties of the state to respect and protect the rights enunciated in this Bill of Rights and that this Bill is to be considered fundamental to principles of international law and of the national law of each of the member states of the United Nations.

Ms. Roosevelt then appointed a representative drafting committee which appointed Mr. Cassin, "the true father of human rights" (Szabo, 1982, p. 23) to condense the Secretariat's document and consider also a Bill submitted by the United Kingdom during this time.

Input from the UNESCO Committee on the Philosophic
Basis for Human Rights

This committee of the United Nations Educational, Scientific and Cultural Organization (UNESCO) asked a number of prominent thinkers and philosophers their opinions on human rights. At the second session of the Commission on Human Rights, UNESCO made a summary of these opinions available which may have influenced the Commission. Professor E.H. Carr, for example, a distinguished political scientist, noted that the idea of human rights dated historically from the eighteenth century and was primarily, though not entirely, associated with the American and French Revolutions. According to him, the more modern version of rights which is associated with the Russian Revolution stresses not only the political rights of the previous revolutions, but now the economic and social rights which also inspired the UN Charter. Benedetto Croce, a world famous philosopher, stressed that the idea of human rights expressed manifestations of human needs of a particular historical period and attempts to satisfy these needs. Arthur H. Compton, winner of the Nobel Prize in physics in 1927 and author of the *Freedom of Man*, noted basic rights that a society should endeavor to ensure, such as the right to a healthy life, the right to work effectively, the right to choose wisely the objectives of one's efforts, and the obligations of the individual to society.

Jacques Maritain, philosopher and French Ambassador to the Holy See, saw human rights as exemplifying the practical conclusions of the disciples of Locke, Rousseau, Thomas Paine, Roman Catholicism, Marx-Leninism, Humanitarian Socialism, Existentialism, Rationalism, Greek Orthodoxy, Calvinism, Gandhiism, and Confucianism.

One final example is Mohandas Gandhi, the father of India's Independence, who had learned from his illiterate but wise mother that all rights to be deserved came from duty well done. To Ghandi, the very right to live accrued only when one also does the duty of citizenship to the world.

Developments Before the Third Session of the Commission

It was at this second session in December 1947 that the meaning of the term "International Bill of Human Rights" became clearer. This Bill, therefore, should definitely contain a Declaration, a Covenant, and Measures of Implementation.   At this session, the Commission came up with a Draft International Covenant on Human Rights and a Draft International Declaration on Human Rights.   The draft declaration was the Commission's revision of Cassin's drafting committee's document.   The Commission then requested comments on this Draft International Declaration from every member government and such organs of the United Nations as the United Nations Conference on Freedom of Information, the Sub-Commission on the Prevention of Discrimination and the Protection of Minorities, and Commission on the Status of Women.   There were so many proposals for revision that the Commission rewrote the draft declaration word for word. At the end of June 1948 this preliminary task was completed (UN. Dept. of Pub. Inf., 1950).

The Commission on Human Rights also had the benefit of the American Declaration of the Rights and Duties of Man written at the Ninth International Conference of American States in Bogota on March-May, 1948. This declaration was the first intergovernmental statement of human rights in history (Green, 1956).

Briefly, this document contained twenty eight articles on the rights of the individual, and ten articles on duties. It covered both negative and positive freedoms and concluded with an article of general limitations: "The rights of man are limited by the rights of others, by the security of all, and by the just demands of the general welfare and the advancement of democracy." It is not within the scope of this discussion to reproduce, these three revisions of the Secretariat's document (i.e. of the drafting committee, the commission's revision and then its subsequent revision upon comments from UN governments and agencies).   However, some issues which arose among the member states are noteworthy.

The USSR, Byelorussian SSR, Ukrainian SSR, and Yugoslavia, for instance, felt that the Declaration should emphasize the duty of man to the state and to the community, and urged that the Declaration contain more explicit safeguards of the sovereign rights of the democratic state. Their second major concern was the degree of emphasis to be given the individual-personal rights on the one hand and the so-called economic-social rights on the other. All nations wanted both types of right affirmed. The only differences concerned emphasis and subordination.

The Soviet Union interpreted the problem of human rights as essentially that of the economic and social rights of the broad masses of the people and the duty of the states to guarantee these rights to them. The United States and the United Kingdom, on the other hand, laid greater stress on the more traditional individual liberties. However, these two states would not have the state alone responsible for ensuring the economic and social rights to the people.

China, the United States, and the United Kingdom, while calling for a positive and simple declaration of rights, felt that all restrictions and limitations should be left to the Covenants (UN Dept. of Pub. Inf., 1950).

Brazil wanted to omit Article 1 because it reflected philosophical postulates from 1946-47).

The eastern European countries also expressed the outdated theories of natural law and therefore Article 1 should be omitted. (*Yearbook of the United Nations* need for the Declaration not only to spell out rights and freedoms, but also to state clearly what actions were to be taken to secure their enjoyment. They also wanted that document to contain limitations to a number of particular rights and wanted these rights to be denied to nazis, fascists, and anyone working against democratic interests. They also expressed concern for a statement that the realization of these rights and freedoms are to be in accordance with the laws of the countries concerned (UN Dept. of Pub. Inf., 1950).

This draft declaration, as completed by the Commission on Human Rights in June 1948, was sent by the Economic and Social Council to the third session of the General Assembly, which met in Paris in September 1948. There, despite the exhaustive analysis which was already given to it during the preceding two years the Third Committee, which is responsible for Social and Humanitarian Affairs of the General Assembly and consists of representatives of all member states of the UN, revised it again almost entirely line by line and even word by word. So meticulous was its consideration that at the end of the first seventeen days' debate, only the first two articles had been adopted (UN Dept. of Pub. Inf., 1950).

The chairperson Eleanor Roosevelt's comments on the Universal Declaration are pertinent here:

Naturally it is not a perfect document....Being, as it must be, a composite document to meet the thoughts of so many different peoples, there must be a considerable number of compromises. On the whole, however, it is a good document. We could never hope for perfection no matter how many times we revised the Declaration, for one could always see something a little better that one might do. (UN Dept. of Pub. Inf., 1950, pp. 15-16)

The Final Debates

These debates consisted of the Third Committee's and General Assembly's considerations of the Draft International Declaration of Human Rights drafted by the Commission on Human Rights at their third session.

Previously, I had chosen certain articles from various human rights documents. To do adequate justice to this important discussion on the Universal Declaration of Human Rights itself, which is my standard of comparison for contemporary state and federal constitutions, it appears necessary, therefore, to highlight key issues brought up by member states for *each* of the articles. Discussions of each article will also accent the numerous political compromises involved, which are the consequence of some of the historical-philosophical traditions previously discussed.

For the sake of the reader's convenience, I have chosen to briefly paraphrase in parentheses following the article under discussion its essential themes. For a fuller appreciation of the debates concerning the article, however, it may be worthwhile to again refer to the copy of the Universal Declaration of Human Rights at the end of Chapter One. In cases of substantial discrepancy between the Commission's draft at its third session and the final article of the Universal Declaration, furthermore, I will, in order to provide a more fruitful understanding of key issues, reproduce the entire draft article.[7]

Concerning Article 1 (on human dignity, equality of rights, the endowment of reason and conscience in all persons and the need to act towards one another in the spirit of brotherhood), South Africa[8] felt that certain portions of the draft propounded a thesis which would destroy the whole basis of the multi-racial structure of the Union of South Africa. It felt that South Africa could not possibly accept the proposition that human dignity would be impaired if a person was told that he could not reside in a particular area. The right to participate in government, furthermore, was not universal. It was conditioned not only by nationality but also by qualifications of franchise.

Belgium and China proposed to delete the words "by nature" in the Draft Declaration which read: "[Humans] are endowed by nature with reason and conscience." Some governments wished to say that man is endowed by God with reason and conscience. "By nature" was deleted.

Civil and Political Rights.

Concerning Article 2 (that people should have all rights irregardless of race, color, sex, language, religion, political opinion, national origin, property, birth, or other status and that no distinction should be made on the international status of the country to which a person belongs), the Soviets proposed to add the word "class" to the phrase "property and other status." The Committee chose to include "birth," as the appropriate translation in English and French of the sense of the Soviet text.

Article 3 (on the rights to life, liberty, and security) was adopted unanimously, but only after a week of debate. The USSR had recommended a two part amendment that the state should guarantee the right to life and that capital punishment should be abolished. It spoke of lynching in the United States, and famine in India where the life expectancy is 26.9 years. France retorted with a comment about slow death in concentration camps which is as "truly a death penalty as death by hanging." The USSR responded that "properly run concentration camps and penal institutions did not lead to death, but rather to the reform of persons temporarily deprived of their liberty." Belgium was fearful that traitors could not be shot in time of peace.

Concerning Articles 4 and 5 (on the abolition of slavery and torture respectively), the Soviets proposed a two-part amendment: "Slavery and the slave trade are prohibited in all their aspects; and all violations of this principle, whether they may be of an overt or clandestine nature, must be punished according to law."

The USSR said that Thomas Jefferson wanted to abolish slavery, but the US Congress failed to listen. The USSR stated that possibly as much as eight million people lived in conditions of slavery and it was necessary to state clearly that slavery and the slave trade be prohibited. Poland referred to a report by the Trusteeship Council that stated that the practice of selling small female children is still being carried on in one of the Trust Territories. France pointed out the importance of the word "servitude" which would cover such matters as Nazi treatment of prisoners of war and traffic in women and children.

Concerning Article 6 (on the right to recognition as a person before the law) France expressed a major concern that even apart from the countries which pursued a policy of systematic oppression, there were others with more liberal legislations which had tended to deprive aliens living within their territory of the exercise of fundamental rights, such as the right to enter into marriage, to acquire property or to take legal proceedings. France felt that this article would combat this disastrous tendency, that the right to recognition as a person before the law was sufficient.

Pertaining to Articles 7 and 8 (on the rights to equal protection of the law and to an effective remedy by competent national tribunals) the Commission's draft read:

> All are equal before the law and are entitled without any discrimina-
> tion to equal protection of the law against any discrimination in
> violation of this Declaration and against any incitement to such
> discrimination.

Here much comment was made upon South Africa's treatment of its black population. France declared that laws considered discriminatory by most of the representatives on the Committee existed in South Africa and that the portion of the Trusteeship Council's report dealing with the mandated territory of South-West Africa supported that opinion.

South Africa responded by saying that legislation in South Africa guaranteed to everyone, without discrimination on the grounds of race, age, sex, or religion, the most equality of law. South Africa stated that it is a highly developed country with legislation which combined harmoniously certain elements of Roman law and Dutch law in a very modern system. The judges, whose professional competence and high moral qualities were beyond question, equitably protected all citizens.

It noted, however, that it could not be claimed that the Declaration included all rights, and that the concept of equality before the law should not be limited to the principles laid down in the Declaration. South Africa proposed to delete from the Article the phrase, "against any discrimination in violation of this Declaration and against any incitement to such discrimination."

France felt that the South African amendment would rob the article of its substance. France commented, furthermore, that the natives of South-West Africa had no share in the administration of the territory; although they represented 90 percent of the population, only 10 per cent of the budget was allocated to their needs.

Poland asked why, if there were no discrimination in South African courts, would that country object to the prevention of discrimination appearing in the Declaration? Members appealed to South Africa to withdraw the amendment.

South Africa withdrew the amendment, but felt that the committee had made little attempt to understand the difficulty which European civilization was facing in its struggle for survival in that country.

France, however, had urged South Africa to retain the amendment feeling that a rejection of the amendment would let the world know that racial discrimination as practiced in South Africa was strictly unacceptable.

Mexico also proposed an additional paragraph reading: "There should likewise be available to every person a simple, brief procedure whereby the Courts will protect him from acts of authority that, to his prejudice, violate any fundamental constitutional rights." It was generally felt that Mexico's proposal would widen the scope of the phrase "equal protection of the law." The French delegation, however, felt that it should appear in the Covenant on Human Rights, not in the Declaration. Mexico's proposal was accepted as Article 8, the right to remedies.

Article 9 (that no one shall be subjected to arbitrary arrest, detention, or exile) of the Commission's draft read: "No one shall be subjected to arbitrary arrest or detention." Here there were two main considerations: that everyone should have the right to test the legality of his or her arrest and that the wording should be broadened to protect an individual from arbitrary exile.

Many amendments were offered such as: "No one may be deprived of his freedom, nor exiled" (Cuba, Ecuador and Uruguay) "except in cases and according to the procedure prescribed by prior legislation" (Cuba, Ecuador, USSR, Uruguay); "Anyone deprived of his freedom should have the right to be informed without delay of the grounds of his detention...to have his case brought before the court without undue delay or to be liberated" (Cuba, Ecuador, France, USSR, Uruguay); and "No one may be deprived of his freedom on account merely of failure to carry out obligations of a purely civil character" (Cuba, Ecuador, Mexico USSR, Uruguay) "or violation of a work contract" (Cuba, Ecuador, Mexico Uruguay). All amendments except for "No one may be exiled" were defeated.

Concerning Article 10 (that everyone shall have a fair and public hearing by an independent and impartial tribunal), the Commission's draft did not include the words "and public" before the word "hearing." Cuba introduced the addition of those words. Representatives appeared anxious to ensure maximum protection of this important right. The USSR, for instance, proposed an amendment embracing five points, such as equality before the law, the independence of judges, the necessity for public hearings and an accused person's right to use his own language.

The Soviet Proposal was rejected because of Greece and Belgium's opinion that their effect would be to place in the Declaration a series of regulations to govern public administration. Both countries felt that these amendments were important, but they did not fit into the Declaration.

Article 11 (that a person shall be presumed innocent, until proven guilty at a public trial and given all guarantees necessary for defense, and that a person shall neither be held guilty of an offense, which was not an offense at the time it was committed, nor given a heavier penalty which was applicable at the time the offence was committed) of the Commission's draft was similar to the present article except that the sentence, "nor shall a heavier penalty be imposed than the one that was applicable at the time the penal offence" was omitted. Panama proposed that addition which was accepted.

Here the Nuremberg trials entered into the discussion. Belgium stated that at the Nuremberg trials the principle that a man could not be condemned for crimes under laws not existing when the crimes were committed was rejected in favor of the idea that unwritten laws of humanity were more important than the written laws of states. It proposed to include such a statement about these higher laws that took precedence over man made ones.

Cuba pointed out that the problem of the Nuremberg trials had been raised in the General Assembly in 1946 when the United States asked for affirmation of the principles of international law contained in the Charter and the judgment of the Nuremberg Tribunal. Cuba felt that it would be better not to include any reference to the trial which would weaken the article and might be considered as an indirect criticism of the trial.

Belgium, however, believed that the legality of the Nuremberg trials could not be challenged. The legal standing of these trials was securely founded on General Assembly Resolution 95(1) of 1946 which affirmed the "principles of international law recognized by the charter of the Nuremberg Tribunal." It thought that the future Declaration of Human Rights should include such an article, notwithstanding the guarantees given in the General Assembly's resolution. Belgium's idea was rejected.

The Commission's draft of Article 12 (that noone shall be subjected to arbitrary interference with privacy, family, home, correspondence nor to attacks upon one's reputation, and that he or she shall have legal protection against such interference or attacks) read: "No one shall be subjected to unreasonable interference with his privacy, family, home, correspondence or reputation." Amendments were proposed in order to extend a person's privacy even further. The United Kingdom, for instance, proposed: "the right to the protection of the law against attacks upon his honour and reputation." The USSR offered to reword the Article to read: "No one shall be submitted to arbitrary interference with his privacy, family, home, correspondence, honor and reputation. Everyone has the right to the protection of the law against such interference." The Soviet proposal was accepted.

The Commission's draft of Article 13 (on the rights to freedom of movement and residence within the borders of each state and to leave and return to one's country) was similar to the present article except that 13(2) did not include the words "and return to his country." Lebanon proposed that addition which was accepted.

Belgium commented that the principles of freedom of movement and freedom of residence have to be stressed at this time, because the war and its resulting upheavals have demonstrated the extent to which the principle could be trodden underfoot. To Belgium, the ideal was to return to a time when a person could travel round the world armed only with a visiting card. Haiti also commented that the world belongs to all mankind.

A Soviet proposal to add: "in accordance with the laws of the state," and a Cuban and Egyptian proposal to give a national the right to leave "only of his own accord," were rejected. A Lebanese amendment "and to return to his country" was accepted.

The issues concerning Article 14 (on the right to enjoy asylum from persecution except for crimes committed, which were non-political or contrary to the purposes of the United Nations) centered around questions such as: could a group of persecuted persons, no matter how large, *demand* the right to enter any country? Would such an attempt prove an embarrassing dislocation of immigration laws? If a country wanted to get rid of a minority, would it not be possible to persecute them to the point of mass exodus to another country?

The United Kingdom felt that the text of that article revealed defeatism. If the Declaration envisaged an ideal life for members of society, the article admitted the existence of persecution within that society. It said that Great Britain was ready to guarantee that any persecuted person asking for refuge would be treated with sympathy. But no state could accept the responsibilities imposed by the Article as it stood. Consequently, it proposed that "to enjoy" be substituted for "to be granted" in the Commission's draft.

Netherlands commented that in 1938 its country had admitted thousands of German Jews driven out of their own country, but had not found it possible to receive all those who wished to enter. The United Kingdom's proposal was accepted.

France, in commenting upon Article 15 (on the right to a nationality and the right to change one's nationality), declared flatly that every human being has a right to a nationality. It proposed, therefore, an amendment to the Commission's draft, "No one shall be arbitrarily deprived of his nationality or denied the right to change his nationality." That amendment was accepted.

France also proposed an amendment stating that it was the duty of the UN to prevent stateless persons and to concern itself with the plight of stateless persons. The USSR felt that this second amendment would make it the duty of the UN to assume functions which would be in contradiction with the provisions of the Charter and could not be fulfilled. They felt, furthermore, that the UN would have to assume the financial implications and special organizations and special funds would have to be considered.

Another issue in Article 15 concerned naturalized citizens. Australia and the United Kingdom felt that a government was entitled to revoke the nationality of naturalized citizens who had obtained that nationality either by fraud or with the intent of overthrowing the government in question.

The USSR amendment that "No one shall be arbitrarily deprived of his nationality...in any other manner or in any other case than as provided for in the laws of the country concerned" was rejected.

The Unites States also emphasized that this article was designed to make clear first, that individuals should not be subjected to the situation which happened during the Nazi regime when thousands had lost their nationality through arbitrary government action and that no one should be forced to keep a nationality which he did not want and be denied the right to change his nationality.

Saudi Arabia felt that Article 16 (on the rights to marry by full consent of intending spouses and to found a family, and that the family is the fundamental group of society and is entitled to protection by society) took into consideration only the standards of marriage recognized by western civilization and had ignored more ancient civilizations whose institutions, such as marriage had proven their wisdom through the ages. It also felt that marriage laws are not the same in all parts of the world and the phrase should be "legal matrimonial age."

Some countries appeared adamant in keeping the word "divorce" out of the article. France mentioned that divorce did not exist in certain parts of the world and that the term "as to marriage" was a better broad general formula. Netherlands mentioned that it would be deplorable to mention divorce for it was a disrupting factor in society and to include it in the Universal Declaration would imply that the UN approved of divorce on the same footing as marriage.

Concerning Article 17 (on the right to own property and the right not to be arbitrarily deprived of one's property), Sweden thought it "not always wise" that the right to own property should be unlimited, especially when the property consisted of large interests in a foreign country.

The USSR reminded members that various countries have widely differing views regarding the ownership of property. In the USSR, for example, certain categories of properties were allowed to individuals, but all large units of property, such as mines, means of communication, banks, and large industrial and commercial enterprises were owned either by the state, which meant the people as a whole, or by smaller groups, like cooperatives. The USSR proposed, therefore, that the Article should be drafted in general terms so as to include all concepts of ownership. In order to ensure equality in international law for the different social structures in the world, the article should contain specific reference to the laws of the country concerned. That amendment was rejected.

The USSR brought forth five amendments concerning Article 18 (on the right to freedoms of thought, conscience, and religion). One of these amendments was that everyone be guaranteed freedom of thought and freedom to perform religious services "in accordance with the laws of the country concerned and the requirements of public morality."

The USSR noted that it had placed particular emphasis on freedom of thought, which it felt was necessary to sanction in order to promote the development of science and take account of the existence of free-thinkers, whose reasoning had led them to discard all the old fashioned beliefs and religious fanaticism. It contended, furthermore, that certain religious practices represented a real danger to society. In South Africa, for example, religious practices had until recently taken the form of human sacrifice. National legislation had to put an end to these inhuman and barbaric practices. In the Far East, the Soviet Union added, there exist sects whose religious fanaticism leads to savage mortification. It wanted to condemn such public ceremonies.

Saudi Arabia had something critical to say about missionaries. Throughout history it declared, missionaries have often abused their rights by becoming the forerunners of political intervention, and there were many instances of murderous conflicts resulting from missionary efforts.

The clause "this right includes freedom to change his religion or belief" was strongly opposed by some of the Moslem countries. They pointed out that the Qur'an forbids a Moslem to change his faith. They also criticized the Christian missionaries for their efforts to win converts in Mohammedan countries. Saudi Arabia felt obliged to abstain on the final vote because of this clause. France felt that this clause might result in a certain lowering of respect for religion.

Some Moslem states were content merely to register their objections. Pakistan, however, defended the article on the ground that the Moslem faith is itself a missionary religion (Green, 1956).

Greece was concerned that the phrase "freedom to manifest his religion" might lead to unfair practices of proselytizing.   Uruguay pointed out that freedom of conscience is not a concept that can be legislated upon and was out of place in a legal document.

All of these amendments were rejected.

In Article 19 (on the rights to freedom of opinion and expression and to receive and impart information through any media), the USSR moved two amendments that would have replaced the Commission's draft article:

> 1. In accordance with the principles of democracy and in the inter-
> ests of strengthening international collaboration and world peace,
> everyone must be legally guaranteed the right freely to express his
> opinions and, in particular, freedom of speech and the press and also
> freedom of artistic expression. Freedom of speech and the press
> shall not be used for purposes of propagating fascism, aggression,
> and for provoking hatred as between nations.
> 2. a) For the purpose of enabling the wider masses of the people
> and their organizations to give free expression to their opinions, the
> state will assist and cooperate in making available the material
> resources (premises, printing presses, paper, etc.) necessary for the
> publication of democratic organs of the press and b)Everyone has
> the right to freedom of thought and its expression, wherein is in-
> cluded freedom of conviction and freedom of access to sources of
> information and means of communication for the transmission of
> information in the territory of his own country and also in other
> countries, within limits corresponding to the interests of national
> security.

In support of these proposals, the USSR said that freedom of speech for the propagation of aggression could not be permitted and it accused sections of the American press of encouraging a war psychosis. It admitted, however, that not all the United States press was guilty and that this policy of aggression did not reflect the views of the American people.

None of the countries, except eastern European states, offered much support for the Soviet viewpoint. The Philippines said that the Soviet amendment would create a controlled press such as existed in all totalitarian countries. France asked the USSR to define fascism. The Soviet Union replied "the bloody dictatorship of the most reactionary section of capitalism and monopolies."

The Soviet proposals were rejected.

The Commission's draft of Article 20 (on the right to freedom of peaceful assembly and that no one may be compelled to belong to an association) read: "Everyone has the right to freedom of assembly and association." Most of the delegates felt that the wording here was too "terse and compact."

Uruguay proposed an amendment that "No one may be compelled to belong to an association." The United Kingdom objected to this amendment because it felt that the notion of compulsion was not clear nor was the meaning of association in this context. If it could mean a trade union, then the amendment could be interpreted to prohibit the closed shop.

New Zealand supported this view and added that in some cases it was essential, in the interests of particular groups, to impose conditions for belonging to an association and it was sometimes necessary to demand that all members of the group concerned should belong to the association. It gave as an example professional associations responsible for supervising the conduct of those carrying on some special profession, as the bar associations. Despite these objections, Uruguay's amendment was accepted.

The USSR felt it should be specified that all gatherings of an anti-democratic nature should be forbidden by law. Steps had to be taken to ensure that "the monster of fascism" did not rise again. Haiti thought that in every country there are associations of evil-doers and that they could justify their activities under this article. Lebanon said that if the text were read in conjunction with Article 30, then Haiti's fears would be dissipated. But Haiti replied that if the meaning of each article could not be understood without reference to other parts of the Declaration then the document would not be simple enough to be understood by all peoples.

Uruguay also felt that the word "peaceful" be added before assembly. This proposal was accepted.

The Commission's draft of Article 21 (on the rights to take part in government directly or through chosen representatives, to equal access to public service and that the will of the people shall be the basis of the authority of government) read:

> 1. Everyone has the right to take part in the government of his country, directly or through his freely chosen representatives. 2. Everyone has the right of access to public employment in his country. 3. Everyone has the right to a government which conforms to the will of the people.

Few of the members seemed satisfied with this wording. Sweden said the Article should make clear how the will of the people should find expression. It proposed an addition to the third paragraph: "manifested in general and free elections or in equivalent voting procedures." The latter phrase was included to take account of the fact that some primitive peoples were not accustomed to elections.

Costa Rica and Columbia stated that there should be a statement of the right to oppose the government and to take steps to replace it by legal means. The USSR hesitated to accept this amendment because it might make it possible for fascist elements to overthrow the government.

China proposed to add the statement "the will of the people shall be the basis" of the authority of government. It felt that this would be the proclamation of a right, rather than a statement of fact which existed in "The will of the people is the source of authority."

Several speakers wanted clarification and the authors of many amendments got together unofficially and prepared a joint text. A "compromise text" was accepted.

Economic, Social, and Cultural Rights.

The Commission's draft of Article 22 (on the right to social security in general) read:

> Everyone as a member of society, has the right to social security and is entitled to the realization, through national effort and international cooperation, and in accordance with the organization and resources of each State, of the economic, social and cultural rights set out below.

A major issue here was the phrase "social security." Peru, France and Chile declared that it means, in this case social justice in the broad sense, not the protection of the individual from want in the narrow technical sense.

The USSR emphasized that this article would serve as a preamble to stress the importance of the following economic and social rights. Their inclusion in the Declaration was a result of social progress in the 19th and 20th centuries. The Soviets commented that these rights had not appeared in any of the previous declarations of the rights of man.

The Soviets proposed an amendment containing the idea that the state and society must *ensure* to the individual the realization of social, economic and cultural rights, and that they must give him or her a real opportunity to enjoy all the other rights enunciated in the Declaration. This proposal was rejected.

The United States emphasized the importance that essential elements of the article were "through national effort and international cooperation" and "in accordance with the organization and resources of each state." Cuba proposed to delete "set out below" and add "indispensable for his dignity and the free development of his personality." Cuba's proposal was accepted.

The fourth draft of Article 23 (on the rights related to work) read:

> 1. Everyone has the right to work, to just and favorable conditions of work and pay and to protection against unemployment. 2. Everyone has the right to equal pay for equal work. 3. Everyone is free to form and join trade unions for the protection of his interests.

The Committee had great difficulty with this article. The difficulty did not arise from lack of agreement on a person's right to work, but on the state's responsibility in the matter and whether a person should have the right or the obligatory duty to join a trade union.

The USSR commented that unemployment is one of the great misfortunes of the working class. Between 20 to 30 million people, not counting those of the East, are permanently unemployed, and even in a country as wealthy as the United States official figures put the number of unemployed at over two million. According to the Soviet Union, unemployment was impossible owing to the socialist economy and the absence of private property and exploitation.

Poland commented that if the Declaration were to go beyond the ideas proclaimed in the 18th century it must lay down clearly the obligations of the state and society to prevent unemployment. Any omission of the obligations of the state and society to prevent unemployment would make this article "meaningless and abstract."

New Zealand noted that the draft article implied that the individual was free to join or not to join trade unions. It could not accept any text which left any doubt about the power to compel workers to join trade unions. It noted that in 1936 a law had been passed in New Zealand making it illegal for employers covered by the Industrial Conciliation and Arbitration Act to employ non-union members.

Bolivia felt that in view of inflation the word "real" before the word "pay" ought to be included. It was important to state that remuneration for work should have a certain purchasing power. Others thought it important that the right to choose one's work should be stated specifically.

A subcommittee came up with the final version which only the United States voted against because it felt that the Article was so badly drafted that it would take many years to determine the meaning of the expression "an existence worthy of human dignity." Noteworthy, however, is the United States' definition of the right to work:

> The right to work, in this Declaration meant the right of the individual to benefit from conditions under which those who were able and willing to work would have the possibility of doing useful work, including independent work, as well as the right to full employment and to further the development of production and of purchasing power. (Robinson, 1958, p. 135)

The Commission's draft of Article 24 (on the rights to rest, leisure, reasonable limitation of working hours, and periodic holidays with pay) read: "Everyone has the right to rest and leisure."

Here several states pointed out that rest and leisure are important to a person's well-being, both physical and mental. The problem was whether the inclusion of such a right be misinterpreted as implying a right to laziness. Many thought, however, that the right should be amplified to include mention of the complementary subject of working hours and conditions. Some members thought it especially important to protect the rights for working men and women, but this in turn raised the general question of specifying the right to rest and leisure for the self-employed, such as housewives and doctors.

The United Kingdom said that the right to rest and leisure would be hollow unless holidays with pay and similar facilities for enjoying rest and leisure were guaranteed. The Philippines stressed that rest means cessation of activity, while leisure is simply a period of unengaged time, the latter giving an opportunity for cultural development. New Zealand proposed the final draft which was approved.

The Commission's draft of Article 25 (on the rights related to a standard of living adequate for the health and well-being of a person and his or her family) read:

> 1. Everyone has the right to a standard of living, including food, clothing, housing and medical care, and to social services, adequate for the health and well-being of himself and his family and to security in the event of unemployment, sickness, disability, old age or other lack of livelihood in circumstances beyond his control. 2. Mother and child have the right to special care and assistance.

Discussion of this article was directed chiefly toward a sharper definition of the rights to security. Yugoslavia mentioned that discrimination against children born out of wedlock has led, in some countries, to serious infringements of human rights. This problem was serious because in some countries as many as 30 percent of all children were illegitimate. That meant that thousands of citizens were held responsible for a state of affairs that was completely beyond their control. The Declaration could not ignore that form of inequality. It moved an amendment to correct this omission. The United States opposed the amendment because the word children in paragraph 2 would include illegitimate children.

The USSR was more concerned with the social security of the worker and thought it important that workers should be covered by social insurance either at the expense of the state or the employer, according to the conditions prevailing in each country.

A Chinese amendment which slightly amplified the Commission's draft and a Norwegian amendment mentioning illegitimate children was adopted.

The Commission's draft of Article 26 (on the rights related to education) read:

> 1. Everyone has the right to education. Elementary and fundamental education shall be free and compulsory and there shall be equal access on the basis of merit to higher education. 2. Education shall be directed to the full development of the human personality, to strengthening respect for human rights and fundamental freedoms and to combating the spirit of intolerance and hatred against other nations and against racial and religious groups everywhere.

There was general agreement among the states that education should be free and that it should be compulsory.

Mexico objected to the second paragraph because it was "too negative, too pessimistic." Mexico, in joint sponsorship with the United States, introduced the following amendment: "Education should be directed...to the promotion of understanding, tolerance, and friendship among all peoples, as well as the activities of the United Nations for the maintenance of peace." Lebanon hoped that the phrase "racial and national groups" would also be inserted in that proposal. Both proposals were adopted.

On the rights of parents over the education of their children, the Netherlands said it was logical that the family should be given primary responsibility for education, because it was in the family that the child first learned to live as a member of the community. The family could not be replaced by any public or private institution.

Netherlands continued that the rights of children were sacred, because children could not demand implementation of their rights; parents were the most natural persons to do so, and parents would be unable to bear that primary responsibility unless they were able to choose the kind of education their children should have. Nazi Germany, where the Hitler Youth Movement deprived parents of control over their children, had provided an experience which should never be permitted again.

Turkey also felt that primary education must be compulsory and that secondary and higher education must be open to all able to profit by it. Lebanon stated that secondary and higher education must also be free, otherwise it could not be said that there should be equal access to it on the basis of merit.

All of these concerns were expressed in an amended version of the Commission's draft.

The Commission's draft of Article 27 (on the rights to participate in the cultural life of the community) read: "Everyone has the right to participate in the cultural life of the community, to enjoy the arts and to share in scientific advancement."

Mexico felt that no article so far had dealt with the rights of the intellectual worker. Without such recognition of the contribution of that important form of activity, no social progress would be possible. Mexico noted that the Declaration had already recognized the rights of the wage earner, the family, the mother and the child. If the Committee wished to avoid a serious omission, the rights of the individual as an intellectual worker, scientist, or writer must be recognized.

It, therefore, moved for an amendment that would ensure protection of the moral and material interests in any invention, literary, scientific, or artistic work of which an individual was the author. That amendment was accepted.

The USSR proposed that the development of science must serve the interests of progress and democracy and the cause of international peace and cooperation. Uruguay noted, however, that science should follow a process of independent evolution and should not depend on political considerations which, very often, were influenced by science. The Soviet proposal was rejected. A compromise text offered by China was adopted.

On Duties and Solidarity Rights.

The Commission's draft of Article 28 (on the right to a social and international order in which human rights can be realized) read: "Everyone is entitled to a good social and international order in which the rights and freedoms set out in this Declaration can be fully realized."

An interesting debate ensued on a USSR amendment that the word "good" should be deleted before the words "social and international order." It noted that even if all the rights and freedoms set out in the Declaration were fully realized, there was still no ground to conclude that the resulting social and international order would necessarily be good, even if the formal realization of a right did not necessarily mean much in practice. The Soviet Union emphasized, furthermore, that the principle of equality had once been of the greatest importance, having led to the abolition of serfdom and slavery. But the USSR felt that as long as society is divided into exploiters and exploited, and as long as there is private ownership of the means of production, the social order could not possibly be a good one.

The Soviet Union did not ask that the Committee approve the Soviet social order. What it did ask, since two conflicting views were involved, was that there should be no moral evaluation in the Declaration of either order. The final verdict should be left to history.

Australia felt that it had never regarded this Article as endorsing the capitalist system, but for drafting reasons would accept that amendment. Canada observed that should the rights set forth in the Declaration be achieved, the social and international order would be good, whether it related to capitalism, communism, feudalism, or any other system. The United States felt that any order that permitted individuals to achieve the rights set out in the Declaration would be a good one, so although it did not think the Soviet amendment necessary, it had no objection to it.

The Commission's draft of Article 29 (on duties to the community and limitations to rights in order to secure these rights and freedoms to others and to meet just requirements of morality, public order and the general welfare in a democratic society) was similar to the final text except that there was no mention that "These rights and freedoms may in no case be exercised contrary to the purposes and principles of the United Nations."

Most representatives agreed with the ideas in that text, but disagreed upon the wording. Uruguay said that this article must make clear that human rights could only be restricted for certain reasons. While it was necessary to have a police force to maintain public order, police power could only be exercised in conformity with the laws of the country.

France agreed that this article could give rise to certain arbitrary acts. However, the law did not always ensure the protection of human rights. It proposed, therefore, the insertion of the word "legitimate" before requirements. It also thought it would be appropriate to include a reference to the purposes and principles of the United Nations.

The United States pointed out that if this article were not included, it would be necessary to lay down specific limitations to the preceding articles.

The USSR said that the most important task concerning human progress was to find the proper balance between the interests of the individual and the interests of society.

Cuba said that, while it was important to defend the individual against the State, he should also be reminded that he was a member of society, and must affirm his right to be deemed a human being by recognizing the duties which were corollaries of his rights. A solemn declaration of social solidarity would be a safeguard against the exaggerated individualism which had done so much ill.

It was generally realized that individual liberty had to be balanced with the liberty of other individuals and with the reasonable demands of the community. Belgium noted, furthermore, that the article mentions duties to the community, but that there is no mention of duties to one's neighbor, family or self. It added that in dealing with that subject, mankind has as yet been unable to improve upon the Ten Commandments, the cornerstone of which was "Thou shalt love thy neighbor as thyself."

Article 30 (that nothing in the Declaration should be interpreted that any state, group, or person can engage in any activity aimed at the destruction of any of the rights and freedoms stated in the Universal Declaration) produced fewer amendments than probably any of the others. Belgium noted that it was essential to include this article because the rights granted in the Declaration might be nullified unless there were a provision stating that no activity should be aimed at their destruction. It also felt that it should be made clear that the Declaration did not grant anyone the freedom to endanger the freedom of others.

Belgium appeared to echo the general consensus of the member states who were firmly convinced of the necessity of stopping the activities of subversive groups and preventing a repetition of the experience of a number of countries in the years immediately before the war.

Additional Proposals.

Two additional articles on the Right of Petition and the Fate of Minorities were also considered.

The Commission on Human Rights did not include the former article in the body of the Declaration because it had not discussed measures of implementation. Nevertheless, it submitted it at this time to the General Assembly. This article stated: "Everyone has the right, either individually, or in association with others, to petition or to communicate with the public authorities of the State of which he is a national or in which he resides, or with the United Nations."

France stated that the Commission felt that this right could not be accepted before measures of implementation had been studied. It claimed that it was essential that individuals should know that their petitions would receive a hearing. It felt, however, that this text was too lengthy and there was the danger of infringing on sovereignty of States and the risk of being flooded by petitions. However, it added that it would be questionable whether the Declaration could be considered complete without the statement of such a right.

Cuba agreed with France, noting that the right of petition was a right in itself and not merely a measure of implementation. It was already recognized in the law of many countries and it thought it should appear in the Declaration. Cuba felt, however, that such a right would raise difficulties. At this time, therefore, it appeared premature.

Mexico appealed for caution in considering the proposed article and mentioned that the United Nations had no machinery to deal with petitions from states which were not members. To include this right, might set a form of international jurisdiction above the sovereign jurisdiction of states. The Chairman reminded Mexico that in Article 56 of the Charter members pledged themselves to take joint and separate action in cooperation with the UN for the promotion of universal respect for human rights.

The United States emphasized that it had not as yet examined the text of this right, but would consider it when it examined measures for implementation. Only Ecuador, Chile and New Zealand wanted to include this article.

Rather than include this article, they accepted a United Kingdom proposal to ask the Economic and Social Council and the Commission on Human Rights to examine the problem of petitions. In this resolution was also included a Cuban amendment that "the right of petition is an essential human right."

Concerning the Fate of Minorities, each of the early drafts of the Declaration included an article proclaiming the rights of ethnic, linguistic or religious minorities which stated:

> Persons belonging to such groups shall have the right, as far as is compatible with public order and security, to establish and maintain their schools and cultural or religious institutions, and to use their own language and script in the press, in public assembly and before the courts and other authorities of the State, if they so choose.

France noted that this right was dropped from the Commission of Human Rights' third session because the Declaration had already proclaimed the equality of all men everywhere and therefore the rights of minorities were for the large part covered. It also felt that the problem of minorities was complicated by the different structure of the various States and the various texts were too general in character.

Syria pointed out that the principle of the protection of minorities had often been used as a political excuse to subject or interfere with the people of other nations. If it were incorporated in the declaration it was afraid that some nations would again feel justified in abusing that principle.

Haiti proposed that the Sub-commission on the Prevention of Discrimination and the Protection of Minorities should be asked to study the question of a convention on international machinery to ensure effective protection of minorities. This proposal was accepted. Member states also adopted a draft resolution noting that, while the United Nations could not remain indifferent to the fate of minorities, it recognized the difficulty of adopting a uniform solution of this complex and delicate question.

Of the 56 member states of the United Nations at that time the Universal Declaration of Human Rights was adopted by 48 votes. There were 8 abstentions by Byelorussian SSR, Czechoslovakia, Poland, Saudi Arabia, Ukrainian SSR, Union of South Africa, USSR, and Yugoslavia (*Yearbook of the United Nations*, 1948-49).

BEYOND THE UNIVERSAL DECLARATION
1949-THE PRESENT

Since the adoption of the Universal Declaration by the General Assembly, the idea of human rights has reached unprecedented heights.

This massive acceptance seems to have occurred in spite of the hesitation of many governments, beginning as early as the League of Nations and continuing to the present day, to articulate standards and implementation methods. The "lack of time" at the San Francisco Conference, the notion of the Commission on Human Rights as a "rudimentary receptacle" and lack of inclusion of the Right to Petition in the Universal Declaration are examples which suggest this reluctance.

Yet, the latter half of the twentieth century has witnessed an extraordinary proliferation of *non*-governmental organizations [NGO's] who are steadily forming global, comprehensive, and systematic movements to investigate and reform human rights abuses. This growth of NGO's is not surprising, however, since it is the world's governments who are to be prosecuted.

Yet, if "The will of the people shall be the basis of [their] authority," (i.e. Article 21 in the Universal Declaration), it appears reasonable to expect governmental sensitivity to citizens' concerns. Furthermore, it was the persistent pressure of such NGO's as Amnesty International on the UN General Assembly to adopt a Convention Against Torture and Other Cruel, Inhumane, or Degrading Treatment or Punishment and the American Jewish Committee to win the General Assembly's acceptance of a Declaration on the Elimination of All Forms of Intolerance and of Discrimination Based on Religion or Belief (Claude and Weston, 1989). The work of NGO's strongly suggests that global popular movements are the driving forces behind the cause of human rights.

United Nations Developments

Member states had agreed that the drafting of legal instruments which would also contain enforcement procedures would follow the Universal Declaration. Work began, therefore, in 1949 on what later became the International Covenant on Civil and Political Rights and the International Covenant on Economic, Social and Cultural Rights. Both covenants were open for signature in 1966 and went into force in 1976.

As the debates on the Universal Declaration indicated, there were deep ideological differences, emanating from different philosophical and cultural histories, among member states. This situation necessitated the drawing up of these two core legal documents (Trubek, 1985) which reflected these disparities.

The content of the two covenants appears fairly similar to that of the Universal Declaration, although more detailed language is sometimes used (Blaustein, 1987). The Covenant on Economic, Social and Cultural Rights, for example, while proclaiming the right to just and favorable conditions of work, corresponding to Article 23 of the Universal Declaration, elaborates in Article 7:

> [This right should] ensure...Fair wages and equal remuneration for work of equal value without distinction of any kind, in particular women being guaranteed conditions of work not inferior to those enjoyed by men, with equal pay for equal work; [and] equal opportunity for everyone to be promoted in his employment to an appropriate higher level, subject to no considerations other than those of seniority and competence.

Both covenants, however, do not contain a right to own property (Article 17 of the Universal Declaration). This right was not included because the numerous philosophical and political traditions represented in the UN could not agree on its scope and definition (Buergenthal, 1988).

The Covenants both begin by stating in Article 1: "All peoples have the right to self-determination." This inclusion at the outset seems to dramatically symbolize the tremendous importance for decolonization in the work of the UN (Blaustein, 1987).

Other basic differences with the Universal Declaration are that they both provide for implementation mechanisms for states that have ratified them. They mention, for example, that "States Parties to the present Covenant [shall]...submit reports on the measures they have adopted which give effect to the rights recognized" (in Part IV of the Covenant on Civil and Political Rights).

The major difference between implementation measures of both covenants is that the Covenant on Civil and Political Rights requires that these reports are submitted to a "human Rights Committee...consist[ing] of eighteen members...composed of nationals of the States Parties to the present Covenant who shall be of high moral character and recognized competence in the field of human rights" (in Article 28).

This committee "may respond to allegations by one state party that another state party is not fulfilling its obligations under the covenant." If the committee cannot resolve the issue, then an ad hoc conciliation committee reports its findings in order to find an amicable solution (Weston, 1989).

The Covenant on Civil and Political Rights also contains an Optional Protocol. State parties to this document further recognize the competence of the Human Rights Committee to act upon communications from individuals claiming to be victims of covenant violations.

The Covenant on Economic, Social, and Cultural Rights, however, is not geared to immediate implementation. State parties having agreed only "to take steps" toward "achieving progressively the full realization of the rights recognized in the...Covenant" and then subject to "the maximum of available resources."

State parties submit reports to the Economic and Social Council rather than to a Human Rights Committee on the progress they have made in achieving the enumerated rights. Primarily, however, it appears a promotional convention which requires implementation over time, rather than immediately.

Whereas the above measures are applicable only to states that have ratified the Covenants, there are two procedures which appear applicable to all governments. These approaches, the "1235" and the "1503" procedures, both examine consistent patterns of gross, massive violations of human rights. The former approach however, discusses these issues in a public forum and concerns itself essentially with violations *as exemplified* by South Africa's policy of apartheid; the latter method examines in a confidential setting *all* infringements of human rights violations as defined by the Commission on Human Rights (Newman and Weissbrodt, 1990).

Other mechanisms of implementation include: the establishment of specialized theme mechanisms to take effective action often on an emergency basis on several critical human rights problems such as disappearances, summary executions, torture, and religious intolerance; the appointment of Special Rapporteurs to examine conditions in individual countries, which, in 1991 include Afghanistan, Chile, El Salvador, Iran, and Romania; the expansion of the activities of new supervisory committees that monitor compliance with human rights treaties; the expansion of advisory service programs that provide technical assistance in human rights; and the development to expand UN public information on human rights concomitant with an advancing awareness of rights in the global arena (Tessitore and Woolfson, 1991).

These implementation mechanisms appear integrated to varied extents in subsequent conventions. On the whole, however, these mechanisms appear extremely weak and currently most human rights advocates agree that the major challenge is to strengthen the implementation and enforcement of human rights standards developed over the years (Tessitore and Woolfson, 1991).

Often, however, complaints can unfortunately be fostered by non-humanitarian and other hidden agenda. According to Van Boven (1981), Director of the Human Rights Commission (1977-1982), for example, when the United Kingdom and the United States recently moved to draft a resolution concerning the fate of the dissident Dr. Sakharov in the Soviet Union, the USSR countered with a proposal to examine human rights in Northern Ireland and among the indigenous people in the United States. Whereas all these issues appear legitimate human rights concerns, they appear to emanate from political rather than purely humanitarian motives, a recurring theme throughout the history of the idea of human rights. With the evident end of the Cold War between the United States and the newly formed Commonwealth of Independent States, it remains to be seen if this previous, basically East-West polemic will lead to a North-South confrontation with political, rather than humanitarian concerns, motivating the advancement of human rights.

During approximately the first forty years, furthermore, the UN human rights program concentrated primarily on standards setting (Stamatapoulou,

1989). In addition to the two covenants the United Nations has also generated numerous other human rights conventions.

These conventions include: *topically specific conventions*, intended to guard against particular human rights abuses such as genocide, war crimes, slavery, traffic in persons, forced labor, and torture. Some examples are: Convention on the Prevention and Punishment of the Crime of Genocide (Dec. 9, 1948), Convention for the Suppression of the Traffic in Persons and of the Exploitation of the Prostitution of Others (March 21, 1950), and Convention Against Torture and Other Cruel, Inhumane or Degrading Treatment or Punishment (Dec. 10, 1984).

There are also *conventions on group protection* which correspond to needs of special groups such as refugees, stateless persons, migrants, workers, women, children, combatants, prisoners, and civilians in time of armed conflict. Some examples are: Convention Relating to the Status of Refugees (July 28, 1951), Convention Concerning Migrations in Abusive Conditions and the Promotion of Equality of Opportunity and Treatment of Migrant Workers (June 4, 1975), Convention Concerning Freedom of Association and Protection of the Right to Organize (July 9, 1948), and, most recently, the Convention on the Rights of the Child (Nov. 20, 1989).

Finally, there are *conventions prohibiting discrimination* based on race or sex in education, employment, and occupation. Some examples are: The International Convention on the Elimination of All Forms of Racial Discrimination (Mar. 7, 1966), The International Convention Against Apartheid in Sports (Dec. 10, 1985) and The Convention on the Elimination of All Forms of Discrimination Against Women (Dec. 18, 1979).

Regional Developments

Supplementing the globally-oriented human rights activity of the United Nations, are regional human rights developments, sometimes called "human rights regimes" which are playing an increasing part in the development of international human rights law and policy.

The first regional development was the European Convention for the Protection of Human Rights and Fundamental Freedoms. Agreed to by the Council of Europe on November 4, 1950, which was developed in large measure as a protection against a revival of totalitarian dictatorships, the purpose of the European Convention is to ensure in the region the enforcement of certain rights stated in the Universal Declaration of Human Rights (Weston, Lukes, and Hnatt, 1989). The opening of the Human Rights Building in Strasbourg, France in June, 1995 and decisions which the European community appears to take rather seriously (Newman and Weissbrodt, 1996), such as *Dudgeon v. United Kingdom*, 45 Eur. Ct. H.R. (ser. A) (1982), which asserted that treatment of homosexuals in Northern Ireland was discriminatory, suggests that this system is the most developed. The *Dudgeon* decision led Northern Ireland to pass the Criminal Law (Sexual Offenses) Act (1993) which decriminalized homosexual acts between consenting adults over 17.

In 1959, within the framework of the Organization of American States (OAS), which assisted in the adoption of the American Declaration of the Rights and Duties of Man (1948), the Inter-American Commission on Human Rights was created. The main function of this commission is to develop "awareness of human rights, making recommendations to OAS Member States, preparing studies or reports, requesting information from OAS Member States, responding to and advising OAS Member States on matters relating to human rights, and submitting annual reports to the OAS General Assembly" (Weston et. al., p. 213). This "regime" 's influence appears to be growing as evidenced in part by its "country reports," that, according to Newman and Weissbrodt (1996, p. 447) "have helped...to confront gross and massive human rights violations in the region, even in those countries where the Commision was denied government consent to conduct an on-site investigation."

In 1981 the African Charter on Human and Peoples' Rights was adopted. The provisions of this Charter go beyond its European and Inter-American counterparts by recognizing the rights of peoples, which include third generation or solidarity rights (Weston et. al., 1989).

Some examples from this charter also referred to as the Banjul Charter on Human and Peoples' Rights are:

> (Article 19) All peoples shall be equal; they shall enjoy the same respect and shall have the same rights. Nothing shall justify the domination of a people by another; (Article 20 [1]) All peoples have the right to existence. They shall have the unquestionable and inalienable right to self-determination....[and] (Article 21 [1]) All peoples shall freely dispose of their wealth and natural resources. This right shall be exercised in the exclusive interest of the people. In no case shall a people be deprived of it. (Blaustein, 1987, pp. 632-645)

Because African customs and traditions favor mediation and conciliation, this regional development does not entertain the more adversarial and adjudicative procedures common to European legal systems (Weston, 1989). It has also established a Commission on Human and People's Rights. In March 1995 this Commission passed a resolution for the establishment of an African Court on Human Rights in part because "some scholars have criticized the African system for its inadequate implementation of procedures" (Newman and Weissbrodt, 1996, p. 465) as evidenced by, for example, only 17 states having submitted reports from 49 that have ratified the Banjul Charter.

Asia appears to have only begun to establish regional human rights institutions due in large measure to an extremely diverse religious, cultural, and philosophical heritage. The 1983 Declaration of the Basic Duties of ASEAN (Association of Southeast Asian Nations Peoples and Governments) (Blaustein, 1987) and the recent formations of sub-regional structures, such as the South Pacific Forum (SPF) and the South Asia Association for Regional Cooperation (SAARC). There is now a proposal for a Pacific Charter on Human Rights (Newman and Weissbrodt, 1996).

Consistent with Gandhi's notions of human rights, excerpts from the 1983 Declaration appears unique in the human rights field because it couches its principles in terms of duties rather than rights. More than half of the provisions of this Declaration begin with the words: "It is the duty of government." Other provisions dictate duties for individuals and people, for example:

> (Article 1) It is the duty of every government to insure and protect the basic rights of all persons to life, a decent standard of living, security, dignity, identity, freedom, truth, due process of law and justice...and other rights and freedoms of individuals and of peoples set forth in - the Universal Declaration of Human Rights....(Article 3)...It is the duty of government to eradicate nepotism, favoritism, corruption, and waste in public life. It is the duty of government officials to lead a simple and modest life, and to set an example of impartiality, integrity and service to the people...(Article 5) Social Justice...It is the duty of the people to respect the dignity of all kinds of labor and services rendered by workers and employees. (Blaustein, pp. 646-657)

Human rights have also been addressed by the Arab and Islamic states who in 1968 established a Human Rights Commission. In 1994 this league adopted an Arab Charter on Human Rights, but as of January 1995, there have been no ratifications. Another initiative was the Cairo Declaration on Human Rights (1990) of the Organization of the Islamic Conference (OIC), which Muslim governments belong. It is in this context of regional developments that I would like to mention the current debate concerning "cultural relativism," where the issue is most pronounced. Article 6(b) of the Cairo Declaration states, for example, "The husband is responsible for the support and welfare of the family." While it is true that there is no similar statement in western documents, nevertheless, economic, social, cultural, and solidarity rights as a general rule are often forgotten, most particularly in the United States which often engages in a "torrent of self-praise" in regards to its upholding of human rights standards and is also the world's largest arms supplier (Chomsky, 1997, p. 13).

Theoretical Developments

The realm of theory seems to have lagged far behind the elaboration of human rights standards and, to some extent, mechanisms of implementation in conventions at the United Nations and the regional developments. Undeniably, the theorists discussed from the Ages of Enlightenment and Industrialization were vital to the establishment of such documents as the Declaration of Independence and the Soviet Constitution which, in turn, were influential in the development of the Universal Declaration. The importance of social theorists in the area of human rights, however, during the last four decades does not appear as substantial.

Nevertheless, John Rawls's contribution is noteworthy. Also of significance are the contributions of Pope John Paul II and a group of lesser known individuals, such as human rights scholars Theodoor Van Boven, Rajni Kothari, and Raúl Ferrero, who have added to the debate on the meaning of solidarity rights in the context of the New International Economic Order. Finally, contributions by such organizations as the World Council of Churches and Worldwatch deserve comment.

Although Rawls in *A Theory of Justice* (1971) does not mention the term "human rights," his work is widely acclaimed as a substantive contribution to the inquiry into an adequate basis for a philosophy of rights (Martin, 1985). Rawls seems to pose an alternative to Jeremy Bentham's notion of a just society as the "greatest good for the greatest number" (i.e. utilitarianism) which Rawls sees as the dominant systematic moral view for the past two hundred years. His general conception of justice, however, is one of *fairness* which provides that all "social primary goods," such as liberty and opportunity, income and wealth, are to be distributed equally unless an unequal distribution of any of these goods is to the advantage of the least favored (Shestack, 1985).   In Rawls's theory, primary goods are "things that every rational [person]...is presumed to want" (1971, p. 62), deliberating under a "veil of ignorance" and in an "original position" of equality. Behind this veil and in this position, therefore, no one is aware "of his place in society, his class position or social status, nor does any one know his fortune in the distribution of natural assets and abilities, his intelligence, strength and the like" (p. 12).

Injustice to Rawls, therefore, is simply inequalities of these primary goods, which every rational person should want that are not to the benefit of everyone.

Rawls feels, therefore, that each person, even the least favored, possesses an inviolability founded on justice that even the welfare of society as a whole cannot overrule. Consequently, Rawls would not interpret concepts such as "the general welfare" or "justice" in terms of Bentham's formulation, but rather to the extent that they benefit *everyone*, including the least advantaged.

Rawls also emphasizes duties. He states, for example: "Duty has two parts: first, we are to comply with and to do our share in just institutions when they exist and apply to us; and, second, we are to assist in the establishment of just arrangements when they do not exist" (p. 334). To Rawls, if these conceptions of justice are applied, ideas of respect and human dignity are given more definite meaning. Respect for persons is shown by treating them in ways that they can see are justifiable.

My observations suggest strong affinities with the Universal Declaration in Rawls's concern for *everyone's* welfare, and his concern for duties and human dignity. More importantly, however, his theory of justice seems to have placed on the academic and political agenda not only an alternative to utilitarianism, but also, a realization that philosophy can help articulate notions of a just society in which social and economic inequalities can be arranged so that they are to the greatest benefit of the least advantaged.

It is easy, furthermore, to apply Rawls's notion to arrange inequalities to the greatest benefit of the least advantaged to the global community. The poorest peoples of the world, usually referred to as the Third World, often speak, for example, of the global maldistribution of wealth and call for *international* distributive justice in order to participate in some of the wealth of the richer nations.

The notion of solidarity rights as expressed particularly in Article 28 of the Universal Declaration, which asserts the right "to a social and international order in which the rights and freedoms set forth in the Declaration can be fully realized," expresses in part this demand for international distributive justice.

I had previously commented that these new rights to solidarity are still in the process of conceptual elaboration. The following thinkers and organizations represent some contributions to the articulation of this concept.

Pope John Paul II, for example, has often expressed concern that the recent changes in Eastern Europe should not take the world's attention from the plight of the poorer countries of the world (i.e. the Third World). In his encyclical *Laborem Exercens (On Human Work)* (1981) he expresses the need to examine the phenomenon of work within the broader context of human rights. Acknowledging the interdependence of all nations in contemporary times, he calls for international collaboration among states by treaties and agreements and movements of solidarity among workers in order to use the world's natural resources more efficiently. Global mismanagement of the world's resources has resulted in the violation of dignity of human work, generating huge numbers of unemployed, underemployed, and countless peoples suffering from hunger. In his most recent encyclical, *Centissimus Annus (The Hundredth Year)*, which commemorates the hundredth anniversary of *Rerum Novarum*, the Pope continues his plea for a just social and international order:

> Many...people, while not completely marginalized, live in situations in which the struggle for a bare minimum is uppermost. These are situations in which the rules of the earliest period of capitalism still flourish in conditions of ruthlessness in no way inferior to the darkest moments of the first phase of industrialization.....It is still possible today, as in the days of Rerum Novarum, to speak of inhuman exploitation....Unfortunately, the great majority of people in the third world still live in such conditions. (Steinfels, 1991)

Van Boven (1982) notes that on the global level, a most striking development has recently been a concern for collectivist (i.e. solidarity) rather than an individualist approach to human rights. Such rights include the right of peoples to self-determination, the right of underprivileged groups to a fair share in the world's resources, the right to development, and the right to peace.

He regards, furthermore, the Proclamation of Teheran of 1968, as a significant development of this trend, which referred to the widening gap between the developed and developing countries which is a tremendous impediment to the realization of human rights in the international community. The African Charter and the ASEAN Declaration are two further developments of this new trend toward solidarity.

Rajni Kothari (1989) expresses rather forcefully some of the issues involved in rights based on a New International Economic Order noting that the human rights debate is now in the "throes of acute controversy" and is not confined merely to the traditional dichotomy between first and second generations of rights. This controversy has deepened because there has been little progress in restructuring an unjust international order. There continues to be an historical and ever increasing pattern of Northern command over the world's resources which includes lavish and exploitative lifestyles of the industrialized world at the expense of the living standards of the developing countries. Speaking specifically of a growing sense of threat to cultural identity and civilizational values in Asia, Africa and Latin America, he feels that their traditions of lifestyle and sharing of a common heritage are being undermined.

To Kothari, "The crux of the matter....is the whole question of lifestyle" (p.137). He sees a global restructuring of the relationship between resources and human beings in which a minority of nations in pursuit of a "parasitic and wasteful" style no longer shores up the majority of world's resources. While he is pessimistic that this restructuring will be long and drawn out, he, nevertheless, offers wisdom to attain a more just order recalling Gandhi's notion that there can be no freedom without a measure of self-control and sacrifice:

> Gandhi put his finger on the most crucial dimension of moving
> towards a just social order when he called for a limitation of wants
> and warned his countrymen against falling prey to an industrial
> machine that not only reduces a majority of men to laboring slaves,
> but also dictates what and how they should eat, wear, dress, sing
> and dance. (p. 139)

Another author is Raúl Ferrero (1986) who, as Special Rapporteur for the Commission on Human Rights' Sub-Commission on Prevention of Discrimination and Protection of Minorities, writes in his study, *The New International Economic Order and the Promotion of Human Rights,* that the present order is a serious obstacle to the realization of human rights as proclaimed in the Universal Declaration, especially Article 25 which declares that everyone has the right to an adequate standard of living.

Noting that the "gap between the levels of living of developed and developing countries continues to widen-from roughly 10:1 in the 1950s to 14:1 at the end of the 1970s," (p. 40) he explains, that the industrialized nations are trying to solve their social problems, such as unemployment and inflation at the expense of the poorer countries.

Ferrero also stresses the importance of the indivisible and interdependent nature of all human rights, in which priority is not given to any category in particular. The main difficulty to him, however, is how to establish a flexible relationship between generations of rights, taking each country's level of socio-economic development fully into account.

Acknowledging that the concept of human rights has evolved gradually and then relating briefly the development of first and second generation rights, he recognizes that:

> Only in recent times has the need been maintained to recognize the
> existence of the "rights of solidarity"- which include the right to
> development, to a healthy environment, to peace and to the common
> heritage of mankind, and other rights that make up what could be
> called the third generation in this evolution. These rights, however,
> have scarcely taken shape and to implement them will require a
> major effort along a difficult road ahead. (p. 42)

He concludes his study by emphasizing that the basic challenge is to ensure that the establishment of the new international economic order and promotion of respect for human rights, are approached in ways which ensure that concepts of human dignity and solidarity are the guiding principles.

The World Council of Churches has, in addition, always demanded "authentic solidarity" with the poor which means: "accompanying them in their struggles against the injustices which they suffer and those who generate them, [and]....that we must cease our solidarity with those who often oppress the poor and denounce their injustice" (De Santa Ana, 1979, p. 106). Since its Fifth Assembly meeting in Nairobi, Kenya in 1975, the Council seems to have shifted its emphasis from providing programs for the poor, to finding ways to change unjust economic and social structures which result in the maldistribution of goods. Basing its mission on numerous scriptural references to justice and liberation, it stresses the priority of the right to development which minimizes dependence and encourages people to control their own destinies and realize their full potentials (United Nations, 1981).

The Worldwatch Institute under the directorship of Lester Brown (1991) publishes reports concerning the *State of the World*. The United Nations and the international community in general concerned with development issues rely heavily upon its work. In its recent report for 1991, Worldwatch acknowledges that the Gross National Product (GNP) of nations throughout the world is approximately thirty-three percent higher in *constant* dollars from a decade ago. Stock prices, furthermore, have reached all-time highs on some financial exchanges.

It states, however, that the GNP can no longer be a satisfactory indicator of progress. Using other indicators which also take into consideration such factors as long-term environmental damage, it concludes that this unprecedented "growth" in the GNP is at the expense of later generations. Air pollution, for example, an externality of "progress" has officially reduced U.S. crop production by 5-10 percent. Similarly, deforestation has led to an increasing frequency of flood-damaged harvests. Brown (1989) has also commented that since the drought of 1988 which depleted U.S. grain surpluses, Americans are leading a hand-to-mouth existence. Unless immediate actions, such as taxing environmentally destructive activities, are taken to reverse environmental trends which are undermining the welfare of individuals throughout the world, dreams for future generations will become nightmares. Its 1992 report emphasizes, furthermore, that as the next century approaches, this period is undoubtedly the "decisive decade" to begin developing viable alternatives ("Worldwatch Report," 1992).

Five years after the UN Conference on Environment and Development in Rio de Janeiro in 1992, it appears, however, that this summit at least "set in motion historical processes that will bear fruit fordecades to come" (Flavin, 1997, p. 19). Yet, these processes are in danger of becoming "empty vessels," unless governments transform the conventions that resulted from the conference, like the Framework Convention on Climate Change into "tough, legally binding effective aggrements" (p. 21). Worldwatch certainly reflects the concern of many organizations today for international and intergenerational cooperation in order to fully realize rights to solidarity.

The Vienna Declaration of Human Rights to the
Fiftieth Anniversary of the Universal Declaration

Perhaps the pivotal turning point in human rights work was the 1993 World Conference on Human Rights in Vienna, which resulted in the Vienna Declaration and Programme of Action. That conference was one of other rather successful international conferences sponsored by the UN, such as the Rio conference already mentioned, the International Conference on Population and Development (Cairo, 1994), World Summit for Social Development (Copenhagen, 1995), the Fourth World Conference on Women (Beijing, 1995), the Food Summit (Rome, 1996) and Habitat II (Istanbul, 1996) which also emphasized various aspects of human rights. Needless to say, while global awareness of such issues, like development in Copenhagen, food in Rome, and housing in Istanbul, increased, the United States never asserted that development, food, or housing were human rights.

The Vienna Declaration, however, emphasized: first increased coordination on human rights within the U.N. system; second, equality, dignity and tolerance, with emphasis upon racial discrimination, xenophobia: persons belonging to national or ethnic, religious and linguistic minorities: the equal status and human rights of women: the rights of the child: freedom from torture: and the rights of the disabled person; third, cooperation, development, and strengthening of human rights, in particular the development of action plans by states, which incorporate grassroots organizations into the debates and in accordance with U.N. human rights guidelines; fourth, implementation and monitoring methods to improve reporting mechanisms; fifth, human rights education to include "peace, development, democracy and social justice" in curricula of "all learning institutions in formal and informal settings"; and finally, follow-up on the program of action .

Overseeing much of this human rights work is the newly appointed position, United Nations High Commissioner for Human Rights, also a result of the Vienna Conference. It is noteworthy that the United States was a major advocate for that position. Presently, it is held by the former President of Ireland, Mary Robinson, who began this work on September 15, 1997. She was also a keynote speaker at the First Joint European Seminar "Culture and identity: Social Work in a Changing Europe," August 1997. She is extremely sympathetic to economic, social, cultural, and solidarity rights and most recently emphasized that "the normative work is largely done. The international human rights standards are in place. The task for us all, [now] will be to implement them" (The Romanes Lecture, Oxford University, the

United Nations Human Rights Website, www3.unicef.ch/html/intlist.htm) .
Many human rights activists are hopeful that she will continue to strengthen
burgeoning notions of human rights.

An examination of UN documents after the Vienna Declaration strongly
suggest that many of the goals of the Declaration are slowly becoming reality.
These documents appeared to emphasize proactive measures, such as the
"identification of early warning signs" in regards to human rights violations
perhaps as a response to unconscionable genocide in Rwanda in 1994. In
addition, documents such as "Human rights questions: Alternative approaches
for improving the effective enjoyment of human rights- National institutions for
the promotion and protection of human rights," (UN, 1995); "Progress report of
the intergovernmental group of experts on the right to development" (UN,
1997); "Follow-up to the World Conference on Human Rights: Report of the
UN High Commissioner for Human Rights, building a partnership" (UN, 1997)
and "Implementation of the Programme of Action for the Third Decade to
Combat Racism: Seminar on the role of the Internet with regard to the
provisions of the International Convention on the Elimination of All Forms of
Racial Discrimination (1997) strongly suggest that the visions, along with the
growth of public sentiment in support of human rights, may be becoming
realities.

Yet, it would be absurd to think that now the world is on the road to
recovery. Quite the contrary. The Universal Declaration of Human Rights and
its progeny may have "shaken" us. But, human rights work will always be a
struggle. Recent attempts to draft a "Human Rights Defenders Declaration" are
perhaps proofs that governments are slowly beginning to listen. Government
reluctance, however, is still evident in the United States as reports to the
Human Rights monitoring committees to the Conventions Against Torture and
the Elimination of All Forms of Racial Discrimination are two years late.

In conclusion, although the idea of human rights is riddled with notions of
natural law, humanitarian intervention, various hidden agenda, and cultural
relativism when unjust international orders, tyrannical monarchs or
governments attempted to thwart human needs, individuals have banded
together to produce documents that may assist them in the realization of these
needs. The United Nations Universal Declaration of Human Rights is one such
document. While this idea of human rights has given "birth" to other human
rights declarations and conventions, and "human rights regimes" into the next
century the Universal Declaration should still continue to be the authoritative
definition of human rights. The celebration of its 50th anniversary is an
excellent opportunity to expand even further awareness about that document, as
well as, its progeny. Largely, the task ahead is now one of implementation, or
what might be called programs of action to realize human rights for all.

Notes - Chapter Three

[1] Unless otherwise noted, this summary of key issues is taken from United Nations Department of Public Information, 1950, *These Rights and Freedoms*, pp. 17-86 and the *United Nations Weekly Bulletin*, November 1, 1948 (Articles 1-2), November 15, 1948 (Articles 3-6), December 1, 1948 (Articles 7-15), December 15, 1948 (Articles 16-23)and January 15, 1949 (Articles 24-30).

[2] Because all representatives were under directives from their governments (Green, 1956), I have chosen to refer by name to the specific state rather than its representative.

PART TWO

A HUMAN RIGHTS ANALYSIS

IMPLICATIONS FOR

SOCIAL POLICY

Whenever there is in any country, uncultivated lands and unemployed poor, it is clear that the laws of property have been so far extended as to violate natural right. The earth is given as a common stock for man to labour and live on. If for the encouragement of industry we allow it to be appropriated, we must take care that other employment be provided to those excluded from the appropriation.

- *Thomas Jefferson*

CHAPTER FOUR

📖📖📖📖📖📖📖📖📖📖📖📖📖📖📖📖📖📖📖📖📖

COMPARISON OF THE UNITED STATES CONSTITUTION WITH THE UNIVERSAL DECLARATION OF HUMAN RIGHTS

This chapter and the following one present the analysis of United States' constitutions in comparison with the Universal Declaration. In this chapter I will consider only the Federal Constitution which will include not only a textual comparison, but also Supreme Court decisions guaranteeing rights not explicitly defined in the United States Constitution, and an examination of the "general welfare" and "establish justice" clauses of the Constitution. The following chapter analyzes the texts of the 50 state constitutions in relation to the Universal Declaration.

Concerning the textual comparisons, my method consists of listing all basic provisions in the Universal Declaration and then identifying the relevant phrase or phrases in the Constitution which correspond to these basic provisions. For example, Article 18 of the Universal Declaration states:

> Everyone has the right to freedom of thought, conscience and religion; this right includes freedom to change his religion or belief, and freedom, either alone or in community with others, to manifest his religion or belief in teaching, practice, and in public or private worship and observance.

On the matter of religion the United States Constitution states in Article 1 of the Bill of Rights: "Congress shall make no law respecting an establishment of religion, or prohibiting the free exercise thereof." Although the language of both articles is different, and their correspondence is not total or precise, in my judgment they appear to express in substance and sense the right of an individual to practice his or her religion.

In like fashion, I will match basic provisions of all articles to ascertain similarities between the Universal Declaration and United States' constitutions. Occasionally, moreover, some articles seem to express more than one right. Article 3 of the Universal Declaration states, for instance: "Everyone has the right to life, liberty and security of person." For the purposes of this analysis, therefore, I have chosen to divide this article (and others expressing more than one right) into three parts: a) Everyone has the right to life, b) liberty, and c) security of person, before making a comparison.   At the end of this analysis I will discuss major issues, including summative statements about the relation between these two documents.

On the matter of Supreme Court decisions guaranteeing rights not spelled out in the United States Constitution, I have chosen to list what appears a major case and the phrase or phrases that the Supreme Court has referred to in the Federal Constitution, in order to give sustenance to a basic right. Article 13(2) of the Universal Declaration states, for example: "Everyone has the right to leave any country, including his own, and to return to his country." In my consideration of relevant phrases, I will list the case as well as the pertinent phrase which the Supreme Court has referred to in establishing a basic right, in this case the right to travel. Next to the right to travel, for example, I will list:

> *Shapiro v. Thompson* make or enforce any law which shall (1969): (AmXIV,S1)No state shall abridge the privileges and immunities of citizn of the United States...nor deny to any person within its jurisdiction the equal protection of the laws.

An explanation of abbreviations, such as (P) for Preamble or (Am) for Amendment can be found below in Table 2. I will consider the general welfare and establish justice clauses in a separate section of this chapter.

Table 2.
Explanation of Abbreviations

Abbreviation	Explanation
Am	Amendment
Ar	Article
BR	Bill of Rights
Ch	Chapter
DR	Declaration of Rights
E	Education
GA	General Assembly
P	Preamble
Pr	Paragraph
Pt	Part
S	Section

ANALYSIS OF THE UNITED STATES CONSTITUTION
IN COMPARISON WITH THE
UNIVERSAL DECLARATION OF HUMAN RIGHTS

The Universal Declaration of Human Rights	The United States Constitution
Article 1	Relevant Phrase
a)All human beings are born free and	(P) We, the people of the United States, in order to...secure the blessings of liberty...do ordain and establish this Constitution. (AmV,S1) No person shall...be deprived of...liberty. (AmXIV,S1) No state shall...deprive any person of...liberty.
b) equal in dignity	
c) and rights	(AmXIV,S1) No state shall...deny to any person within its jurisdiction the equal protection of the laws
d) They are endowed with reason and conscience	(AmI,S1) Congress shall make no law respecting an establishment of religion

e) and should act towards one another
in a spirit of brotherhood

Article 2

a) Everyone is entitled to all the rights and freedoms set forth in this Declaration, without distinction of any kind such as race, color, sex, language, religion, political or other opinion, national or social origin, property, birth, or other status.

(AmXIV, S1) No state shall make or enforce any law which shall abridge the privileges or immunities of citizens of the United States...nor deny to any person within its jurisdiction the equal protection of the laws.

b) Furthermore, no distinction shall be made on the basis of the political, jurisdictional or international status of the country or territory to which a person belongs, whether it be independent, trust, non-self governing or under any other limitation of sovereignty.

(AmXIV,S1) No state shall make or enforce any law which shall abridge the privileges or immunities of citizens of the United States...nor deny to any person within its jurisdiction the equal protection of the laws.

Article 3

a) Everyone has the right to life

(AmV,S1) No person shall...be deprived of life, liberty or property.
(AmXIV,S1) No state shall...deprive any person of life, liberty or property.

b) liberty and   "

c) security of person

(AmIV,S1) The right of people to be secure in their persons... shall not be violated.

Article 4

a) No one shall be held in slavery or

(AmXIII,S1) Neither slavery nor

servitude;

b) slavery and the slave trade shall be prohibited in all their forms.

involuntary servitude...shall exist in the United States

"

Article 5

a) No one shall be subjected to torture or

(AmIV,S1) The right of the people to be secure in their persons...shall not be violated. (AmV,S1) No person shall be...deprived of life, liberty or property without due process of law. (AmVI) The accused shall enjoy the right to a speedy and public trial by an impartial jury. (AmXIV,S1) No state shall...deprive any person of life, liberty or property, without due process of law. (AmVIII,S1) No cruel and unusual punishments shall be inflicted.

b) to cruel inhuman or degrading treatment or punishment.

"

Article 6

a) Everyone has the right to recognition everywhere as a person before the law.

(AmI,S1) Congress shall make no law respecting...the right of the people...to petition the government for a redress of grievances. (AmV,S1) No person shall...be deprived of life, liberty, or property without due process of law. (AmXIV,S1) All persons born...in the United States...and subject to the jurisdiction thereof are citizens of the United States....No state shall enforce any law which shall abridge the privileges of immunities of citizens of the United States...nor deny to any person within its jurisdiction the equal protection of the laws.

Article 7

a) All are equal before the law and are entitled without any discrimination to equal protection of the law. All are entitled to equal protection against any discrimination in violation of this Declaration and against any incitement to such discrimination.

(AmXIV,S1) No state ...shall deny to any person within its jurisdiction the equal protection of the laws.

Article 8

a) Everyone has the right to an effective remedy by the competent national tribunals for acts violating the fundamental rights granted him by the constitution or by law.

Article 9

a) No one shall be subjected to arbitrary arrest, detention or exile.

(AmIV,S1) The right of the people to be secure...against unreasonable searches and seizures shall not be violated. (AmXIV,S1) No state shall...deprive any person of life, liberty, or property without due process of law. (ArI,S9.2) The privilege of the writ of habeas corpus shall not be suspended unless when in cases of rebellion or invasion, the public safety may require it.

Article 10

a) Everyone is entitled in full equality to a fair and public hearing by an independent and impartial tribunal, in the determination of his rights and

(AmVI,S1) The accused shall enjoy the right to a speedy and public trial by an impartial jury. (AmVII,S1) In suits of common law...the right of trial by jury shall be preserved.

obligations and of any criminal charge against him.

(AmXIV,S1) No state shall...deny any person...equal protection of the laws.

Article 11

(1) (a) Everyone charged with a penal offence has the right to be presumed innocent until proved guilty according to law in a public trial

(AmV,S1) No person shall...be deprived of life, liberty, or property, without due process of law. (AmVI,S1) The accused shall enjoy the right to a speedy and public trial, by an impartial jury. (AmXIV,S1) No state shall...deprive any person of life, liberty, or property without de process of law.

b) at which he has had all the guarantees necessary for his defense

(AmVI,S1) The accused shall...be informed of the nature and cause of the accusation...be confronted with the witnesses against him...have compulsory processes for obtaining witnesses in his favor and...have assistance of counsel for his defense.

(2) (a) No one shall be held guilty of any penal offence on account of any act or omission which did not constitute a penal offence, under national or international law, at the time when it was committed.

(ArI,S9.3) No bill of attainder or ex post facto law shall be passed.

(b) Nor shall a heavier penalty be imposed than the one that was applicable at the time the penal offence was committed.

(AmVIII,S1) Excessive bail shall not be required, nor excessive fines imposed, nor cruel and unusual punishments inflicted.

Article 12

(a) No one shall be subjected to arbitrary interference with his privacy, family, home or correspondence,

(AmIV,S1) The right of the people to be secure in their persons, houses, papers and effects, against unreasonable searches and seizures, shall not be violated. *Griswold v.*

Connecticut (1965): (AmV,S1) [No person shall] be compelled to be a witness against himself, nor be deprived of life, liberty or property without due process of law. (AmIX,S1) The enumeration in the Constitution of certain rights shall not be construed to deny or disparage others retained by the people.

b) nor to attacks upon his honor and reputation. Everyone has the right to the protection of the law against such interference or attacks.

(AmXIV,S1) No state shall deprive any person of life, liberty, or property without due process of law.

Article 13

(1) Everyone has the right to freedom of movement and residence within the borders of each State

Shapiro v. Thompson (1969): (ArIV,S2.1) The citizens of each state shall be entitled to all privileges and immunities of citizens in the several states. (AmXIV,S1) No state shall make or enforce any law which shall abridge the privileges or immunities of citizens of the U.S.

(2) Everyone has the right to leave any country, including his own, and to return to his country

Shapiro v. Thompson (1969): (ArIV,S2.1) the citizens of each state shall be entitled to all privileges and immunities of citizens in the several states. (AmXIV,S1) No state shall make or enforce any law which shall abridge the privileges or immunities of citizens of the U.S.

Article 14

(1) Everyone has the right to seek and to enjoy in other countries asylum from persecution

(ArIV,S2.1) The citizens of each state shall be entitled to all privileges and immunities of citizens in the several states. (AmXIV,S1) No state shall make or enforce any law which shall abridge the privileges or immunities of citizens of the U.S.

(2) (a) This right may not be invoked in the case of prosecutions genuinely arising from non-political crimes or

"

(b) from acts contrary to the purposes and principles of the United Nations

"

Article 15

(1) Everyone has the right to a nationality. No one shall be arbitrarily deprived of his nationality nor denied the right to change his nationality.

(AmXIV,S1) All persons born or naturalized in the United States and subject to the jurisdiction thereof, are citizens of the United States and of the State wherein they reside. No state shall make...any law which shall abridge the privileges and immunities of the citizens of the US: nor deprive any person of life, liberty or property without due process of law; nor deny to any person within its jurisdiction equal protection of the laws.

Article 16

(1) (a) Men and women of full age, without any limitation due to race, nationality or religion, have the right to marry and to found a family.

Loving v. Virginia (1967): (AmXIV,S1) No state shall...deprive any person of life, liberty, or property, without due process of law; nor deny to any person within its jurisdiction the equal protection of the laws.

b) They are entitled to equal rights as to marriage, during marriage and at its dissolution.

(AmXIV,S1) No state shall...deny to any person within its jurisdiction equal protection of the laws.

(2) Marriage shall be entered into only with the free and full consent of the intending spouses.

(AmXIV,S1) No state shall...deny to any person within its jurisdiction equal protection of the laws

(3) The family is the natural and fundamental group unit of society and is entitled to protection by society and the State.

Article 17

(1) Everyone has the right to own property alone as well as in association with others.

(AmIV,S1) The right of the people to be secure in their persons, houses, papers and effects,against unreasonable searches and seizures shall not be violated. (AmV,S1) No person shall be deprived of life, liberty or property without due process of law. (AmXIVS1) No state shall...deprive any person of life, liberty, or property without due process of law.

2) No one shall be arbitrarily deprived of his property.

"

Article 18

a) Everyone has the right to freedom of thought, conscience and religion; this right includes freedom to change his religion or belief, and freedom, either alone or in community with others and in public or private, to manifest his religion or belief in teaching, practice, worship and observance.

(AmI,S1) Congress shall make no law respecting an establishment of religion, or prohibiting the free exercise thereof;or abridging the freedom of speech, or of the press;or the right of the people peaceably to assemble.

Article 19

Article 19

a) Everyone has the right to freedom of opinion and expression; this right includes freedom to hold opinions without interference and to seek, receive and impart information and ideas through any media and regardless of frontiers.

(AmI,S1) Congress shall make no law...abridging the freedom of speech, or of the press.

Article 20

(1) Everyone has the right to freedom of peaceful assembly and association.

(AmI,S1) Congress shall make no law...abridging...the right of the people peaceably to assemble.

(2) No one may be compelled to belong to an association.

(AmI,S1) Congress shall make no law respecting...the establishment of religion...or the right of the people peaceably to assemble. (AmIX,S1) No state shall...deprive any person of life, liberty, or property, without due process of law,; nor deny to any person within its jurisdiction the equal protection of the laws.

Article 21

(1) Everyone has the right to take part in the government of his country directly or through freely chosen representatives.

(ArI,S2.1) The House of Representatives shall be composed of members chosen every second year by the people of the several states. (AmI,-S1) Congress shall make no law... abridging the right of the people...to petition the government for a redress of grievances. (AmXII,S1) The electors shall meet in their respective states and vote by ballot for President and Vice President. (AmXVII,S1)

The Senate of the US shall be...elected by the people thereof. (AmXV,S1) The right...to vote shall not be denied- ...on account of race, color or previous condition of servitude. (AmXIX,S1) The right...to vote shall not be denied ...on account of sex. (AmXXVI,S1) The right of citizens...who are eighteen years of age or older, to vote shall not be denied.

(2) Everyone has the right of equal access to public service in his country.

(AmXIV,S1) No state shall...deny any person...the equal protection of the laws.

(3) (a) The will of the people shall be the basis of the authority of government;

(P) We, the people of the United States...do ordain and establish this Constitution.

(b) This will shall be expressed in periodic and genuine elections which shall be by universal and equal suffrage and shall be held by secret vote or by equivalent free voting procedures.

(ArI,S2.1) The House of Representatives shall be composed of members chosen every second year by the people of the several states. (Ar2,- S1.1) [The President]...shall hold his office during the term of four years and, together with the Vice President, chosen for the same term be elected. (AmXII,S1) The electors shall meet in their respective states and vote by ballot for President and Vice President. (AmXVII,S1) The Senate of the US shall be...elected by the people thereof for six years. (P) We the people of the US, in order to...establish justice...promote the general welfare...to ourselves and to our posterity, do ordain and establish this Constitution.

Article 22

a) Everyone as a member of society has the right to social security and is entitled to realization, through national effort and international cooperation and in accordance with the organization and resources of each State, of the economic, social and cultural rights indispensable for his dignity and the free development of his personality.

Article 23

(1) (a) Everyone has the right to work,
b) to free choice of employment,
c) to just and favorable conditions of work and
d)to protection against unemployment.

(2)Everyone, without any discrimination, has the right to equal pay for equal work.

(3) (a) Everyone who works has the right to just and favorable remuneration ensuring for himself and his family an existence worthy of human dignity, and
b) supplemented, if necessary, by other means of social protection.

(4) Everyone has the right to form and to join trade unions for the protection of his interests.

Article 24

a) Everyone has the right to rest and leisure, including
b) reasonable limitation of working hours and
c) periodic holidays with pay.

Article 25

(1) (a) Everyone has the right to a standard of living adequate for the health and well-being of himself and his family, including
b) food,
c) clothing,
d) housing and
e) medical care and
f) necessary social services, and
g) the right to security in the event of unemployment,
h) sickness,
(i) disability,
j) widowhood,
k) old age or
l) other lack of livelihood in circumstances beyond his control.

(2) a) Motherhood and childhood are entitled to special care and assistance.
 b) All children, whether born in or out of wedlock, shall enjoy the same social protection.

(AmXIV,S1) No state shall...deny to any person...the equal protection of the laws.

Article 26   (1) (a) Everyone has the right to education.
b) Education shall be free, at least in the elementary and fundamental stages.
c) Elementary education shall be compulsory.
d) Technical and professional education shall be made generally available and
e) higher education shall be equally accessible to all on the basis of merit.

(2) (a) Education shall be directed to the full development of the human personality and
b) to the strengthening of respect for human rights and fundamental freedoms.
c) It shall promote understanding, tolerance and friendship among all nations, racial or religious groups, and
d) shall further the activities of the United Nations for the maintenance of peace.

(3) Parents have a prior right to choose the kind of education that shall be given to their children.

Article 27

(1) (a) Everyone has the right freely to participate in the cultural life of the community,
b) to enjoy the arts and

c) to share in scientific advancement and its benefits.

(2) Everyone has the right to the protection of the moral and material interests resulting from any scientific, literary or artistic production of which he is the author.

(ArI,S8.8) [The Congress shall have power]...to promote the progress of science and useful arts, by securing for limited times to authors and inventors the exclusive right to their respective writings and discoveries.

Article 28

a) Everyone is entitled to a social and international order in which the rights and freedoms set forth in this Declaration can be fully realized.

Article 29

(1) (a) Everyone has duties to the community in which alone the free and full development of his personality is possible.

(2) (a) In the exercise of his rights and freedoms, everyone shall be subject only to such limitations as are determined by law solely for the purpose of securing due recognition and respect for the rights and freedoms of others and of meeting the just requirements of morality, public order and the general welfare in a democratic society.

(3) These rights and freedoms may in no case be exercised contrary to the purposes and principles of the United Nations.

Article 30

a)   Nothing in this Declaration may
be interpreted as implying for any
State, group or persons any right to
engage in any activity or to perform
any act   aimed at the destruction of
any of the rights and freedoms set
forth herein.

Discussion

In this discussion I will consider major issues as they arose sequentially in
the foregoing analysis. Then, I will offer summative statements about the
comparison. For the sake of brevity, I will not duplicate the articles considered,
although I will briefly state their main thrust. If a more in depth description of
the article is desired, I would recommend referring to the preceding pages.

The first major point is the equal protection clause found in Amendment
XIV, Section 1, which I stated as roughly corresponding to Article 2 of the
Universal Declaration. Whereas the original intent of the framers of that
amendment in the wake of the Civil War was the protection of racial
minorities, specifically individuals now referred to as African-Americans, its
importance appears to have expanded tremendously. In *Levy v. Louisiana*
(1968), for example, the Supreme Court invoked that clause to acknowledge the
right of illegitimate children to recover damages for the wrongful death of their
mother; in *Plyer v. Doe* (1982) the Supreme Court invoked that clause to allow
undocumented school age children the right to a free public education.

My point is that my reading of the equal protection clause is more
consistent with contemporary meanings, rather than with the original
intentions of the framers. Such a view is also consistent with constitutional
scholar Bernard Schwartz (1990) who states: "Original intention, even where
clear and unambiguous, cannot be the determinative factor in constitutional
interpretation when it completely fails to meet the 'felt necessities of the time'"
(p. 14).   Supreme Court Justice Cardozo, has also commented: "The
Constitution states, not rules for the passing hour, but principles for an
ever-expanding future" (Schwartz, p. 10).

I have chosen, however, to include Article 2 of the Universal Declaration
in my comparison with the state constitutions because I think that despite the
"ever-expanding" meanings of the equal protection clause, it appears important
to determine which states *explicitly* mention whether race, color, sex, language,

religion, political affiliation etc. as stated in Article 2 can be grounds for claiming discrimination.

Another major point concerning the equal protection clause is that this clause in the United States Constitution states explicitly, "equal protection *of the laws* [italics added]." In other words, a person has equal protection only for the rights contained in the United States Constitution. He or she, therefore, cannot be discriminated against when it comes to the right to due process (Amendment V), but not when it comes to the right to health care which is not a guarantee defined in the United States Constitution or by the Supreme Court.

Concerning the right to remedies (Article 8), I am aware, furthermore, that Supreme Court Chief Justice Marshall stated in *Marbury v. Madison* (1803): "The essence of civil liberty certainly consists in the right of every individual to claim the protection of the laws, whenever he receives an injury." He later quoted Blackstone who said "It is a general and indisputable rule, that where there is a legal right, there is also a legal remedy by suit, or action at law, whenever that right is invaded." Concerning human dignity (Article 1), it is also true that some constitutional scholars, such as Paust (1983), citing references to Supreme Court decisions which have referred to human dignity, declare that human dignity is a constitutional right.

I have chosen, however, not to note correspondences between the right to a remedy, apparently guaranteed by Marshall's statement, or a right to human dignity seemingly guaranteed by the United States Constitution. To be sure, a legal or constitutional scholar may take issue with my judgment in this matter. However, this book is decidedly an intelligent layperson's reading of United States' constitutions. I do not think that constitutional interpretation should be left to legal scholars alone. It does not appear reasonable that a person must have a doctorate in jurisprudence to know that the constitution guarantees the right to human dignity. To reemphasize, I think that the people should be able to interpret constitutions. As a layman, therefore, I *know* that I presently have such freedoms as the right to marry or the right to travel which Supreme Court decisions have affirmed. As evidenced by such "injuries" (i.e. social problems), however, like unemployment or homelessness, it does not seem that the legal system has seriously entertained the apparent rights to remedies or human dignity. If a person had served a prison sentence for a number of years, furthermore, and was then found innocent, would he or she have the right to receive compensation for lost years of life? If a hungry child were denied adequate food, because he or she did not qualify for a federal nutritional supplement program, is this grounds for a right to remedy? My purpose is not to answer questions such as these, but rather to point out that rights to remedies or human dignity do not appear to be easily recognizable.

Concerning Article 12(b) which allows everyone the right to honor and reputation, *New York Times Co. v. Sullivan* (1964) does *not* exempt public officials from criticisms even if such criticisms result in defamation of character. The sustenance of that ruling comes from Amendment I of the Constitution which permits freedom of speech and the press even if it is directed against government officials. It appears, however, that according to the ruling of that case, private individuals do have the right to a good reputation if, in exercising one's First Amendment rights, there is not total disregard for the truth. I have chosen, therefore, to conclude that overall the Federal Constitution does guarantee the right as stated in Article 12(b) of the Universal Declaration.

Another question concerns whether the phrase "We, the People" is sufficient enough to correspond to Article 3(a) of the Universal Declaration which states that the will of the people shall be the basis of government. Although there is some correspondence, I view this resemblance as having no major substance, especially because James Madison had proposed that the Federal Constitution include a more substantive statement that "All power is originally vested in, and consequently derived from, the people. That government is instituted and ought to be exercised for the benefit of the people" (Chafee, 1952b, p. 48). The First Congress rejected his proposal. Furthermore, as I will soon discuss below, the Supreme Court has ruled in *Jacobson v. Massachusetts* (1905) that the spirit of the Preamble cannot be invoked as a basis for claiming a right.

Although my research did not reveal any Supreme Court cases which guaranteed economic and social rights as defined in Articles 22 to 27 of the Universal Declaration, it is necessary to mention the relatively well known case of *Brown v. Board of Education* (1954). In that case, the Supreme Court did state, for example:

> Education is perhaps the most important function of state and local governments....It is the very foundation of good citizenship....It is the principal instrument in awakening the child to cultural values, in preparing him for later professional training, and in helping him to adjust normally to his environment....[and]It is doubtful that any child may reasonably be expected to succeed in life if he is denied the opportunity of an education. (Gunther, 1985, p. 637)

Despite the importance that the Court placed on education, I noticed no assertion that education is a human right, that it is the obligation of government to provide for this right. Consequently, I chose not to include education as a right guaranteed by the United States Constitution.

Concerning Article 27(2) of the Universal Declaration which expresses the right of an author to the protection of interests resulting from his or her scientific and artistic productions, Article I, S8.8 of the United States

Constitution states that Congress has *the power* to secure to authors the right to their respective writings and discoveries. Since one of the first acts of Congress was to establish a patent office in 1790, and because it has consistently enacted legislation to protect the rights of authors and inventors (Bouvier, 1914; Patents, 1984), I decided, despite the qualification by the words "the power to," that there is a correspondence between these articles.

The following summative statements can be made about the Federal Constitution in relation to the Universal Declaration of Human Rights. First, it does refer to the freedom of the individual at birth who is endowed with reason and conscience. My analysis suggests neither mention of the dignity of the individual nor notions of brotherhood as stated in the Universal Declaration.

It appears almost entirely consistent with notions of civil and political rights as stated in Articles 2 through 21 of the Universal Declaration. The only exceptions appear to be the right to an effective remedy as defined in Article 8 and that the will of the people shall be the basis of the authority of government as stated in Article 21.

Apart from extremely weak phraseology of the general welfare and establish justice clauses of the Federal Constitution, there appear no correspondences with the positive rights as described in Articles 22 through 27. The only exception is in Article 27 which states that an individual has the right to protection of moral and material interests resulting from scientific, literary or artistic production which he or she authored.

There are no correspondences with notions of duties and solidarity rights as defined in Articles 28-30 of the Universal Declaration.

Discussion of the General Welfare and Establish Justice Clauses

The question now is if an analysis of Supreme Court interpretations of these two clauses can enlighten this discussion on the comparison of the United States Constitution with the Universal Declaration. In order to examine these two phrases, as a major part of my research, I accessed LEXIS, a computerized system for legal research, requesting information on Supreme Court cases which utilized the two phrases "establish justice" and "general welfare."

My research revealed, first of all, that the "Supreme Court long ago determined that the preamble *by itself* [italics added] affords no basis for a claim either of governmental power or of private right (*Jacobson v. Massachusetts*, 197 U.S. 11)" (Chase, 1984, p. 367). In that case, the Supreme Court decided that the plaintiff Mr. Henning Jacobson could be fined for not complying with a state statute ordering him to have a vaccination against an epidemic of smallpox in Cambridge Massachusetts. It appeared, however, that the Court based its ruling not because protecting the general welfare necessitated the plaintiff's vaccination, but rather because Mr. Henning's personal liberty secured by the U.S. Constitution in the 14th Amendment against state deprivation was not infringed by the Massachusetts statute requiring compulsory vaccination. It contended furthermore, that although the public welfare of the community was at stake which may have necessitated his vaccination, "The Spirit of the Federal Constitution or its preamble cannot be invoked, apart from the words of that instrument, to invalidate a state statute" (197 U.S. 643). After reading the cases that have, however, utilized these two clauses as they appear in the Preamble, my overall impressions are that phrases in the Preamble can bolster or lend support to judicial decisions which invoke other phrases in the body of the Constitution. Although *by themselves* these phrases do not appear to have value, they, nevertheless, do have some interpretive significance.

When the Supreme Court, moreover, referred to the general welfare clause as stated in Article I, Section VIII, "The Congress shall have Power to lay and collect Taxes, Duties and Imports and Excises, to pay the Debts and provide for the common Defense and general Welfare of the United States" it appeared most concerned in determining the appropriateness of Congress's interpretation of that clause.

In this analysis, therefore, I will relate my understanding of basic themes along with major cases which seem representative of predominant interpretations of these clauses according to opinions of the Supreme Court, whether they appear in the Preamble or in Article I, Section VIII. My concerns are only with cases which appear related to clauses in the Universal Declaration. I will emphasize, furthermore, only those aspects of cases which help illuminate the meanings of Supreme Court interpretations.

The General Welfare Clause.

It appears that the first major theme is that promoting the general welfare means that some individuals must be burdened more than others, at least as related to public appreciation of cultural landmarks. In *Penn Central Transportation Co. v. New York City* (1978), for example, the Supreme Court held that the designation of Grand Central Terminal as a landmark building by New York City, which therefore precluded any major modifications of that railroad terminal which would destroy its cultural significance, did not constitute an arbitrary taking of property. To quote the opinion of the Court:

> It is, of course, true that the Landmarks Law has a more severe
> impact on some landowners than on others, but that in itself does
> not mean that the law effects a "taking." Legislation designed to
> promote the general welfare commonly burdens some more than
> others. (57 L.Ed.2nd 654)

Although the designation of this building as a cultural landmark might cut into the profits of its owner, Penn Central Transportation, the Supreme Court commented that it was necessary for Penn Central to sacrifice these profits in order that the community benefit from the enjoyment of this cultural landmark.

Promoting the general welfare also means non-discrimination "based on race, color, religion, or national origin in...public accommodations" (13 L.Ed.2nd 262). In *Heart of Atlanta v. United States* (1954) the Supreme Court invoked that clause by referring to that phrase in the Civil Rights Act of 1957 and determined that the owner of Heart of Atlanta Motel must rent rooms to blacks.

Another theme emanating from the general welfare clause is that individuals are entitled to an uninterrupted provision of public assistance, unless a pre-termination evidentiary hearing holds otherwise. Public assistance, furthermore is "not mere charity, but a means to 'promote the general welfare'" and "guards against the societal malaise that may flow from a widespread sense of unjustified frustration and insecurity" (25 L.Ed. 297). In *Goldberg, Commissioner of Social Services of the City of New York v. Kelly* (1970), a welfare recipient contested what he felt was the arbitrary termination of his welfare benefits. Despite Goldberg's claim to conserve governmental fiscal and administrative resources, the Court determined that the plaintiff's interests to the "basic demands of subsistence" far outweighed New York City's concerns.

In *Helvering v. Davis* (1937), the Supreme Court upheld the constitutional notion that the discretion to spend for the general welfare, unless done arbitrarily, is up to Congress. The Court, therefore, concurred with a congressional program which taxed covered employers and employees in order to provide for old age benefits under the Social Security Act of 1935. The opinion of the Court asserted for example:

> Congress did not improvise a judgment when it was found that the award of old age benefits would be conducive to the general welfare....The existence of such a system is a bait to the needy and dependent elsewhere, encouraging them to migrate and seek a haven of repose. Only a power that is national can serve the interests of all. (81 L.Ed. 1315, 1317)

In a number of cases, the Court also seems to have been faced with very basic issues concerning individual rights, specifically the right to property, vs.

the welfare of the community, such as access to products and the development of projects that are in the public interest. In *Nebbia v. New York* (1934), for example, the Court acknowledged that promoting the general welfare is inherent in government, and that "correlative rights, that of the citizen to exercise exclusive dominion over property and freely to contract about his affairs, and that of the state to regulate the use of property and the conduct of business, are always in collision" (78 L.Ed. 949). In this case, therefore, it was permissible for the State of New York to fix prices on milk, thereby cutting grocers' profits, because that commodity was vital to the public interest. Also, in *Ivanhoe Irrigation District v. Mc Cracken* (1958), the use of federal monies for "largescale projects for reclamation, irrigation, or other internal improvement" which are for "a valid public and national purpose, the promotion of agriculture (2 L.Ed.2nd 1327)" is consistent with the promotion of the general welfare.

Often the Supreme Court was asked to consider state interpretations of the phrase "to promote the general welfare." In *Green v. Frazier* (1920) it agreed with the Supreme Court of North Dakota which stated that taxes to provide homes for people was consistent with this phrase and did not constitute a taking of property without due process. In *Butler v. Michigan* (1957), however, it disagreed with the state of Michigan which insisted that "By...quarantining the general reading public against books not too rugged for grown men and women in order to shield juvenile innocence, it is exercising its power to promote the general welfare" (1 L.Ed.2nd 414).

My analysis, therefore, of major themes pertinent to the general welfare clauses and cases, which appear representative of these motifs, suggests that Supreme Court interpretations of this clause do not conclusively guarantee other rights than those already stated in the United States Constitution. I did not find the *Penn Central* decision as consistent with Article 27 of the Universal Declaration which speaks of the right to freely "participate in the cultural life of the community." *Heart of Atlanta's* ruling against non-discrimination in public accommodations can already be subsumed under the equal protection clause. *Goldberg* guarantees only due process before public assistance is terminated. I noticed no statement which guaranteed in substance the "right to a standard of living adequate for the health and well-being" of a person and his or her family as stated in Article 25 of the Universal Declaration. In *Helvering*, old age benefits are only for covered employees and not for *all.*

My analysis suggests, however, that while the general welfare clause alone cannot be the basis for claiming a right, it can nevertheless, be used as a vehicle to justify regulation and taxation in order to promote the public interest. The Supreme Court, for example, regarded foods such as milk *(Nebbia)*, public housing projects, *(Green)*, and some development projects *(Irrigation)*,*Ivanhoe* as worthwhile spheres to regulate and tax in order to promote the general welfare. Overall, however, I did not regard these specific instances as enough evidence to state definitively any comparison between the United States Constitution and Article 29 of the Universal Declaration which asserts that rights can be subject to limitations for the "purpose of securing due recognition and respect for the rights and freedoms of others and of meeting the just requirements of morality, public order, and the general welfare in a democratic society."

The Establish Justice Clause.

Like the general welfare clause, this clause did not reveal any direct correspondences with rights as guaranteed by the Universal Declaration. The phrase, "establish justice," however, as invoked by the Supreme Court, did seem to justify limitations to certain freedoms in some instances. To quote the opinion of the Supreme Court in *Montana Company v. St. Louis Mining*, for example, (1894):

> To "establish justice" is one of the objects of all social organizations, as well as one of the declared purposes of the Federal Constitution, and if, to determine the exact measure of the rights of parties it is necessary that a temporary invasion of the possession of either for purposes of inspection be had, surely the lesser evil of a temporary invasion of one's possession should yield to the higher good of establishing justice. (38 L.Ed. 400)

On the matter of excise taxes, furthermore, the Court in *Ward v. Maryland* (1870), stated:

> Excise taxes...may be imposed by the States, if not in any sense discriminating; but it should not be forgotten that the people of the several States live under one common Constitution, which was ordained to establish justice, and which, with the laws of Congress, and the treaties made by the proper authority, is the supreme law of the land; and that that supreme law requires equality of burden, and forbids discrimination in State taxation when the power is applied to the citizens of the other States. (20 L.Ed. 453)

While the Supreme Court, therefore, has regarded it "just" in *Montana Company* to inspect a mine in order to assess its true value and in *Ward* to spread the burden of taxation to all states equally, thereby prohibiting a state to require a license by non-residents to sell certain articles, I did not perceive these opinions to substantively reflect notions as described in Article 29 of the

Universal Declaration. In addition, no judicial opinion referred to notions of economic and social justice or elaborated upon notions of positive rights as described in the Universal Declaration when referring to the establish justice clause.

Of significance perhaps is that these two cases just mentioned come *before* the *Jacobson* decision which declared that the Preamble could not be solely invoked as a justification to claim a right. Not one case after *Jacobson* seemed to use the phrase "establish justice" as the basis for any entitlement. Whereas these two cases are not entitlements per se, the limitations of rights they speak of have some relevance to Article 29 of the Universal Declaration. I find it ironic that the Supreme Court Justices cannot refer to the need to establish justice by referring to the Preamble, the only place in the United States Constitution which speaks directly about justice. Although this phrase can be used with other clauses in the body of the Constitution, apparently the Supreme Court has chosen essentially not to invoke that clause to assist in establishing the basis for a right.

Overall, therefore, an examination of these two phrases reveals that they do not extend any of the rights in the United States Constitution already described as comparable with the Universal Declaration.

It does the cause of human rights no good to inveigh against civil and political rights deviations while helping to perpetuate illiteracy, malnutrition, disease, infant mortality, and a low life expectancy among millions of human beings. All the dictators and all the aggressors throughout history, however, ruthless, have not succeeded in creating as much misery and suffering as the disparities between the world's rich and poor sustain today.
- Shridath Ramphal, Commonwealth Secretary-General to the United Nations

CHAPTER FIVE

COMPARISON OF STATE CONSTITUTIONS WITH THE UNIVERSAL DECLARATION OF HUMAN RIGHTS

This chapter considers rights provisions in the Universal Declaration, which the United States Constitution does not contain, in comparison with state constitutions.

I will compare, therefore, only those clauses in the Universal Declaration which do not already correspond with provisions in the Federal Constitution. The previous analysis demonstrated, for example, that the clause "Everyone has the right to freedom of peaceful assembly and association" in Article 20 of the Universal Declaration concurred with Amendment I in the Federal Constitution: "Congress shall make no law... abridging...the right of the people peaceably to assemble." Consequently, I will not consider that clause and others which correspond to provisions in the Universal Declaration. I will, however, compare clauses, such as "Everyone has the right to work" and "Everyone has the right to rest and leisure," in Articles 23 and 24 of the Universal Declaration respectively, which do not correspond with phrases in the Federal Constitution.

My reason for considering only those clauses in the Universal Declaration which do not correspond with the Federal Constitution is because state constitutions are already bound by the principles of the Federal Constitution. They can, however, extend the guarantees of the United States Constitution. The purpose of this section, therefore, is to determine the extent that state constitutions have gone beyond the Federal Constitution in relation to the Universal Declaration of Human Rights. I obtained these state constitutions by writing the governors of each state in August 1989. All states responded except for Delaware, Indiana, Kansas, Connecticut, West Virginia, and Oklahoma. For these remaining states I consulted *Constitutions of the United States: National and State* (Grad, Stearns, Hustace, & Frishman, 1990). In this revised edition, I read again only the select constitutions chosen below. Bold type will connote additional rights found, which were only in Rhode Island. A discussion of major considerations, including summative statements concerning the comparison, will follow.

ANALYSIS OF STATE CONSTITUTIONS IN COMPARISON WITH
THE UNIVERSAL DECLARATION OF HUMAN RIGHTS

The New England States

Maine

The Universal Declaration of Human Rights	**The Constitution of Maine**
Article 8	Relevant Phrase
a) Everyone has the right to an effective remedy by the competent national tribunals for acts violating the fundamental rights granted him by the constitution or by law	(ArI,S19) Every person, for an injury done him in his person, reputation, property or immunities, shall have remedy by due course of law; and right and justice shall be administered freely and without sale, completely and without denial, promptly and without delay.
Article 21	
(3) (a) The will of the people shall be the basis of the authority of government;	(ArI,S2) All power is inherent in the people; all free governments are founded in their authority and instituted for their benefit; they have therefore an unalienable and indefeasible right to institute government, and to alter, reform, or

totally change the same, when their safety and happiness require it.

Article 26

(1) (a) Everyone has the right to education.

(ArVIII,PtI,S1) The legislature are authorized...and it shall be their duty to require, that several towns make suitable provision, at their own expense, for the support and maintenance of public schools.

b) Education shall be free, at least in the elementary and fundamental stages.

"

d) Technical and professional education shall be made generally available.

(ArVIII,PtI,S1) It shall further be their [the legislature's] duty to encourage and suitably endow, from time to time, as the circumstances of the people may authorize, all academies, colleges and seminaries of learning within the state

New Hampshire

The Universal Declaration of Human Rights

The Constitution of New Hampshire

Article 8

Relevant Phrase

a) Everyone has the right to an effective remedy by the competent national tribunals for acts violating the fundamental rights granted him by the constitution or by law.

(PtI,Ar14) Every subject...is entitled to a certain remedy, by having recourse to the laws, for all injuries he may receive in his person, property or character; to obtain right and justice freely, without being obliged to purchase it; completely and without any denial; promptly, and without delay; conformably to the laws.

162 *Human Rights and Social Policy in the 21st Century*

Article 21

(3) (a) The will of the people shall be the basis of the authority of government;

(PtI,Ar1) All government of right originates from the people, is founded in consent. (PtI,Ar7) The people of this state have the sole and exclusive right of governing themselves as a free, sovereign, and independent state. (PtI,Ar8) All power residing originally in, and being derived from, the people, all...officers of government are accountable to them. Government, therefore, should be open, accessible, accountable and responsive. To that end, the public's right of access to governmental proceedings and records shall not be unreasonably restricted. (PtI,Ar10) Whenever the ends of government are perverted, and public liberty manifestly endangered, and all other means of redress are ineffectual, the people may, and of right ought to reform the old, or establish a new government. The doctrine of nonresistance against arbitrary power and oppression, is absurd, slavish and destructive of the good and happiness of mankind.

Article 29

(1) Everyone has duties to the community in which alone the free and full development of his personality is possible.

(PtI,Ar12) Every member of the community has a right to be protected by it...he is therefore bound to contribute his share in the expense of this protection and to yield his personal service when necessary.

(2) (a) In the exercise of his rights and freedoms, everyone shall be subject

(PtI,Ar3) When men enter into a state of society, they surrender up some of

only to such limitations as are determined by law solely for the purpose of securing due recognition and respect for the rights and freedoms of others and of meeting the just requirements of morality, public order and the general welfare in a democratic society.

their natural rights to that society, in order to ensure the protection of others.

Massachusetts

The Universal Declaration of Human Rights

Article 1

(All human beings are born free and equal in dignity):

c) and rights

Article 2

a) Everyone is entitled to all the rights and freedoms set forth in this Declaration, without distinction of any kind such as race, color, sex, language, religion, political or other opinion, national or social origin, property, birth, or other status.

The Constitution of Massachusetts

Relevant Phrase

(Am,ArCVI) All people are born free and equal and have certain natural, essential and unalienable rights.

(Am,ArCVI) Equality under the law shall not be denied or abridged because of sex, race, color, creed or national origin. (Am,ArCXIV) No otherwise qualified handicapped individual shall, solely by reason of his handicap, be excluded from the participation in, denied the benefits of, or be subject to discrimination under any program or activity within the commonwealth.

Article 8

a) Everyone has the right to an effective remedy by the competent national tribunals for acts violating the fundamental rights granted him by the constitution or by law.

(PtI,ArXI) Every subject...ought to find a certain remedy, by having recourse to the laws, for all injuries or wrongs which he may receive in his person, property, or character. He ought to obtain right and justice freely, and without being obliged to purchase it; compleatly, and without any denial;promptly, and without delay; conformably to the laws.

Article 21

(3) (a) The will of the people shall be the basis of the authority of government;

(P) The end of the institution...of government is to secure the existence of the body-politic... to furnish the individuals who compose it, with the power of enjoying...their natural rights...whenever these great objects are not obtained, the people have a right to alter government. The Body-Politic is...a social compact, by which the whole people covenants with each citizen, ...that all shall be governed by certain laws for the common good. (PtI,ArV) All power residing originally in the people, and being derived from them...the officers of government...are at all times accountable to them. (PtI,ArVII) The people alone have an...unalienable... right to institute government; and to reform...the same when their protection, safety prosperity and happiness require it. (PtI,ArXIX) The people have a right...to consult upon the common good [and to] give instructions to their representatives. (PtI,ArIV) The people of this Commonwealth have the sole and exclusive right of governing themselves, as a free, sovereign, and independent state. (Am,-ArLXXXIX,S1) It is the intention of this article to reaffirm the customary and traditional liberties of the people with respect to the conduct of local government and to grant and confirm to the people the right of self-government.

Article 29

(1) Everyone has duties to the community in which alone the free and full development of his personality is possible.

(P) It is the duty of the people to provide for an equitable mode of making laws. (PtI,ArX) Ea(P) It is the duty of the people to provide for and each individual has a right to be protected by [society]...he is obliged, consequently, to contribute his share to the expense of this protection; to give his personal service or the equivalent, when necessary.

Rhode Island

The Universal Declaration of Human Rights

The Constitution of Rhode Island

Relevant Phrase

Article 2

a) Everyone is entitled to all the rights and freedoms set forth in this Declaration, without distinction of any kind such as race, color, sex, language, religion, political or other opinion, national or social origin, property, birth, or other status.

(ArI,S2) **No otherwise qualified person shall, solely by reason of race, gender, or handicap be subject to discrimination by the state....such discrimination is untenable in a democratic society.**

Article 8

a) Everyone has the right to an effective remedy by the competent national tribunals for acts violating the fundamental rights granted him by the constitution or by law.

(ArI,S5) Every person within this state ought to find a certain remedy, by having recourse to the laws, for all injuries or wrongs which may be received in one's person, property or character. Every person ought to obtain right and justice freely, and without purchase, completely and without denial;promptly and without delay; conformably to the laws.

Article 21

(3) (a) The will of the people shall be the basis of the authority of government;

(ArI,S1) In the words of the Father of this Country, we declare that "the basis of our political system is the right of the people to make and alter their constitutions of government; but that the constitution which at any time exists, till changed by an explicit and authentic act of the whole people, is sacredly obligatory upon all." (ArXIIIS1) It is the intention of this article to grant and confirm to the people of every city and town in this state the right of self government in all local matters.

Article 26

(1) (a) Everyone has the right to education.

(ArXII,S1) The diffusion of knowledge, as well as of virtue among the people, being essential to the preservation of their rights and liberties, it shall be the duty of the general assembly to promote public schools and public libraries and to adopt all means which it may deem necessary and proper to secure to the people   the   advantages   and opportunities of education.

b) Education shall be free, at least in the elementary and fundamental stages.

"

Article 29

(1) Everyone has duties to the community in which alone the free and full development of his personality is possible.

(ArI,S2) All free governments are instituted for the protection, safety and happiness of the people. All laws, therefore, should be made for the good of the whole; and the burdens of the state ought to be fairly distributed among its citizens

Connecticut

The Universal Declaration of Human Rights

The Constitution of Connecticut

Article 1

Relevant Phrase

(All human beings are born free and equal in dignity):

c) and rights

(ArI,S1) All men when they form a social compact, are equal in rights.

Article 2

a) Everyone is entitled to all the rights and freedoms set forth in this Declaration without distinction of any kind, such as race, color, sex, language, religion, political or other opinion, nation or social origin, property, birth or other status

(ArI,S20)   No   person   shall be...subjected   to   segregation   or discrimination in the exercise or enjoyment of his or her civil or political rights because of religion, race, color, ancestry, national origin or sex. (ArXXI) No person shall be

Article 8

a) Everyone has the right to an effective remedy by the competent national tribunals for acts violating the fundamental rights granted him by the constitution or by law.

denied equal protection of the law because of...physical handicap.

(ArI,S10) All courts shall be open and every person, for an injury done to him in his person, property or reputation shall have remedy by due course of law and right and justice administered without sale, denial or delay.

Article 21

(3) (a) The will of the people shall be the basis of the authority of government;

(ArI,S2) All political power is inherent in the people and all free governments are founded on their authority and instituted for their benefit; and they have at all times an undeniable and indefeasible right to alter their form of government in such manner as they may think expedient.

Article 26

(1) (a) Everyone has the right to education.

(ArVIII,S1) There shall always be free public elementary and secondary schools in the state. (ArVIII,S4) The fund, called the School Fund...shall be inviolably appropriated to the support and encouragement of the public schools and for the equal benefit of the people thereof.

b) Education shall be free, at least in the elementary and fundamental stages.

"

d) Technical and professional education shall be made generally available and

(ArVIII,S2) The state shall maintain a system of higher education, including the University of Connecticut which shall be dedicated to excellence in higher education.

e) higher education shall be equally accessible to all on the basis of merit.

"

Vermont

The Universal Declaration of Human Rights

The Constitution of Vermont

Article 8

Relevant Phrase

a) Everyone has the right to an effective remedy by the competent national tribunals for acts violating the fundamental rights granted him by the constitution or by law.

(ChI,Ar4) Every person within this state ought to find a certain remedy, by having recourse to the laws, for all injuries or wrongs which he may receive in his person, property or character; he ought to obtain right and justice freely, and without being obliged to purchase it; completely and without any denial; promptly and without delay; conformably to the laws.

Article 21

3(a) The will of the people shall be the basis of the authority of goverment;

(ChI,Ar6) All power being originally inherent in and consequently derived from the people...all officers of government...[are] at all times accountable to them. (ChI,Ar7) The community hath an indubitable, unalienable, and indefeasible right, to reform or alter government, in such manner as shall be, by that community, judged most conducive to the public weal.

Article 26

1(a) Everyone has the right to education.

(b) Education shall be free, at least in the elementary and fundamental stages.

(ChII,S68) A competent number of schools ought to be maintained in each town.

"

Article 29

(1) Everyone has duties to the community in which alone the free and full development of his personality is possible.

(ChI,Ar9) That every member of society hath a right to be protected...therefore is bound to contribute his proportion towards the expense of that protection and yield his personal service.

The reader may wish to refer to the 1992 edition of this book, which does a comparison of all the fifty states and the proposed state constitution of the State of New Columbia, presently the District of Columbia. As a research-action strategy, to be discussed more in depth later in this book, she/he may wish to compare other world constitutions to determine discrepancies between them and the Universal Declaration. Then telling the world about these violations ought to assist in changing public sentiment to be in accord with the rights of the Declaration. The table at the end of this chapter, which includes findings from my most recent reading, however, lists correspondences between all state constitutions and the Declaration.

Discussion

In comparing these documents I chose words such as "provide" and "promote" as characteristic of human rights which necessitated positive interventions on the part of governments to take care of human needs. I excluded, therefore, words of lesser impact such as "encourage" or "cherish" which do not appear to demonstrate the obligations of governments. Article IX, Part 2, Section 3, for example, of Iowa's Constitution states: "The General Assembly shall *encourage* [italics added], by all suitable means, the promotion of intellectual, scientific, moral and agricultural improvement." Similarly, the Constitution of Massachusetts states in Chapter V, Section II that the Legislature shall:

> Cherish the interests of literature and the sciences and all seminaries of them; especially the university at Cambridge, public schools and grammar schools in the towns; [and] to encourage private societies and public institutions rewards and immunities, for the promotion of agriculture, arts, sciences, commerce, trades, manufactures, and a natural history of the country.

I did not, therefore, regard these statements as comparable with the Universal Declaration's provisions on the right to share in scientific advancement and its benefits (in Article 27) and the right to education (Article 26) respectively. They do not appear, furthermore, to correspond with my main criteria of substance and sense to basic provisions in the Universal Declaration.

Concerning elaboration of the equal protection clause, moreover, I chose only to consider statements which spoke of nondiscrimination generally of rights as contained in the state constitution, not merely rights related to specific instances, such as the right not to be discriminated against in employment or public accommodations. While these rights are undoubtedly important, I was more concerned with exclusive statements, such as in Wyoming's constitution which states in Article I, Section 3: "Since equality in the enjoyment of natural and civil rights is only made sure through political equality, the laws of this state affecting the political rights and privileges of its citizens shall be without distinction of race, color, [or] sex." I, therefore, also excluded more specific statements of nondiscrimination such as in Illinois's constitution in Article I, Section 17 which states: "Persons shall have the right to be free from discrimination on the basis of race, color, creed, national ancestry and sex in the hiring and promotion practices of any employer or in the sale or rental of property."

Another point to consider is related to the right to work. Some constitutions such as Florida, express this right as follows: "The right of persons to work shall not be denied or abridged on account of membership or non-membership in any labor union or labor organization" (ArI,S6). Although this statement does mention a right to work, however, I did not see it as comparable with this right as defined during the debates concerning the

Universal Declaration which emphasized the right to do useful work and to further the development of production and purchasing power.

I also excluded statements such as "may provide" or "shall have the power to provide for." Some examples are: New York, "The legislature may provide...for low rent housing and nursing home accommodations for persons of low income" (ArXVII,S1); California, "The Legislature shall have the power to grant aid to needy blind persons" (ArXIV,S2[3])....[and] "to grant aid to needy physically handicapped persons" (ArXVI,S2[4]); and Hawaii, "The state shall have the power to provide financial assistance, medical assistance and social services for persons who are found to be in need of and are eligible for such assistance and services as provided by law"(ArIX,S3)...."The state shall have the power to provide for, or assist in housing, slum clearance and the development or rehabilitation of substandard areas" (ArIX,S5)....."The state shall have the power to provide for the treatment and rehabilitation of handicapped persons" (ArIX,S2)...."The state shall have the power to provide for the security of the elderly by establishing and promoting programs to assure their economic and social well-being" (ArIX,S4).

While these provisions acknowledge certain human rights of the Universal Declaration, they do *not* explicitly guarantee them. Article 25 of the Universal Declaration, for example, expresses the *right* (not the power to provide for a right) to a standard of living adequate for one's health and well-being including food, clothing, housing, medical care, necessary social services, and security in the event of disability and old age.

Partial Rights.

Because the purpose of this book is to highlight correspondences between the Universal Declaration and United States' constitutions, I chose not to compare rights which partially correspond with guarantees in the Universal Declaration. Briefly, however, an example of a partial right is: "[Concerning] placing out, adoption or guardianship, the child shall be committed or remanded or placed, when practicable, in an institution or agency governed by persons, or in the custody of a person, of the same religious persuasion as the child" (New York, ArVI,S32). Some state constitutions, furthermore, like Michigan (ArIV,S50), Alaska (ArVII,S5), and Hawaii (ArIX,S6) have provisions for public health. Michigan, for example, states: "The public health and general welfare of the people of the state are hereby declared to be matters of primary public concern. The legislature shall pass suitable laws for the protection and promotion of the public health."

Although these rights could be subsumed under provisions in Articles 25 and 28 which provide for special protections for motherhood and children and the right to medical care, they were not as all-inclusive as their prospective counterparts in the Universal Declaration.

There are also some partial rights expressed in state constitutions related to the need for a social and international order in which human rights can be realized as stated in Article 28 of the Universal Declaration. New Hampshire, for example, speaks of the right of the people to "be protected against all monopolies and conspiracies" (Pt2,Ar83). Montana states: "The legislature shall provide protection and education for the people against harmful and unfair practices by either foreign or domestic corporations, individuals, or associations" (ArXIII,S1). Idaho and Colorado state in similar language that "The police powers of the state shall never be...construed as to permit corporations to conduct their business in such manner as to infringe the equal rights of individual or the general well-being of the state" (ArXI,S8 and ArXV,S8 respectively).

Massachusetts (ArXCVII), Pennsylvania (ArI,S27), Illinois (ArXI,S2), Louisiana (ArIX,S1), and Montana (ArII,S3), furthermore, express the right to a clean environment. Massachusetts, states, for example: "The people shall have the right to clean air and water, freedom from excessive and unnecessary noise, and the natural scenic, historic, and esthetic qualities of their environment" (ArXCVII). In these and other instances, however, there was no conclusive statement that everyone is entitled to a just social and international order.

Summative Statements.

This reading, therefore, of the state constitutions in comparison with the Universal Declaration revealed the following major summative statements. On the notions of human dignity only two states, Louisiana and Montana, noted its importance. Massachusetts, Connecticut, Rhode Island, Missouri, Kansas, Louisiana, Texas, Wyoming, Oregon, and Alaska expressed notions of equality of rights.

On the elaboration of the equal protection clause of the Federal Constitution, Massachusetts recognized sex, race, color, creed, national origin, and disability; Connecticut - religion, race, color, ancestry, national origin, sex and physical handicap; Rhode Island - race, gender, handicap; New York - race, color, creed and religion; Illinois - sex; Michigan - religion, race, color, national origin, aliens; Virginia - religious conviction, race, color, sex, and national origin; North Carolina - race, color, religion, and national origin; Florida - race, religion, and physical handicap; Louisiana - race, religion, national ancestry, age, sex, birth, political opinion, and physical condition; Texas - sex, race, color, creed, and national origin; Montana - race, color, sex, culture, social origin or condition, and political or religious ideas; Wyoming -

race, color, sex, and any "circumstance or condition whatsoever other than individual incompetency or unworthiness duly ascertained by a court"; Alaska - race, color, creed, sex, and national origin; and Hawaii - race, religion, sex and ancestry.

The two basic civil and political provisions of the Universal Declaration (i.e. the right to remedies [Article 8] and the will of the people as the basis of government [in Article 21]) which did not appear to be expressed in the Federal Constitution were generally expressed in the state constitutions. The exceptions to Article 8 were: New York, Michigan, Iowa, Virginia, Georgia, Texas, Arizona, Nevada, California, Washington, Alaska, and Hawaii. There were no exceptions to the above provision in Article 21 although New York and California's constitutions, while acknowledging that "We, the people" like other state constitutions ordained their constitutions, nevertheless, had relatively "weak" statements in accordance with the will of the people as the basis of government. New York stated, for example, only that "Effective local self-government...are purposes of the people of the state; California noted that "The people have the right to instruct their representatives, petition government for redress of grievances and assemble freely to consult for the common good." Georgia and Idaho were the only states that recognized the importance of the family. The aim of government, for example, was to "promote the interest and happiness of the citizen and...the family" similar to Article 16 of the Universal Declaration.

On the notions of economic, social, and cultural rights no state, apart from Illinois and Louisiana, had provisions which corresponded to Article 22 of the Universal Declaration which served as an introduction to the economic and social guarantees which followed. In Illinois and Louisiana's preambles, for example, there appeared to be general statements about the need for economic and social justice. The preamble of the Illinois constitution states, for example:

> We the people...in order to provide for the health, safety and welfare of the people....eliminate poverty and inequality; assure legal, social and economic justice; provide opportunity for the fullest development of the individual...do ordain and establish this constitution.

Because these preambles speak, therefore, of the need to provide for the health, safety and welfare of the people they appear to be the only constitutions which correspond to provisions in Article 25 of the Universal Declaration which also speaks of these rights. Hawaii's constitution which states that government has "the power to provide for" health care, was not included as a definitive statement of health care.

Certain provisions related to the right to work in Article 23 can be found in Missouri, North Carolina, Florida, Oklahoma, Alaska, and Oregon which assert generally that people have the rights to the enjoyment of the gains of their own industry, to the enjoyment of the fruits of their own labor, and to just compensation for services rendered. Wyoming asserts that the right of labor shall have just protection through laws calculated to secure to the laborer proper rewards for his service and to promote the industrial welfare of the state. Utah also asserts the right of labor but only to the extent that it promotes the industrial welfare of the state. New York, New Jersey, Missouri, Florida, and Hawaii contain rights to collective bargaining in their constitutions. New York, Montana, Colorado, and Arizona provide for limitations of employment to eight hours per day.

All constitutions expressed the right to education except for New Hampshire, Massachusetts, Indiana, Tennessee, Alabama, and California. Virginia, North Carolina, Oklahoma, Idaho, New Mexico, Utah, and Nevada had provisions for compulsory attendance.

Virginia, Louisiana, Montana, and Hawaii's constitutions expressed the need for individuals to participate in the cultural life of the community as expressed in Article 27 of the Universal Declaration.

On the notions of duties and solidarity rights as expressed in the last few articles of the Universal Declaration, New Hampshire, Vermont, Massachusetts, Rhode Island, Illinois, Maryland, Virginia, Montana, Alaska, and Hawaii express the need for corresponding obligations to the people and the state.

In neither the United States Constitution nor the state constitutions were the following guarantees expressed. First, no constitution endorsed the notion of the "spirit of brotherhood" as stated in Article 1.

No state had a provision recognizing property as a reason not to discriminate in order to enjoy fundamental rights.

Apart from certain provisions noted above, no constitution contained definitive statements relating to the right to work, to free choice of employment, and to protection against unemployment. Neither was there a right to equal pay for equal work nor an acknowledgment of the need to supplement one's income if necessary to ensure an existence worthy of human dignity. No constitution acknowledged the right to rest and leisure.

Apart from the two exceptions noted above in Illinois and Louisiana, none of the states guaranteed any of the rights contained in Article 25 which speak of the rights to food, housing, medical care, necessary social services, and security in the event of unemployment, sickness, disability, widowhood, old age, or other lack of livelihood beyond one's control. No provision in the state constitutions declared that motherhood and childhood are entitled to special care and assistance.

No constitution spoke of the need for a just social and international in order to realize human rights. Finally, and understandably, there was no mention of the Universal Declaration or the United Nations as stated in the last two articles of the Universal Declaration.[1]

There did not appear to be any significant major differences among groups of states. A summary of these major findings can be found in Table 3 at the conclusion of this chapter.

Of interest, however, is that concern for indigenous people's rights becomes more pronounced in the western states, particularly Hawaii. There are regional differences, furthermore, related to the protection of workers in specific industries, which are common to a geographic region, such as mining, metallurgy, and agriculture.

One final observation is that there were many economic and social guarantees, too numerous to mention, in the form of retirement and other benefits, such as health care and compensation for disabilities, for veterans, judges, state representatives, and state officials in general. It appeared, therefore, that if a person were to engage in combat, if he or she should survive, then the veteran would have certain economic and social guarantees. It is as if the old feudal order in which the serf engages in combat for the Lord, in exchange for certain benefits was still generally apparent in state constitutions.

My impressions also are that the aphorism that laws are made by and for the lawmakers is true. Yet, for the "least of these," such as children there was *no* mention of economic and social guarantees. Can this account in large part why the first nationwide study of the level of childhood hunger in the United States says: "One child in eight under the age of 12-5.5 million-goes hungry each day and another 6 million live in families that do not have enough money to spend for food and are at risk for being hungry" (Kurkjian, 1991)?; why, in 1989, according to the Census Bureau 22.5% of all children and 50% of all black children under 6 in the US live in poverty ("U.S. Reports", 1990)?; or why, according to the Children's Defense Fund, "The United States lags behind most other industrialized countries, and behind some Third World nations, in indicators of children's health, educational achievement and economic well-being" (Ribadeneira, 1991)? Why is it, finally, that "children are the hardest hit by hunger" in the United States, having "double the rate of hunger" in this age group than "any other industrialized nation." Ironically, worldwide hunger is going down worldwide and in Africa, but in the United States it is going up (Karger and Stoesz, 1998, p. 421).

The last chapter will examine the implications of these analyses of United States constitutions for social policy, in comparison with the Universal Declaration and within the context of the historical-philosophical underpinnings of the idea of human rights.

Table 3

Summary of State Constitutions' Major Correspondences with Articles in the Universal Declaration of Human Rights, not Guaranteed by the United States Constitutions

(Article) Right	# of States with Relevant Guarantees	Identified States
1(b)Human Dignity	2	LA, MT
(c) Equality of Rights	9	MA, CT, MO, AK LA, TX, WY, OR, AK
2. Elaboration of the Equal Protection Clause Categories:	14	MA, CT, NY, IL, MI, VA, NC, FL, LA, TX, MT, WY, AK, HI
Race	14	MA, CT, RI, NY, MI, VA, NC, FL, LA, TX, MT, WY, AK, HI
Religion	12	MA, CT, NY, MI, VA, NC, FL, LA, TX, MT, AK, HI
Color	10	MA, CT, NY, MI, VA, NC, TX, MT, WY, AK
Sex	11	MA, CT, RI,IL, VA, LA, TX, MT, WY, AK, HI
National Origin	9	MA, CT, MI, VA, LA, NC, TX, AK, HI
Physical Handicap	4	CT, RI, FL, LA
Political Opinion	2	MT, LA

(Article) Right	# of States with Relevant Guarantees	Identified States
Social Origin or Condition	1	MT
Birth	1	LA
Disability	1	MA
Aliens	1	MI
Court Determined Circumstance	1	WY
8. Right to an Effective Remedy	38	All *except* NY, MI, IA, VA, GA, TX, AZ, NV, CA, WA, AK, HI
16(3) The Importance of the Family	2	GA, ID
21(3)(a) The Will of the People as the Basis of Government	50	All states
22. General Statements About Economic and Social Justice	2	IL, LA
23(1)(c) Right to Favorable Conditions of Work	2	WY, UT
23(3)(c) Right to Favorable Remuneration for Work	6	MO, NC, FL, OK, AK, OR
23(4) Right to Join Trade Unions	5	NY, NJ, MO, FL, HI
24(b) Reasonable Limitations of Working Hours	4	NY, MT, CO, AZ

Table 3. (continued)

(Article) Right	# of States with Relevant Guarantees	Identified States
25(1)(e) Right to Medical Care	2	IL, LA
26(1)(a) Right to Education	44	All *except* NH, MA, IN, TN, AL, CA
26(1)(c) Compulsory School Attendance	7	VA, NC, OK, ID, NM, UT, NV
27(1)(a) Right to Participate in Cultural Life	4	VA, LA, MT, HI
29(1)(a) Need for Duties	10	NH, VT, MA, RI, IL, MD, VA, MT, AK, HI

Table 3. (continued)

Note. Provisions of articles as stated are brief paraphrases of original articles. Abbreviations for states are official two-letter Postal Service abbreviations.

Note - Chapter Five

[1] The proposed constitution for the State of New Columbia, presently Washington, D.C. can be found in the 1992 edition. Briefly, and in comparison with the Universal Declaration, it extends rights found in state constitutions by including property as a basis for nondiscrimination and by providing for an income to meet basic human needs if unable to work, equal pay for equal work, and security for the disabled and the elderly. That constitution in its preamble also "reaches out to the people of the world in a spirit of friendship and cooperation."

The search for a more human and effective way to deal with poverty should not be limited to short-term reform measures....Special attention is needed to develop new efforts that are targeted on long-term poverty....Proposals should be part of a creative and ongoing effort to fashion a system of income support for the poor that protects their basic dignity.

• *United States Catholic Bishops*, Economic Justice For All

CHAPTER SIX

IMPLICATIONS FOR SOCIAL POLICY

This study has revealed that United States' constitutions concur fundamentally with the Universal Declaration's first generation or negative rights, which consist of civil and political guarantees. There appear minor correspondences, most notably in states' guarantees for education, with the Universal Declaration's second generation or positive rights, which consist of economic, social, and cultural rights. Apart from some states' concerns for duties to the community, there are no correspondences with the Universal Declaration's third generation or solidarity rights which consist essentially of the right to a just social and international order in which human rights can be realized.

This concluding chapter will suggest recommendations for social policy based on this analysis. In this section, I will also reiterate some basic issues and occasionally elaborate upon them in order to underscore the significance of these suggestions.

The primary recommendation of this study is that United States' constitutions should include those guarantees found in the Universal Declaration of Human Rights which federal court justices and legal scholars have increasingly referred to as customary international law. There also needs to be a slow and gradual incorporation of all the rights of the Universal Declaration into American jurisprudence in general. At present, according to the *Restatement (Third) of the Foreign Relations Law of the United States* some of the provisions which the Universal Declaration contains, such as the prohibitions against slavery and torture have customary international law status in American courts. Gradually, all the rights contained in that document, such as the rights to shelter, food, and health care need to be incorporated into the American legal system.

Because the Ninth Amendment to the Federal Constitution clearly states, furthermore: "The enumeration in the Constitution, of certain rights, shall not be construed to deny or disparage others retained by the people," it is conceivable that the legal system can refer to all the provisions of the Universal Declaration as standards for other rights which are retained by the people. The United States delegation signed that document on December 10, 1948. The United States, therefore, ought to comply with its commitment.

The Constitution, furthermore, is a "living" document, which, according to Supreme Court Justice Cardozo, contains principles for an ever-expanding future that must meet the felt necessities of the time. The recent disapproval of presidential nominee to the Supreme Court, Robert Bork, who opposed the idea of a living constitution and advocated "framer's intents" and "original understanding arguments" suggests that contemporary legislative bodies are amenable to the idea of a living Constitution.

Yet, at the recent confirmation hearings of the current Supreme Court Justice Clarence Thomas, questions related to economic, social, cultural, and solidarity rights were barely mentioned. While questions related to affirmative action in the workplace were discussed, notions of the right to work for all, or, for that matter, human rights to health care or shelter, did not appear to be seriously entertained. This paucity of questioning on such rights, therefore, suggests that, if legislators are truly representatives of the people, such notions of rights are not, at present, embedded in the American consciousness. Certainly, as we approach the twenty-first century, much work is necessary to realize the rights of the Universal Declaration.

Assimilation of internationally recognized rights in United States' constitutions or the legal system in general would, thereby, serve to legitimate claims by individuals or groups who felt that some of their basic human needs were not being realized. Undeniably, if public consciousness were strong enough to take care of people's needs, an easy argument could be made not to have these rights in constitutions. However, in this world where constitutions have legal impact, the incorporation of these rights appears necessary for the fulfillment of human needs.

It may be easy to dismiss this basic suggestion as wishful thinking or utopian. In fact, United States Ambassador to the United Nations Jeane J. Kirkpatrick, in reference to the Universal Declaration exclaimed that it is "a letter to Santa Claus....Neither nature, experience, nor probability informs these lists of 'entitlements,' which are subject to no constraints except those of the mind and appetite of their authors" (Laqueur and Rubin, 1990, p. 364).

As the Chairperson of the Commission on Human Rights and Representative of the United States Eleanor Roosevelt expressed, however, the Universal Declaration is "a common standard of achievement for all peoples of all nations" (Green, 1956, p. 31). My point is that incorporation of its rights in United States' constitutions would represent strivings or goals. It may be naive to think that these goals can be immediately realized. Nevertheless, that must not be an excuse to expend every effort to begin the implementation of these aims as defined by the Universal Declaration. The barons at Runnymede or the drafters of the United States' Bill of Rights, for example, persisted in their realistic demands to have some basic human needs realized. Today their legacy is evident in numerous legal codes which guarantee such rights as freedoms of speech, religion, or the press. Striving for the realization of these goals, has undoubtedly enriched the lives of many Americans.

In the final debates, moreover, the United States delegation exclaimed that the most important phrase in the Universal Declaration is in Article 22 which states that rights can be realized only "in accordance with the organization and resources of each State." In other words, the Universal Declaration is a practical document which acknowledges that human needs can only be realized within the context of a state's resources.

There also appears a burgeoning political movement to endorse internationally accepted standards. Clearly, many people appear increasingly cognizant of the importance of such principles. One third of all nations, for example, especially those which emerged from colonialism after World War II, have modeled their rights provisions on the Universal Declaration of Human Rights (Claude and Weston, 1989). The City Council of Burlington, Iowa also, in September 1986, adopted an ordinance which added substantive provisions of the UN International Convention on the Elimination of All Forms or Racial Discrimination to the City's basic legal structure (Farer, 1989). New York City, on November 21, 1989, one day after the General Assembly of the United Nations adopted the Convention on the Rights of the Child, passed a resolution pledging to uphold the convention as law for city agencies (Castelle & Nurske, 1990). It is also apparent that many eastern European countries are incorporating internationally recognized rights into their new constitutions, such as rights to work, rest, regular paid holidays, and health care (Kaufman, 1991).

STRATEGIES TO MODIFY UNITED STATES' CONSTITUTIONS

The United States Constitution can only be changed through an amendment process; state constitutions it appears can be modified by adding amendments or changing the text itself (May, 1990). Since the ratification of the United States Constitution in 1789, of 5,000 proposed amendments, only 26 were adopted (Toner, 1989). Of all proposed substantive changes for state constitutions from 1982 through 1989, however, on the average 69.3% of these changes were adopted in these constitutions (May, 1990, p. 22). In state constitutions' Bill of Rights, an average of 87.5% of substantive changes were adopted (May, 1990, p. 22). For example, as of January 1, 1990 Massachusetts residents adopted 116 out of 143 amendments submitted; Alaskans adopted 22 out of 31; and New Yorkers adopted 207 out of 274 (Council of State Governments, 1990, p. 40).

Clearly, state constitutions are easier to modify than the Federal Constitution. I would suggest, therefore, that state residents consider the modification of their constitutions. That way, states can act, in the words of Supreme Court Justice Louis Brandeis, as "laboratories," or experiments which may assist in the guaranteeing of human rights and, consequently, the fulfillment of human needs. Despite the comparative difficulty in amending the United States constitution, however, I would recommend that efforts continue in that direction. My reasons are first, that nationwide campaigns would illuminate public consciousness, an essential ingredient for constitutional change, on a scale far greater than on the state level. Secondly, upon federal constitutional modification, states would automatically be bound to abide by the new guarantees.

Already, there are movements for constitutional change on state and national levels to extend rights contained in these documents. On the state level, in 1986-87 the total number of propositions concerning policy articles was nearly double that of the past biennium (Sturm and May, 1988). Of 29 proposals, over half of them (19) concerned education which reflected a growing public concern for state responsibility to improve education. Residents approved 79% (15) of these proposals. In 1988-89, furthermore, the number of proposals (21) and adoptions (19) to states' Bills of Rights reached a record-high for the decade (May, 1990).

Examples of some movements to expand rights on the federal level are Resolution S139 (1985) emanating from the Massachusetts legislature and Bill H.R. 2870 (1987) introduced in the House of Representatives. The former resolution urged Congress to:

Enact legislation presenting to the states a proposed constitutional amendment wherein the right to employment shall be guaranteed to every person in the United States in accordance with his (*sic*) capacity, at a rate of compensation sufficient to support such individual and his (*sic*) family in dignity and self-respect. (Gil, 1990a, p. 281)

The purpose of the latter Bill, introduced by Representatives Hayes and Hawkins was: "to help and improve the quality of life for all people of the United States by setting forth an economic bill of rights." This bill included *inter alia*: "the right of every family to a decent home....the right to adequate medical care and the opportunity to achieve and enjoy good health....the right to adequate protection from the economic fears of old age, sickness, accident and unemployment....[and] the right to a good education."

Specific Recommendations For Constitutional Change

As this research has suggested, phrasing that is too general or unclear, such as the general welfare and establish justice clauses of the United States Constitution does not necessarily result in judicial interpretation that can result in the realization of human needs. The Supreme Court justices did not construe these phrases, for example, to include certain notions of economic and social justice as defined by the Universal Declaration, which includes such rights as health care, education, and shelter. In addition, failures of the United States' Constitutions to state clearly that individuals had, for instance, rights to marry and to travel resulted in the imprisonment of individuals desiring interracial marriages and the denial of welfare payments to emigrants from other states. Judicial interpretation of ambiguous phrasing such as "equal protection" and "privileges and immunities" seems to have come too late.

I would urge, therefore, that United States' constitutions consider phrasing which lacks ambiguity in order that every intelligent layperson be able to understand his or her human rights. This recommendation is consistent with the intents of the framers of the Universal Declaration who wanted a document that all people could easily understand.

Other recommendations are first, that the phrases "human dignity" and "spirit of brotherhood" as expressed in the Universal Declaration and conspicuously absent in the Federal Constitution and the majority of state constitutions ought to be addressed. Taken with the numerous references to individual liberty in these constitutions, it seems that the "common good" is subordinated to the needs of the individual. An analysis of the general welfare and establish justice clauses of the Federal Constitution, suggests, in addition, that although the Supreme Court has acknowledged that individual and group rights "are always in collision," the Court did not appear to resolve the issue in any substantive sense. Although I do not think that the pendulum should swing in the other direction and totally regard the good of the community in deference to individual rights, nevertheless, it appears that a more substantive acknowledgement of the common good in words comparable with human dignity and fraternity would correct an apparent one-sided emphasis upon individual liberties.

On the notion of negative freedoms, (i.e. civil and political liberties), the United States Constitution appears exemplary. The only areas which the Constitution and Supreme Court judicial interpretation do not appear to substantively reflect, (i.e. the right to remedies and the will of the people as the basis of government), are taken up by the majority of state constitutions. I would suggest, however, that in the final analysis it would be important to have these two areas substantively reflected in all state constitutions and the Federal Constitution.

Rather than rely on the vagaries of the "equal protection clause," the United States Constitution ought to clearly state, as in the Universal Declaration, that none of the rights which it contains shall be denied on account of race, color, sex, language, religion, political or other opinion, national or social origin, property, birth or other status. While some state constitutions have gone beyond the Federal Constitution in this regard, I would also recommend more congruence with these categories as expounded upon in the Universal Declaration.

On the notion of positive freedoms (i.e. economic, social and cultural rights) United States' constitutions are sorely lacking. In the Federal Constitution, for example, there are neither general statements nor Supreme Court decisions which speak about these rights. Apart from authors' protection for their scientific or literary productions there is no mention of any positive freedoms as specified by the Universal Declaration.

State constitutions, however, do expand upon this one positive right guaranteed in the Federal Constitution. Almost all of them guarantee the right to education (see Table 3). Two states speak in general terms of the need to eliminate poverty and to work for economic and social justice. Five states guarantee the right to join trade unions. There are some provisions in state constitutions which express the right to favorable conditions of work and favorable remuneration for work. Two states assert that the people of their state shall promote health. Four states guarantee the right to participate in the cultural life of the community.

Based on this analysis, therefore, it would appear appropriate, first for the United States Constitution to incorporate all the rights which the states have extended in their constitutions. Secondly, United States' constitutions, preferably the Federal Constitution, need to incorporate other basic guarantees as defined by the Universal Declaration which to briefly reiterate are: the right to social security in accordance with the organization and resources of each state in order to ensure the economic, social and cultural rights indispensable to human dignity and the free development of personality; the rights to work, to free choice of employment, to protection against unemployment, to equal pay for equal work, and to the supplementation of one's wages, if necessary, by other means of social protection in order to ensure an existence worthy of human dignity; the rights to rest and leisure and periodic holidays with pay; the right to a standard of living adequate for the health and well-being of oneself and his or her family, including food, clothing, housing, necessary social services, sickness, disability, widowhood, old age or other lack of livelihood in circumstances beyond one's control; the right for motherhood and childhood to be given special care and assistance; and the right to an education which shall be directed to the strengthening of respect for human rights and fundamental freedoms.

Concerning state constitutions that use phrasing, such as "may provide for" or "has the power to provide for" in regard to rights like housing, medical care, or security for the elderly, I would recommend that they assert more emphatically that they should *provide for* these and other guarantees which will assist in the fulfillment of human needs. In regard to constitutions which provide for rights that only partially satisfy criteria of the Universal Declaration, such as the promotion and protection of public health, I would recommend that these and other states which speak to partial rights expand upon these notions. In these instances, for example, a right to public health ought to be expanded to include a right to medical care. Future research, furthermore, should examine all of the partial rights in United States' constitutions and the extent that judicial decisions and social policies in general are in accordance with rights as stated in United States' constitutions.

On the notions of duties and solidarity rights, the United States Constitution does not mention the importance of the need for responsibility to the community. Only ten states express the importance of responsibilities to the community. The paucity of constitutions which reflect this right ought not to be dismissed lightly because, every right has a corresponding duty. The right to speak, for example, necessitates a corresponding duty to listen; the right to food requires the duties to assist in the production of food and not to overconsume. Notions of duties, therefore, ought to be incorporated in the remaining state constitutions and the Federal Constitution.

Although some states have recognized partial rights to a just social and international order, such as the right to a clean environment (Massachusetts, ArXCVII) and the right to be treated fairly by domestic and international corporations (Montana, ArXII,S1), my recommendation is to incorporate into

United States' constitutions, the phrasing of Article 28 in the Universal Declaration. I think that such a statement would address the more encompassing goal that individuals and governments cooperate on an international level in stewardship of the world's resources.

Additional Strategies

In order to incorporate human rights principles as defined by the Universal Declaration in United States' constitutions, it is necessary to begin at the grassroots level. It is of utmost importance, therefore, that public sentiment be in accordance with these principles. I think that it is necessary that Americans expand their consciousness in regards to current notions of rights which seem to emphasize civil and political guarantees. I am not saying that it is important to "win converts" to the cause of human rights, or to convince others that human rights are in their interest. As the philosopher Frederick Nietzsche once glibly noted, that the proof of the pudding is in the eating (Kaufmann, 1982), people in time will come to know whether the principles of the Universal Declaration can positively affect their lives. Yet, the burgeoning interest in that document seems to stand as testimony to its affirmative impact on people's consciousness. Certainly, Americans should be informed that there are other rights than those claimed in the United States' Bill of Rights and that these rights, as stated in the Universal Declaration, are increasingly considered customary international law.

To inform the public of these rights I would suggest first, that education about these principles begins in school. Although I had learned about civil and political rights during grammar school, high school, and college, I had never heard of the concept of economic, social, or cultural rights! So-called civic education courses in grammar school, American history classes in high school, and political science courses in college are just a few instances where teachers and students can discuss these rights. In addition, because these concepts are interdisciplinary in character, they can easily be integrated into other classes.

I am not simply advocating reform in educational curricula. To do justice to the Universal Declaration, it will be necessary to evaluate the current "social and international order" to determine if human rights are indeed realized in contemporary American society. Students would need to determine, for example, if a society that encourages monetary gain from capital, rather than from work, or that has an average unemployment rate of 7.1% in approximately the last hundred years (Harvey, 1989) is conducive to the realization of human dignity. Taking the Universal Declaration seriously, would mean that schools would become creative workplaces to establish a just society, rather than bastions of unquestioning acceptance of the status quo in preparation for a world which tends to abrogate the fulfillment of human needs.

It will be necessary also to appeal to mass audiences, not only to groups that may be most receptive to human rights issues such as organizations concerned with fair labor practices, homelessness, poverty, or infant mortality. One method might be to utilize the media, by writing, for example, letters-to-the-editor, op-ed pieces, or articles directed to mass audiences. The arts, such as films, plays, and music can also play a part in expanding people's consciousness about human rights. In the 1990s, moreover, the decade that celebrated the 200th anniversary of the Bill of Rights on December 15, 1991, articles, documentaries, and various other productions related to rights are evident in the media. Furthermore, a recent poll conducted by Research USA Inc. stated "Nearly three out of four who responded to the survey said they would like the Constitution to guarantee adequate health care for all Americans" ("Poll Finds," 1991). The time is ripe to talk about rights.

In the early 1990s there is also a growing concern for United Nations' resolutions and human rights issues in general. Considering this climate, it seems appropriate to refer to the United Nations Universal Declaration as a document of customary international law. Should this climate change, it may be more appropriate to refer to some of its principles as emanating from traditional religious and philosophical perspectives. Only five years ago, references to the Universal Declaration might have brought consternation. But, with an apparent termination of the cold war among Eastern and Western Bloc nations, people appear more receptive to such United Nations' documents as the Universal Declaration of Human Rights. It would appear worthwhile, therefore, to refer to contemporary concerns about health care, employment opportunities, education, and the global maldistribution of wealth as international human rights issues. Even the growing public awareness of duties to the environment could be framed within the context of human rights. A faltering environment can also be seen as symptomatic of an unjust social and international order which is the result, for example, of faulty economic policies which emphasize excess profiteering.

It might also be effective to discuss positive freedoms as having strands in United States culture which go back to President Franklin D. Roosevelt who spoke of an "eternal linkage" between freedom from fear and freedom from want. In more recent times United States Secretary of State Cyrus R. Vance announced that the United States government should make the advancement of human rights a central part of United States foreign policy which includes "the right to the fulfillment of such vital needs as food, shelter, health care, and education" (Weston, 1989, p. 19). The hope is that public awareness of human rights standards will eventually encompass all of the rights in the Universal Declaration. Only by encouraging dialogue among individuals about ways to create a less unjust society can movements begin which question established social orders that have deleterious side-effects.

Apart, therefore, from this essential component of public concern for the advancement of human rights principles, individuals can submit proposed constitutional changes, which are in accordance with internationally accepted standards, to elected officials or to the electorate itself. I have previously discussed some strategies which occurred, for example, in Massachusetts (Resolution 139). The submission of these proposed changes could also act as a means to educate the public in regard to human rights issues.

On the international arena, furthermore, disenfranchised groups can appeal to international bodies, for example, the United Nations HumanRights Commission or the regional organizations, such as the Inter-American Commission on Human Rights. Human rights groups, like Amnesty International or Helsinki Watch, ought to also expand their mandates to include all of the rights proclaimed in the Universal Declaration of Human Rights. Expansion of their mandates may also provide an impetus for governments and international human rights commissions to take *all* the rights of the Universal Declaration seriously.

Certainly, these strategies will require time. It would be naive to think that constitutional and other legal changes can occur immediately. Even if these changes did occur it is no guarantee that individuals would then exercise their rights. Constitutional change, however, seems an important step in a long process. As Philip Alston (1990) states:

> No specific analysis is offered to support the assumption that formal guarantees will inevitably be hollow and meaningless and that a society which makes such undertakings will therefore fail to honor them....There will always be governments that make empty promises and some will even clothe those promises in the garb of formal guarantees. But many other governments have given carefully worded guarantees and delivered as well. (pp. 376-377)

As a case in point, recent Assistant Secretary of State Richard Schifter made an argument against the enactment of human rights documents when he once asked a representative of a Third World country: "If children in your country are starving would they want a United Nations declaration on the right to food or would they want something to eat?" According to Schifter, "What the world needs regarding economic and social development is action-oriented programs, not declarations." (Alston, 1990, p. 376).

But it appears that Schifter, was speaking in order to suggest reasons for the United States not to ratify the International Covenant on Economic, Social, and Cultural Rights. Ratification of that Covenant would necessitate a fundamental shift in United States human rights policy (Alston, 1990). Similarly, incorporation of human rights principles in United States' constitutions and American jurisprudence will in due time demand major transformations of ways to meet human needs. A well-known story in the field of mental health primary prevention about the rescue of drowning people from a river may also illustrate the point that the effects of constitutional change upon people's lives may require time. Yet, the results should be more effective than strategies which demonstrate only immediate results.

Having successfully administered first aid to a drowning person, a rescuer spots another struggling person and pulls her out, too. After a half dozen repetitions, the rescuer suddenly turns and starts running away while yet another person is seen floundering. "Aren't you going to rescue that fellow?" asks a bystander. "Heck no," the rescuer replies. "I'm going upstream to find what's pushing all these people in." It takes time to travel upstream and no results are immediately discernible. This approach, however, to stop the flow of drowning people by examining the source of the trouble seems in the long run to be far more productive.

Upstream are United States' constitutions, which have emanated from historical and philosophical traditions, emphasizing civil and political rights at the expense of economic and social guarantees. Modification of these constitutions in accordance with human rights principles of the Universal Declaration should leave less people floundering in the waters, that is less homelessness, infant mortality, and unemployment. In the final analysis, because these rights are for *everyone*, no one should drown in the miseries which an unjust social and international order inflicts.

IMPLICATIONS FOR PRACTICE IN THE HUMAN SERVICES

The Universal Declaration of Human Rights can also serve to legitimate the work of human service practitioners. While many human service workers, for example, acknowledge that social problems, such as homelessness, high infant mortality rates, and unemployment are unjust, this awareness often emanates from a social consciousness which may also include an "intuitive sense" that these social ills are blatantly "wrong." The Universal Declaration, however, by succinctly stating rights acknowledged by the world community, gives this intuitive sense significant quasi-legal status.

As this research has demonstrated, furthermore, many social ills in the United States are not illegal. It may be illegal, for example, to interfere with a person's right to practice his or her religion, but it is not unlawful for governments to abdicate their responsibility to provide for such basic human needs as security in the event of unemployment, sickness, or disability. Using the Universal Declaration as the standard, however, a social ill, such as

192   *Human Rights and Social Policy in the 21st Century*

homelessness may challenge governments to provide for basic human needs, in this case, the right to shelter.

Human service practitioners, therefore, can integrate these internationally recognized principles into their work by alerting governments of the rights in the Universal Declaration, a document referred to as customary international law. They can engage in movements which may culminate in the acceptance of some or all of the provisions of the Universal Declaration of Human Rights as law for a specific locale, or for that matter, the United States. The recent Universal Declaration of Human Rights Project, which I, along with David Gil had initiated should be a major step in that direction. Essentially, its goals are to expand people's awareness of the Universal Declaration of Human Rights; to use the Declaration as a frame of reference to assess progress toward the realization of internationally acknowledged human rights; draw attention to significant violations; and suggest avenues to overcome such violations.

Because the Universal Declaration does not contain sophisticated and often technical language which is common to many disciplines in the human services, such as psychology, sociology, psychiatry, and medicine, human service workers will also be able to transcend the confines of their own specialties. Working together to ensure basic human rights easily understood by individuals, will also not necessitate traditional cleavages among human service workers into such categories as expert, professional, or paraprofessional. While these categories may at times serve some purposes, they will become subordinated, if not irrelevant, among human service practitioners and any other workers in the quest for the realization of human rights for all people.

In the pursuit of the fulfillment of human needs it would furthermore, be senseless for a sociologist to view him or herself as an expert in group processes, a psychologist in intrapsychic processes, or a lawyer in legal matters. Paradoxically, however, all disciplines will need to cooperate and, when appropriate, borrow upon the experience and knowledge of other disciplines in order to determine ways that human rights can be realized. However, mere knowledge of the rights in the Universal Declaration should be sufficient to provide clearly stated goals and harness energies of all people to work toward the satisfaction of human needs.

Working together, therefore, human service and other workers can promote legislation, educate the general public, and conduct research in ways that will expand people's consciousness in regard to human rights. In addition to developing strategies which will incorporate internationally recognized rights into legal codes, they can conduct workshops or hold classes on human rights, and determine reasons for poor implementation of human rights principles. If human service and other workers were successful enough to include a right to health care, in a state constitution, for example, the next step would be to determine how to implement this right. In the meantime, it may be important to discover which states that have said the legislature "may provide" for housing or health care, have enacted legislation to provide for such rights. The next step would be to determine the impediments to the realization of such rights. It may be found, for example, that certain judges or law enforcement personnel were incognizant of certain statutes. An interventive measure then would be, for instance, education.

Many human service workers are often involved with "treating" such "mental disorders," as alcohol abuse, anti-social personality, or anxiety disorders of childhood or adolescence as defined in the *Diagnostic and Statistical Manual of Mental Disorders*. While I do not deny that it is still important to treat such individuals in ways that will help them fulfill their potential as human beings, it also appears important to recognize the social order which may have played a substantial part in the development of such disorders. Human service workers, through some of the strategies already mentioned, can also play a part in the establishment of a social order more conducive to the flowering of the human personality.

The Universal Declaration can also act as a guide for one's conscience. The human service worker can refuse to participate in endeavors which may not be conducive, for example, to ensuring "a family an existence of human dignity" (as in Article 25). While many social service programs barely provide enough assistance to families for such basic necessities as food and shelter, the committed human service worker can decline the mere dispensing of such meager support. Thus, he or she can attempt to augment this assistance in order to provide for a dignified existence. An increase in assistance will not only include a monetary augmentation, but also an attempt to provide for other rights, such as the right to work and the need for a social order in which human rights can be realized. I am not saying that a human service worker ought to be "all things to all persons." Yet, he or she can realize the inadequacies of many social welfare programs in relation to the rights as described in the Universal Declaration. Cognizant of these deficiencies, the human service worker can conscientiously, in accordance with internationally recognized human rights principles, work toward the fulfillment of human needs.

Finally, while the idea of human rights has emerged as a very powerful construct to advance the cause of human needs, human service workers could additionally benefit from other approaches, which are beyond the scope of this work, that may also enhance human potential and growth. Because the primary aim of effective social policies is to match human needs with available resources, any approach which performs this function without violating the dignity and integrity of the human person, is a worthwhile effort. However, to neglect the growing acceptance of internationally recognized human rights standards, such as found in the Universal Declaration is to dismiss an extremely powerful strategy.

PROBLEMS INVOLVED IN ADVANCING HUMAN RIGHTS

As the history of the idea of human rights has illustrated, hidden agenda can riddle attempts to advance the cause of human rights. It appears that a major difficulty may be that the concern for human rights can actually mask exploitation. Noble crusades, even the cause of human rights, have always aroused public opinion. The "noble" right to private property, for example, may have served as a pretext to deprive indigenous peoples of their lands. The granting of freedom of religion by the English monarchy to the American colonists appeared actually an attempt to entice cheap labor to the New World in order to transport gold back to England.

Descriptions of torture or other abuses of individuals at the mercy of tyrannical governments, furthermore, may serve as "just" causes for humanitarian intervention which, in reality, may be attempts to regain lost territories or preserve the wealth of elites. Governments might also condemn human rights abuses in countries inimical to their interests, not from humanitarian concerns, but rather to mobilize world opinion against them. Political leaders may also criticize human rights violations in other countries, while ignoring violations in their own countries. It can also be contentiously argued that Amnesty International's concern for torture victims in foreign countries and the public's concern for such genocidal atrocities as the Holocaust and the Killing Fields (after the fact!) is an example of government propaganda to divert attention from human rights abuses at home, such as homelessness, lack of health care, and high infant mortality rates.

In the above situations, motives may be other than the fulfillment of human needs. In these cases, Jeremy Bentham's pithy statement that talk about rights is "nonsense on stilts" may have some validity. However, the history of the idea of human rights has demonstrated that humans have banded together with the purest of motives when unjust monarchs, governments, and social orders have thwarted human needs. The barons at Runnymede, the drafters of the United States Constitution's Bill of Rights, and the numerous NGO's at the San Francisco Conference are a few examples of committed individuals desirous of documents advancing the cause of human rights and human needs.

It appears, therefore, that concern for advancement of human rights will always require vigilance. It would be most disparaging, for instance, if monstrous wars erupted in order to secure human rights, resulting not in the assurance of human rights, but rather the untold loss of human lives. Yet, it is also heartening to know that documents such as the Magna Carta, the Bill of Rights, and the Universal Declaration of Human Rights have served as bases for legitimate claims against political authorities for failure to fulfill human needs. Nietzsche's comments in his last work, *Twilight of the Idols*, written toward the end of the twentieth century, may have some relevance as the dawn of the twenty-first century approaches. He acknowledges, for instance, that the doctrine of equality has often been surrounded by "gruesome and bloody events" (Kaufmann, 1982, p. 553). Another problem is that concern for a specific right or groups of rights may lessen concern for other rights. A difficulty may arise, for example, if one works to include a specific right such as the right to work or the right to health care in the federal or state constitutions. Surely, these rights, are interdependent and indivisible. Workers need to be healthy to perform a job; the healthy need work to do. Despite this difficulty, I think, however, that it may be appropriate to work for the inclusion of specific rights such as employment, health care, shelter, and education but, only if one does not lose sight of the "forest for the trees." That is, the aim is the eventual inclusion of all rights contained in the Universal Declaration, because they are *all* important. Another problem is that trying to incorporate rights in United States constitutions such as equal rights for women, or people with disabilities or economic and social rights for children or the elderly can have the unfortunate consequence of setting up one group against another. The recent shift in poverty from the elderly to children is one evidence of this possible confrontation among groups in vying for rights. The question becomes, therefore, how to coalesce all groups so that society doesn't rob Peter to pay Paul. Certainly, women, people with disabilities, children, the elderly and other groups need to have their needs met.

To resolve this issue, I think that all groups should strive for a just "social and international order" as stated in Article 28 which implies a fair distribution of wealth and the dissemination of monies to those most in need. These funds, therefore, would not come from other groups in need, but rather from an elite one-half percent of the population who, according to a recent report on the concentration of wealth in the United States by the Joint Economic Committee of the U.S. Congress, own approximately half of the United States' wealth (Kolby, 1987). Surely, the resources are there.

Undoubtedly, efforts to inform individuals about their human rights will be difficult largely because concern for human rights is threatening to the small minority of elites who own much of the country's wealth and control most of the media. Despite such efforts, the world will continually be filtered through the eyes of these elites, thereby assuring that the majority of the population believe that governments already provide individuals with enough goods and services to satisfy their needs.

A final issue, briefly touched upon previously, perhaps more in need of elaboration is the problem of cultural relativism. The search for universal norms may, for example, be inimical to some cultures. Surely, some traditions, espouse other rights than those proclaimed by the Universal Declaration. Although I pretend in no way to speak for indigenous peoples who traditionally have not had written traditions, I can easily imagine their concern that the Universal Declaration and other human rights documents are a few of many other written documents which non-indigenous peoples abuse. It is also necessary to listen to the concerns of some poorer nations of the world related to the gross maldistribution of global wealth. From their perspective, which often emanates from different cultural traditions, it is inconceivable to give their northern counterparts recognition for the founding of human rights as defined in the Universal Declaration when the poorer countries of the world must live in hunger and poverty. Although the Universal Declaration has enormous possibilities to improve the quality of life for all, openness to other cultural viewpoints is essential to understanding the occasional limitations of this "good document."

In conclusion, incorporation of the principles of the Universal Declaration in United States' constitutions would be a significant stride in the realization of a less unjust society. Because of the legal status of constitutions, people could then refer to them as legitimate claims in order to have their basic human needs met. Judiciary, legislative, and executive branches of government and law enforcement personnel would also refer to them as standards for the development and implementation of just social policies.

Governments, which proclaim to represent the will of the people, would therefore, distribute resources in ways that best matched human needs. This distribution would be accomplished by a just social order evidenced in part by equitable tax structures based on human need. Furthermore, many of the guarantees discussed throughout this book, such as the right to join trade unions, special protections for motherhood and children, the right to work, and the right to security in old age would eventually become reality. In such a world, there would be no need for social welfare programs as presently known, such as Medicaid, Medicare, food stamps, unemployment, or health insurance. Social policies will already be integrated into the structure of the society in order to prevent systemic breakdowns like poverty, unemployment, infant mortality, illiteracy, drug abuse, and domestic violence.

Living up to the principles of the Universal Declaration would, therefore, eradicate many of the aforementioned by-products of the failure to meet human needs. Quite often, for instance, fear of losing one's job or inability to cope with poor working conditions can result in the displacement of frustration and anger from work to the home situation resulting in domestic violence and child abuse

(Gil, 1990b). Surely, there is a sense of urgency to realize its rights, for the Universal Declaration emphatically asserts: "Disregard and contempt for human rights have resulted in barbarous acts, which have outraged the conscience of mankind."

The Universal Declaration of Human Rights represents valuable goals now and for the twenty-first century. Because it is in *everyone's* interest to realize these goals, their incorporation in United States' constitutions is a worthwhile effort. There is no guarantee that their inclusion in United States' constitutions will secure all human rights. However, as the common struggles of humans in the face of tyranny throughout history has revealed, it is the *striving* toward these clearly defined goals, which provides the most hope for a more humane and socially just world.

BIBLIOGRAPHY

(CHAPTERS ONE TO SIX)

Ali, A. (Trans.). *The Holy Qur-an* Hyderabad No. 500002, India: Husami Book

Abrahamson, S. S. (1987). State constitutional law. In R. Janosik (Ed.), *Encyclopedia of the American judicial system* (Vol. 3). (pp. 1271-1287). New York: Charles Scribner.

Adler, M. J. (1967). *The difference of man and the difference it makes.* New York: Holt, Rinehart, and Winston.

Adler, M. J., & Gorman, W. (1975). *The American testament.* NewYork: Praeger.Depot.

Allen, J. (1951). *A history of political thought in the sixteenthcentury* (3rd. ed.). London: Methuen.

Alston, P. (1985). The shortcomings of a "Garfield the Cat"approach to the right to development. *California Western International Law Journal, 15,* 510-518.

_____. (1989). International law and the right to food. In R. P. Claude & B. H. Weston (Eds.), *Human rights in the world comunity* (pp. 142-150). Philadelphia: University of Pennsylvania Press.

_____. (1990). U.S. ratification of the covenant on economic, social and cultural rights: The need for an entirely new strategy. *American Journal of International Law, 84,* 365-393.

Alston, P., & Vasak, K. (Eds.) (1982). *The international dimensions of human rights* (Vols. 1-2). Westport, CT: Greenwood.

Althusser, L. (1982). *Montesquieu, Rousseau, Marx.* (B. Brewster, Trans.). London: Verso Editions.

American Psychiatric Association. (1980). *Diagnostic and statistical manual of mental disorders* (3rd ed.). Washington,DC: Author.

Amnesty International. (1991). *Amnesty International Report 1991.*New York: Author.

Atkinson, A. (1983). *Social justice and public policy.* Cambridge, MA: MIT Press.

Arkes, H. (1990). *Beyond the Constitution.* Princeton: Princeton University Press.

Artz, F. (1953) *The mind of the Middle Ages*. New York: Alfred A. Knopf.

Asher, R. E., Kotschnig W. M., Brown, W. A., Green, J. F., Sady, E. J. & Associates. (1957). *The United Nations and promotion of the general welfare*. Washington, DC: The BrookingsInstitution.

Babbie, E. (1986). *The practice of social research* (4th ed.). Belmont, CA: Wadsworth.

Barber, S. (1986). Inherent powers. In L. Levy, L. & K. Larst, (Eds.), *Encyclopedia of the American Constitution* (Vol 3). (p.   982). New York: MacMillan.

Barron, J., & Dienes, C. (1986). *Constitutional law*. St. Paul, MN: West.

Bay, C. (1989). Human rights on the periphery: No room in the ark for the Yanomami? In R. P. Claude & B. H. Weston (Eds.), *Human rights in the world community* (pp. 104-114). Philadelphia: University of Pennsylvania Press.

Bayles, M. (1978). *Principles of legislation*. Detroit: Wayne State University Press.

Bayliff, R. E, Clark, E., Easton, L., Grimes, B., Jennings, D., &   Leonard, N. H. (1954). *Readings in social policy* (2nd ed.). Dubuque, Iowa: Wm. C. Brown.

Beard, C. A. (1929). *An economic interpretation of the Constitution of the United States*. New York: Macmillan.

Behrens, C. (1985). *Society, government and the Enlightenment*. The German Democratic Republic: Thames and Hudson.

Benditt, T. (1982).*Rights* . Totowa, NJ: Rowman and Littlefield.

Benn, S. I. (1967) Rights. In P. Edwards (Ed.), *Encyclopedia of philosophy* (Vol. 7) (pp. 195-199). New York: MacMillan.

Berelson, B. (1952). *Content analysis in communications research*.   Glencoe, IL: Free.

Berger, P. (1972). *Sociology*. New York: Basic Books.

Berger, P. L. & Luckmann, T. (1971*)*. *The social construction of reality*. New York: Doubleday. Berlin, I. (1956). *The Age of Enlightenment*. Boston: Houghton Mifflin.

_____. (1959). *Karl Marx: His life and environment*. (2nd. ed.). New York: Oxford University Press.

_____. (1979). *Against the current: Essays in the history of ideas*. New York: Viking.

Birn, D. (1981). *The League of Nations Union: 1918-1945*. Oxford: Clarendon.

Bishop, C. H. (1974) *How Catholics look at Jews*. New York: Paulist.

Black, H. C., Nolan, J. R., Nolan-Haley, J. M., Connolly, M. J., Hicks, S. C., & Alibrandi, M. N. (1990*)*. *Black's law dictionary* (6th ed.). St. Paul, MN: West.

Blaustein, A. P., Clark R. S., & Sigler, J. A. (Eds.). (1987). *Human rights sourcebook* New York: Paragon House.

Bloed, A., & Van Dijk, P. (Eds.). (1985). *Essays on human rights in the Helsinki Process*. Boston: Martinus Nijhoff.

Bloom, A. (Ed.). (1990). *Confronting the Constitution*.Washington, DC: American Enterprise Institute.

Bobbitt, P. (1982). *Constitutional fate: Theory of the New Constitution* York: Oxford University Press.

Bodin, J. (1956). *Six books on the commonwealth*. (M. J. Tooley, Trans.). Oxford: Basil Blackwell.

Bork, R. H. (1990). *The tempting of America*. New York: Simon and Schuster.

Bouvier, J. (1914). *Bouvier's law dictionary*. Kansas City, MO: Vernon Law Books.

Braddock, D., Hemp, R., Fujiura, G., Bachelder, L., & Mitchell, D. (1989, May). Third national study of public spending formental retardation and developmental disabilities: Summary (Report No. 45). *Public Policy Monograph Series: Institute for the Study of Developmental Disabilities, 45.* Chicago: University of Illinois Press.

Brennan, W. (1977). State constitutions and the protection of individual rights. *Harvard Law Review, 90,* 3, 489-504.

Britannica world data annual. (1991). The nations of the world (pp. 538-739). Chicago: Encyclopedia Britannica.

Britt, A. (1938). *Great Indian chiefs.* Freeport, NY: Books for Libraries Press.

Brown, L. (1989, November 8-11). Closing address at the *National Conference on the United States and the United Nations.* Washington, DC. (Available from UNA-USA, 485 Fifth Avenue, NY, NY 10017-6104).

Brown, L., Durning, A., Flavin, C., French, H., Jacobson, J., Lenseen, N., Lowe, M., Postel, S., Renner, M., Ryan, J., Starke, L., & Young, J. (1991). *State of the world.* New York: W.W. Norton.

Brown, R. (1956). *Charles Beard and the Constitution.* Princeton: Princeton University Press.

Brown v. Board of Education. 98 L.Ed. 873 (1954).

Brownlie, I. (Ed.). (1971*). Basic documents on human rights.* Oxford: Clarendon.

Buchanan, S. (1962). *Rediscovering natural law.* Santa Barbara, CA: The Fund for the Republic.

Buergenthal, T. (1988). *International human rights law.* St. Paul, MN: West.

Burckhardt, J. (1990). *The civilization of the Renaissance in Italy.* (S. Middlemore, Trans.). London: Penguin Books.

Bury, J. (1932). *The idea of progress: An inquiry into its origin and growth.* New York: Dover.

Burke E., & Paine, T. (1973*). Reflections on the revolution in France and the rights of man.* Garden City: Anchor.

Butler v. Michigan. 1 L.Ed.2nd (1957).

Butterfield, B. (1990, April 22). Child labor endangers a new generation. *The Boston Globe,* pp. 1, 22-23.

Campbell, T., Goldberg, D., McLean, S. & Mullen, T. (Eds.). (1986). *Human rights: From rhetoric to reality.* New York: Basil Blackwell.

Cassirer, E. (1948*). The Renaissance philosophy of man.* Chicago: University of Chicago Press.

_____. (1951). *The philosophy of the Enlightenment.* (F. C. Koelln & J. P. Pettegrove, Trans.). Princeton: Princeton University Press.

Castelle, K., & Nurske, D. (1990, December 1). Time for U.S. to back rights of children. [Letter to the editor]. *The New York Times,* p. A24.

Center for the Study of the Presidency. (1989) Foreign policy, human rights, and political alignment, 1789-1989 [Special issue]. *Presidential Studies Quarterly, 19*(4).

Chafee, Z. (1952a). *Documents on fundamental human rights* (Vols. 1-3). Cambridge: Harvard University Press.

_____. (1952b). *How human rights got into the Constitution.* Boston: Boston University Press.

Chalk, F., & Jonassohn, K. (1990). *The history and sociology of genocide.* New Haven: Yale University Press.

Chase, H. (1984). General welfare (pp. 367-368). In *Guide to American law* (Vol. 5). St. Paul, MN: West.

Chomsky, N. (1989). *Necessary illusions.* Boston: South End.

_____. (1997). *The United States and the challenge of relativity.* (Paper available from Professor Noam Chomsky, Department of Linguistics and Philosophy, MIT, Cambridge, MA 02138).

Churchill, W. (1994). *Indians are us?* Monroe, ME: Common Courage.

Cicero, M. T. (1967) *On moral obligation.* (J. Higgenbotham, Trans.). Berkeley: University of California Press.

Clark, R. (1987). International human rights law. In R. Janosik (Ed.), *Encyclopedia of the American judicial system* (Vol. 1). (pp. 334-346). New York: Charles Scribner.

Claude, R., P. (1976). *Comparative human rights.* Baltimore: John Hopkins University Press.

_____. (1983). The Case of Joelito Filartiga and the Clinic of Hope. *Human Rights Quarterly, 5,* 275-95.

Claude, R. P., & Weston B. (Eds.). (1989). *Human rights in theworld community.* Philadelphia: University of Pennsylvania Press.

Cleary, E. (Ed.). *Path from Puebla: Significant documents of the Latin American Bishops since 1979.* (P. Berryman, Trans.). Washington, DC: United States Catholic Conference.

Coate, R. A., & Rosati J. A. (Eds.). (1988). *The power of human needs in world society.* Boulder, CO: Lynne Rienner.

Cobban, A. (1964). *Rousseau and the modern state* (2nd. ed.). Hamden, CT: Archon.

Cogley, J. (1971). *Natural law and modern society.* Freeport, NY: World.

Cohen, M. (1985). *Legal research.* St. Paul, MN: West.

Cohen, C. (1995). In B. Franklin (Ed.), *The handbook of children's rights: Comparative policy and practice.* London: Routldege.

Collins, R. (1985). Selected state constitutional law provisions including comparative charts and tables. In S. Livermore (Ed.), *The American bench* (pp. 2485-2523). Sacramento, CA: Reginald Bishop Forster.

Commager, H. (Ed.). (1960). *The era of reform.* Princeton, NJ: D. Van Nostrand.

Committee on the District of Columbia House of Representatives 98th Congress.(1983) *District of Columbia Statehood Constitution.* (Serial No. S-1). Washington, DC: US Government Printing Office.

Connor, W. (1988). *Socialism's dilemma's.* New York: Columbia University Press.

Council of state governments. (1988). *Book of states.* Lexington, KY: Author.

_____. (1990). *Book of states.* Lexington, KY: Author.

Cranston, M. (1961). *Locke.* London: Longmans & Green.

_____. (1983). Are there any human rights? *Daedalus, 112*(4), 1-17.

_____. (1990). What are human rights? In W. Laqueur & B. Rubin (Eds.), *The human rights reader* (pp. 17-25). New York: New American Library.

Crawford, J. (Ed.). (1990). *The rights of peoples.* Oxford: Clarendon.

Crocker, L. (Ed.). (1969). *The Age of Enlightenment.* New York: Walker.

Curtis, M. (Ed.). (1981a). *The great political theories* (Vol. 1). New York: Avon.

_____. (Ed.). (1981b). *The great political theories* (Vol. 2). New York: Avon.

Daes, E. (1986). Sub-Commission on Prevention of Discrimination and Protection of Minorities. *Principles, guidelines and guarantees for the protection of persons detained on grounds of mental ill-health or suffering from mental disorder.* (E/CN.4/Sub.2/1983/17/Rev.1). New York: United Nations.

Daughters of St. Paul. (1979). *U.S.A. The message of justice, peace and love: JohnPaul II.* Boston: St. Paul Editions.

Davis, G. (1992). *Passport to freedom: A guide for world citizens.* Cabin John, MD: Seven Locks.

Deane, H. A. (1963). *The political and social ideas of St. Augustine.* New York: Columbia University Press.

D'Entreves, A. (1959) *The medieval contribution to political thought.* New York: Humanities.

Department of State. (1989). *United States participation in the UN: Report by the President to the Congress for the year 1988* (Publication No. 9712). Washington, DC: Government Printing Office.

De Santa Ana, J. (1979). *Good news to the poor: The challenge of the poor in the history of the Church.* Maryknoll, NY: Orbis.

Dillow, A. (1986) Human rights and peace. In L. Pauling (Ed.), *World encyclopedia of peace* (pp. 423-427). New York: Pergamon

Donnelly, J. (1989). *Universal human rights in theory and practice.* Ithaca, NY: Cornell University Press.

Donnelly, J. & Howard R. (1987). *International handbook of human rights.* New York: Greenwood.

Draper, E. (Ed.). (1982). *Human rights.* New York: H.W. Wilson.

Dred Scott v. Sandford. 19 How. 393 (1856).

Drinan, R. (1987) *Cry of the oppressed: The history and hope of the human rights revolution.* San Francisco: Harper and Row.

Ducat, C. (1987) Constitutional interpretation. In R. Janosik (Ed.) *Encyclopedia of the American judicial system* (Vol. 3). (pp. 972-985). New York: Charles Scribner.

Dworkin, R. (1978). *Taking rights seriously.* Cambridge: Harvard University Press.

Ebenstein, W. (Ed.). (1960). *Great political thinkers* (3rd. ed.). New York: Holt, Rinehart, and Winston.

Economic Bill of Rights Act. (1987, July 1). House of Representatives (Bill #2870). 100th Congress, 1st Session.

Edwards, P. (Ed.). (1968). *Encyclopedia of philosophy* (Vols. 1-8). New York: Mac Millan.

Eide, A. (1987). United Nations Commission on Human Rights. *Report on the right to adequate food as a human right.* (E/CN.4/Sub.2/1987/23). New York: United Nations.

Eliade, M. (Ed.). (1987). *The Encyclopedia of religion.* New York: Mac Millan.

Elton, G. (Ed.). (1971). *The new Cambridge modern history Volume   II: The Reformation 1520-59*. London: Cambridge University Press.

Encyclopedia brittanica. (1991). Jefferson (pp. 349-53). Chicago: Author.

European convention on human rights: Collected texts. (1987) Boston: Martinus Nijhoff.

Evolution of human rights. (1946, December 10) *UN Weekly Bulletin*, pp. 12-15.

Excerpts from the Charter of Paris for a new Europe as signed yesterday. (1990, November 22). *The New York Times*, p. A16.

Farer, T. (1989). The United Nations and human rights: More than a whimper. In R. P. Claude & B. H. Weston (Eds.), *Human rights   in the world community* (pp. 194-208). Philadelphia: University of Pennsylvania Press.

Farhang, M. (1988). Fundamentalism and civil rights in   contemporary middle eastern politics. In L. Rouner (Ed.)   *Human rights and the world's religions* (pp. 63-75). Indiana: University of Notre Dame Press.

Fast, H. (1946). *The selected works of Tom Paine and citizen Tom   Paine*. New York: Random House.

Ferrero, R. (1986). Sub-Commission on Prevention of Discrimination and Protection of Minorities. *The new   international economic order and the promotion of human rights*. (E/CN.4/Sub.2/1983/24/Rev.1). New York: United Nations.

Filartiga v. Pena-Irala. 630 F. 2d 876 (1980).

Fisher, E. & MacKay. (1996). *Gender justice: Women's rights are human rights*. Cambridge, MA: Unitarian Universalist Service Committee.

Flavin, C. (1997). The legacy of Rio. In L. Brown, C. Flavin, H. French, J. Abramovitz, C. Bright, G. Gardner, A Mc Ginn, M. Renner, D. Roodman, L. Starke (Eds.) *State of the world, 1997*. NY: W.W. Norton.

Foreman, J. (1972). *Socialism: Its theoretical roots and present day development*. New York: Franklin Watts.

Fraenkel, O. (1971) *The rights we have*. New York: Thomas   Crowell.

Frank, T. M. (1982). *Human rights in third world perspective* (Vols. 1-3). New York: Oceana.

Fremantle, A. (Ed.). (1956). *The papal encyclicals in their historical context*. New York: Mentor.

Fresia, J. (1988). *Towards an American revolution: Exposing the Constitution and other illusions*. New York: South End.

Friedelbaum, S. H. (1988). *Human Rights in the states; New directions in constitutiona policymaking*. New York: Greenwood.

Friedman, J. and Wiseberg, L. (1981). *Teaching human rights*. Washington, DC: Human Rights Internet.

Frost, S. (1942). *Basic teachings of the great philosophers*. Philadelphia: Blakiston.

Gagarin, M. (1989). *Early Greek law*. Berkeley: University of California Press.

Galie, P. (1988a). Social services and egalitarian activism. In S. Freidelbaum (Ed.), *Human rights in the states; New directionsIn constitutional policymaking* (pp. 108-120). New York: Greenwood.

_____. (1988b). State courts and economic rights. In J.   Kincaid (Ed.), *The Annals of the American Academy of Political and Social Science* (pp. 76-87). Newbury Park, CA: Sage

Gallagher, M. (1985). *Becoming aware: Human rights and the family*. Paris: UNESCO.

Germino, D. (1972). *Machiavelli to Marx: Modern western political thought*. Chicago: University of Chicago Press.

Gibbons, J. (Ed.). (1963). *Pacem in Terris*. New York: Paulist Press.

Gierke, O. (1951). *Political theories of the Middle Ages*. (F. Maitland, Trans.). Cambridge, London: University Press.

Gil, D. (1973). *Violence against children: Physical child abuse in the United States*. Cambridge: Harvard University Press.

_____. (1976) *The challenge of social equality: Essays on social policy, social development and political practice*. Cambridge: Schenkman.

_____. (1977). *Social policy and the right to work. Social thought*. Washington: National Catholic Conference of Charities.

_____. (1990a). *Unravelling social policy* (rev. 4th ed.). Cambridge: Schenkman.

_____. (1990b, September, 2-6). *Have we really overcome Hitler?* Keynote address at the International Congress on Child Abuse and Neglect, Hamburg, West Germany. For inquiries contact: Dr. David Gil, Heller School, Brandeis University, Waltham, MA 02254-9110.

Gil, D., & Gil, E. (Eds.). (1985). *The future of work*. Rochester, VT: Schenkman.

Gilmore, M. (1952). *The world of humanism*. New York: Harper.

Giorgi, A., Murray, E., & Von Eckartsberg, R. (Eds.). (1971). *Duquesne Studies in Phenomenological Psychology* (Vol 1). Pittsburgh: Duquesne University Press.

Glennon, M. (1990). *Constitutional diplomacy*. Princeton: Princeton University Press.

Goldberg, Commissioner of Social Services of the City of New York v. Kelly. 25 L. Ed. 287 (1970).

Goldmann, L. (1973). *The philosophy of the Enlightenment: The Christian burgess and the Enlightenment*. Cambridge, MA: MIT Press.

Goldstein, R. (1987). The United States. In J. Donnelly & R. E. Howard. *International handbook of human rights* (pp. 429-456). New York: Greenwood.

Gooch, G. P. & Laski, H. J. (1954). *English democratic ideas in the seventeenth century* (2nd. ed.). Cambridge: At the University Press.

Gorbachev, M. (1985). *A time for peace*. New York: Richardson and Stigerman.

_____. (1988, December 7). Address to the General Assembly of the United Nations. New York: United Nations.

Gough, J. (1973). *John Locke's political philosophy*. Oxford: Clarendon.

Grad, F.P., Stearns, L., Hustace, T & Frishman, A. (Eds.). (1990). *Constitutions of the United States: National and state*. New York: Oceana.

Graubard, S. (Ed.). (1983). Human rights. [Special issue]. *Daedalus, 10*(4).

Green, J. F. (1956). *The U.N. and human rights*. Washington: Brookings Institute.

Green v. Frazier. 64 L.Ed. 878 (1920).

Gremillion, J. (1981). *The gospel of peace and justice: Catholic social teaching since Pope John*. Maryknoll, NY: Orbis Books.

Griswold v. Connecticut. 14 L.Ed.2nd 510 (1965).

Grodin, J. (1989). *In pursuit of justice: Reflections of a state supreme court justice*. Berkely: University of California Press.

Gunther, G. (1985). *Constitutional law* (11th Edition). Mineola, NY: Foundation.

Gurvitch G. (1946). *The bill of social rights.* New York: International Universities.
Hadas, M. (Ed.). (1965). *Essential works of stoicism.* New York: Bantam Books.

Hannum, H. (1984). *Guide to international human rights practice.* Philadelphia: University of Pennsylvania Press.
Hannum, H. & Fischer, D. (1993). *U.S. ratification of the internationa covenants on human rights.* Irvington-on-Hudson, NY: Transnational Press.
Harrington, M. (1972). *Socialism.* New York: Saturday Review.
_____. (1989). *Socialism past and future.* New York: Arcade.
Harvard Law Review. (1982). Developments in the law: The interpretation of state constitutional rights, *95,* 1325-1502.
Harvey, P. (1989). *Securing the right to employment.* Princeton: Princeton University Press.
Hassan, R. (1982). On human rights and the Qur'anic perspective. In A. Swidler (Ed.), *Human rights in religious traditions.* (pp. 51-65). New York: Pilgrim.
Hayes, C. (1948). *A political and cultural history of modern Europe: Vol. 1; Three centuries of predominantly agricultural society 1500-1830.* New York: Macmillan.
Hazeltine, H. D. (1917). The influence of Magna Carta on American constitutional development. In H. Malden, *Magna Carta commemoration essays* (pp. 180-226). Aberdeen: The University press.
Hearnshaw, F. (Ed.). (1928). *The social and political ideas of some great mediaeval thinkers.* New York: Barnes and Noble.
_____. (1949a). *The social and political ideas of some representative thinkers of the age of reaction and reconstruction.* New York: Barnes and Noble.
_____. (1949b). *The social and political ideas of some great thinkers of the sixteenth and seventeenth centuries.* New York: Barnes and Noble.
_____. (1949c). *The social and political ideas of some great thinkers of the Renaissance and the Reformation.* New York: Barnes and Noble.
_____. (1950). *The social and political ideas of some representative thinkers of the revolutionary era.* New York: Barnes and Noble.
Heart of Atlanta v. United States. 13 L. Ed.2nd 258 (1964).
Heilbroner, R. L. (1961) *The worldly philosophers* (rev. ed.). New York: Simon and Schuster.
Heller, A. (1978). *Renaissance man.* (R. Allen, Trans.). Boston: Routledge and Kegan Paul.
Helton, T. (Ed.). (1961). *The Renaissance: A reconsideration of the theories and interpretations of the age.* Madison: University of Wisconsin Press.
Helvering v. Davis. 301 U.S. 619 (1937).
Henkin, L. (1978). *The rights of man today.* Boulder, CO: Westview.
Henle, R. (1980). A Catholic view of human rights. In A. Rosenbaum (Ed.), *The philosophy of human rights: International perspectives* (pp. 87-93). Westport, CT: Greenwood.
Hennessey, E. (1990, April 6). State courts are holding the line on individual rights. *The Boston Globe,* op. ed. page.

Heymann, P. B., & Liebman, L. (1988*). The social responsibilities of lawyers.* Westbury, NY: Foundation Press.

Higgenbotham, J. (Trans.). (1967*). Cicero: On moral obligation.* Berkeley: University of California Press.

Higgins, K. (1990, November 24). Liberation theology and the new world order. *America*, pp. 389-393.

Hill, W. & Marks, M. (1986). *1984 annual survey of American law.* Dobbs Ferry, NY: Oceana.

Hodes, N. & Hays, M. (1995). *The United Nations and the world's religions.* Cambridge, MA: Boston Research Center for the 21st Century.

Hollenbach, D. (1988). *Justice, peace, and human rights: American Catholic social ethics in a pluralistic context.* New York: Crossroad.

Holman, F. (1949). International proposals affecting so-called human rights. *Law and Contemporary Problems, 14,* 479-489.

Holsti, O. (1969*). Content analysis for the social sciences and humanities.* Reading, MA: Addison-Wesley.

The Holy Bible. (1961). New York: Benziger.

Hook, S. (1980). *Philosophy and public policy.* Carbondale: Southern Illinois University Press.

Howland, C. W. (1997). The challenge of religious fundamentalism to the liberty and equality rights of women: An analysis under the U.N. Charter, *Coumbia Journal of Transnational Law, 35,*(2), 271-376.

Hudelson, R. (1990). *Marxism and philosophy in the twentieth century: A defense of vulgar Marxism.* New York: Praeger.

Hunt, E. K. & Sherman, H. J. (1986). *Economics: An introduction to traditional and radical views* (5th Ed.). New York: Harper and Row.

Human rights internet. (1991). *For the record: Indigenous peoples and slavery in the United Nations.* Ontario: Author.

Human rights treaty update.(1991, Spring). *Human rightsadvocacy interest group newsletter: American society of international law, 2*(1) p. 2.

Humphrey, J. (1976). The International Bill of Rights: Scope and implementation. *William and Mary Law Review, 17,* 524-541.

Ingraham v. Wright. 430 U.S. 651 (1977).

International Bill of Rights to be drafted. (1947, June 17). *UN Weekly Bulletin*, pp. 639-643.

International Planned Parenthood Association. (1996). *Charter on Sexual and Reproductive Rights.* London: Author.

Ivanhoe Irrigation District v. Mc Cracken. 2 L.Ed. 1313 (1958).

Jackson, S. (Ed.). (1910). *The new Schaff and Herzog encyclopedia of religious knowledge. New York: Funk and Wagnall.*

Jacobson v. Massachusetts. 49 L.Ed. 643 (1905).

Janosik, R. (Ed.). (1987). *Encyclopedia of the American judicial system* (Vols. 1-3). New York: Charles Scribner.

Jarrett, B. (1914). *Medieval socialism.* New York: Dodge.

_____. (1942). *Social theories of the Middle Ages*. Westminster, MD: Newman Books.

Jones, W. (1952). *A history of western philosophy*. New York: Harcourt Brace.

Joyce, J. (1978). *The new politics of human rights*. New York: Mac   Millan.

Kagan, D. (1965). *Sources in Greek political thought*. New York: Free.

Kamenka, E. (Ed.). (1983). *The portable Karl Marx*. London: Viking.

Kaplan, A. (1980). Human Relations and Human Rights in Judaism. In A. Rosenbaum (Ed.), *The philosophy of human rights: International perspectives* (pp. 53-85). Westport, CT: Greenwood.

Karger H. & Stoesz, D. (1998). *American social welfare policy: A pluralist approach*.

Kaufman, J. (1991, April 7). The collective good. *The Boston Globe Magazine*, pp. 20-27.

Kaufmann, W. (Trans. & Ed.). (1976). *The portable Nietzsche*. New York: Penguin.

Katz, M.B. (1986). *In the shadow of the poorhouse: A social history of welfare in America*. New York: Basic.

Kincaid, J. (1988). State constitutions in a federal system. *The   Annals of the American Academy of Political and Social Science. [Special Edition]*, *496*, Newbury Park, CA: Sage.

King, P. (Ed.). (1983). *The history of ideas: Introduction to method*. Totowa, NJ: Barnes and Noble.

Kiss, A. (1988). The role of the Universal Declaration of Human Rights in international law. In United Nations Center for Human Rights, Fortieth Anniversary of the Universal Declaration of Human Rights [Special issue]. *Bulletin of Human Rights*, 47-52.

Kly, Y. (1997). *Societal development: Minority rights*. Atlanta: Clarity.

Kolakowski, P. (1983). Marxism and human rights. *Daedalus, 112*(4), 81-92.

Kolby, J. (1987, September). The growing divide: Class polarization in the 1980s. *Monthly Review*, 1-8.

Koren, H. (1967). *Marx and authentic man*. Pittsburgh: Duquesne University Press.

Kothari, R. (1989). Human Rights as a North-South Issue. In R. P.   Claude & B. H. Weston (Eds.), *Human rights in the world community* (pp. 134-142). Philadelphia: University of Pennsylvania Press.

Kristol, I. (1990) Human rights: The hidden agenda. In W. Laqueur   and B. Rubin (Eds.), *The human rights reader* (pp. 391-404). New York: New American library.

Kurkjian, S. (1991, March 26). Widespread child hunger is found. *The Boston Globe*. p. 3.

Lane, D. (1989). Human rights under state socialism. In R. P.   Claude & B. H. Weston (Eds.), *Human rights in the world community* (pp. 123-134). Philadelphia: University of Pennsylvania Press.

Laski, H. (1920). *Political thought in England from Locke to Bentham*. New York: Henry Holt.

_____. (1925?) *A defence of liberty against tyrants*. (J. Brutus, Trans.). New York: Harcourt Brace.

Laqueur, W., & Rubin, B. (Eds.). (1990). *The human rights reader* (rev. ed.). New York: New American Library.

Lauterpacht, H. (1950) *International law and human rights*. London: Stevens and sons.

Lawyers Committee for Human Rights. (1989) *The Reagan administration's record on human rights in 1988*. New York: Human Rights Watch.

Legesse, A. (1980) Human rights in African political culture. In K. Thompson (Ed.).*The moral imperatives of human rights: a world survey*. Washington D.C.: University Press of America.

Lenin, V. I. (1964) *The teachings of Karl Marx*. New York: International Publishers.

Lerner, M. (1986). *Surplus powerlessness*. Oakland, CA: The Institute for Labor and Mental Health.

Levy, L. and Larst, K. (1986*). Encyclopedia of the American Constitution.* New York: MacMillan.

Levy v. Louisiana. 391 US 68 (1968).

Lewis, E. (1954). *Medieval political ideas*. New York: Alfred A. Knopf.

Lichteim, G. (1970). *A short history of socialism*. New York: Praeger.

Lillich, R. (1989). The Constitution and international human rights. *American Journal of International Law, 83, 4*, 851-862.

_____. (1990) The United States Constitution and international human rights law. *Harvard Human Rights Journal, 3*, 53-82.

Lillich, R. and Newman, F. (1979). *International human rights: Problems of law and policy*. Boston: Little, Brown.

Little, D., Kelsay, J., and Sachedina, A. (1988). *Human rights and the conflict of cultures: Western and Islamic perspectives on religious liberty*. Columbia: University of South Carolina Press.

Livermore, S. (Ed.). (1985*). The American bench: Bills and declarations of rights digest.* (3rd ed.). Sacramento, CA: Reginald Bishop Forster.

Lloyd-Jones, H. (1971). *The justice of Zeus*. Berkeley: University of California Press.

Locke, J. (1990). Second treatise of government. In W. Laqueur and B. Rubin (Eds.), *The human rights reader* (pp. 62-67). New York: New American library.

Loving v. Virginia. 18 L. Ed.2nd 1010 (1967).

Lovejoy A. (1957). *The great chain of being: A study of the history of an idea*. Cambridge: Harvard University Press.

Lutz, E., Hannun, H., & Burke, K. (1989*). New directions in human rights.* Philadelphia: University of Pennsylvania Press.

Mac Iver, R. (Ed.). (1950*). Great expressions of human rights.* New York: The Institute for Religious and Social Studies.

Mac Manus, S., & Van Hightower, N. (1989, May/June). Limits of state constitutional guarantees: Lessons from efforts to implement domestic violence policies. *Public Administration Review*, May/June, pp. 269-287.

Maestro, M. (1972*). Voltaire and Beccaria as reformers of criminal law.* New York: Octagon.

Mahoney, D. (1986) Preamble. In L. Levy and K. Larst (Eds.), *Encyclopedia of the American Constitution* (pp. 1435-1436). New York: MacMillan.

Malden, H. (1917). *Magna Carta: Commemoration essays*. Aberdeen: The University Press.

Mangone, G. (1951). *The idea and practice of world government*. NY: Columbia University Press.

Marbury v. Madison. 2 L. Ed. 60 (1803).

Maritain, J. (1947, November 18) The rights of man. *United Nations Weekly Bulletin,* pp. 672-674.

_____. (1951). *Man and the state.* Chicago: University of Chicago Press.

Marks, T., & Cooper, J. (1988). *State constitutional law.* St. Paul, MN: West.

Marquardt, D. (1977). *A guide to the Supreme Court.* Indianapolis: Bobbs-Merrill.

Martenson, J. (1988) Introduction. In United Nations Center for Human Rights,Fortieth anniversary of the Universal Declaration   of Human   Rights [Special Issue].*Bulletin of Human Rights* (pp. 1-3). Geneva: United Nations.

Martin, R. (1985). *Rawls and rights.* Lawrence: University of Kansas Press.

Marx, K. (1978). On the Jewish question. In R. C. Tucker (Ed.),   *The Marx-Engels reader* (pp. 26-52). New York: W.W. Norton.

May, J.C. (1990). State constitutions and constitutional   revision: 1988-89 and the 1980s. In the council of state   governments, *Book of states* (pp. 21-39). Lexington, KY: Council of state governments.

Maynard, E. (1989). The bureaucracy and implementation of U.S.   human rights policy. *Human Rights Quarterly, 11,* 175-248.

Mazlish, B. (1984). *The meaning of Karl Marx.* New York: Oxford   University Press.

McIlwain, H. (1917a). Magna Carta and common law. In H. Malden   (Ed.), *Magna Carta: Commemoration essays* (pp. 122-179).   Aberdeen: The University Press.

_____. (1917b). Magna Carta: An address delivered on its   seventh centennary, to the Royal Historical Society and the   Magna Carta celebration committee. In H. Malden, H. (Ed.).   *Magna Carta: Commemoration essays* (pp. 1-25). Aberdeen: The University Press.

McKechnie, W. (1914). *Magna Carta: A commentary on the Great Charter of King John* (rev. 2nd ed.). Glasgow: James Maclehose.

Meron, T. (Ed.). (1985). *Human rights in international law: Legal and policy issues.* Oxford: Clarendon.

_____. (1986). *Human Rights law-making in the United Nations: A critique of instruments and process.* Oxford: Clarendon.

_____. (1989). *Human rights and humanitarian norms as customary law.* Oxford: Clarendon.

Minogue, K. (1990). The history of the idea of human rights. In W. Laqueur & B. Rubin (Eds.), *The human rights reader* (pp. 3-25). New York: New American Library.

Mihesuah, D. (1996). *American Indians: Stereotypes and realities.* Atlanta: Clarity.

Mitgang, H. (1991, January 2). The First Amendment and rebels it   protects. *The New York Times,* p. C15.

Montana Co. v. St. Louis Mining. 38 L.Ed. 398 (1894).

Morris, C., & Morris, M. (1924). *A history of political ideas.*   London: Christophers

Mosk S. (1988). The emerging agenda in state constitutional rights law. In Kinkaid (ed.) In J.Kincaid (Ed.), *The Annals   of the American Academy of Political and Social Science: State Constitutions in a Federal System* (Vol.496) (pp. 54-65).   Newbury Park, CA: Sage.

Mott, R. (1926). *Due process of law.* Indianapolis: Bobbs-Merrill. Movement for humanity. (1990, April 10). *The New York Times,* p.   A12.

Mower, A. (1979). *The United States, the United Nations and human rights.* Westport, CT: Greenwood.

_____. (1985). *International cooperation for social justice: Global and regional protection of economic/social rights.* Westport, CT: Greenwood.

Moynihan, D. P. (1990). *On the law of nations.* Cambridge: Harvard University Press.

Murphy, S.P. (1991, June 18). Rights cases shift to state courts. *The Globe, Boston* pp. 17, 19.

Myers, D. (1930). *Handbook of the League of Nations since 1920.* Boston: World Peace Foundation.

Nasr, S. (1980) The concept and reality of freedom in Islam and Islamic civilization. In A. S. Roseenbaum (Ed.), *The philosophy of human rights: International perspectives* (pp. 95-101). Westport, CT: Greenwood.

Nearing, S. (1919). *Labor and the League of Nations.* New York: Rand School of Social Science.

Nebbia v. New York. 78 L.Ed. 940 (1934).

Nelson-Pallmeyer, J. (1997). *School of Assassins.* Maryknoll, NY: Orbis.

New York Times v. Sullivan. 11 L.Ed.2nd 686 (1964).

Newman, F., & Weissbrodt D. (1996). *International human rights: Law, policy, and process.* Cincinnati: Anderson.

Nickel, J. (1987). *Making sense of human rights.* Berkeley:: University of California Press.

Oates, W., & Murphy, C. (1944). *Greek literature in translation.* New York: Longmans, Green.

Olson, M. (1983). A less ideological way of deciding how much should be given to the poor, *Daedalus, 112*(4), 217-236.

Orwin, C., & Pangle, T. (1984). The philosophical foundation of human rights. In M. Plattner, (Ed.), *Human rights in our time* (pp. 1-22). Boulder, CO: Westview.

Orwin, C., & Stoner, J. (1990). Neoconstitutionalism? Rawls, Dworkin and Nozick. In A. Bloom (Ed.), *Confronting the Constitution* (pp. 437-470). Washington, DC: American Enterprise Institute.

Padover, S. (1983). *The living Constitution* (2nd rev. ed.). New York: New American Library.

Palumbo, M. (1982). *Human rights: Meaning and history.* Malabar, FL: Krieger.

Parry, C., & Grant J. (Eds.). (1986). *Encyclopaedic dictionary of international law* (Vols. 1-3). New York: Oceana.

Patents. (1984). *The guide to American law* (Vol. 8) (pp. 141-145) St. Paul, MN:West.

Paul, D. (1993). *We were not the savages: A Micmac perspective on the collision of European and Aboriginal civilization.* Halifax, NS: Nimbus.

Pauling, L. (Ed.). (1986). *World encyclopedia of peace.* New York: Pergamon.

Paust, J. J. (1983). Human dignity as a constitutional right: A jurisprudentially based inquiry into criteria and content. *Howard Law Journal, 27,* 144-225.

_____. (1987). The president is bound by international law. *American Journal of International Law, 81,* 378-390.

_____.(1988). Self-executing treaties. *American Journal of International Law, 82,* 760-783.

_____. (1989). On human rights: The use of human rightsprecepts in U.S. history and the right to an effective remedy in domestic courts. *Michigan Journal of International Law, 10,* 543-652.

_____. (1989). Congress and genocide: They're not going to get away with it. *Michigan Journal of International Law,* 11, 90-104.

Penn Central Transportation Co. v. New York City. 57 L.Ed.2nd 633 (1978).

Perry, R. L., & Cooper, J. C. (Ed.). (1959). *Sources of our liberties.* New York: Associated College Presses.

Physicians for Human Rights. (1990). *Operation "Just Cause": The human cost of military action in Panama.* Somerville, MA: Author.

Pickthall, M. (1979). *The meaning of the glorious Koran.* New York: New American Library.

Plattner, M. (Ed.). (1984). *Human rights in our time.* Boulder: Westview.

Plyer v. Doe. 72 L.Ed.2nd 786 (1982).

Polish, D. F. (1982). Judaism and human rights. In A. Swidler (Ed.), *Human rights in religious traditions* (pp. 40-50). New York: Pilgrim.

Pollis, A., & Schwab, P. (Eds.). (1979). Human rights: A western construct with limited applicability. In A. Pollis & P. Schwab (Eds.), *Human rights: Cultural and ideological perspectives* (pp. 1-18). New York: Praeger.

Pope John Paul II. (1981) *On human work.* Boston: Daughters of St. Paul.

Popkin, R. (Ed.). (1966). *Philosophers of the 16th and 17th centuries.* New York: Free.

Porter, M. (1982). *State supreme courts: Policymakers in the federal system.* Westport, CT: Greenwood.

Potter, G. (Ed.). (1971). *The new Cambridge modern history Vol. I: The Renaissance.* London: Cambridge University Press.

Pritchard, K. (1989) Political science and the teaching of human rights. *Human Rights Quarterly, 11,* 458-475.

Rankin, R. (1960). *State constitutions: Bill of rights.* New York: National Municipal League.

Raphael, D. (1967). *Political theory and the rights of man.* Bloomington: Indiana University Press.

Rawls, J. (1971). *A theory of justice.* Cambridge: Harvard University Press.

Reisman, M. (1990). Sovereignty and human rights in contemporary international law. *American Journal of International Law, 84,* 866-876.

Ribadeneira, D. (1991, November 8). Candidates pressed on children's needs. *The Boston Globe,* p. 23.

Riehm, J. (1987). *Glasnost: How open?* New York: Freedom House.

Rimlinger, G. (1983). Capitalism and human rights. *Daedalus, 112, (4),* 51-79.

Rist, J. (Ed.). (1978). *The Stoics.* Berkeley: University of California Press.

Roberts, J. (1987). *History of the world.* London: Penguin.

Robinson, N. (1958). *The Universal Declaration of Human Rights: Its origin, significance and interpretation.* New York: Institute of Jewish Affairs.

Rosenbaum, A. (Ed.). (1980). *The philosophy of human rights: International perspectives.* Westport, CN: Greenwood.

Rosenbaum, S. (1989). Lawyers *pro bono publico*: Using international human rights on behalf of the poor. In E. L. Lutz, H. Hannum, & K. J. Burke (Eds.), *New directions in human rights* (pp. 109-133). Philadelphia: University of Pennsylvania Press.

Rosenstock-Huessy, E. (1969). *Out of revolution: Autobiography of western man.* Norwich, VT: Argo.

Rosenzweig, M. (1988). Psychology and United Nations human rights efforts. *American Psychologist, 43*, 79-86.

Ross, W. (1961). *The works of Aristotle translated into English* (Vol X). London: Clarendon.

Rotblat, J. (Ed.). (1997). *World citizenship: Allegiance to humanity.* NY: St. Martin's.

Rouner, L. (1988). *Human rights and the world's religions.* Indiana: University of Notre Dame.

Royce, J. R. (1964). *The encapsulated man--An interdisciplinary essay on the search for meaning.* New York: Van Nostrand.

Rimlinger, G. (1983). Capitalism and human rights. *Daedalus, 112(4)*, 51-79.

Sabatini, R. (1924). *Torquemada and the Spanish Inquisition.* New York: Houghton ifflin.

Sachs, B. F. (1980). *Constitutions of the United States: National and state - fundamental liberties and rights - a 50-state index.* New York: Oceana.

Sanford, E. (1917). *History of the Reformation.* Hartford, CT: S.S. Scranton.

Santillana, G. (1957). *The age of adventure: The Renaissance philosophers.* Boston: Houghton Mifflin.

Schaeffer, J. (1983, January). Presentation by John Schaeffer, President of the Northwest Alaska Native Association (NANA) at a shareholders meeting. For inquiries contact NANA corporation, Kotzebue, Alaska 99752.

Schauer, F. (1989). *Supplement to constitutional law*, (Gunther,11th ed.). Westbury, NY: Foundation.

Schifter, R. (1988). Human rights: A western cultural bias? In W. Laqueur & B. Rubin (Eds.), *The human rights reader* (pp. 440-441). New York: New American Library.

Schwartz, B. (1980a). *The roots of the bill of rights* (Vol. 1). New York: Chelsea House.

_____. (1980b). *The roots of the bill of rights* (Vol. 2). New York: Chelsea House.

_____. (1980c). *The roots of the bill of rights* (Vol. 3). New York: Chelsea House.

_____. (1990). *The new right and the Constitution.* Boston: Northeastern University Press.

Schwelb, E. (1986). Human rights. In D. Sills (Ed.), *International encyclopedia of social sciences* (Vol. 6) (pp. 540-545). New York: Free.

Schwoebel, R. (Ed.). (1971). *Renaissance men and ideas.* New York: St. Martin's.

Scoble, H., & Wiseberg, L. (Eds.). (1985). *Access to justice.* London: Zed.

Severid, M. (1950?) Interview with Eleanor Roosevelt. *The United Nations Today (film).* Presented at the National Conference on the United States and the United Nations (November 8-11, 1989). For inquiries contact: UNA-USA, 485 Fifth Avenue, NY, NY 10017-6104.

Seville Statement on Violence (1990) *American Psychologist, 45*, 1167-1168.

Shapiro v. Thompson. 22 L.Ed.2nd 600 (1969).

Shestack, J. (1985). The jurisprudence of human rights. In T. Meron (Ed.), *Human rights in international law* (pp. 69-113). Oxford: Clarendon.

Shirley, F. (1949). Richard Hooker and contemporary political ideas. London: SPCK.

Silbey, S. & Sarat, A. (1990*). Studies in law politics, and society* (Vol. 10). Greenwich, CT: Jai.

Sills, D. (Ed.). (1986). *International encyclopedia of the social sciences.* New York: Free.

Skurski, R. (1983). *New directions in economic justice.* Notre Dame: University of Notre Dame Press.

Smith, T., & Grene, M. (Eds.). (1957). *From Descartes to Locke.* Chicago: University of Chicago Press.

Spend fairly for schools. Then what? (1990, June 6*) New York Times,* p. A22.

Spitz, L. (1962). *The Reformation: Material or spiritual?* Boston: D.C. and Heath.

Stamatapoulou, E. (1989, November 8-11). The UN's role in   protecting human rights. Presentation at the *National Conference on the United States and the United Nations.* Washington, DC. (Available from UNA-USA, 485 Fifth Avenue, NY, NY 10017-6104).

Staniforth, M. (Trans.). (1984) *Marcus Aurelius: Meditations.* New York: Penguin.

Steinfels, P. (1991, May 3). Papal encyclical urges capitalism to shed injustices. *The New York Times,* pp. A1, A10.

Steward Machine Co. v. Davis. 301 U.S. 548 (1937).

Stone, D. (1988). *Policy paradox and political reason.* Boston: Scott Foresman.

Staunton, M., Fenn S., & Amnesty International U.S.A.. *The Amnesty International Handbook.* Clarement, CA: Hunter House.

Strauss, L. (1952). *The political philosophy of Hobbes: Its basis and genesis.* Chicago: University of Chicago Press.

Stringham, R. (1966). *Magna Carta: Fountainhead of freedom.* Rochester, NY: Aqueduct.

Steiner, H. J. (1991). *Diverse partners: Non-governmental organizations in the human rights movement.* Cambridge: President and Fellows of Harvard College.

Sturm, A. L., & May, J.C. (1988). State constitutions and constitutional   revision: 1986-87. In the Council of state governments, *Book of states* (pp. 3-13) Lexington, KY: Council of State Governments.

Suetonius. (1957). *The 12 Caesars.* (R. Graves, Trans.). Baltimore: Penguin.

Suro, R. (1990, March 11). Courts ordering financing changes in public schools. *The New York Times,* pp. A1, A28.

Sussman, D., & Abrahamson, S. (Eds.). (1989). *Constitutions of the United States: National and state.* New York: Oceana.

Swedish Institute. (1990, May). *Constitutional protection of rights and freedoms in Sweden.* (Classification: FS 4 e Oc.01). Stockholm: Author.

Swindler, W. (1965). *Magna Carta: legend and legacy.* New York: Bobbs-Merrill.

Szabo, I. (1982). Historical foundations of human rights and subsequent developments. In K. Vasak (Ed.), *The international dimensions of human rights.* (Vol. 1) (pp. 11-41). Westport, CT: Greenwood.

Tarr G., & Porter, C. (1988). *State supreme courts in state and nation.* New Haven: Yale University Press.

Taylor, H. (1914). *The mediaeval mind* (Vols. 1-2) London: Macmillan.

Tessitore, J., & Woolfson, S. (Eds.). (1990). *Issues before the 45th General Assembly of the UN.* Lexington, MA: D.C. Heath.

_____ (Eds.). (1991). *Issues before the 45th General Assembly of the UN.* Lexington, MA: D.C. Heath.

Thompson, K. (Ed.). (1980). *The moral imperatives of human rights: A world survey.* Washington, DC: University Press of America.

Thomson, J. (Ed. & Trans.). (1953). *The ethics of Aristotle.* London: George Allen.

Tolley, H. (1987). *The UN Commission on Human Rights.* Boulder, CO: Westview.

Toner, R. (1989, July 2). Spirit of 89: The uproar over what America owes its first allegiance to. *The New York Times,* S4, p. 1.

Trials-and error-in China. (February 1, 1991*). The New York Times,* p. A28.

Tribe, L. (1985*). God save this honorable court: How choice of Supreme Court justices shapes our history.* New York: Random House.

Trubek, D. (1985). Economic, social and cultural rights in the third world: Human rights law and human needs programs. In T. Meron (Ed.), *Human rights in international law* (pp. 205- 271). Oxford: Clarendon Press.

Tucker, R. (1978). *The Marx-Engels reader* (2nd ed.). New York: W.W. Norton.

United Nations. (1981, December 31). *The regional and national dimensions of the right to development as a human right.* (E/CN.4/1488). New York: Author.

_____. (1988). General Assembly, 45th Session. *Question of a convention on the rights of the child.* (Agenda Item 13) Geneva: Author.

_____. (1988) General Assembly, 43rdSession. *Report of the human rights committee.* (Supp. No. 40). New York: Author.

United Nations Center for Human Rights. (1988). Fortieth Anniversary of the Universal Declaration of Human Rights [Special Issue]. *Bulletin of Human Rights.* Geneva: Author.

United Nations Commission on Human Rights. (1996, June 28). *The realization of economic, social, and cultural rights: Final report on human rights and extreme poverty, submitted by Mr. Leandro Despouy.* NY: Author.

_____. (1994) *United Nations action in the field of human rights.* NY: Author.

United Nations Department of Public Information. (1950*). These rights and freedoms.* (Sales # 1950.1.6). New York: Author.

_____. (1986) *Everyone's United Nations* (10th ed.). New York: Author.

United Nations Development Program. (1996). *Human development report.* New York: Author.

UNESCO, Henry Dunant Institute. (1988) *International dimensions of humanitarian law.* The Netherlands: Martinus Nijhoff.

UNESCO yearbook on peace and conflict studies. (1989). New York:Greenwood.

United Nations General Assembly—44th session. (1990, March 1).*Resolution adopted by the General Assemby - Human rights based on solidarity.* (A/RES/44/148-Agenda item 15). New York: Author.

United Nations General Assembly —50th session. (1995, September 20). *Human rights questions,including alternative approaches fo improving the effective enjoyment of human rights and fundamental freedoms: National institutions for the promotion and protection of human rights.* (A/RES/50/452-agenda item 114). NY: Author.

United Nations High Commissioner for Human Rights. (1997, November 11). *Realising human rights: Take hold of it boldly.* www3.unicef.ch/html/menu2/3/e/12nov97.htm

United Nations Information Organization. (1945). *Documents of the United Nations conference on international organization at San Francisco, 1945* (Vol. 6) (published in cooperation with the Library of Congress).

United Nations Library and the Graduate Institute of International Studies. (1983) *The League of Nations in retrospect.* New York: Walter de Gruyter.

United States Catholic Bishops. (1986). *Economic justice for all: Catholic social teaching and the U.S. economy.* The Catholic Telegraph.

United States Congress. (1935). *Act to provide for the general welfare by establishing a system of federal old age benefits.* Washington, DC: U.S. Government Printing Office.

Valle R., & Halling S. (1989). *Existential-phenomenological perspectives in psychology.* New York: Plenum.

Van Boven, T. (1981). A People's Commission. In R. Claude & B. Weston (Ed.), *Human rights in the world community* (pp. 188 -189). Philadelphia: University of Pennsylvania Press.

_____. (1982). Distinguishing criteria of human rights. In K. Vasek and P. Alston (Eds.), *The international dimensions of human rights* (Vol. 1) (pp. 43-59). Westport, CT: Greenwood.

Van Wormer, K. (1997). *Social welfare: A world view.* Chicago: Nelson-Hall.

Vasak, K. (1977). *A 30-year struggle: The sustained efforts to give force of law to the Universal Declaration of Human Rights.* New York: United Nations.

_____. (1982). Distinguishing criteria of human rights. In K. Vasak and P. Alston (Ed.), *The international dimensions of human rights* (Vol. 1) (pp. 3-10). Westport, CT: Greenwood.

Vasak, K., & Alston, P. (Eds.). (1982*). The international dimensions of human rights* (Vols. 1-2), (rev. ed.). Westport, CT: Greenwood.

Veatch, R. (1983). Minorities and the League of Nations. In United Nations Library, *The League of Nations in retrospect* (pp. 369-383). New York: Walter de Gruyter.

Verdross, A. (1979). The journey of an idea. *Human Rights Journal, 8(3),* 21-23.

Verhovek, S. H. (1991, May 6). Poorer New York school districts challenging state aid as unequal. *The New York Times,* pp. A1, B4.

Volpe, G. (1978*). Rousseau and Marx* (J. Fraser, Trans.). Atlantic Highlands, NJ: Humanities.

Voltaire, M. (1849) *Philosophical dictionary* (Vols 1-2). London: L.A. Lewis.

Von Eckartsberg, R. (1972). An approach to experiential social psychology. In A. Giorgi, E. Murray, & R. Von Eckartsberg (Eds.),*Duquesne Studies in Phenomenological Psychology* (Vol. 1) (pp. 325-372). Pittsburgh: Duquesne University Press.

Von Leyden, W. (1985). *Aristotle on equality and justice.* London: MacMillan.

Wagner, R. (1989). *Redefining the welfare state: To promote the general welfare.* San Francisco: Pacific Research Institute for Public Policy.

Ward v. Maryland. 20 L.Ed. 449 (1870).

Waring, L. (1978). *Political theories of Martin Luther.* Port Washington, NY: Kennikat.

Warren, C. (1978). *Congress as Santa Claus or national donations and the general welfare clause of the Constitution.* New York: Arno.

Watson, A. (1987). *Roman slave law.* Baltimore: John Hopkins University Press.

Weinreb, L. L. (1987). *Natural law and justice.* Cambridge: Harvard University Press.

Weimer, D. L., & Vining, A. R. (1989). *Policy analysis; Concepts and practice.* Englewood Cliffs, NJ: Prentice Hall.

Werhane, J. (1986). *Philosophical issues in human rights: Theories and applications.* New York: Random House.

Wernham, R. (Ed.). (1971). *The new Cambridge modern history Vol. III: The Counter Reformation and price revolution.* London: Cambridge University Press.

West, G. (1981). *The national welfare rights movement--The social protest of poor women.* New York: Praeger.

Weston, B. H. (1989). Human rights. In R. Claude and B. Weston (Eds.), *Human rights in the world community* (pp. 12-29). Philadelphia: University of Pennsylvania Press.

Weston, B., Lukes, R., & Hnatt, K. (1989). Regional human rights regimes: A comparison and appraisal. In R. Claude and B. Weston (Eds.), *Human rights in the world community* (pp. 208 -220). Philadelphia: University of Pennsylvania Press.

Whalen, L. (Ed.). (1989). *Human rights: A reference book.* Santa Barbara, CA: ABC-CLIO.

White, M. (1978). *The philosophy of the American revolution.* New York: Oxford University Press.

Whitney, C. R. (1990, November 11). The legacy of Helsinki: European Magna Carta? *The New York Times,* pp. A1, A6. Wiener, P. (1973). *Dictionary of the history of ideas.* Charles Scribner: New York.

Williams, P. (Ed.). (1981). *The International Bill of Human Rights.* Glen Ellen, IL: Entwhistle.

Wiseberg, L. (Ed.). (1989). *Human rights internet reporter, 13* (1). Cambridge, MA: Harvard Law School.

_____. (1991). *Human rights internet reporter, 14* (1). Ottowa, CN: University of Ontario.

Wolff, H. (1982). *Roman law: An historical introduction.* Norman, OK: University of Oklahoma Press.

Wollman, N. (1985). *Working for peace.* San Luis Obispo, CA: Impact.

World encyclopedia of nations. (1971). New York: John Wiley.

218   *Human Rights and Social Policy in the 21st Century*

Yearbook of the United Nations. (1946-47). Lake Success, NY: United Nations Department of Public Information.

_____. (1948-49). Lake Success, NY: United Nations Department of Public Information.

Zinn, H. (1970). *The politics of history.* Boston: Beacon.

_____. (1980). *A people's history of the United States.* New York: Harper and Row.

_____. (1990). *Declarations of independence: Cross-examining American ideology.* New York: Harper-Collins.

PART THREE

ESSAYS TOWARD THE CREATION

OF A

HUMAN RIGHTS CULTURE

The orators prophesy; the professors sharpen their pens...Where are the counselors of the people? Have they nothing to offer but their regrets?

• *Maurice Merleau-Ponty,* Signs

CHAPTER SEVEN

ᗰᗰᗰᗰᗰᗰᗰᗰᗰᗰᗰᗰᗰᗰᗰᗰᗰᗰᗰᗰᗰᗰᗰ

CREATING A HUMAN RIGHTS CULTURE*

A United Nations document that has gone largely unknown to Americans for 46 years may hold thekey to the creation of a fairer and more humanitarian world. cember 10, 1948, the United Statesigned and the U.N. General Assembly endorsed with no dissenting vote the Universal Declaration of Human Rights. The chair of the drafting committee, Eleanor Roosevelt, (who later became a professor at Brandeis) referred to it as a new Magna Carta for humanity. The U.N. Human Rights Commission asserts that it is the authoritative definition of human rights standards left undefined by the U.N. Charter, which alleges only a vague commitment to human rights. World leaders, such as Pope John Paul II, have called it a "milestone in the long and difficult struggle of the human race."

---

* Originally published in the *Brandeis Review,* Winter 1995, 28-31, reprinted with permission.

Despite its world acclaim and burgeoning legal status, most Americans have never heard of this document. And if they have, they seem unaware of the scope of rights it contains. Human rights violations are more than what appears generally understood to occur in such far away places as Tiananmen Square in China, or the jungles of Somalia.

Originally meant to be merely a hortatory document, today it is of burgeoning global significance and increasingly referred to as *customary international law* by human rights scholars and even Federal Judges. In the case precedent, *Filartiga v. Pena* (1980), a United States court ruled against a military commander for torturing and murdering a 17 year old high school student, Joelita Filartiga, in Paraguay. Federal Judges Kaufman, Kearse, and Feinberg of the Second Circuit reached the following conclusion:

> Official torture is now prohibited by the law of nations. This prohibition is clear and unambiguous and admits no distinction between treatment of aliens and citizens....This prohibition has become part of customary international law, as evidenced and defined by the Universal Declaration of Human Rights. (630 F.2d 884-885)

The ruling was against Pena, a military commander. After the torture, Joelita's father and Pena had moved to the United States. Upon learning of Pena's whereabouts, Dr. Filartiga filed suit. The ruling came after extremely long litigation. What has become known as the "Filartiga" principle has been used against torturers from other countries, who have tried to settle in the United States. Recently, a Massachusetts court ruled against General Hector Gramajo, a former Minister of Defense in Guatemala, who ordered, among other things, the disembowelment of children in front of their parents.

The Filartiga case spawned numerous articles and commentary in such journals as the *Harvard Human Rights Journal* and the *American Society of International Law,* which argued that in addition to the prohibition against torture, other rights contained in the Universal Declaration should be considered part of customary international law. According to human rights scholar, Richard Lillich, noting that "numerous judges and litigants have already invoked the Declaration, arguments that other human rights now are part of customary international law can be expected to be made with increasing frequency.

In brief, The Universal Declaration of Human Rights consists of 30 articles, written as the drafting committee wanted it, not for the doctorate in jurisprudence, but for the everyday layperson in understandable language that is easy to read. It consists basically of four crucial notions. The first is Human dignity, as emphasized in the first article.

The second is civil and political rights supported in Articles 2 through 21. These are known as negative rights, as they emphasize government's responsibility *not* to interfere in such basic human rights as freedoms of speech, the press, religion, and assembly. They are also known as first generation rights, because they arose primarily in the 18th century in response to the abuses of such tyrannical monarchs, as King George. The American Bill of Rights exemplifies these fundamental freedoms.

The third is economic and social rights covered in Articles 22 through 27. These are known as second generation or positive rights, because they stress governments' responsibility to provide for certain basic human needs like shelter, health care, education, employment, and security in old age. They arose primarily in response to the abuses of industrialization, in the 19th and 20 the centuries, which in essence replaced the previously abusive monarchs. The Soviet Constitution of 1917 emphasizes these freedoms.

The fourth crucial notion is that of solidarity rights or third generation rights. Although still in the process of conceptual elaboration, they emphasize first the notion of duties. The right to food, for instance, requires the duty not to overconsume. In essence, they stress the need for individual and international cooperation to realize such rights as a clean environment, peace, and international distributive justice. They have arisen from the failure of domestic sovereignty to solve such global issues.

The creation of the Universal Declaration of Human Rights is the culmination of struggle. In 1938 at the Conference of Evian called largely upon the initiative of the United States, many nations of the world stood horrified at Hitler's atrocities against its own citizens. As it turned out, the world's outrage, however, was not so much over the horrors of the Third Reich, but rather, the gall of other countries to intervene in another's domestic affairs. The conference concluded that no country had that right. What occurred was one of the most dreadful pogroms in history, more commonly known as the holocaust, resulting in the wanton massacre of 10 million innocents, primarily Jews, but also such groups as homosexuals, gypsies, Poles and people with disabilities.

From the ashes of World War II, in order not to let such a bloodbath to ever happen again, countries formed a "United Nations" at the San Francisco Conference in June 1945. But still many governments appeared hesitant at that time to include detailed provisions of "human rights," a term which the U.N. Charter officially coined. The Soviet Union, after all, had its Gulag, the United States its numerous racial problems and sprawling ghettos, and Europe its many colonial empires. But, according to John Humphrey, first Director of the Division of Human Rights, were it not for the efforts of a few deeply committed delegates and representatives of some forty-two *non-governmental* organizations, representing primarily labor and religious groups and called in largely by the United States, human rights would have received "only a passing reference."

The Universal Declaration of Human Rights may be described, therefore, as truly a "people's document," which is also a philosophical and political compromise among divergent beliefs, countries, and traditions.   Today, no government would dare say that they are against human rights.

Research for my doctoral dissertation at the Heller School, which eventually evolved into a book, *Human rights and Social Policy in the 21st Century: a history of the idea of human rights and comparison of the Universal Declaration of Human Rights with United States Federal and state constitutions*, revealed first, that in our federal constitution, human dignity is nowhere mentioned and while exemplary in regard to civil and political rights, in the area of economic, social, cultural and solidarity rights, it is sorely lacking.   Apart from general protection for an author's interests, there is *no* mention of such fundamental rights as shelter, food, employment, health care, education, special protections for children, security in old age, and a clean environment.   The majority of state constitutions mention *only* education as a human right.   If, as often stated, constitutions can legally mandate the fulfillment of human need, can these lacks account for our many hungry, homeless, and unemployed, whom Thomas Jefferson had asserted were "excluded from the appropriation...of the earth as a common stock to labor and live on."   In these twilight years of the 20th century, would it not be wise, to heed the words of Justice Louis Brandeis who urged in his famous phrase that states act as "laboratories of democracy," to expand the rights found in the Federal Constitution?

While it is easy to contend that the United States is a rights based culture- it does after all sustain the legacy of its Bill of Rights, a beautiful, but nevertheless, limited statement of fundamental freedoms-advancing human rights here will not be easy.   As Philip Alston, Chairperson of the United Nations Committee on Economic, Social, and Cultural Rights has commented, anyone trying to advance economic and social rights in the United States will undoubtedly meet with much resistance.   Individuals, such as Robert Bork, who was against the Filartiga decision, have expressed fear, moreover, that notions of "customary international law" will revolutionize society.   Jeanne Kirkpatrick, former U.S. Ambassador to the United States referred to the Universal Declaration as "a letter to Santa Clause...neither nature, experience, nor probability informs these lists of 'entitlements,' which are subject to no constraints except those of the mind and appetite of their authors."   The former United States Representative to the U.N. Human Rights Commission Morris Abrams, furthermore, stated that the official position of the United States was the "priority" of civil and political rights.   This position is antithetical to the official U.N. position that rights are interdependent and indivisible.   What is freedom of speech, for instance, if a person is unemployed, homeless and hungry?

We need a "human rights culture," what I call a "lived awareness" of the principles of the Universal Declaration of Human Rights, not to mention the long train of covenants and declarations which have followed it, like the Conventions Against Torture and the Rights of the Child. We have ratified neither, though Congress is presently deliberating over the Convention Against the Elimination of Discrimination Against Women. It is here where education, broadly defined, may play a key role as I just argued in "Human rights in the United States: An educational agenda for the 21st century" in the *Journal of Moral Education*. Thus, not only must we know cognitively, that we need "a social and international order," as the Declaration asserts, in which human rights can be realized, but we must also engage in social movements to guarantee basic human rights and carry these principles into our everyday lives.

Public sentiment then, is the key to advancing the principles of the Universal Declaration. We need to work to expand the mandates of such fine organizations as Amnesty International and local, state and other human rights commissions. Such commissions, for example, often limit themselves to such issues as affirmative actions programs, rather than employment for all. We need to have ordinances endorsing the principles of the Universal Declaration. In addition to monitoring only limited notions of rights in 191 foreign countries, as in the Department of State's *Country Reports on Human Rights Practices for 1993*, we need to respect, as well, the ancient injunction to look at the log in our own eye, before plucking out the spec from another's. Should we not begin to examine ourselves?

I have begun with Dr. David Gil The Universal DeclaratnofHuman Rights Project, a joint project of Brandeis University and Springfield College, where I teach, which commits itself to raise awareness of the Universal Declaration, monitor compliance with it, and suggest ways to overcome violations. Results would not be in vain, for as Dr. Gil in *Violence Against Children*, has found unemployment is a major predictor of domestic violence; lack of education, according to Dr. Williams at the Heller School in *Black Teenage Mothers: Pregnancy and Child Rearing From Their Perspective* is a major predictor of teenage pregnancy.

This challenge is a challenge for all citizens of the world, but particularly to the Brandeis community, which traditionally has had a strong commitment to these rights, let alone the visions of its namesake. Given the Clinton administration's endorsement, among other things, of the 1993 Vienna Declaration, which referred to the Universal Declaration as a "timeless document" and his initiatives for universal health care, the time appears ripe to form "partnerships of empowerment" with all people to create a more humane and socially just world.

ロ ロ

Human Rights and Social Policy in the United States:
An Educational Agenda for the 21st Century*

ABSTRACT Education has tended in the human rights arena to emphasize, at least in the United States, civil and political rights. Into the next century, this moral educational agenda ought to be expanded to include more emphasis upon economic, social, and solidarity rights and the notion of the interdependency of human rights, the official position of the U.N. Human Rights Commission. The Universal Declaration of Human Rights, reaffirmed at the recent World Conference on Human Rights, is the authoritative definition of human rights standards, and increasingly referred to as customary international law. That document should provide an adequate grounding for human rights education, which should facilitate a "human rights culture." It is argued here that moral education should not seek "converts" to the principles of the Declaration, but rather emphasize open discussion, and scholarship in order that students *choose* their values. This expansion in people's consciousness in regard to a comprehensive understanding of human rights principles could directly impact constitutional change, social policy, and the fulfillment of human needs.

The Universal Declaration as the Centerpiece of Human Rights

The General Assembly of the United Nations endorsed the Universal Declaration of Human Rights with no dissenting vote on December 10, 1948. This document, a milestone on the long and difficult path of the human race (Pope John Paul II, 1979) is also the authoritative definition of the basic human rights *(United Nations Chronicle*, 1985). According to Rene Cassin, referred to as the Father of Human Rights (Szabo, 1982), it ought to be the centerpiece of human rights work. He argued that the human rights structure of the United Nations ought to be like a triptych. The central panel is the Declaration, with the two side panels the various conventions and the covenants on the one hand, and the implementation measures on the other (Szabo, 1982). Furthermore, its significance is evident in the words of Eleanor Roosevelt, the Chairperson of the Drafting Committee of the Universal Declaration, who declared it a Magna Carta (Green, 1956) for humanity.

However, this document, originally meant to be hortatory, is increasingly referred to in the United States as "customary international law" (Buergenthal, 1988; *Filartiga v. Pena*, 1980; Humphrey, 1976; Kiss, 1988; Lillich, 1989, 1990;

---

*Originally published in the *Journal of Moral Education*, Spring 1994, [Special Human Rights issue], *23*, 261-272, reprinted with permission.

Reismam, 1990; Rosensweig, 1988; Vasak, 1982; Wronka, 1992). In *Filartiga v. Pena*, for instance, a United States court ruled against Pena, a military commander, for torturing and murdering a high school student, Joelita Filartiga in Paraguay! The court composed of Federal Chief Justice Feinberg of the Second Circuit and Circuit Judges Kaufman and Kearse, reached the following conclusion:

> Official torture is now prohibited by the law of nations. This prohibition is clear and unambiguous and admits no distinction between treatment of aliens and citizens....This prohibition has become part of customary international law, as evidenced and defined by the Universal Declaration of Human Rights. (*Filartiga v. Pena* 630 F.2d, 884-885)

Since that ground breaking decision, other suits based on the "Filartiga principle," as it has become known, have been applied to government officials allegedly participating in acts of torture from Chile, Ethiopia, Guatemala, and the Philippines. Recently, a Massachusetts court declared General Hector Gramajo, a former Minister of Defense in Guatemala, in default in two Filartiga suits against him (Rohter, 1991).

The Universal Declaration, while not having authoritative legal status in the United States, nevertheless, is beginning to substantively impact U.S. jurisprudence (Lillich, 1990). The document generally considered by the legal community as definitive of norms of customary international law is now the *Restatement (Third) of the Foreign Relations Law of the United States* (D. Vagts, Professor of International Law, Harvard University, June 1990). Presently, this *Restatement* acknowledges the prohibition against torture, (as in *Filartiga*), genocide, slavery, murder, the causing of disappearances, prolonged arbitrary detention, systematic racial discrimination, and consistent patterns of gross violations of internationally recognized human rights as violations of customary international law. These standards emanate not only from the Universal Declaration, but also from human rights treaties signed by the United States which pertain to slavery, the political rights of women, the law of war and refugees, and genocide (Lillich, 1989).

The Universal Declaration, however, is the first all-inclusive statement on human rights which has, in part, attained legal status in United States courts. Furthermore, the Declaration is often cited "consistently" and "frequently," as a basic criterion for a norm becoming customary international law (Meron, 1989). It appears only a matter of time before other human rights recognized in the Universal Declaration, which numerous litigants and judges continue to invoke, (Lillich, 1990) become part of customary international law. According to Lillich (1990) "Arguments that other human rights now are part of customary international law can be expected to be made with increasing frequency" (p. 73). The opinion of the court in *Filartiga*, moreover, seemed hopeful that other internationally accepted human rights may be forthcoming in United States jurisprudence: "International law confers fundamental rights upon all people vis-a-vis their own governments...the ultimate scope of those rights will be subject for continuing refinement and elaboration" (630 F.2d 884-885).

A Philosophical-Historical Overview of the Declaration

Because discussions about human rights education cannot take place in a philosophical vacuum, it is first necessary to examine the Declaration within the contexts of its historical underpinnings. As the ensuing discussion will demonstrate, a thorough examination of human rights principles, may be antithetical to commonly accepted definitions, thereby, initially provoking resistance among educators. Yet, the "moral educator...must be personally and professionally competent and...willing to take the risks that moral education promises to provide" (Fuhrmann, 1990, p. 112). In the final analysis, these promises ought to result in a just society characterized by the fulfillment of human needs (Gil, 1992).

The Declaration consists, therefore, of four crucial tenets: the basic right to human dignity; civil and political rights; economic, social, and cultural rights; and solidarity rights. The first concept of human dignity, emphasized in Article 1, appears to emanate from the Judaic-Christian tradition (Drinan, 1987) indicative of the preponderance of western nations involved in the drafting of the Declaration. Thus, Genesis 1:27 states: "God created man in His image," which according to Talmudic scholar, Ben Azzai, embodies the "ultimate and supreme worth" of the individual (Kaplan, 1980, p. 55). Christians also accept the sanctity and dignity of the human person, proclaimed in Genesis (Henle, 1980). Similarly, The Holy Koran asserts in Sura 17:70, "Verily, we have honored every human being." According to Muslim scholar, Riffat Hassan (1982): "The sanctity and absolute value of human life is upheld by the Koran" (p. 55).

The second notion is the liberty to pursue this quest for human dignity against the abuse of political authority, emphasized primarily in Articles 2-21, most commonly referred to as civil and political rights. These freedoms, also called "first generation" or "negative" rights (Weston, 1989), include, for example, freedoms of speech, the press, and religion. They arose primarily in response to the abuses of some of the tyrannical monarchs of the seventeenth and eighteenth centuries resulting in such documents as the American Declaration of Independence and the United States Constitution's Bill of Rights. Major thrusts behind these documents were Enlightenment theorists, such as John Locke (1632-1704), who emphasized, for instance, the rights to life and liberty (i.e. freedom from arbitrary rule). These fundamental freedoms stress essentially the need for government *not* to interfere with basic human needs to express one's self or practice one's religion.

Economic, social, and cultural, otherwise known as, "second generation" or "positive" rights (Weston, 1989), which underscore the idea that government provide for basic necessities to ensure an existence worthy of human dignity, are primarily in Articles 22 through 27. Examples are rights to health care, education, employment, special protections for motherhood and children, and security in old age. They arose predominantly in reaction to the abuses of industrialization increasingly evident in the nineteenth century resulting, for instance, in massive poverty among affluence. The Soviet Constitution of 1936 exemplifies such rights. Theorists, such as Graccus Babeuf (1760-1797), Thomas Paine (1737-1809), and Karl Marx (1818-1883) appeared influential in the development of positive rights. Thomas Paine is exemplary. In the *Rights of Man* he advocates for the prevention of poverty in order that:

> The hearts of the humane will not be shocked by ragged and hungry children, and persons of seventy or eighty years of age, begging for bread. The dying poor will not be dragged from place to place to breathe their last. [and]....Widows will have a maintenance for their children and not be carted away, on the deaths of their husbands, like culprits and criminals. (Fast, 1946, pp. 255-256)

Solidarity rights, Articles 28-30, comprise the last crucial notion in the Declaration. Whereas these rights are still in the process of conceptual elaboration (Weston, 1989) they are the result of the failure of domestic sovereignty, most noticeable at the final years of the 20th century, to solve such global problems as pollution, war, and international distributive justice. They emphasize the basic human right to intergovernmental cooperation (E. Stamatapolou, Director of the Liaison Office for the U.N. Human Rights Commission, April 1990) and the notion that every right has a corresponding duty (Vasak, 1977). International cooperation to distribute food, therefore, as well as, the individual duty not to overconsume (Alston, 1989) should assist in providing for social justice on the global scale. The noted philosopher Immanual Kant (1724-1804), recognizing the hypocrisy of nations in his *Project for a Perpetual Peace* (Crocker, 1969) and accentuating that "An action to have moral worth, must be done from duty" (Curtis, 1981, p. 40), in *Fundamental Principles of the Metaphysic of Morals* seems to have paved the way for an inclusion of the idea of solidarity in human rights discussions.

A Contemporary Emphasis - The Interdependence of Rights

During the debates involved in the drafting of the Universal Declaration it appeared primarily that capitalist oriented countries emphasized first generation rights; socialist countries stressed the second generation. The poorest countries of the world, commonly referred to as the Third World were barely represented. As a consequence, therefore, the United Nations gave only scant attention at that time to rights to solidarity (U. N. Department of Public Information, 1950; *United Nations Weekly Bulletin*, 1948; Wronka, 1992).

Only recently, however, has it become pivotal to the human rights movement to recognize that rights are indivisible and interdependent (The Carter Center, 1993; Donnelly, 1989; Stamatapolou, 1989; Weston, 1989; Wronka, 1992), a "fundamental tenet of the United Nations approach to human rights" (Eide, 1987, p. 10). To illustrate, the right to travel, (a civil and political right), is possible only if one has worked (an economic and social right), earning enough wages to afford the fare to move freely. Similarly, the right to vote is meaningless if the voter lacks education, is illiterate, and/or uninformed; the right to food also implies corresponding duties to be productive and not to overconsume (Alston, 1989).

As Shridath Ramphal, (1982) Commonwealth Secretary-General to the United Nations, eloquently asserts, furthermore:

> It does the cause of human rights no good to inveigh against civil and political rights deviations while helping to perpetuate illiteracy, malnutrition, disease, infant mortality, and a low life expectancy among millions of human beings. All the dictators and all the aggressors throughout history, however, ruthless, have not succeeded in creating as much misery and suffering as the disparities between the world's rich and poor sustain today. (p. 1)

To be sure, these crucial tenets of the Declaration only briefly examined in their historical and contemporary contexts, are simplified expressions of a complex reality. Nevertheless, these demarcations should provide the necessary contours to understand the social policy implications of the Universal Declaration of Human Rights and the importance of establishing an ongoing moral educational agenda necessary to implement its principles into the next century.

Social Policy Implications

Social policies, if they are socially just, seek to create a social and international order which can effectively match human needs with available resources (Gil, 1992). A common misperception is to equate social policies with social welfare programs like Aid to Families with Dependent Children, Medicaid, or Medicare. Because a social order ought to prevent poverty, it would be better if there were no need for such programs. There ought to be no poor to help.   Social policies, therefore, are dependent upon human choices to effectively distribute rights and responsibilities in the creation of a just social and international order to realize human needs.   Whereas some species of animals, for instance, may be genetically programmed to have a caste system, humans can choose their societal arrangements (Gil, 1992). Most often, constitutions represent these choices.

Constitutions can have the potential to significantly affect social policies. State Supreme Courts in Montana, Kentucky, and Texas (Suro, 1990), for instance, recently struck down their states' school financing systems, citing "unconstitutional disparities" in what is spent for rich and poor districts. The State of New Jersey also insisted that New Jersey "provide enough aid to poor districts to allow them to provide a 'thorough and efficient' education as guaranteed by the State Constitution ("Spend Fairly," 1990). Also, in Hawaii approximately 6% of the population lack health insurance; nationwide this lack is 37%.

After researching all the U.S. state constitutions, I observed that Hawaii was the only one that recognized in the body of its constitution that health care is a human right (Wronka, 1992). Moreover, Braddock, Hemp, Fujiura, Bachelder, and Mitchell (1989) cite statistically significant differences between human rights "innovative and non-innovative" states for expenditures that benefit the developmentally disabled. There are also some national constitutions, such as those of Sweden and Cuba, which emphasize certain economic and social rights, including the rights to work, health care, shelter, and education. In those countries health care, for example, is paid for by taxes and available to everyone.

Given this visible relation between constitutions and social policies, the challenge into the next century is to incorporate the principles of the Universal Declaration into U.S. federal and state constitutions. This challenge is obvious. A comparison of the U.S. constitution, for instance, with the Declaration revealed that, while there were exemplary correspondences with civil and political rights, there were no similarities with economic, social, and solidarity rights, with the exception of protection of an author's interests (Wronka, 1992). Can these disparities account, in part, for why in the United States there are approximately 35 million who lack health insurance, approximately 3 million homeless, an average 7.1% of unemployment (Harvey, 1989), evidence of functional illiteracy at 15% *(Encyclopedia Britannica World_Data Annual,* 1993) and, according to the Children's Defense Fund (1992) approximately 28% of American children live in poverty?

State constitutions, which Supreme Court Justice Louis Brandeis urged ought to act as experiments or laboratories to expand upon the rights of the federal constitution, do not appear, however, to significantly extend these rights. Although the majority of states recognize education as a human right, and a few recognize other rights like collective bargaining or favorable remuneration for work:

> No constitution contained definitive statements relating to the right to work, to free choice of employment, and to protection against unemployment. Neither was there a right to equal pay for equal work nor an acknowledgement of the need to supplement one's income if necessary to ensure an existence worthy of human dignity. No constitution acknowledged the right to rest and leisure....none of the states guaranteed...rights to food, housing, medical care, necessary social services, and security in the event of unemployment, sickness, disability, widowhood, old age, or other lack of livelihood beyond one's control...[nor were] motherhood and childhood entitled to special care and assistance. (Wronka, 1992, p. 215)

Whereas ten states do assert the need for duties, none speak of the importance of the rights to solidarity or inter-governmental cooperation.

The Significance of the Educational Dimension

Incorporating human rights principles of the Declaration in the U.S. constitutions to positively affect social policy development, is not possible unless public sentiment is favorable to the idea. Consequently, it is important to develop a "human rights culture" (The Carter Center, 1993), which, utilizing the Declaration as the frame of reference, can rigorously entertain such notions as economic, social, and solidarity rights and the interdependency of rights. It is here that moral education can play a pivotal role.

In the United States it has become apparent, however, that civil and political rights tend to dominate human rights discussions. The official policy of the United States, for example, is the "priority of civil and political rights" (Abrams, 1990). Also, an official government publication which The Commission on the Bicentennial of the United States (1989) distributed to high school classes for the recent bicentennial celebration of the United States Constitution, although entitled "Human Rights Under the Constitution," makes no mention of economic, social, or solidarity rights. I know of no high school student or text acknowledging that Thomas Jefferson was a proponent of the right to employment. Similarly, on the college level, a classic text by Gunther (1992) examining basic issues of American law gives only scant attention to other than first generation rights.

I can also recall my own experience with both high school and college texts which refer to thinkers like Babeuf or Marx as "utopian idealists." Later, I would learn that these and other "idealists" advocated health care, education, and full employment. Can it be that education, which may mask ideology, has tended to socialize me and other Americans into accepting what has become known as "structural violence" (Gil, 1992) (i.e. a social order inhospitable to the fulfillment of human needs)? While I do not doubt the importance of civil and political rights, I am, nevertheless, inclined to agree with Philip Alston (1990), Chairperson of the United Nations Committee on Economic, Social, and Cultural rights who states: "Any U.S. group that might contemplate taking economic rights seriously in the future would have to bear in mind that a significant segment of public opinion would be actively opposed to the idea" (p. 389).

Teaching human rights in psychology, social policy, and research classes for the past five years has also taught me that students are, initially, resistant, if not resentful, to the acceptance of other than first generation rights. (I amply document these experiences in V.K. Kool [1993], *Non-violence: Social and psychological issues).* Words like "socialism," "idealism," or claims that "humans are basically selfish" tend to dominate discussions. I have previously demonstrated (Wronka, 1992) that despite its growing significance worldwide, there is significant resistance to the Declaration in U.S. government leaders. For example, the U.S. representative to the United Nations, Ms. Jeanne Kirkpatrick referred to it as a "letter to Santa Clause" (Laquer and Rubin, 1990, p. 364). These ideas surely have affected the U.S. culture in the United States and this is seen in students' resistance in the classroom. Although my focus here is the Declaration when I teach human rights, I also mention some of the many human rights covenants following it, like the Convention Against Torture. I discuss the fact that the U.S. has still not ratified the Torture Convention, in part, because ratification would invalidate the *Ingraham V. Wright* (1977)   Supreme Court decision allowing corporal punishment in schools ("Human Rights Treaty Update," 1991). Despite students' resistance to these uncomfortable issues, I can honestly say that by the conclusion of the semester, most students are ardent supporters of human rights as advocated by the Universal Declaration.

I cannot precisely account for this transformation. To be sure, I offer the Declaration as a framework for discussion, not indoctrination.   Thus, I acknowledge as did Eleanor Roosevelt that it is a good document (U.N.

Department of Public Information, 1950), not a perfect one. It has its limitations. It may be too "eurocentric," for instance. As the debates prior to its drafting revealed, some Moslem countries felt that freedom of religion may lessen the value of Islam and be used as a pretext for political activism from more economically secure countries. Also, some cultures do not believe that a person has the right to marry. Rather, individuals are betrothed or marriages arranged between families.

While one thus has to acknowledge that the Universal Declaration may have its limitations, it remains noteworthy that its worldwide significance has grown, especially since the recent World Conference on Human Rights in Vienna reaffirmed its principles (Riding, 1993). It is becoming more apparent, therefore, that there is a connection among the various kinds of rights (civil, political, economic, social, and solidarity). As one thinks beyond civil and political right as the only set of rights to be recognized as universal human rights, one will begin to question specific economic policies and actions, such as mass transfers of wealth through capital gain, stock market speculation, rather than through "the sweat of one's brow."

And one may also wonder whether the cultural belief that humans are "intrinsically" selfish, may conveniently cater to established elites or to a social order that values competition, rather than cooperation. Noteworthy also is that unemployment can lead to child abuse (Gil, 1973) and lack of education is a prime predictor of adolescent pregnancy (Caldas, 1993). These examples indicate that one needs to consider economic and social rights, as well as, civil and political rights, if one interprets the frequently mentioned interdependence and indivisibility of human rights to mean that human rights are expressive of a comprehensive moral concern for human well being.

This comprehensive understanding of human rights is required for adopting an educational perspective on human rights. Far more is at issue than mere legalisms. At issue is human rights education that must have "lived meaning" (Colaizzi, 1976) for students, a comprehensive set of principles that individuals can choose to apply in their daily lives.

Educators must make every effort to assume the task of embracing the moral perspective entailed in human rights. This choice could result in a human rights culture which would strengthen public sentiment toward modifying constitutions, thereby, impacting social policies toward more humanitarian directions. But, such a culture is possible only through scholarly analysis, and open debate of the many issues which the Universal Declaration engenders. Rather than seeking "converts" to the Declaration, it is necessary to expand people's consciousness concerning a comprehensive, rather than limited definition of human rights.

In addition to the opportunities available in the formal educational setting, possibilities are endless in regard to promulgating the Universal Declaration of

Human Rights. I have, for instance, recently initiated "The Universal Declaration of Human Rights Project" which aims to use the Declaration as a frame of reference, assess progress toward the realization of internationally acknowledged human rights, draw attention to significant violations, and suggest avenues to overcome such violations. I have also begun developing a curriculum with both cognitive and experiential exercises illustrating, for instance, the interconnection between rights and duties. Articles pointing to gaps between the Universal Declaration and U.S. and other constitutions are useful as well. One may also attempt to develop strategies to place some of the principles of the Universal Declaration on the ballot like the right to health care, to come up with city proclamations endorsing its principles, or to form a local human rights task force. Considering that increasingly, the idea of human rights is widely accepted among the general populace (Drinan, 1987; Henkin, 1978; "Movement for Humanity," 1990; Ring, 1993; Trials and Error," 1991), people in general appear amenable to examining in depth the Universal Declaration. I invite the reader to creatively tap into this growing public concern for human rights.

A Final Caveat

The doctrine of humanitarian intervention seems to have become a troublesome, yet influential, principle in the promulgation of human rights. Promoted by Hugo Grotius (1583-1645) it recognizes "as lawful the use of force by one or more states to stop the maltreatment by a state of its own nationals when that conduct was so brutal and largescale as to shock the conscience of the community of nations" (Buergenthal, 1988, p. 3). As such, human rights, a definite humanitarian goal, may be a pretext to engage in war, masking, therefore, a "hidden agenda" (Kristol, 1990). Was the primary purpose of the American Civil War to free the slaves or to encourage the migration of cheap labor to the growing industrial North? Did the United States invade Iraq, because of the human rights abuses of Saddam Hussein, or was oil at stake? While my purpose is not to answer questions such as these, it is to demonstrate that violent methods to promote human rights are counterproductive, leading to endless suffering. Violence, according to Martin Luther King, only begets more violence.

If, indeed, the Universal Declaration of Human Rights is a Magna Carta for humanity, then human rights educators and activists can learn from the lessons of the original Magna Carta of 1215. The Barons at Runnymede could have easily and violently killed the abusive King John and his entourage. Yet, for reasons still unclear, they chose instead to draw up an "eternal" document, the Magna Carta. Many of the rights it contained like trial by jury, the right to travel, and representative government (Stringham, 1966) remain with us today, their timelessness, a living testimony to the efficacy of non-violence. Similarly, only non-violent measures can advance the principles of the United Nations Universal Declaration of Human Rights to promote and ensure now and into the 21st century a more humane and socially just world.

REFERENCES

ABRAMS, M. (1990) *On the economic and social rights of the Universal Declaration of Human Rights.* For inquiries contact: Mr. Martin Abrams, U.S. Representative to the U.N. Human Rights Commission, Geneva, Switzerland.

ALSTON, P. (1990) U.S. ratification of the covenant on economic, social and cultural rights: The need for an entirely new strategy. *American Journal of International Law, 84,* 365-393.

ALSTON, P. (1989) International law and the right to food. In R. P. Claude & B. H. Weston (Eds.), *Human rights in the world community* (pp. 142-150). Philadelphia: University of Pennsylvania Press.

BRADDOCK, D., HEMP, R., FUJIURA, G., BACHELDER, L., & MITCHELL, D. (1989, May) Third national study of public spending for mental retardation and developmental disabilities: Summary (Report No. 45). *Public Policy Monograph Series: Institute for the Study of Developmental Disabilities, 45.* Chicago: University of Illinois Press.

BUERGENTHAL, T. (1988) *International human rights law.* St. Paul, MN: West.

CALDAS, S. J. (1993) Current theoretical perspectives on adolescent pregnancy and childbearing in the United States. *Journal of Adolescent Research, 8* (1), 4-20.

THE CARTER CENTER FOR HUMAN RIGHTS. (1993) *The Atlanta Statement.* Atlanta, GA: Author.

CHILDREN'S DEFENSE FUND. (1992) *The state of America's children.* New York: Author.

COLAIZZI, P. (1976). A phenomenological approach to learning In Valle, R. & Halling, S. (Eds.). *Existential-phenomenological alternatives to psychology* (pp. 78-92). New York: Plenum.

THE COMMISSION ON THE BICENTENNIAL OF THE UNITED STATES CONSTITUTION. (1989) Human rights under the constitution (Unit two). *Constitution: Let's talk about it.* Washington, DC: Author *The*

CROCKER, L. (Ed.). (1969) *The Age of Enlightenment.* New York: Walker.

CURTIS, M. (Ed.). (1981) *The theories great political* (Vol. 2). New York: Avon.

DONNELLY, J. (1989) *Universal human rights in theory and practice.* Ithaca, NY: Cornell University Press.

DRINAN, R. (1987) *Cry of the oppressed: The history and hope of the human rights revolution.* San Francisco: Harper and Row.

EIDE, A. (1987) United Nations Commission on Human Rights. *Report on the right to adequate food as a human right.* (E/CN.4/Sub.2/1987/23). New York: United Nations.

ENCYCLOPEDIA WORLD DATA ANNUAL (1993). Chicago, IL: Author.

FAST, H. (1946) *The selected works of Tom Paine and citizen Tom Paine.* New York: Random House.

FILARTIGA V. PENA-IRALA. 630 F. 2d 876 (1980).

FUHRMANN, B. (1990) *Adolescence, adolescents.* Glenview, IL: Scott, Foresman.

GIL, D. (1973) *Violence against children: Physical child abuse in the United States.* Cambridge, MA: Harvard University Press.

Gil, D. (1992) *Unravelling social policy* (rev. 5th ed.). Cambridge: Schenkman.

GREEN, J. F. (1956) *The U.N. and human rights.* Washington: Brookings Institute.

GUNTHER, G. (1992) *Constitutional law* (12th Edition). Mineola, NY: Foundation.

HARVEY, P. (1989) *Securing the right to employment.* Princeton: Princeton University Press.

HASSAN, R. (1982) On human rights and the Qur'anic perspective. In A. Swidler (Ed.). *Human rights in religious traditions* (pp. 51-65). New York: Pilgrim.

HENKIN, L. (1978) *The rights of man today.* Boulder, CO: Westview.

HENLE, R. (1980) A Catholic view of human rights. In A. Rosenbaum (Ed.), *The philosophy of human rights: International perspectives* (pp. 87-93). Westport, CT: Greenwood.

HUMAN RIGHTS TREATY UPDATE. (1991, Spring) Human rights advocacy interest group newsletter: American society of international law, *2* (1) p. 2.

HUMPHREY, J. (1976) The International Bill of Rights: Scope and implementation. *William and Mary Law Review, 17*, 524-541.

INGRAHAM V. WRIGHT. 430 U.S. 651 (1977).

JEFFERSON, T. (1991) In the *Encyclopedia Britannica* (pp. 349-53). Chicago: Encyclopedia Britannica Press.

KAPLAN, A. (1980) Human Relations and Human Rights in Judaism. In A. Rosenbaum (Ed.), *The philosophy of human rights: International perspectives* (pp. 53-85). Westport, CT: Greenwood.

KISS, A. (1988) The role of the Universal Declaration of Human Rights in international law. In United Nations Center for Human Rights, Fortieth Anniversary of the Universal Declaration of Human Rights [Special issue]. *Bulletin of Human Rights,* 47-52.

KOOL, V.K. (1993) *Non-violence: Social and psychological issues.* Lanham, MD: University Press of America.

KRISTOL, I. (1990) Human rights: The hidden agenda. In W. Laqueur and B. Rubin (Eds.), *The human rights reader* (pp. 391-404). New York: New American Library.

LAQUEUR, W., & RUBIN, B. (Eds.). (1990) *The human rights reader* (rev. ed.). New York: New American Library.

LILLICH, R. (1989) The Constitution and international human rights. *American Journal of International Law, 83, 4*, 851-862.

_____. (1990) The United States Constitution and international human rights law. *Harvard Human Rights Journal, 3*, 53-82.

MERON, T. (1989) *Human rights and humanitarian norms.* Oxford: Clarendon.

MOVEMENT FOR HUMANITY. (1990, April 10) *The New York Times*, p. A12.

POPE JOHN PAUL II. (1979) *U.S.A. The message of justice, peace,and love.* Boston: Daughters of St. Paul.

RAMPHAL, S. (1982) Address to the United Nations. For inquiries contact: Shridath Ramphal, Commonwealth Secretary-General to the United Nations. New York, New York.

REISMAN, M. (1990) Sovereignty and human rights in contemporary international law. *American Journal of International Law, 84,* 866-876.

RESTATEMENT (THIRD) OF THE FOREIGN LAW OF THE UNITED STATES. (1987) For inquiries contact: Professor D. Vagts, Associate Reporter, Harvard School of International Law, Harvard University, 02138.

RIDING, A. (1993, June 26) *The New York Times,* p. 2.

ROHTER, L. (1991, November 15) Ex-dictator of Haiti is facing human rights suit. *The New York Times,* p. 3.

ROSENZWEIG, M. (1988) Psychology and United Nations human rights efforts. *American   Psychologist, 43,* 79-86.

SPEND FAIRLY FOR SCHOOLS. THEN WHAT? (1990, June 6) *New York Times,* p.A22.

STAMATAPOULOU, E. (1989, November 8-11) The UN's role in protecting human rights. Presentation at the *National Conference on the United States and the United Nations.* Washington, DC. (Available from UNA-USA, 485 Fifth Avenue, NY, NY 10017-6104).

STRINGHAM, R. (1966) *Magna Carta: Fountainhead of freedom.* Rochester, NY: Aqueduct.

SURO, R. (1990, March 11) Courts ordering financing changes in public schools. *The New York Times,* pp. A1, A28.

SZABO, I. (1982) Historical foundations of human rights and subsequent developments. In K. Vasak (Ed.), *The international dimensions of human rights.* (Vol. 1) (pp. 11-41). Westport, CT: Greenwood.

TRIALS AND ERROR IN CHINA. (February 1, 1991) *The New York Times,* p. A28.

THE UNITED NATIONS. (1948) *The United Nations Weekly Bulletin.* New York: Author.

THE UNITED NATIONS. (1950) Department of Public Information. New York: Author.

THE UNITED NATIONS. (1985) *The United Nations Chronicle.* New York: Author.

VASAK, K. (1977) *A 30-year struggle: The sustained efforts to give force of law to the Universal Declaration of Human Rights.* New York: United Nations.

VASAK, K. (1982) Distinguishing criteria of human rights. In K. Vasak and P. Alston (Ed.), *The international dimensions of human rights* (Vol. 1) (pp. 3-10). Westport, CT: Greenwood.

WESTON, B. H. (1989) Human rights. In R. Claude and B. Weston (Eds.), *Human rights in the world community* (pp. 12-29). Philadelphia: University of Pennsylvania Press.

WRONKA, J. M. (1992) *Human rights and social policy in the 21st century: A history of the idea of human rights and comparison of the United Nations Universal Declaration of Human Rights with United States federal and state constitutions.* Lanham, MD: University Press of America.

ᄆᄆᄆᄆᄆᄆᄆᄆᄆᄆᄆᄆᄆᄆᄆᄆᄆᄆᄆᄆᄆᄆᄆ

"SCIENCE" AND INDIGENOUS CULTURES*

ABSTRACT: This article assesses the expert-oriented approach of the social sciences and helping professions. This orientation, which appears embedded in Western approaches to science, emphasizes that those who have mastered the workings and intricacies of scientific method and helping are professionals or experts. Given the recent experiences and background of the author who worked in the mental health and alcoholism fields primarily with Eskimos and Athabascan Native Americans in the Arctic and Sub-Arctic regions of Alaska, this essay stresses the relevance/irrelevance of scientific findings to indigenous peoples. Without discounting "Science" completely, the author examines alternative modes-of-being-with-others in a communal way, rather than as "objects" in a scientific study. Bringing attention to the reaffirmation of the Universal Declaration of Human Rights at the recent World Conference on Human Rights in Vienna and the United Nations Declaration of 1993 as The International Year for the World's Indigenous Peoples, this essay ends with a call to consciousness in regard to the ongoing situation of indigenous peoples worldwide.

Science and the Problem of the Expert

An expert-oriented mentality permeates western science and the helping professions in general. It has given us a sense of "surplus powerlessness." By giving deference to experts, we have undermined our confidence in ourselves to solve our own problems as individuals and as members of a community. As Michael Lerner (1985) states in *Surplus Powerlessness* in a chapter appropriately entitled "Science Legitimating Domination":

---

*Originally published in the *Humanistic Psychologist*, 21, 341-353, reprinted with permission.

Many people feel even more unsure of themselves, because they can't quite understand what the experts are really saying, garbed as it often is in the language of obscurity.....but who constitutes the experts as experts? Supposedly this is done by some entity called 'Science'...The problem is that science is not the only, or even the best way to organize our experience according to our current needs. In failing to understand the real limits of science as an approach to reality, we tend to disempower ourselves. (p. 203)

Science, therefore, does not appear the *only*, or even the best way to organize our experience. An examination of some of the limits of scientific "findings" as they relate to indigenous peoples should help illuminate how traditionally oriented scientific methods have tended to distort the lived experience of indigenous peoples. While my purpose is not to discredit science completely, it is rather to provoke discussion and dialogue concerning broader questions of the relationship between more traditional ways of knowing (i.e. science, from the Latin *scio* meaning "to know") and human rights and social justice, with particular attention to indigenous peoples.

I do not believe, therefore, that much of the *sine qua non* of scientific method which consists of operationalizing of variables, setting of confidence levels, assumption of the null hypothesis are the *only* ways to look for truth. Certainly, this method *may* be one way to ascertain an aspect of the reality of a phenomenon.   Phenomenological approaches, sometimes referred to as "Heuristic" (Moustakas, 1990; Babbie, 1992; Tyson, 1992), while not hostile to such a method, tend to urge viewing such findings in context. Similarly, as it is increasingly well known in academia, Giorgi (1971), analyzing the assumptions of the social sciences, which emulate the methods of the natural sciences, calls for a "human" rather than "social" scientific approach to phenomenon, which in varying situations should be more fecund.

Much, if not all, of the helping professions predicates itself on the assumption that "we" are the professionals, experts if you will, "administering" its services to the population at large in order to "cure" them of their ills. The problem of the expert is long embedded in the humanistic tradition. Keen (1972), for has examined this problem seeking other alternatives to "Freudian Consciousness," which also stresses the need for the expert. and More recently, Katz (1981;1982; 1983/84) has written about the problem of the expert-oriented mentality which appears at odds with communal healing practices among the Kalahari !Kung. According to Katz (1981), "current education and training of community mental health workers in the West have focused on the accumulation of knowledge and on healing technology" in contradistinction to the !Kung healer who disavows "the accumulation of power" (p.57).

1993 as the International Year for Indigenous Peoples

Concern for issues pertaining to indigenous peoples today, who, if living in the United States are often referred to as Native Americans, also appears especially relevant in light of the United Nations Declaration of this year as The International Year for Indigenous Peoples. The theme is this year is "Indigenous Peoples-A New Partnership" (United Nations, 1993). Furthermore, decrying the consumerist and individualist orientation of the world's dominant cultures (of which science is a part) in Europe and the United States, Worldwatch Institute (1993) urging support for indigenous people worldwide, recognizes that "They may offer living examples of cultural patterns that can help revive ancient values within everyone: devotion to future generations, ethical regard for nature, and commitment to community among people" (p. 100).

Background of the Author

It is important to point out at the outset, however, that I am male, white and middle class. Consequently, I am aware that my perceptions are biased, subjective and emanate from a particular perspective. However, rather than claiming "objectivity" and then purporting to find "truth" via rejection of a "null hypothesis," I will attempt to provoke discussion of these issues by relating to some of my work and other experiences in the Arctic and Sub-Arctic regions of Alaska. I had lived in Alaska from 1981-1987 where I, among other things, developed a Generalist Counseling Program that was to be "culturally sensitive" to the Eskimo population of the region and was Director of a Mental Health/Substance Abuse Treatment Center in a predominantly Athabascan community.

Descriptions of Helping

Unfortunately, therefore, the very notions of "professionalism" and the "expert," in disciplines that are to help, rather than hinder, appears to have set up a hierarchical relationship, in itself a western ideology, which is at odds with non-western cultures that espouse more communal and non-hierarchical treatment methodologies. Although some elders have spoken of shamans who, at times, would instill fear in individuals, communal ways of healing appear to have been much more permeating and widespread.

When I asked elders (as well as some of my students recounting stories from their elders), for instance, to describe traditional Eskimo ways of helping those in need, if possible, prior to the arrival of the "White Man," responses did not appear to emphasize "experts" *over* "non-experts," or notions of "mental health professional" or "learned person" over the "inept," but rather a kind of "struggling together" in the face of the many hardships that life in the Arctic produced. In times of starvation, for example, individuals would at times share what they found in their "honey buckets." Sometimes even persons would cut off parts of their skin which they in turn, would share with other members of the community. It is well known how a hunter in this present day shares the meat from a "kill," rather than hoard it for him or herself.

Also, upon the introduction of alcohol to the community, some elders discussed with sadness how people would follow tracks in the snow which appeared "wobbling." Then, if they would find a person drunk or unconscious and "everyone would give him [or her] much love." Noteworthy also was that notions of "orphaned child" appeared totally absent from the worldview of the Eskimo. It was difficult, for example, to get the idea across of "orphan." According to one elder, all children were loved and like gifts to the community.

Not one person talked about anything akin to "talking cures," or "free association." People didn't sit with one person for something similar to a fifty-minute session. I learned in fact of a phenomenon known as "white man's disease." This "disease" is when "Whites," as they are sometimes called, "use big words, sound important, and speak fast." In addition, it appears that children are treated with utmost respect and are socialized into a strong sense of mutual responsibility. According to some elders, for instance: "Do not shove a child around. A child that gets shoved around at an early age like that always ends up feisty, getting into fights"; and "When we were kids are parents told us...to help people.... We should we kindly to all people" (Craig and Skin, 1983, pp. 11-12). In fact, my impressions were that overall in order to "help," one could prevent misfortune by a strong sense of community, characterized by mutual responsibility and caring.

Recent Developments

Currently, in Native American cultures, there are sweatlodges, which are ways to purify one's self and pow-wows, where Native Americans discuss communal issues and celebrate a sense of community through dance. Noteworthy also is what appears to be an extremely effective community approach towards alcoholism in the population at Alkali Lake (The Honour of All, 1984), a predominantly Native American community. In that locale, an approximately 90% alcoholism rate among the population was reduced to approximately 5% By enlisting the help of concerned clergy, businesspeople, "everyday townsfolk" *and* human service providers, an all out effort was attempted to once and for all eradicate alcoholism in that town. It was undoubtedly a communal effort to achieve a "quality" sobriety.

I am reminded here of the words of Mr. John Schaeffer (personal communication, January, 1983), an Eskimo leader and recently president of The Northwest Arctic Native Association who lamented the fact that despite the influx of helping professionals during the last twenty years, alcoholism, substance abuse, suicide, and domestic violence rates had remained constant. My point certainly is not to "romanticize" the Native American, to embellish the idea of the"noble savage," nor to claim entirely that "their" approach is "better" than a "Western" approach. Yet, it is necessary to recognize that in some contexts assumptions of science and helping should not go unquestioned.

Following the example of Alkalai Lake, then, Native American communities appear to have adopted a more communal approach, consistent with their apparent ways of socialization, rather than rely *solely* on western healers and therapies. For example, in schools, some individuals, Native Americans themselves, have instituted an hour a week for students, from the first to the twelfth grades simply to talk about things that might be bothering them. The rationale, according to the originator of this idea, Rudy Hamilton, himself a Native American, was that he felt that Native children had a tendency to hold things in. When they became older they might escape through depression, alcoholism, and in the worst of cases, suicide.

Since the program was initiated, there was not one suicide attempt in his village. Prior to that program there was on the average one attempt every two years for the past ten years. Although one cannot draw a direct causal relationship between that program along with other communal "healing" attempts in that village, nevertheless, there were undoubtedly changes in the village. These changes were brought about when, like in Alkali Lake, the individuals; white, red, or brown, united in a cause, and decided to "empower" themselves. Through a mysterious, if not spiritual process of "collective passion," (Rosenstock-Huessy, 1972), they were *determined* improve their lot.

The Paradox of the Utilization of Mental Health and Alcoholism Services

My experiences in Alaska seemed to indicate a kind of paradox with the utilization of state funded mental health and alcoholism programs. On the one hand, most residents undoubtedly respected many of the human service professionals' dedication and concern for their problems; on the other hand, my impression was that quite often these programs were underutilized. Certain *individuals* whether White or Native, were sought after rather than specific programs.

It is significant then that the problem of underutilization appeared to be not so much the service providers, but rather the strategies and programs which emanated from these policies. These policies, in turn, were steeped in scientific ideologies that were problematic. The problem then was not the many dedicated and caring helping professionals who practiced in the field, but rather an issue endemic to the helping professions in general.

As a whole then, the helping professions appeared steeped and embedded in western ideology. Treatment methodologies, consequently, tended to carry much conceptual baggage and scientific bias. Putting aside the more obvious fact of dedicated and culturally sensitive providers versus less dedicated and culturally insensitive ones, could there be other explanations for an apparent "failure" of human service programs on the whole among indigenous populations?

Could one explanation be that despite the fact that the helping professions tend to decry the "infiltration" of middle class values in "their" programs, nevertheless, they continue to provide programs that are essentially middle class in orientation? The ethical standards for the American Psychological Association, for example, urge that "treatment" should be culturally relevant. Nevertheless, the very fact that treatment is set up as a hierarchical relationship, (i.e. therapist-patient) appears culturally irrelevant. A credo, for example, in the human services is that people come to practitioners because they are "professionals," the experts. But, if successful treatment methodologies such as Alkali Lake do not assume "professionalism," but rather "community" as primary to the healing process, can it not be said that the basic philosophical assumptions of some of the helping professions tend to be misguided?

Inupiat Ilitqusiat as an Example

I would like to illustrate the embededness of treatment methods in western ideology and scientific method by way of another example. *Inupiat Ilitiquisiat* is a kind of "spirit movement" among the Inupiat Eskimo of Northwest Alaska. This movement, which stresses tribal identification, asserts that survival of the Eskimo community "depends on our ability to restore our traditional values ad take on our responsibilities to ourselves and to others" (Christensen, 1982, p.11) As part of this movement, the elders drew up a list of "Inupiaq Values." These values are: Knowledge of Language, Sharing, Respect for Elders, Love for Children, Hard Work, Knowledge of Family Tree, Avoid Conflict, Respect for Nature, Spirituality, Humor, Family Roles, Hunter Success, Domestic Skills, Humility and Responsibility to Tribe.

It is noteworthy that one value is to "Avoid Conflict." In this case, the questions then becomes to what extent should one teach "assertiveness" as a highly esteemed goal of psychotherapy, in western cultures. No study seems to scientifically validate assertiveness as essential to one's being, although studies do point to a lowering of self-esteem as a failure to assert oneself (Wallace, 1984, p.10). This one "truth" among many other problematics of human existence has been supposedly "found," by one or even a plethora of scientific studies that have been duplicated and found to be "valid" and "reliable." The helping professions which purport to have developed their treatment approaches on scientific evidence, continue with the dissemination of this "truth" despite the fact that it *might* not be culturally relevant.   Thus, the question of assertiveness training courses in cultures where avoiding conflict is a value, might be culturally "inappropriate." Only, the community can decide the relevance or irrelevance of such a course.

Science and Social Justice

At its worst, scientific enterprise could be described as a form a colonialism and imperialism.   Although these words have tended to have pejorative meanings and to be associated with radical social movements, they, like all explanations need to be looked at, if we are to truly have a society based on the most decent of values, human rights and social justice.   In 1978 a national report was compiled on the mental health problems of American Indians.   The report found:

> Without reservation...alcoholism and alcohol abuse affects directly and indirectly the entire national Indian community...and, the concept of the colonized and colonizer relationship found in Indian countries is probably the most appropriate way to view these issues. (Blauner, 1972, p.5)

That report was submitted to the President's Commission on Mental Health! Many leading scholars of colonialism point to the fact that even the best quality care of the colonizer subverts its positive effects.   In the end:

> Alienation manifests itself both through the fact that my means of recovery belongs to another, that the object of my desire (in this case sobriety) is the inaccessible property of another, and through the fact that each object as well as my own activity is alien to itself, since everything and everybody, the capitalists not excluded is dominated by an inhuman fee...(Zaher, 1974, p.5)

Thus, even if one recovers, it can also be seen as a kind of "spiritual" death (Colorado, 1986). The helping professions then, by leaning upon the findings of science as well as mastering the intricacies of their professions and taking on the toga of expert need to be critically evaluated as to the relevance and/or irrelevance for a particular culture, in this case, indigenous peoples.

Two Contrasting Approaches

One example of a "typical" scientific study of indigenous peoples is *Psychodynamic Problems of Adaptation Among the MacKenzie Delta Eskimos* by Lubart (1970). The rather complex and meaningful world of the Eskimo is immediately seen in terms of scientific constructs. For example: "This report is an attempt to correlate observed patterns of social disturbance among Mackenzie Delta Eskimos with factors in basic personality. Particular emphasis is placed on points of potential conflict implicit in the structure of Eskimo character" (Lubart, 1970, p. xi). Its methodology consisted essentially of the "detached" and "objective" scientist studying his "subjects," (i.e. the Eskimo), in typical scientific fashion:

> Aside from general observations of behaviour, about 60 depth interviews were obtained in serial sessions. Together with many less formal interviews and spontaneous discussions, these provided life histories and furnished a great deal of material for psychoanalytic interpretation. (Lubart, 1970, p. xii)

It is not within the scope of this paper to cite this study in depth. However, some of its conclusions are noteworthy: "Hedonism has always been a part of Eskimo culture and is the route to relief from tension in many cultures when an individual's goals of validation are confused, non-operational and immature" (p. 44) He continues: "Pathological patterns and potentials related to the system of permissive child reading...can be disastrous" (p. 44).

Given the "scientific" findings of this study, should human service providers and policy makers, therefore, set up programs that "decrease" hedonism or that teach parent "effectiveness" training in order to counteract the deleterious effects of "permissive" child rearing "found" to exist among the Eskimo population?

By using such value laden terms such as "hedonism" and "permissive" isn't that an attempt to "force" a western interpretation of an extremely complex culture into pejorative labels? Couldn't one say that such labels are, at their worst, examples of colonialism? To construct programs from these value laden labels, despite their supposed scientific objectivity, which experts "discovered", could possibly be considered even further forms of colonialism.

One shouldn't be quick, however, to totally dismiss science as a worthless effort. Robert Coles (1977), for example, in his classic work *Eskimos, Chicanos and Indians* astutely acknowledged his own biases and tried to come up with a more descriptive, rather than categorical and pejorative study. He was aware that considering people as "objects" in a scientific study tended to dehumanize them. Thus, he perceived as severely limiting the effort to "get"

information from individuals in order to label and make abstract generalizations about "them".
Coles writes, for example:

> I am, or at least I have wanted to be, exceedingly wary about categorical, overinclusive descriptionsancertainly, causative links: *this* (in the home, the culture, the larger society) leads to *that* in Eskimo children or adults....If mere abstract remarks are the essence of what the reader ends up taking away from this book, then I will have, by my lights, failed miserably. The whole point of this work has been to put myself (body, mind and I pray but cannot at all be sure, heart and soul) in a position, with respect to a number of children, that offers them a chance to indicate a certain amount about themselves to me, and through me, to others. But each life, as we ought know, has its own history, its own authority, dignity, fragility, rock-bottom strength. (p. 77)

Thus, he appears to have adopted an interpretation of science that opts for participant-observation. In more academic parlance, one could say that his research was descriptive and qualitative. Whereas Lubart's study was also descriptive and qualitative, to a major extent, it nevertheless, failed to relinquish its own scientistic assumptions which resulted, in a simplistic and rather pejorative explanation of the Eskimo's world. Coles's study furthermore, appears to reject a basic assumption of research in the social sciences, to predict and control. Instead, he seeks more phenomenological criteria, such as understanding. This is not to totally discount other quantitative approaches and even qualitative approaches of which Lubart's study was but one example. Rather, both Coles's and Lubart's works were examples of scientific studies based on different assumptions.

A Call for Consciousness

The problem which I have tried to point out in this paper concerns itself with a rather erroneous supposition on the part of the expert that he/she is the sole founder of "truth" which was arrived at by means of a particular scientific method. Thus, helping modalities, social policies, and programs become based on these experts' statements rather than emanating from the social consciousness or what I have described as "collective passions" of the community at large. As a case in point, one of my Eskimo students woefully lamented: "They make life too easy for us now. Before we used to go hunting and fishing to eat. We would hunt animals like fox ad ear for clothing, too. Some of us would even make raincoats from whale intestines. We used to cut down trees and burn the wood to warm us up. Now we go to the local store and buy everything with food stamps. Often, governments just give us money to buy some of the things we need. We have lost our subsistence lifestyle and our culture."

To speculate concerning reasons for an apparently unprecedented belief in scientific expertise, Peter Berger's (1967) concept of "theodicy" appears significant. This concept refers to beliefs of people throughout the centuries about certain value systems and theological deities. People have taken these beliefs as doctrines of faith or morals. It seems that in the 1980's beliefs in science have replaced beliefs in God, Allah or Jehovah. Thus, as technology has come rushing through and challenged traditional creeds, it has supplanted old dogma with a new one. As with all belief systems, it needs to be reevaluated and assessed as to its relevance for contemporary times. If this new belief system, (i.e. science), is not assessed critically, which I have tried to initially do in this paper, it is in danger of becoming a kind of "second order level of abstraction" (Merleau-Ponty, 1962), divorced from the experience of a "lived" community. Scientific findings, therefore, may tend to obscure the richness of the lived experience of the Eskimo's world.

The World Conference on Human Rights meeting in Vienna in June of this year recently reaffirmed the principles of the Universal Declaration of Human Rights. This Declaration, signed by the United States in 1948 is increasingly referred to as customary international law and a document with burgeoning legal status for governments (Wronka, 1992). That document which stresses the little known economic and social rights (i.e. rights to health care, shelter, employment, security in old age etc.), and even lesser known, solidarity rights (i.e. rights to self-determination, intergovernmental cooperation, humanitarian disaster relief etc.) can serve as an effective primary prevention strategy to enhance well-being and mental health.

Lack of employment, for instance, is directly related to domestic violence and substance abuse (Gil, 1973; 1992). Similarly, the apparent failure of governments to provide for self-determination of Indigenous Peoples worldwide, that is, to control their own destiny, appears related to many of the problems which they face. Certainly, science with its emphasis upon the "expert" and the "professional" seems to play a major role in diminishing this sense of control among indigenous peoples. Only science as a means to empower, rather than a method which creates surplus powerlessness, will provide hope for a socially just and more humane world.

REFERENCES

Babbie, E. (1992). *The practice of social research* (rev. 6th ed.). Belmont, CA: Wadsworth.
Berger P. (1967). *The sacred canopy.* Garden City, NY: Anchor.

Blauner, R. (1972). *Racial oppression in America.* Berkely, CA.: Harper and Row.

Christensen, J. (Ed.). (1982). *Inupiat Ilitqusiat: Yesterday, today, and tomorrow.* Kotzebue, AK: Maniilaq.

Coles, R. (1977). *Eskimos, Chicanos, and Indians.* Boston, MA.: Little, Brown.

Colorado, P. (1986). *Native American alcoholism: An issue of survival.* Unpublished doctoral dissertation. Waltham, MA: The Heller School, Brandeis University.

Craig, R. & Skin, R. (1982). *Algaqsruutit: Words of wisdom.* Kotzebue, AK: Maniilaq.

Gil, D. (1973). *Violence against children: Physical child abuse in the United States.* Chicago: Harvard University Press.

_____. (1992). *Unravelling social policy.* Rochester, VT: Schenkman.

Giorgi, A. (1970). *Psychology as a human science* NY, NY: Harper and Row.

The Honor of All. (1984). Phil Lucas Productions. Available from: 800-328-9000.

Katz, R. (1981). Education as transformation: Becoming a healer among the !Kung and the Fijans. *Harvard Educational Review, 51,* 57-78.

_____.(1982). *Boiling energy: Community healing among the Kalahari !Kung.* Cambridge, MA: Harper and Row.

_____. (1983/84). Empowerment and synergy: Expanding the community's healing resources. *Prevention in Human Services, 3,* 201-226.

Lerner, M. (1985). *Surplus powerlessness.* Oakland, CA: The Institute of Labor and Mental Health.

Lubart, J. (1970). *Psychodynamic problems of adaptation among the Mac Kenzie Delta Eskimos.* Ottawa, Canada: Department of Indian Affairs.

Merleau Ponty, M. (1962). *The phenomenology of perception.* NY, NY: Humanities Press.

Moustakas, C. (1990). *Heuristic research: Design, methodology, and applications.* Newbury Park, CA: Sage.

Rosenstock-Huessy, E. (1972) *Out of revolution: Autobiography of western man.* Norwich, VT: Argo.

Tyson, K. (1992). A new approach to relevant scientific research for practitioners: The heuristic paradigm. *Social Work, 37*(2), pp. 541-556).

United Nations Department of Public Information. (1993, April). New York: Author.

Wallace, C. (1984). *Behavior modification.* Los Angeles, CA: Behavioral Systems Association for Advanced Training in the Behavioral Sciences.

Wronka, J. (1992*). Human rights and social policy in the 21st century: A history of the idea of human rights and comparison of the United Nations Universal Declaration of Human Rights with United States federal and state constitutions.* Lanham, MD: University Press of America.

Zaher, M. (1974). *Colonialism and alienation.* NY, NY: Monthly Review Press.

Recall the face of the poorest and most helpless person you have seen and ask yourself if the next step you contemplate is going to be of any use to that person.
- *Mahatma Gandhi*, M. K. Gandhi's wit and wisdom.

CHAPTER EIGHT

ꗈꗈꗈꗈꗈꗈꗈꗈꗈꗈꗈꗈꗈꗈꗈꗈꗈꗈꗈꗈꗈꗈꗈ

SOCIAL ACTION IN THE STRUGGLE FOR HUMAN DIGNITY

HUMAN RIGHTS*

In 1938 at the Conference of Evian, called largely upon the initiative of the United States, international leaders gathered to consider Hitler's atrocities against German citizens. Instead of condemning the horrors of the Third Reich, however, the conference concluded that no country had the right to intervene in another's domestic affairs. The result was one of the most dreadful pogroms in history, more commonly known as the holocaust, in which 10 million people, primarily Jews, but also homosexuals, gypsies, Poles, and people with disabilities were massacred.

To prevent such a massacre from happening again, the United Nations (UN) was formed in June 1945. However, many governments at that time appeared hesitant to include detailed provisions of human rights in the U.N. Charter. The Soviet Union, had its Gulag; the United States its numerous

---

* Originally published in R. Edwards (Ed.). the *Encyclopedia of Social Work*, (NASW Press, 1995), 1404-1418 reprinted with permission.

racial problems and sprawling ghettos; and Europe its many colonial empires (Buergenthal, 1988).   Therefore, were it not for the efforts of a few deeply committed delegates and representatives of some forty-two *non-governmental* organizations (NGO's), human rights would have received "only a passing reference" (Farer, 1989, p. 195).

Status in the 1990s

Currently, as the result of such human rights groups as Helsinki Watch, Children's Rights International, and Amnesty International, the idea of human rights is so widespread and commonly accepted (Henkin, 1978; Drinan, 1987; "A Movement for Humanity," 1990; Trials and Error," 1991; Eide, 1992; "On Human Rights Day," 1993), that no government would say that it is against human rights. To do so, would create a public outcry, if not rebellion. .

However, government reluctance appears to continue. At the 1993 World Conference on Human Rights in Vienna some have claimed "cultural relativism" in a seeming attempt to thwart human rights developments. Again, NGO's and the people in general have not accepted such explanations (Henkin & Hargrove, 1994).   As an illustration, the 1989 slaughter inTiananmen Square, may be rationalized, given an alienable duty of people to obey government, an idea historically embedded perhaps in the tradition of an emperor's divine right (Information Office, 1991). The world's outcry over that meaningless slaughter, however, demonstrates the frailty of such reasoning. Yet, although tradition and societal acceptance largely account for the practice of genital mutilation, which U.N. human rights conventions have condemned (Tomasevski, 1993), it may be that the challenge is how to enhance dialogue with culturally diverse groups, to promote understanding of this custom as part of an entire social fabric (Dawit and Mekuria, 1993, p. A12).

Given social work's commitments to the promotion of the general welfare and social justice, the prevention and elimination of discrimination, and the assurance of access to resources, and services for *all persons* (NASW, 1994a), the relevance of human rights to the profession is particularly evident. Moreover, the policy statement of NASW's Peace and Social Justice Committee has asserted unequivocally to "Support implementation of the Universal Declaration of Human Rights" (NASW, 1994b, p. 203).   The International Federation of Social Workers and the International Association of Schools of Social Worker (1992) also declared the importance of international human rights instruments that "recognize and uphold the dignity and worth of the human persons" to all persons and "more especially those trained and skilled in the helping professions, to promote these principles through their actions" (p. "a"). Finally, the International Policy on Human Rights of the International

Federation notes, finally, a "special responsibility on the social work profession to advance the cause of human rights throughout the world" (Van Soest, 1992, p. 207).

Relationship Between Human Rights and Needs

The idea of human rights is a social construct (Wronka, 1992). It emerged as the human species evolved, in an effort to fulfill human needs, which are rooted in nature. Although the knowledge of human needs is imperfect, the human beings generally tends to have the following interrelated basic needs for growth and development: *biological-material* (to eat and have shelter); *social-psychological* (to feel affiliated and loved); *productive-creative* (to work and create); *security* (to have privacy and be secure in one's person); and *spiritual* (to worship and find meaning in one's existence) (Gil, 1992; 1993a).

Human rights are legal mandates to fulfill these needs. Thus, the rights to food, housing and clothing as found in Article 25 of the Universal Declaration should require society to provide for biological-material needs; the freedom of assembly in the United States Bill of Rights mandates society not to interfere with a person's needs for affiliation. These mandates to fulfill human need, at times represented in constitutions appear to be particular to the human condition, which is especially vulnerable to the vicissitudes of life, due in large measure because of the lack of genetic programming of the human species (Gil, 1992).

To be sure, needs are often culturally elaborated. Writing on the right to food, for instance, Special Rapporteur, Asbjorn Eide (1987) states:

> Food is a basic need for all human beings. Everyone requires access to food which is a) sufficient, balanced and safe to satisfy nutritional requirements, b) *culturally acceptable* [italics added] and c) accessible in a manner which does not destroy one's dignity as human beings. (p. 12)

A slice of wheat bread to an Inuit child may be as abhorrent as seal oil to a European. Furtherng human rights, therefore, requires understanding and fulfilling human needs in their culturally diverse contexts, another major commitment of social work.

Rights as Ideals, Enactments, or Exercised Rights

Ideals.

Rights then can be asserted as ideals, enactments, or exercised (Wronka, 1992). *Ideals* are goals that members of a society view as important to meet individual or group needs. The assertion of equality in the United States Declaration of Independence is one example. It is in this case that human rights scholar Maurice Cranston's (1983) criteria of rights are most applicable. To Cranston, rights must be: *universal, practicable,* and *of paramount importance.* Being universal, they ought to be based not upon status, privilege, sex, occupation, race, class or any other accidental characteristic, such as sexual orientation but rather upon the essence of being human. Society should also have the economic and other means to provide for such a right. For example, the right to education would be meaningless, if society did not have the resources to provide for equal opportunity for it. Finally, to be of paramount importance, the right must be essential to advance survival of the human species, (for example, like employment or health care) rather than trivial (for instance, the right to a candy bar).

Enactments.

The codification of these ideals into documents, usually legal instruments, such as constitutions or statutes (enactments), is a way to transform them into reality. Therefore, there are laws in the United States, that prohibit the free exercise of religion. Often, however, these codes of conduct do not have to be in written form. Distributive justice and strong commitments to community, for instance, are cultural ethics throughout much of Africa (Legesse, 1980) and indigenous cultures (Wronka, 1993b; Stamatapolou, 1994).

Exercised Rights

Rights as exercised are rights actually enjoyed. They are needs satisfied regardless of their source. The ultimate aim is to exercise, or more commonly stated, especially in the field of social policy, to *implement* human rights.

Certainly, mandating human rights, that are universal, practicable, and of paramount importance, and ultimately implementing these rights, will not only fulfill human needs, but also influence the overall quality of life for all. For example, when the need for education is fulfilled, the incidence of teenage pregnancy decreases(Williams, 1991; Caldas, 1993; Brown, 1994). Similarly, when the need for employment is fulfilled, domestic violence and child abuse decline (Gil,1973; 1992).

Universal Declaration of Human Rights

The authoritative definition of human rights standards (*United Nations Chronicle*, 1985) is the Universal Declaration of Human Rights which the U.N. General Assembly endorsed with no dissenting vote on December 10, 1948. World leaders have also praised that document, in particular, Pope John Paul II who referred to it as a milestone on the long and difficult path of the human race (1979). According to Rene Cassin, referred to as the Father of Human Rights (Szabo, 1982), it ought to be the centerpiece of human rights work. He argued that the human rights structure of the United Nations is like a triptych. The central panel is the Declaration, with one side panel being the various conventions and the covenants on the one hand, and the other being the implementation measures (Szabo, 1982). Furthermore, its significance is evident in the words of Eleanor Roosevelt, the Chairperson of the Drafting Committee of the Universal Declaration, who declared it a Magna Carta for humanity (Green, 1956).

Customary International Law.

However, this document, which was originally meant to be hortatory, is increasingly referred to, at least in the United States, as "customary international law" (Humphrey, 1976; *Filartiga v. Pena*, 1980; Vasak, 1982; Buergenthal, 1988; Kiss, 1988; Rosensweig, 1988; Lillich, 1989, 1990; Reismam, 1990; Wronka, 1992; Stamatapolou, 1994). In *Filartiga v. Pena-Irala*, for instance, with the assistance of such human rights groups as Amnesty International, a United States court ruled against Pena, a military commander, for torturing and murdering a high school student, Joelita Filartiga in Paraguay! The court reached the following conclusion:

> Official torture is now prohibited by the law of nations. This prohibition is clear and unambiguous and admits no distinction between treatment of aliens and citizens....This prohibition has become part of customary international law, as evidenced and defined by the Universal Declaration of Human Rights. (*Filartiga v. Pena* 630 F.2d, 884-885)

Since that ground breaking decision, other suits based on the "Filartiga principle," as it has become known, have been applied to government officials allegedly participating in acts of torture from Chile, Ethiopia, Guatemala, and the Philippines. The United States District Court, District of Massachusetts declared General Hector Gramajo, a former Minister of Defense in Guatemala, who ordered, among other things, the disembowellment of children in front of their parents, in default in two Filartiga suits against him (Rohter, 1991).

Impact on U.S. Jurisprudence.

The Universal Declaration, although it does not have authoritative legal status in the United States, nevertheless, is beginning to substantively impact U.S. jurisprudence (Lillich, 1990). The document generally considered by the legal community as definitive of norms of customary international law is now the *Restatement (Third) of the Foreign Relations Law of the United States* (D. Vagts, Professor of International Law, Harvard University, personal communication, March, 1994). Presently, this *Restatement* acknowledges the prohibition against torture, (as in *Filartiga*), genocide, slavery, murder, the causing of disappearances, prolonged arbitrary detention, systematic racial discrimination, and consistent patterns of gross violations of internationally recognized human rights as violations of customary international law. These standards emanate not only from the Universal Declaration, but also from human rights treaties signed by the United States which pertain to slavery, the political rights of women, the law of war and refugees, and genocide (Lillich, 1989).

The Universal Declaration, however, is the first all inclusive statement on human rights which has, in part, attained legal status in United States courts. Furthermore, the Declaration is often cited "consistently" and "frequently," as a basic criterion for a norm becoming customary international law (Meron, 1989). It appears only a matter of time before other human rights recognized in the Universal Declaration, which numerous litigants and judges continue to invoke, (Lillich, 1990) become part of customary international law. According to Lillich (1990) "Arguments that other human rights now are part of customary international law can be expected to be made with increasing frequency" (p. 73). The opinion of the court in *Filartiga*, moreover, seemed hopeful that other internationally accepted human rights may be forthcoming in United States jurisprudence: "International law confers fundamental rights upon all people vis-a-vis their own governments...the ultimate scope of those rights will be subject for continuing refinement and elaboration" (630 F.2d 884-885).

These movements to provide for human rights are not mere legalisms; rather, they represent growing public sentiment and the possibility for the social work profession in concert with the legal system, broadly defined, to advance this "cause that knows no frontiers" ("A Movement for Humanity," 1990). Such sentiment appears in response not only to such social problems as increasing violence and childhood poverty in the United States, but to an increasing awareness of worldwide dilemmas, such as the lack of substitutes for ever depleting biological and water resources (Postel, 1994) so necessary for the survival of the human species.

History of the Idea of Human Rights

Ideas move people (Gil, 1992; Stone, 1988; Wronka, 1992). However, American jurisprudence essentially identifies the idea of human rights with *Filartiga* and the *Restatement (Third)*, as well as, with the Bill of Rights, an important, but, nevertheless narrow definition of human rights. The American public largely perceives human rights similar to the Bill of Rights, as well as, mandates of ever proliferating human rights groups, like Amnesty International (1993) which essentially advocates for the release of political prisoners, abolition of the death penalty, and torture.

As the 21st century approaches, this idea is slowly expanding, however, to include other notions of human rights only briefly discussed. Because human rights discussions cannot take place in an historical-philosophical vacuum, it is necessary at this time to further examine the Universal Declaration of Human Rights and further developments in the human rights structure, in light of these philosophical underpinnings, before discussing research-action strategies for the social work profession in the realization of human rights for all.

Four Crucial Notions of Human Rights.

The Declaration consists of four crucial notions: the basic right to human dignity; civil and political rights; economic, social, and cultural rights; and solidarity rights (Wronka, 1992).
Human Dignity.

The first concept of human dignity, emphasized in Article 1, appears to emanate from the Judaic-Christian tradition (Drinan, 1987) indicative of the preponderance of western nations involved in the drafting of the Declaration. Thus, Genesis 1:27 states: "God created man in His image," which according to Talmudic scholar, Ben Azzai, embodies the "ultimate and supreme worth" of the individual (Kaplan, 1980, p. 55). Christians also accept the sanctity and dignity of the human person, proclaimed in Genesis (Henle, 1980). Similarly, The Holy Koran asserts in Sura 17:70, "Verily, we have honored every human being." According to Muslim scholar, Riffat Hassan (1982): "The sanctity and absolute value of human life is upheld by the Koran" (p. 55).

Civil and Political Rights.

The second notion is the liberty to pursue this quest for human dignity free from the abuse of political authority, emphasized primarily in Articles 2-21, most commonly referred to as civil and political rights. These freedoms, also called "first generation" or "negative" rights (Weston, 1989), include, for example, freedoms of speech, the press, and religion. They arose primarily in response to the abuses of some of the tyrannical monarchs of the 17th and 18th centuries resulting in such documents as the American Declaration of Independence and the United States Constitution's Bill of Rights. Major thrusts behind these documents were Enlightenment theorists, such as John Locke (1632-1704), who emphasized, for instance, the rights to life and liberty (that is, freedom from arbitrary rule). These fundamental freedoms stress essentially the need for government *not* to interfere with basic human needs to express one's self or practice one's religion.

Economic, social, and cultural rights.

These rights, otherwise known as "second generation" or "positive" rights (Weston, 1989), which underscore the idea that government provides for basic necessities to ensure an existence worthy of human dignity, are primarily in Articles 22 through 27. Examples are rights to health care, education, employment, special protections for motherhood and children, and security in old age. They arose predominantly in reaction to the abuses of industrialization increasingly evident in the nineteenth century resulting, for instance, in massive poverty among affluence. The Soviet Constitution of 1936 exemplifies such rights. Theorists, such as Graccus Babeuf (1760-1797), Thomas Paine (1737-1809), and Karl Marx (1818-1883) appeared influential in the development of positive rights. Thomas Paine is exemplary. In the *Rights of Man* he advocates for the prevention of poverty in order that:

> The hearts of the humane will not be shocked by ragged and hungry children, and persons of seventy or eighty years of age, begging for bread. The dying poor will not be dragged from place to place to breathe their last. [and]....Widows will have a maintenance for their children and not be carted away, on the deaths of their husbands, like culprits and criminals. (Fast, 1946, pp. 255-256)

Solidarity Rights.

Solidarity rights, Articles 28-30, comprise the last crucial notion in the Declaration. Whereas these rights are still in the process of conceptual elaboration (Weston, 1989) they are the result of the failure of domestic sovereignty, most noticeable at the final years of the 20th century, to resolve such global issues as pollution, war, the oppression of indigenous and other peoples, and international distributive justice. They emphasize the basic human right to intergovernmental cooperation (personal communiction with E. Stamatapolou, Director of the Liaison Office for the U.N. Human Rights Commission, April 1990) and the notion that every right has a corresponding duty (Vasak, 1977). Therefore, international cooperation to distribute food, therefore, as well as, the individual duty not to overconsume (Alston, 1989) should assist in providing for social justice on the global scale. The noted philosopher Immanual Kant (1724-1804), recognizing the hypocrisy of nations in his *Project for a Perpetual Peace* (Crocker, 1969) and accentuating that "An action to have moral worth, must be done from duty" (Curtis, 1981, p. 40), seems to have paved the way for an inclusion of the idea of solidarity in human rights discussions. Taking solidarity rights seriously would mean a major transformation in thinking in the domestic arena (Agonafer, 1994; "Reconceputalizing Human Rights," 1994; Shepard & Nanda, 1985; United Nations Center for Human Rights, 1981; Wronka, 1994a), because solidarity with all would include equal concern for all atrocities-Asian and African, as well as European (Carter, 1994; Moeller, 1994)

The Interdependency of Rights

During the debates involved in the drafting of the Universal Declaration it appeared primarily that capitalist oriented countries emphasized first generation rights; socialist countries stressed the second generation (Wronka, 1992). The poorest countries of the world, commonly referred to as the Third World were barely represented. Apparently, therefore, the United Nations gave only scant attention at that time to rights to solidarity (Alston, 1994; Drinan, 1987; Ferrero, 1986; Wronka, 1992, 1994a).

However, it has become pivotal to the human rights movement to recognize that rights are indivisible and interdependent (Donnelly, 1989; Stamatapolou, 1989; Weston, 1989; Wronka, 1992, 1994a; The Carter Center, 1993), a "fundamental tenet of the United Nations approach to human rights" (Eide, 1987, p. 10). To illustrate, the right to travel, (a civil and political right), is possible only if one has worked (an economic and social right), earning enough wages to afford the fare to move freely. Similarly, the right to vote is meaningless if the voter lacks education, is illiterate, and/or uninformed; the right to food also implies corresponding duties to be productive and not to overconsume (Alston, 1989; Alston & Tomasevski, 1984).

As Shridath Ramphal, (1982) Commonwealth Secretary-General to the United Nations, eloquently asserted:

It does the cause of human rights no good to inveigh against civil and political rights deviations while helping to perpetuate illiteracy, malnutrition, disease, infant mortality, and a low life expectancy among millions of human beings. All the dictators and all the aggressors throughout history, however, ruthless, have not succeeded in creating as much misery and suffering as the disparities between the world's rich and poor sustain today. (p. 1)

These crucial tenets of the Declaration only briefly examined in their historical and philosophic contexts, are simplified expressions of a complex reality. Nevertheless, these demarcations, with the Universal Declaration as the pivotal point, should provide the necessary contours to understand ensuing developments and research-action strategies for the committed social worker.

Further Developments in the Human Rights Structure

Whereas the Universal Declaration is undoubtedly the centerpiece of human rights work, the other sides of the triptych in this international human rights structure, which Cassin referred to (Szabo, 1982), should not be dismissed. They represent, in essence, the development of normative standards, initiated by the Universal Declaration in 1948 and their implementation.

Other Covenants and Declarations

One side of the triptych, therefore, consists of the International Covenant of Civil and Political Rights (1966), the International Covenant of Economic, Social, and Cultural Rights (1966), and the long train of other conventions and declarations. Some examples are: the Convention on Consent to Marriage, Minimum Age for Marriage and Registration of Marriages (1962); Convention Relating to the Status of Refugees (1966); The Universal Declaration on the Eradication of Hunger and Malnutrition (1974); Declaration on the Rights of Disabled Persons (1975); Convention on the Elimination of All Forms of Discrimination Against Women (1979); Declaration on the Elimination of All Forms of Intolerance of Discrimination Based on Religion or Belief (1981); Convention Against Torture and Other Cruel, Inhuman or Degrading Treatment or Punishment (1984); Convention on the Right to Development (1986); Convention on the Rights of the Child (1989) and Principles for the Protection of Persons with mental Illness and the Improvement of Mental health Care (1991). A number of other conventions and declarations are also presently in process, such as the Universal Declaration on the Rights of the

Rights of Indigenous Peoples (Daes, 1993; "Update on the Draft Universal Declaration,: 1994) and the Convention Against Sexual Exploitation (D'Amato, 1994).

Unlike declarations, conventions, sometimes called covenants, are legally binding. The one exception to date appears the Universal Declaration which has attained burgeoning legal status. To be sure, depending upon the "will of the people" as a basis for government, other declarations may also attain such status. The two International Covenants, however, were open for signature in 1966 and went into force in 1976. If a signatory, a country accepts the plausibility of the document, and its consideration in relevant governmental committees. Ratification means acceptance as legally binding.

U.S. Actions

Amnesty International (1994) documented that the United States has signed and ratified the International Covenant on Civil and Political Rights, but only signed the Economic, Social, and Cultural Rights and the Torture Convention. Failure to ratify the Economic and Social Covenant appears indicative of a cultural legacy in United States that is generally hostile to economic and social rights (Alston, 1990; 1994; Hannum & Fischer, 1993). However, the Clinton Administration, accepting the Vienna Declaration which endorsed economic and social rights and the administration's focus on health care reform and the improvement of educational opportunities, seems to have ended this antagonism (Alston, 1994). Moreover, ratification of the Torture Convention would invalidate the Ingraham v. Wright (1977) Supreme Court decision permitting corporal punishment in U.S. schools ("Human Rights Treaty Update," 1991). Presently, the Clinton administration is seeking Senate advice and consent to ratification of the Convention on the Elimination of All Forms of Racial Discrimination and "is committed to considering other pending human rights treaties in the future" (Department of State, personal communication, June 17, 1994).

It is well known that the United States has neither signed nor ratified the Convention on the Rights of Child. Acording to the annual Progress of Nations report from the United Nations Children's Fund, the U.S. continues to lead the developed world in child poverty, and teen killing is seven times higher for any industrialized nation (Jackson, 1994). According to the U.S. Conference on Mayors, hunger and homelessness continuing unabated in cities across the U.S. in 1993, with a disturbing increase in the proportion of families with children (Holmes, 1993). The U.S. also ranks first in billionaires in the industrialized world (Peterson, 1993).

There is no convention on solidarity rights. However, the Right to Development (1986) with its emphasis on the creation of a social and international order to realize human rights comes the closest to this "third generation." The only veto to that convention was the United States. Furthermore, the U.S. has officially stated that foreign invasion should not be considered a human rights violation ("U.S. Information Regarding," 1993) in its reservations concerning the Vienna Declaration (1993), suggesting that a reversal of that veto is not forthcoming.

Mechanisms for implementing conventions.

Conventions tend to integrate implementation mechanisms for states that have ratified them. They mention, for example, that "State Parties to the present Covenant [shall] ...submit reports on the measures they have adopted which give effect to the rights recognized" (Part IV of the covenant on Civil and Political Rights). These reports are generally submitted to Human Rights Committees whose purposes relate to the implementation of said conventions. The Committee on Economic, Social, and Cultural Rights, for instance, "is composed of 18 experts with recognized competence in the field of human rights serving in their personal capacity....elected for a term of four years (United Nations, 1988, p. 14)."

Procedures.

Briefly, there are also the "1235" and "1503" procedures for all countries in the United Nations, even though they may not have ratified these conventions. Both examine consistent patterns of gross, massive human rights violations. The former, however, discusses these issues in public forum, concerning itself essentially with violations *as exemplified* by apartheid in South Africa; the latter examines in a confidential setting *all* infringements of human rights violations (Newman and Weissbrodt, 1990). Complaints, which individuals and organizations can file, must demonstrate that such situations are a "consistent pattern of gross and systematic violations," (Tomasevski, 1993, p. 113).

Other mechanisms include: the establishment of specialized theme mechanisms to take effective action on an emergency basis on critical human rights problems like disappearances, summary executions, torture, and religious intolerance; the appointment of special rapporteurs to examine conditions individual countries; and the development to expand U.N. public information on human rights concomitant with advancing awareness of rights in the global arena (Tessitore and Woolfson, 1991).

Weaknesses.

Although countries must take these implementation mechanisms seriously (Alston, 1990), what the mechanisms actually do is notoriously weak (Tomasevski, 1993; Sullivan, 1994), apart from the "mobilization of shame" and the weight of world opinion against a particular country. The UN recently created a post of High Commissioner for Human Rights to oversee the overall implementation of human rights standards (Cerna, 1994a). However, this post needs strengthening (Shattuck, 1994). It is perhaps evident here how "hidden agenda"(Kristol, 1990) may mask concern for human rights. The United States, for instance, had often cited the former Soviet Union for its *Gulag* and political use of psychiatry; they retaliated by citing the United States for homelessness, unemployment, childhood poverty, and failure to honor treaties with Native Americans (Van Boven, 1989).

Is it a coincidence that the growing concern to eradicate genital mutilation has occurred primarily during the Somalian conflict, where estimates are that 98 percent of Somali females have undergone the operation ("Born Female," 1994)? This hidden agenda, therefore, may also be a pretext to mobilize public support for armed intervention. Because violence only begets violence only non-violent measures will implement human rights. The most recent attempt of the United States to support "studies to better understand the social-cultural and economic conditions that contribute to female genital mutilation" (Shattuck, 1994c, p. 7), which the United States views as "harmful to women's health and a violation of their right to physical integrity" (Shattuck, 1994c, p. 6), seems however, to be a positive way to deal with violations of human rights. Armed intervention, ostensible to help starving people or, for that matter, to eradicate genital mutilation in Somalia, a strategically located country, can only be counterproductive and antithetical to the spirit of the Universal Declaration of Human Rights, which emphasizes international cooperation and nonviolent intervention (Wronka, 1993c).

Human rights regimes.

In addition to United Nations efforts, various human rights regimes, in such places as Africa, Europe, and the Americas, have also emerged with their own conventions, declarations, and implementation mechanisms. Examples are: the European Convention on Human Rights (1950), the Helsinki Final Act (1975), and the African Charter on Human and Peoples' Rights (1981) (Weston, Lukes, and Hnatt, 1989). In this hemisphere there is The Organization of American States, Inter-American Commission on Human Rights with its American Declaration of the Rights and Duties of Man (1948), and American Convention on Human Rights (1969), with its Petition System.

Yet, a budget of only 1.6 million to attend to the rights of nearly 600 million people in the Western Hemisphere (Center for Human Rights, 1994), suggests the need for more public and governmental support for such valuable and more local human rights networks. Given adequate funding and growing awareness of these regimes, however, it may be that the struggle to advance human rights will increasingly focus on regional bodies (Shattuck, 1994c).

Creating a Human Rights Culture

The principles of the Universal Declaration, as well as, other conventions,declarations, and implementation mechanisms, can only be realized if there is public sentiment in support of human rights in general. Otherwise, efforts will be coercive and bound to fail. They must emanate from the will of the people. Consequently, when advancing human rights, it is imperative *not* to attract converts to the idea, but rather simply engage in open discussion and debate. Often, merely having information about what one's rights are can serve as an effective means of empowerment (Tomasevski, 1993). Yet, only chosen values can endure (Wronka, 1994).

The Need for Human Rights Support Groups.

It is important to emphasize that in the United States, the realization of many of the rights of the Universal Declaration, particularly economic, social, cultural, and solidarity rights will be particularly difficult because as Philip Alston (1990), presently Chairperson of the United Nations Committee on Economic and Social Rights notes "Any U.S. group that might contemplate taking economic rights seriously in the future would have to bear in mind that a significant segment of public opinion would be actively opposed to the idea" (p. 389). This climate is perhaps mirrored in the words of former United Nations Ambassador, Jeanne Kirkpatrick who referred to the Universal Declaration as: a letter to Santa Claus....Neither nature, experience, nor probability informs these lists of 'entitlements,' which are subject to no constraints except those of the mind and appetite of their authors" (Laqueur and Rubin, 1990, p. 364). Recently, U.S. Ambassador to the Human Rights Commission has rejected the notion of positive rights, arguing for the "priority" of civil and political rights (Abram, 1990).

U.S federal and state constitutions, furthermore, while exemplary in regard to civil and political rights, are sorely deficient in acknowledging economic, social, cultural and solidarity rights (Wronka, 1992, 1994a, 1994b). While it is true, therefore, that the U.S. is a "rights-based culture," (Stone, 1988; Wronka, 1992; Chapman, 1993), due in large measure to an emphasis upon the Bill of

Rights, the American conception of rights is constricted. It ought to expand to include all human rights.

Research-Action Strategies.

The following sections present some research-action strategies, with particular attention to the field of social work to advance wht has become known as a "human rights culture" (U.N. Centre for Human Rights, 1988; Eide, 1992; The Carter Center, 1993; Wronka, 1994a, 1994b). Such a culture, furthermore, would not supplant, but rather give impetus to major tenets of some of the world's major religions like Judaism, Christianity, and Islam (Parliament of the World' Religions, 1993).

Human Rights in Advanced Generalist Practice and Inclusion in Social Work Curriculum.

Certainly, human rights work is for every person. However, given social work paradigms, Advanced Generalist Practice appears most amenable for the inclusion of human rights in its curriculum. It is particularly appropriate for primary intervention, otherwise known as the "whole-population" approach, as opposed to secondary (that is, "at-risk population" approach) or tertiary (that is, "counseling" approach) intervention (Springfield College, 1994-1995). Providing for these rights for all, would obviously assist in the prevention of social malaises, like poverty and sickness. It is, of course, also relevant to all areas of social work, as a healthier population would dictate less clinical intervention. It is especially helpful to incorporate human rights notions in required first year courses. Otherwise, students do not tend to understand the relevance and possible impact of this idea.

Relevance of Human Rights to the Social Policy Sequence.

The relevance between human rights and social policy is obvious. Since policies represent values (Gil, 1992, 1994), the creation of a human rights culture would do much to advance a socially just society. It can also be argued as some women's groups have at the World Conference in Human Rights in Vienna that many social issues ought to be viewed through a human rights lens, rather than through the lens of humanitarian social policy (Sullivan, 1994). Thus, the field of social policy may at times carry with it much conceptual baggage, such as "stakeholders," or "policy relevant variables" obfuscating, rather than illuminating basic issues. Most people, for instance, simply do not know that economic, social, cultural, and solidarity rights are not part of the U.S. constitution or barely acknowledged in state constitutions (Wronka, 1992).

An awareness of human rights principles will also ask not merely "what" the extent of homelessness or hunger is (Article 25 of the Declaration), but "how" and "why" (Article 28 which calls for a just "social and international order") such violations occur (U.N. Center for Human Rights, 1981) thereby requiring major structural transformations in society (International Council on social Welfare, 1969; Chapman, 1993; Wronka, 1994).

Merely letting others know about human rights violations and documenting them in a scholarly way, may be sufficient to mobilize public sentiment (Wiseberg, 1990). Because the Declaration was written for the everyday lay person, not for doctorate in jurisprudence so, too must human rights work continue in that spirit. Consequently, this work will seek dialogue with all professions, questioning the value of the "toga of the expert" in the first place (Katz, 1982; Wronka, 1993b) and constantly call for public participation in the formulation of social policy (Chapman, 1993; Mawn, 1994). Human rights is first and foremost a people's movement.

Integral to the human rights movement is the notion that every right has a corresponding duty. As some of this author's Inuit students had commented, government programs had made life easy. Before such programs, the Inuit hunted, fished, and carried on a subsistence lifestyle. Now they go to the local store and buy everything with food stamps (Wronka, 1993b). This lifestyle is hardly the epitome of the right to self-determination. Acknowledging the interdependence of rights, therefore, asks equally how social policies can foster duties, through the reorganization of work.

Certainly, the inclusion of economic, social, cultural, and solidarity rights in constitutions will undoubtedly influence social policy (Wronka, 1992; 1993a, 1994a). The Federal Constitution's failure to provide for a right to employment or education (Wronka, 1992) may account for the fact that U.S. unemployment has averaged approximately 7.1% (Harvey, 1989) or, more surprisingly, according to the U.S. Department of Education, approximately 47% of American adults may be described as functionally illiterate (U.S. Department of State, 1994b; Wilkie, 1993).

Social work, therefore, could engage in movements that question and attempt to change the social order. Why, for instance, is the U.S. only one of three countries that permit advertising on children's television programs (Kaye, 1974, cited in Fuhrmann, 1990)? Does this socialize these defenseless few, to place a priority over "having," rather than "being," which the existential philosopher, Gabriel Marcel (1967) lamented and saw as a growing problem?

Monitoring Human Rights Violations.

The monitoring of human rights violations is also a valuable project (Hannibal, 1993; Schmid & Longman, 1992; U.S. Department of State, 1994a,

1994b). The U.S. Department of State, for instance, in January 1994 drew up a report on human rights violations of 193 countries. However, the United States was missing because according to the Department of State (personal communication, April, 1994) "Congress did not appropriate funds to monitor its own country."

At all times human rights efforts ought to be positive, applauding government efforts to provide for these rights and suggesting ways to overcome violations. In the U.S. it is also worthwhile to acknowledge that it was an American, Eleanor Roosevelt, who spearheaded the Universal Declaration. To advance economic and social rights, it would be worthwhile to acknowledge that Thomas Jefferson was an advocate of the right to employment and therefore economic and social rights (Wronka, 1994). Furthermore, social workers may wish to work in projects, similar to the Universal Declaration of Human Rights Project, a joint undertaking of the Department of Social Work at Springfield College and the Heller Graduate School, Center for Social Change, Brandeis University. The purposes of this project are to expand awareness of the Universal Declaration of Human Rights, monitor movement toward compliance with the Declaration, and suggest ways to overcome violations (Wronka, in press) Social workers must learn from each other in whatever human rights projects they undertake. The need for social work to increasingly collaborate on national and international levels is extremely important, given the profession's "historical engagement in international activities" (Midgley, 1994, p. 165).

Human rights and research.

Given that the major purpose of qualitative research to elicit structures of experience (Moustakis, 1990; Tyson, 1992) from co-researchers (Moustakis, 1990), rather than "subjects," phenomenological descriptions (Valle and Halling, 1989) of "just communities," and/or lived experiences of human rights violations are especially pertinent (Fourth World Movement, U.S.A., 1994a, 1994b). The current failure of the Inter-American Commission on Human Rights to Draft Declaration on Indigenous People because of the insistence of credentialed professionals to distribute questionnaires and tabulate data (Center for Human Rights, 1994), rather than consider essential themes emerging in interchanges among indigenous people, is suggestive of the relevance of qualitative research to human rights work. Quantitative approaches in other contexts, such as bar graphs that illustrate convincingly the race of a victim as a predictor of the death penalty, may also prove worthy (Spirer and Spirer, 1993)

Other possibilities.

Space does not permit a discussion of the numerous other possibilities. However, further suggestions include holding a people's tribunal to try a specific country concerning human rights violations (Blaser, 1992); developing and implementing human rights curriculum in the schools; having cities endorse human rights instruments, particularly the Universal Declaration; integrating human rights work into clinical practice by offering workshops and seminars to staff and the community on human rights (United Nations, 1989); expanding the mandates of local, state, and federal human rights commissions; to have rights of the Declaration placed on state, if not federal, ballots and join in social movements guaranteeing such rights as employment and health care; filing complaints with the U.N. or Inter-American Human Rights Commission (Inter-American Commission, 1994); writing articles, letters to the editor, or even books alerting people in clear and simple terms about human rights violations (Human Rights Internet, 1993); and on graduation to give the student along with a diploma, a copy of the Universal Declaration of Human Rights.

Conclusion

Apart from enthusiasm and perseverance, the key to advancing human rights is what Maurice Merleau-Ponty (1967), called the "happiness of reflecting together." The social worker, grounded in the ethical principles of the profession, must engage in partnerships of empowerment, both locally and worldwide, with other groups, people, and cultures. The present shift, for example, in the United States in poverty from the elderly to children must cease. However, as the Universal Declaration asserts, security in old age is as fundamental a human right as special protections for children. The human rights worker must ask why such inequities continue, as she or he labors in community with others to provide for a socially just world and human rights for *all.*

References

Abram, M. (1990, February 9). *Realization of economic, social, and cultural rights contained in the Universal Declaration of Human Rights* (Agenda item 7: "Rights" Unpublished statement to the 46th session of the UN Commission on Human rights; available from USIA, 1292 Chambesy, Geneva, Switzerland)

Agonafer, M. (1994). *Contending theories of development in the contemporary international-order disorder.* Lanham, MD: University Press of America.

Alston, P. (1990). U.S. ratification of the covenant on economic, social and cultural rights: The need for an entirely new strategy. *American Journal of International Law, 84,* 365-393.

Alston, P. (1989). International law and the right to food. In R. P. Claude & B. H. Weston (Eds.), *Human rights in the world community* (pp. 142-150). Philadelphia: University of Pennsylvania Press.

Alston, P. & Tomasevski (Eds.), (1984). *The right to food.* Utrecht: Martinus Nijhoff.

Amnesty International. (1993). *Report 1993.* New York: Author.

Blaser, A. (1992). How to advance human rights without really trying: An analysis of non governmental tribunals. *Human Rights Quarterly, 14,* 339-370.

Born female-and fettered. (1994, February 2). *The New York Times,* p. 18.

Brown, L. (1994). Facing food insecurity. In L. Brown (Ed.), *State of the World* (pp. 177-197). New York: W.W. Norton.

Buergenthal, T. (1988). *International human rights law.* St. Paul, MN: West.

Caldas, S. J. (1993). Current theoretical perspectives on adolescent pregnancy and childbearing in the United States. *Journal of Adolescent Research, 8* (1), 4-20.

Carter, J. (1994). Address of Jimmy Carter in Columbus Ohio, April 1994. (Available from: The Carter Center, Atlanta, Georgia)

The Carter Center for Human Rights. (1993). *The Atlanta Statement.* Atlanta, GA: Author.

Castelle, K. (1990) *In the child's best interest: A primer on the U.N. Convention on the Rights of the Child.* New York: Defense for Children International-USA.

Center for Human Rights and Humanitarian law, Washington College of Law, the American University. Conference on Defending Human Rights. (1994, April 5). *Defending human rights.* (Available from: Centre for Human Rights, 4400 Massachusetts Ave., N.W. Washington, DC 20016).

Cerna, C. (1994b), Fall) *Human Rights Advocacy Interest Group Newsletter: American Society of International Law, 4*(3), 6-7.

Chapman, A. (1993). *Exploring a human rights approach to health care reform.* Washington, DC: American Association for the Advancement of Science.

Children's Defense Fund. (1993) *The state of America's children.* New York: Author.

Claude, R. & Weston, B. (1989). *Human rights in the world community.* Philadelphia: University of Pennsylvania Press.

Collins, S., Ginsburg, H., & Goldberg, G. (1994). *Jobs for all: A Plan for revitalization of America.* New York: Apex press.

Cranston, M. (1983). Are there any human rights? *Daedalus, 112,(*4), 1-17.

Crocker, L. (Ed.). (1969). *The Age of Enlightenment.* New York: Walker.

Curtis, M. (Ed.). (1981). *The great political theories* (Vol. 2). New York: Avon.

Conference on the Inter-American Commission. (1994). For inquiries contact: Center fo Human Rights, Washington University, Washington, DC.

Daes, E. (1993, July). *Discrimination against indigenous peoples: Explanatory note concerning the draft declaration.* New York: United Nations.

D'Amato, A. (1994, Fall). *Human rights advocacy interest group newsletter: American Society of International Law, 4*(4), 2.

Dawit, S. & Mekuria, S. (1993, December 12). The West just doesn't get it. *The New York Times*, p. A27.

Donnelly, J. (1989). *Universal human rights in theory and practice.* Ithaca, NY: Cornell University Press.

Drinan, R. (1987). *Cry of the oppressed: The history and hope of the human rights revolution.* San Francisco: Harper and Row.

Egan, T. (1994,March 4). An ancient ritual and a mother's asylum plea. *New York Times*, p. A25.

Eide, A. (1987). United Nations Commission on Human Rights. *Report on the right to adequate food as a human right.* (E/CN.4/Sub.2/1987/23). New York: United Nations.

Eide, A., Alfredsson, G., Melander, G., Refhof, L., Rosas, A. & Swinehart, T. (Eds.), (1992). *The Universal Declaration of Human Rights: A commentary.* Oslo: Scandinavian University Press.

Embassy Television. (1982). *Eleanor, first lady of the world* [videotape] Burbank, CA: Columbia Tristar Home Video.

Farer, T. (1989). The United Nations and human rights: More than a whimper. In R.P. Claude and B.H. Weston (Eds), *Human rights in the world community* (pp. 194-208). Philadelphia: University of Pennsylvania Press.

Fast, H. (1946). *The selected works of Tom Paine and citizen Tom Paine.* New York: Random House.

Filartiga v. Pena-Irala. 630 F. 2d 876 (1980).

Fourth World Movement, U.S.A. (1994a). *Families in extreme poverty: Actors in development.* Landover, MD: Author.

Fourth World Movement, U.S.A. (1994b). *The Wresinski Report.* Landover, MD: Author.

Friedan, J. & Wiseberg, L. (1981). *Teaching human rights.* Ottowa: University of Ottowa, human rights internet.

Fuhrmann, B. (1990). *Adolescence, adolescents.* Glenveiw, IL: Scott, Foresman.

Gil, D. (1973). *Violence against children: Physical child abuse in the United States.* Cambridge, MA: Harvard University Press.

Gil, D. (1992). *Unravelling social policy* (rev. 5th ed.). Cambridge: Schenkman.

Gil, D. (1993a). Beyond access to medical care: Pursuit of health and prevention of ills. *Evaluation and the health professions,* 16, 3, 251-277.

Gil, D. (1993b). Oppression and social injustice ad their opposites (chapt. 8). In F. Reamer (Ed.), *The Foundations of Social Work Knowledge.* New York: Columbia University Press.

Green, J. F. (1956). *The U.N. and human rights.* Washington: Brookings Institute.

Hannun, H. & Fischer, D. (Eds.), (1993). *United States ratification of the international covenants on human rights.* Washington, DC: The American Society International Law.

Hannibal, K. (1993). *Taking up the challenge: The promotion of human rights, A guide for the scientific community.* Washington, DC: American Association for the Advancement of Science.

Harvey, P. (1989). Securing the right to employment. Princeton: Princeton University Press.

Hassan, R. (1982). On human rights and the Qur'anic perspective. In A. Swidler (Ed.). Human rights in religious traditions (pp. 51-65). New York: Pilgrim.

Healy, L. (1992). Introducing international development content in the social work curriculum. Washington, DC: National Association of Social Workers.

Henkin, L. (1978). The rights of man today. Boulder, CO: Westview.

Henkin, L. & Hargrove, J. (1994). Human rights: An agenda for the next century. Washington, D.C.: The American Society of International Law.

Henle, R. (1980). A Catholic view of human rights. In A. Rosenbaum (Ed.), The philosophy of human rights: International perspectives (pp. 87-93). Westport, CT: Greenwood.

Hollenbach, D. (1988) Justice, peace, and human rights: American Catholic social ethics in a pluralistic context. New York: Crossroad.

Holmes, S. (1993, December 2). Spread of hunger denied. The New York Times, p. 8.

Human Rights Internet. (1993). funding human rights: An international directory of funding organizations and human rights awards. Ottawa: University of Ottawa, Human Rights Internet.

Human Rights Treaty Update. (1991, Spring) Human rights advocacy interest group newsletter: American society of international law, 2(1) p. 2.

Humphrey, J. (1976) The International Bill of Rights: Scope and implementation. William and Mary Law Review, 17, 524-541.

Hutchins, Soroka, & Dionne. (1994). Update on the Draft Universal Declaration on the Rights of Indigenous Peoples. Nouvelles Internationales HSD International News, 2, 1, 1-6. Available from: 245 St-Jacques St., Montreal, Quebec H2Y 1M6.

Information Office of the State Council of the People's Republic of China. (1991). Human rights in China. Beijing: Author.

Ingraham v. Wright. 430 U.S. 651 (1977).

Inter-American Commission on Human Rights of the Organization of American States. (1994). Human rights: How to present a petition in the inter-american system. Washington, DC: Author.

International Council on Social Welfare. (1969). Social welfare and human rights. New York: Columbia University Press.

International Federation of Social Workers and the International Association of Schools of Social Workers. (1992). Teaching and learning about human rights: A Manual for schools of social work and the social work profession. Geneva: United Nations Centre for Human Rights.

Jackson, D. (1994, June 29). U.S. fals behind on treatment of children. The Boston Globe, p. 17.

Kaplan, A. (1980). Human Relations and Human Rights in Judaism. In A. Rosenbaum (Ed.), The philosophy of human rights: International perspectives (pp. 53-85). Westport, CT: Greenwood.

Katz, R. (1982). Boiling energy: Community healting among the Kalahari Kung. Cambridge: Harvard University Press.

Kaye, E. (1974). The family guide to children's television. New York: Pantheon.

Kiss, A. (1988) The role of the Universal Declaration of Human Rights in international law. In United Nations Center for Human Rights, Fortieth Anniversary of the Universal Declaration of Human Rights [Special issue]. *Bulletin of Human Rights*, 47-52.

Kristol, I. (1990). Human rights: The hidden agenda. In W. Laqueur and B. Rubin (Eds.), *The human rights reader* (pp. 391-404). New York: New American Library.

Laqueur, W., & Rubin, B. (Eds.). (1990) *The human rights reader* (rev. ed.). New York: New American Library.

Legesse, A. (1980). Human rights in African political culture. In K. Thompson (Ed.). *The moral imperatives of human rights: A world survey*. Lanham, MD: University Press of America.

Lillich, R. (1989). The Constitution and international human rights. *American Journal of International Law, 83, 4,* 851-862.

Lillich, R. (1990) The United States Constitution and international human rights law. *Harvard Human Rights Journal, 3,* 53-82.

Marcel, G. (1967). *Homo viator: Introduction to a metaphysic of hope*. Magnolia, MA: Peter Smith.

Mawn, B. (1994). *Women's views on HIV screening during pregnancy and in newborns: Social justice or travesty*. [Microfilm]. Ann Arbor, MI: University Microfilms.

Merleau-Ponty, M. (1967). *Signs*. Chicago: Northwest University Press.

Meron, T. (1989). *Human rights and humanitarian norms*. Oxford: Clarendon.

Midgley, J. (1994). Transnational strategies for social work: Toward effective reciprocal exchanges. In R.G. Meinert, J. T. Pardeck, & W.P. Sullivan (Eds.), *Issues in social work: A critical analysis* (pp. 165-180). Westport, CT: Auburn House.

Moeller, S. (1994, May 20). Human rights and the media at the *Spotlight on Human Rights Conference*, Brandeis University. (For information contact: Dr. Susan Moeller, Director, Department of Journalism, Brandeis University, Waltham, MA 02254)

Moustakis, C. (1990). *Heuristic research: Design, methodology, and applications*. Newbury Park, CA: Sage.

Movement for Humanity. (1990, April 10) *The New York Times*, p. A12.

Mower, A. (1991). *Regional human rights: A comparative study of the west european and inter-American systems*. Westport, CT: Greenwood.

National Association of Social Workers. (1994a). *NASW Code of Ethics*. Washington, DC: Author.

National Association of Social Workers. (1994b). *Peace and social justice*. In *Social work speaks: NASW policy statements* (3rd ed., pp. 200-205) Washington, DC: Author.

Newman F. & Weissbrodt, D. (1990). *International human rights: Law, policy, ad process*. Cincinnati: Anderson.

On Human Rights Day. (December 10, 1993). *The Boston Globe*, p. 26.

Parliament of the World's Religions. (1993). *Towards a global ethic: An initial declaration*. Chicago: Author.

Peterson, J. (1993, April 11). Life in U.S., graded on the curve. *The Los Angeles Times*, p. A1.

Pope John Paul II. (1979) *U.S.A. The message of justice, peace,and love.* Boston: Daughters of St. Paul.

Postel, S. (1994). Carrying capacity: Earth's bottom line. In L. Brown (Ed.), *State of the World* (pp. 3-21). NY: W.W. Norton.

Ramphal, S. (1982) Address to the United Nations. For inquiries contact: Shridath Ramphal, Commonwealth Secretary-General to the United Nations. New York, New York.

Reconceptualizing human rights: a 1994 NGO Summit at Cartegena. (1994, Fall). *The Society for the Study of Social Problems Newsletter, 25,* (3),8.

Reisman, M. (1990). Sovereignty and human rights in contemporary international law. *American Journal of International Law, 84,* 866-876.

Restatement (Third) of the Foreign Law of the United States. (1987) For inquiries contact:Professor D. Vagts, Associate Reporter, Harvard School of International Law, Harvard University, 02138.

Riding, A. (1993, June 26) *The New York Times,* p. 2.

Rohter, L. (1991, November 15) Ex-dictator of Haiti is facing human rights suit. *The New York Times,* p. 3.

Rosenzweig, M. (1988) Psychology and United Nations human rights efforts. *American Psychologist, 43,* 79-86.

Schmid, A. & Jongman, A. (1992). *Monitoring human rights.* University of Leiden: Center for the Study of Social Conflicts, PIOOM (Interdisciplinary program of research on root causes of human rights violations).

Shattuck, J. (1994a, December 10) *Keynote address.* Presented at the Conference on Universal Human Rights: Accountability and Enforcement. Boston. (Available from The coalition for a Strong United Nations, 2161 Massachusetts Ave., Cambridge, MA 02140-1336)

Shattuck, J. (1994b, December 10). The human rights watch. *Boston Globe,* p. 11.

Shattuck, J. (1994c). *Testimony on violations of women's human rights before the House Foreign Affairs Subcommittee on International Security, International Organizations, and Human rights.* Washington, DC: U.S. Department of State, Bureau of Human Rights and Humanitarian Affairs.

Shepard, G. & Nanda, V. (1985). *Human rights and third world development.* Westport, CT: Greenwood press.

Spirer, H. & Spirer, L. (1993). *Data analysis for monitoring human rights.* Washington, DC: American Association for the Advancement of Science.

Springfield College, Department of Social Work. (1994-1995). *Master of Social Work Program's handbook of policies and procedures* (3rd ed.) Springfield, MA: Author.

Stamatapolou, E. (1989, Nov. 8-11). Presentation on the U.N.'s role in protecting human rights at the *National Conference on the United States and the UNited Nations. Washington, DC* (Available from UNA-USA, 485 Fifth Avenue, NY, NY 10017-6104).

Stamatapoulou, E. (1994). Indigenous peoples and the United Nations: Human rights as a developing dynamic. *Human rights quarterly, 16,* 58-81.

Stone, D. (1988). *Policy Paradox and political reason.* Boston: Scott Foresman.

Stringham, R. (1966) *Magna Carta: Fountainhead of freedom.* Rochester, NY: Aqueduct.

Sullivan, D. (1994). Women's human rights and the 1993 World Conference on Human Rights. *American Journal of International Law, 88,* 152-167.

Szabo, I. (1982). Historical foundations of human rights and subsequent developments. I K. Vasak (Ed.), *The international dimensions of human rights.* (Vol. 1) (pp. 11-41). Westport, CT: Greenwood.

Tessitore, J. & Woolfson, S. (Eds). (1991). *Issues before the 45th Geneal Assembly of the U.N.* Lexington, MA: Heath.

Tomasevski, K. (1993). *Women and human rights.* Atlantic Highland, NJ: Zed Books.

Trials and error in China. (February 1, 1991). *The New York Times,* p. 28.

Tyson, K. (1992). A new approach to relevant scientific research for practitioners: The heuristic paradigm. *Social Work, 37,* 541-556.

UN Human Rights Commission. (1989). *The ABC's of teaching about human rights.* Geneva: Author.

The United Nations. (1985) *The United Nations Chronicle.* New York: Author.

The United Nations. (1988). *Human rights machinery.* NY: Author.

United Nations Center for Human Rights (1981). *The regional and national dimensions of the right to development as a human right.* New York: Author.

Update on the draft Universal Declaration on the rights of Indigenous Peoples. (1994). *Nouvvelles Internationales HSD International News, 2*(1), 1-6. (Available from Hutchins, Soroka, & Dionne, 245 St.-Jacques Street, Montreal, Quebec H2Y 1M6)

U.S. Dept. of State. (1994a). *Country reports on human rights practices for 1993)* Washington, DC: U.S. Government Printing Office.

U.S. Dept. of State. (1994b). *International Covenant on Civil and Political Rights: Initial Report of the U.S.A. to the UN Human Rights committee.* Washington, DC: Government Printing Office.

U.S. Information regarding the world conference on human rights. (1993). Available from: The United States Information Service, Geneva Switzerland. (022) 749-4359.

Valle R., & Halling, S. (1989). *Existential-phenomenological perspectives in psychology.* New York: Plenum.

Van Bueren, G. (Ed.). *International documents on children.* Dordrecht, Netherlands: Martinus Nijhoff.

Van Soest, D. (1992). *Incorporating peace and social justice into the social work curriculum.* Washington, DC: National Association of Social Workers Peace and Social Justice Committee.

Van Boven, T. (1989). A people's commission. In R. Claude & B. Weston (Eds.), *Human rights in the world community* (188-189). Philadelphia: University of Pennsylvania Press.

Vasak, K. (1977). *A thirty year struggle: The sustained efforts to give force of law to the Universal Declaration of Human Rights. New York: United Nations.*

Vasak, K. (1982) Distinguishing criteria of human rights. In K. Vasak and P. Alston (Ed.), *The international dimensions of human rights* (Vol. 1) (pp. 3-10). Westport, CT: Greenwood.

Vienna Declaration and programme of action. (June 25, 1993). Available from: The U.N. Human Rights Commission, U.N. Plaza, N.Y., N.Y.

Weston, H. (1989). Human rights. In R. Claude and B. Weston (Eds.), *Human rights in the world community* (pp. 12-29). Philadelphia: University of Pennsylvania Press.

Weston, B., Lukes, R., & Hnatt, K. (1989). Regional human rights regimes: A comparison and appraisal. In R. Claude and B. Weston (Eds.) *Human rights in the world community* (pp. 208-220). Philadelphia: University of Pennsylvania Press.

Wilkie, C. (1993, October 24). Locked out of a world of words. *The Boston Globe,* p. 1.

Williams, C. (1991). *Black teenage mothers: Pregnancy and child rearing from their perspective.* Lexington, MA: Heath.

Wiseberg, L. (Ed.). (1990). *A guide to establishing a human rights documentation center.* Ottowa: University of Ottowa, Human Rights Internet.

Wronka, J. M. (1992). *Human rights and social policy in the 21st century: A history of the idea of human rights and comparison of the United Nations Universal Declaration of Human Rights with United States federal and state constitutions.* Lanham, MD: University Press of America.

Wronka, J. M. (1993a). Human rights, social policy, and indigenous people: A common thread. In *Proceedings from the Sovereignty Symposium VI: The word of the people.* (Available from Oklahoma Supreme Court, Room 204, State Capitol, Oklahoma City, OK 73105).

Wronka, J. M. (1993b). "Science" and Indigenous Cultures. *The Humanistic Psychologist, 21,* 341-353.

Wronka, J. M. (1993c). Teaching human rights in the social sciences. In V.K. Kool (Ed.), *Non-violence: Social and psychological issues* (pp. 259-268). Lanham, MD: University Press of America.

Wronka, J.M. (1994a). Human rights and social policy in the United States: An educational agenda for the 21st century [Special issue on human rights]. *Journal of Moral Education, 23,* 261-272.

Wronka, J.M. (1994b, Spring). Research and teaching human rights. In Earl Babbie (Ed.), *Teaching Methods,* Newsletter to accompany *The Practice of Social Research,* Belmont, Ca: Wadsworth.

Wronka, J. M. (in press). Creating a human rights culture. *Brandeis Review.*

Further Reading

Alexander, Y. (Ed.). (1994). *International Journal on Group Rights, 1*(1) [Entire issue]. Dordrecht, the Netherlands: Martinus Nijhoff.

Alston, P. (Ed.). (1992). *The United Nations and human rights: A critical appraisal.* NY: Oxford University Press.

Blaustein, A., Clark, R., & Sigler, J. (Eds.). (1987). *Human rights sourcebook.* NY: Paragon House.

Castelle, K. (1990). *In the child's best interest: A primer on the UN Convention on the Rights of the Child.* NY: Defense for Children International-USA.

Claude, R. & Weston, B. (Eds.). (1992). *Human rights in the world community.* Philadelphia: University of Pennsylvania Press.

Daes, E. (1986). *Principles, guidelines, and guarantees for the protection of persons detained on grounds of mental ill-health or suffering from mental disorder.* NY: United Nations.

Donnelly, J., & Howard, R. (1987). *International handobok of human rights.* Westport, CT: Greenwood Press.

Freeman, M., & Van Bueren, G. (1994). *International Journal of Children's Rights, 1*(1) [Entire issue]. Dordrecht, the Netherlands: Martinus Nijhoff.

Friedan, J., & Wiseberg, L. (1981). *Teaching human rights.* ottawa: University of Ottawa.

Gallagher, M. (1985). *Becoming aware: Human rights and the family.* Paris: UNESCO.

Human rights internet reporter. (1991). *Master list of human rights organizations and serial publications.* Ottawa: University of Ottawa, Human Rights Internet.

Lauerman, J. (in press). *Health and human rights: An international quarterly journal.* Cambridge, MA: Francois-Xavier Bagnoud Center for Health and Human Rights.

Lawson, E. (1991). *Encyclopedia of Human Rights.* Bristol, PA: Taylor & Francis.

Mower, A. (1991). *Regional human rights: A comparative study of the west European and inter-American systems.* Westport, CT: Greenwood Press.

Newman, F. & Weissbrodt, D. (1990). *Selected international human rights instruments.* Cincinnati: Anderson.

Rocha, R., & Roth, O. (1989). *The Universal Declaration of Human rights: An adaptation for children.* NY: United Nations.

Siegel, R. (1994). *Employment and human rights: The international dimension.* Philadelphia, PA: University of Pennsylvania Press.

United Nations. (1993). *Human rights and disabled persons.* NY: Author.

United Nations. (1994). *Human rights: A compilation of international instruments* (Vols. 1 & 2). NY: Author.

Van Bueren, G. (Ed.). (1993). *International documents on children.* Dordecht, the Netherlands: Martinus Nijhoff.

📖📖📖📖📖📖📖📖📖📖📖📖📖📖📖📖📖📖📖📖

ON THE UN HUMAN RIGHTS COMMITTEE'S CONSIDERATION OF THE INITIAL REPORT OF THE USA ON THE INTERNATIONAL COVENANT ON CIVIL AND POLITICAL RIGHTS... AND BEYOND*

Having attended the Human Rights Committee's Fifty-third session on March 29 and 31, 1995, I would like to share my observations concerning what appeared key issues between the United States and the committee with members of the Human Rights Interest Group. Then I will comment briefly on the new Human Rights Building of the Council of Europe in Strasbourg.

Mr. Aguilar, Chair of the Committee, began the sessions emphasizing that this was not a confrontation with the U.S., but rather the beginnings of a creative dialogue. He then introduced with much praise and as "the youngest survivor of Auschwitz" the US's recent appointee to the committee, Mr. Thomas Buergenthal. Throughout the hearings, committee members consistently welcomed Mr. Buergenthal, praising him for his scholarship and commitment.

Consistent with the rules of the committee, Mr. Buergenthal did not participate in the proceedings. On the 29th, the U.S. gave initial comments, followed by concerns addressed by the committee; on the 31st, the U.S. responded, followed by concluding comments of the committee. Interspersed with observations and some comments, I will try first to condense this interchange among issues that appeared most consistently raised, making note of names and quotes when possible. For expediency, I will comment only upon other issues, less constant it appeared, but, nevertheless, of paramount importance to the committee. Admittedly, this distinction is arbitrary, but I hope will give the reader a basic sense of this historic event.

Only a few copies of the report were available to the public who sat in the balcony. Only printings of the US's initial comments on the 29th, were

---

* Originally published in 5 Human Rights Interest Group Newsletter No. 3, at 14-16 (Fall 1995), copyright by the American Society of International Law, reprinted with permission.

given to the public, which ran out almost immediately. There were no handouts of the committee's concerns, nor of the U.S. responses. Mr. Shattuck, head of the U.S. delegation, commenting that "NGO's [non-governmental organizations] are the backbone of our domestic commitment...[who] will play a key role in the process of implementing the Covenant" urged that those sitting in the balcony could join the delegation and the committee members on the floor as a "symbolic" statement of cooperation.

Ms. Evatt, expert from Australia began the committee's comments, by noting that NGO's were having trouble getting the report. (Committee members, while appointed by their governments, function, nevertheless, in independent capacities.) The U.S. responded that the document is available through the Internet, but is also preparing additional printings.

The Committee's Main Concerns

Throughout, one major concern of the committee was the U.S. pronouncement that the Covenant, while ratified, was still "non self-executing," that is, non-enforceable in U.S. courts. Also brought up was Mr. Buergenthal's scholarly work, which concluded that ratified UN conventions should be enforceable. Briefly, the U.S. response was that its laws were already consistent with the basic provisions of the Covenant. American courts, nevertheless, were not "prevented from seeking guidance from the Covenant in interpreting American law." The Committee, however, while consistently praising the United States for its commitment to civil and political rights as evidenced in particular by its Bill of Rights which has served as a beacon throughout the world, expressed concern that the U.S. was in violation of some of the Covenant's provisions. It is noteworthy, that when one member brought up that the U.S. should be informed that there are other laws than those in the United States, smiles and quite laughter could be perceived among both the U.S. delegation and committee members.

Another basic concern was that "hate speech [in the U.S.] should be raised to the level of an obscenity." The U.S. response was that "no doubt hate speech is a cancer of the soul," but freedom of speech is highly protected in the U.S. and NGO's, in general, have a broad reading of that freedom.

Another major issue was application of the death penalty in general, particularly in regard to minors and the mentally retarded, which was contrary to the "worldwide trend towards abolishing the death penalty," according to the committee. As one member said: "A minor cannot buy a cigarette, but if over 16 can be sentenced to death"! The committee commented that in general, NGO's in the U.S. are against the death penalty. The U.S. felt, however, that the death penalty reflected the general will of the American public, "reflecting a serious deep considerate democratic choice of the American people." The U.S. also responded that it does not keep records on the intelligence level of those executed.

Also of major concern was that reference to state law throughout the report was "higgledy-piggledy" in the words of Mr. Lallah, expert from Mauritius. The report, thus, was not systematically organized to allow examination of states' laws. The U.S. responded that the relationship between federal and state law is "complicated," but that the "Federal government can establish uniform standards, but [ultimately]...cannot tell states how to behave."

According to the U.S., it is "not a dead letter issue...and is an appropriate matter to be resolved."

Of particular note also was a phrase in the report that in the United States, "Money is a form of speech." As Mr. Lallah put it "That is the way it is, but that is not the way it should be." Overall, members feared that this would unduly influence the electoral process, thereby reducing "minority representation in Congress." They also tended to view the election of judges in the U.S. disfavorably influencing the democratic process. The U.S. did acknowledge that poverty can certainly have an "impact" and those without money must be given adequate access to the legal system.

The committee appeared extremely serious about making the provisions of the Covenant law in the United States. They wanted to know, for instance, what was being done to educate the Supreme Court and other legal bodies about its provisions. The U.S. responded that it has informed the Supreme Court and state attorney generals of the Covenant. It also wants to make use of the federal judicial center and well as state judicial centers as means of educating appropriate parties.

The committee appeared especially concerned also with a "checkered history of bias" toward minorities. This included the historical and contemporary mistreatment of African-Americans, who were "six times more likely to be imprisoned [than Whites]" and Native Americans who, as stated in the committee's final comments, have a "high incidence of poverty, sickness and alcoholism...notwithstanding some improvements achieved" with their own self-governance, and Hispanics. According to the committee "poverty and lack of access to education adversely affect persons belonging to these groups in their ability to enjoy rights under the Covenant on the basis of equality." It is within this context of minority concerns that Ms. Evatt brought up rather eloquently that fact that "one in four children in the United States live in poverty." Ms. Rosalyn Higgins, expert from the United Kingdom, was especially concerned if self-governing programs for Native Americans were beginning to work. If so, could comparable programs be provided for other groups, like Latinos and African-Americans. In response to some of these issues, the U.S. did acknowledge that it was indeed "imperfect," and that there did exist "racial, gender discrimination, intolerance, and economic distress in portions of our population."

Additional Concerns

Roughly, of concern also were: reports of burgeoning chain gangs among prisoners, in particular, Alabama; states that would legally imprison consenting adults engaging in homosexual acts; compensation for military, but not civilian victims of nuclear testing; reference to indigenous people from Alaska as Native American, but if from Hawaii, solely as an ethnic group; whether affirmative action programs were indeed working; why, according to the report sterilization is permissible for individuals convicted of grand larceny, but not "mere embezzlers"; workplaces that appeared to allow an imposed "English language only" rule; an undue use and availability of firearms as a possible violation of the right to life; prison overcrowding and conditions, in particular in Oklahoma's supermax prisons where someone may be held indefinitely; "rather disturbing" cases regarding discrimination against women, for instance, a judge stating that a man raping a woman who had fainted was in an "ideal situation"; women prisoners who feared reprisal if they complained about lack of privacy and sexual abuse from male guards; apparent indefinite detention of excludable aliens; treatment of Haitians in Guantanamo; given the separation of church and state, why the U.S. gave educational aid to religious universities and colleges, but not secondary schools; apparent lesser standards of due process for indigent defendants and aliens; insufficient information in the report concerning reasons of scientific experimentation for medical purposes; a seeming lack of concern for the interests of the residents of the District of Columbia (when this was brought up, many cheers could be heard from the audience; an apparent legacy of Mc Carthyism, given the lack of mention of political opinion in the report as grounds for non-discrimination; and too much emphasis upon case law, rather than "facts from the field" in the report.

Space will not permit me to respond to each of these latter, but important, issues. But Mr. David Stewart, legal advisor for the Department of State, who wrote the report, has copies of the US's responses. He and the Department of State, in general, have been most cooperative in releasing information.

Economic, Social, and Cultural Rights

Thus, while obviously the meeting dealt with civil and political rights, (i.e. first generation) economic, social, and cultural rights (i.e. second generation) were brought up rather briefly and almost entirely in the context of the right to self-determination of minorities. I do not recall more "in depth" concerns about other economic and social rights, like homelessness, unemployment, or lack of access to health care, which were concerns of some NGO reports to the committee. I must also comment that, apart from the right to self-determination, solidarity rights (i.e. third generation), like rights to peace, development, and a clean environment were not mentioned. Thus, the human rights committee did not appear to entertain major "structural" issues (i.e. the right to a social and international order as mentioned in the Universal Declaration of Human Rights, the "authoritative definition" of human rights standards). In response to the Vienna Declaration, for instance, the U.S. officially stated that foreign invasion does not constitute a human rights violation. The U.S., furthermore, is the world's largest arms supplier; it also has the greatest percentage of billionaires and children living in poverty in the industrialized world. It is the only country to have vetoed the Declaration on the Right to Development.

At the conclusion of the meeting, some members of the committee, including Mr. Aguilar, the chairperson who had lived in "Beantown," spoke about their positive educational experiences in the United States. They also thanked the U.S. taxpayer. Mr. Aguilar concluded by saying that this creative dialogue will continue in 1998.

Unfortunately, media attention appeared barely negligible. It was neither in any of the major New York newspapers, which I purchased on the 30th nor in that Sunday's New York Times Week in Review. But Bravo to the U.S. delegation and the human rights committee! Good job! It was indeed the beginnings, as Mr. Aguilar hoped, of a creative and constructive dialogue.

If, indeed, the Universal Declaration and the "long train of covenants and declarations," which followed it are "milestone[s] in the long and difficult struggle of the human race" as Pope John Paul II asserted, then certainly this meeting between arguably the most powerful country in the world with other nations, also may have marked a turning point. The struggle continues.

Other Human Rights Experiences

My human rights "shenanigans" this summer took me to the University of Zurich, where I was also fortunate in June to also visit the new human rights building in Strasbourg on the day following its opening. It could be argued that it looks like the triptych of human rights machinery, which Rene Cassin spoke about. Roughly, it is in three sections. The middle is predominantly transparent, where visitors enter; on each side are modern looking relatively round, yet elevated structures, painted in bright silver, which gleamed that day in the sun. (If this makes no sense, sorry. You have to see it yourself. It's really something.)

For lack of a better word, the "vibes" in the building were entirely energetic and hopeful. Everyone seemed most optimistic about this edifice devoted entirely to advance human rights. The building, incidentally, has an excellent, and burgeoning library, with the most helpful librarians. With some informal conversations with lawyers, I was a bit disheartened, however, that their human rights court does not generally tend to hear cases dealing with economic, social, and cultural rights. However, they do have a committee that monitors these rights. Apparently, their decisions are binding as when, for instance, they declared that the Danish Government had to recognize a group of harbor workers' right to strike and that Switzerland could not lower the wages of Italian immigrant workers there, because the lira had gone down. The governments responded positively. Also upon reading some of the speeches from opening day, June 29, which included such notables as Vaclav Havel, President of the Czech Republic and M. Rolv Ryssdal, President of the European Court of Human Rights I would have liked more on economic and social rights. Yet, the thrust of these speeches, was overwhelmingly hopeful, even in these times of Bosnia, Sudan, and Rwanda. As Mr. Ryssdal said, "This new building is...first and foremost the home of those who consider that their rights and freedoms have been infringed and who turn to it in the hope of finding a European response to their questions and difficulties." Can you imagine such a building in the United States?

凹凹凹凹凹凹凹凹凹凹凹凹凹凹凹凹凹凹凹凹凹凹凹凹凹凹凹

SPRINGFIELD COLLEGE
SCHOOL OF SOCIAL WORK
SYLLABUS SPRING 1997

I. COURSE TITLE MSW 324 - HUMAN RIGHTS*

COURSE VALUE Two Semester Credits

INSTRUCTOR Joseph Wronka, Ph.D.
(413) 788-2411
E-mail: joseph_wronka@spfldcol.edu

II. COURSE TEXTS

Required:

International Federation of Social Work. (1994). *Social work and human rights*
New York: United Nations.

Newman, F. & Weissbrodt, D. (1996). *International Human Rights: Law,
policy, and process.* Cincinnati: Anderson.

Tomasevski, K. (1993). *Women and Human Rights.* Boston: Zed Books.

Wronka, J. (1992). *Human rights and social policy in the 21st century. A
history of the idea of human rights and comparison of the United Nations
Universal Declaration of Human Rights with United States federal and
state constitutions.* Lanham, MD: University Press of America.

---

* Originally published in *Global Perspectives in Social Work Education: A Collection
of Course Outlines on International Aspects of Social Work* (Council of Social Work
Education, 1997) 127-134, reprinted with permission.

The following readings, either whole or in part will be available in a packet the first day of class:

Abrams, M. (1991).*On the economic and social rights of the Universal Declaration*. Geneva Human Rights Commission

The Carter Center. (1993). *The Atlanta Statement*. Plains, GA: Author.

Chapman. A. (1993). *Exploring a human rights approach to health care reform*. Washington, DC: Association for the Advancement   of Science.

Cohen, C. (1995). Children's rights: an American perspective. In B.Franklin (Ed.), *Handbook of children's rights* (pp. 163-175). New York: Routledge.

Department of State. (1993). *The Vienna Declaration* and *Response to the Vienna Declaration*.   Washington, DC: Author.

Department of State. (1994). *International Covenant on Civil and Political Rights: Initial report of the .S.A. to the U.N. Human Rights Committee*. Washington: U.S. Government Printing Office.

Human rights and diplomacy. (1997, April 12). *The Economist*, 19-21.

Eide, A. (l987). United Nations Commission on Human Rights. *Report on the right to adequate food as a human right*.(E/CN.4/Sub.2/1987/23). New York: United Nations.

Ferrero, R. (l986). Sub-Commission on Prevention of Discrimination and Protection of Minorities. *The   new international economic order and the promotion of human rights* (E/CN.4/Sub.2/1983/24/Rev.1).   New York: United Nations.

Hiroaka, T. (1996, December). Reasons for the illegalization of nuclear weapons, *Peace and conflict   studies, 3*(2), 72-77.

Langley, W. (1997). The World Court and the legality of nuclear war. (In packet available from the   Coalition for a Strong United Nations.)

Reardon, B. (1995). *Educating for human dignity*. Philadelphia: University of Pennsylvania Press.

UNESCO. (1968). *Some suggestions about teaching human rights.* Geneva: Author.

United Nations. (1981). *The regional and national dimensions of the right to development as a human right. (E/CN.4/1488). New York: Author.*

United Nations. (1993). *Human rights and disabled persons.* Geneva: Author.

United Nations. (1989). *The rights of the child.* Geneva: Author.

United Nations. (1986). *Developmental Social Welfare.* New York: Department of International and   Economic and Social Affairs.

United Nations. (1994). *Declaration on the rights of disabled persons; declaration on the rights of mentally retarded persons; declaration on the protection of persons with mental illness; declaration on the eradication of hunger; declaration   on the rights of people to peace; United Nations Rules for the Protection of Juveniles.* New York: Author.

United Nations. (1995). *Platform for Action of the Fourth World   Conference on Women in Beijing.* New York: U.N. Department of Public Information.

Universal Declaration of Human Rights Project. (1993). *Statement of   Purpose and Action Alert to Repeal the Personal Responsibility and Work Opportunity Reconciliation Act of 1996, Public Law   104-193.* (Available from: Joseph Wronka, School of Social Work, Springfield College, Springfield, MA 01109).

Wronka, J. (1994) Human rights and social policy in the U.S.: An educational agenda for the 21st entury [Special issue on human rights]. *Journal of Moral Education, 23,* 261-272.

Wronka, J. (1995). On the U.N. Human Rights Committee's   consideration of the initial report of the US.A. on the International covenant on Civil and Political Rights. *Human   rights interest group newsletter of the American Society of International Law, 5*(3), 14-16.

Wronka, J. (1995, Winter). Creating a human rights culture. *Brandeis Review.*

Wronka, J. (1995). Human rights. Entry in *The Encyclopedia of   Social Work.* Washington, DC: National Association of Social Workers..

Recommended:

Alston, P. & Tomasevski, K. (1982). *The right to food.* Martinus   Nijhoff.

Claude, R. & Weston, B. (1992). *Human rights in the world community: Issues and action.* Philadelphia: University of Pennsylvania Press.

Franklin, B. (Ed.). (1995). *The Handbook of Children's Rights"   Comparative policy and practice.* New York: Routledge.

Harvard University Francois-Bagnoud Center. (1997).*Journal on Health   and Human Rights (latest edition).* Cambridge, MA: Harvard University Press.

Henkin, L. & Hargrove, J. (1994). *Human rights an agenda for the next century.* Washington, DC: American Society of International /Law.

Journal of Moral Education [Special human rights issue] Vol. 23, No. 3, 1994. (Carfax Publishing, The United Kingdom).

Laqueur & Rubin. (1990). *The human rights reader.* New York: New American Library.

Reardon, B. (1995). *Educating about human dignity: Learning about rights and responsibilities.* Philadelphia: University of Pennsylvania Press.

Siegel, R. (1994). *Employment and Human Rights.* Philadelphia: University of Pennsylvania Press.

United Nations. (1994). *A compilation of international instruments* (Vols. I & II). New York: Author.

U.S. Government Printing Office. (1994). *The International covenant on Civil and Political Rights: Initial Report of the USA to   the UN Human rights committee.* Washington, DC: Department of   State.

Also recommended are packets of readings from conferences at the JFK Library in Boston, in particular: The National Conference on Human Rights on December 10, 1994; the Conference on Reforming the United Nations, December 7, 1995; and the Conference on Individuals, Non-governmental organizations and the U.N. system on March 8, 1997. (Available from:

Coalition for a Strong United Nations: 2161 Massachusetts Avenue, Cambridge, MA 02140-1336).

III. COURSE DESCRIPTION

The purpose of this course is to examine how the idea of human rights can assist in the development of economic and social justice, thereby being a strategy for social change. In addition to the Universal Declaration of Human Rights, it examines some other "state-of-the art" documents, like the Rights of the Disabled, the Convention on the Elimination of Discrimination Against Women, the Rights of Mental Patients, and Youth or the Rights of the Child, which may advance social justice. It also examines strategies that governments, both domestic and foreign, as well as, non-governmental organizations (ngo's) have developed to realize and/or violate human rights. Its approach is that of scholar-practitioner and public-spirited citizen with particular emphasis upon the relevance of human rights to the helping and health professions, in particular, social work.

While it is true that much of the course emphasizes legal issues, its emphasis is upon the interface between the current state of international human rights law, which the serious human rights scholar-practitioner must be aware, and the directions that it appears international human rights law ought to aspire. In particular these directions are to develop social change strategies to fulfill human needs evolving particularly around economic, social, cultural, and solidarity rights. Human rights, after all, is nothing, but a powerful "social construct," moving people to act in the words of Eleanor Roosevelt, that can legally mandate the fulfillment of human need.

IV. COURSE OBJECTIVES

By the end of the course the student will be able to:

1. understand more in depth the Universal Declaration of Human Rights, but also some of its progeny, like the rights of the child, rights of the disabled, and the rights of women;

2. understand how human rights may be integrated into clinical, as well as, advanced generalist practice, that is, micro, mezzo, and macro dimensions of practice;

3. understand the particular relevance of human rights to the profession of social work and the health and helping professions in general;

4. understand ideological bases of United States reports on domestic and foreign compliance with human rights standards;

5. suggest strategies to engender economic, social, cultural and solidarity rights;

6. understand the importance of a people's, rather than elitist approach, to examining human rights standards

7. assess research-action strategies to move governments to comply with internationally recognized human rights instruments;

8. have a lived sense of the idea that every right has a corresponding duty;

9. understand the significance of public sentiment in the promotion of socially just policies;

10. develop public speaking, writing, and interpersonal abilities which should assist in the dissemination of the idea of human rights, in an attempt to expand people's consciousness;

11. understand strategies to teach human rights as "moral education";

12. understand how some governments implement some internationally recognized human rights standards, pertaining to children, the disabled, and of women;

13. understand what non-governmental organizations, like the Carter Center, are doing to advance humanrights;

14. hone our understanding of specific rights like health care, food, peace and to some extent shelter, employment and other rights;

15. have a thorough knowledge of the current state of international human rights law in the U.N., but to a lesser extent the regional systems, in particular the Inter-American system.

16. understand U.S. jurisprudence in the context of international human rights law;

17. understand issues pertaining to cultural relativism and the implementation of U.N. human rights law in general;

18. understand theories pertaining to the causes of human rights violations; and

19. develop strategies to act upon the understanding of human rights issues as discussed in this course.

V. COURSE OUTLINE AND READING ASSIGNMENTS

The format of this course is like a seminar. Thus, students will be able to choose an area of particular interest. They will examine human rights and other documents in this area and also what others are doing in their particular area of interest from which they can develop a research-action strategy. For example, students may be interested primarily in children's rights. Thus, they can become scholars in the area of children's rights, by understanding in depth the Rights of the Child, as well as, government arguments for or against that Convention. Students may also wish to do research into possibilities for funding in their interest area. (That same model can be used for the right to peace, rights of the disabled, rights of women, rights of mental patients etc.)

In addition, however, students must also read the required readings that should give them a "state-of-the-art" appreciation of current issues in the broad area of human rights. Topics with corresponding readings are below. These readings should assist in "lived" understanding of how to promote a "human rights culture," the major thrust of this course.

Module I. Introduction to human rights; Toward the creation of a human rights culture; the interrelationship between human rights and social policy; a history of the idea of human rights; toward the integration of human rights and the micro, mezzo, and macro levels with particular attention to the profession of social work; the interdependence and indivisibility of human rights; the interconnectedness between rights, duties, and a social and international order.

Readings: Wronka (1992), chapters 1 & 2; Wronka (all readings for 1995); International Federation of Social Work (1994).

In packet: Abrams, M. (1991); Eide, A. (1987)

Module II: History of human rights continued with emphasis upon the debates prior to the signing of the Universal Declaration; The human rights triptych; the Universal Declaration of Human Rights as customary international law; A comparison of the Universal Declaration with U.S. federal and state constitutions. The formation of the U.N.; the Nuremberg and Tokyo tribunals; Regional human rights organizations, such as the European and Inter-American System; an introduction to other human rights instruments such as pertaining to juveniles, "mentally retarded persons," "disabled persons"; "mental illness: and the right to peace.

Readings: Wronka (1992), chapters 3-5; Newman and Weissbrodt (1996), chapter 1.
In packet: The Universal Declaration of Human Rights Project (1993); The Carter Center (1993); United Nations (1994).

Module III: The ratification and implementation of human rights treaties; The International Covenant on Economic, Social, and Cultural Rights; international implementation and enforcement mechanisms; the U.N. human rights committees; State reporting under the international human rights treaties with particular attention to the United States; The initial U.S. report to the U.N. committees.

Readings: Newman and Weissbrodt (1996), chapters 2-3.
In packet: Department of State (1993 & 1994)

Module IV: State reporting under international human rights treaties; the situation in Iran; International law prohibiting torture; the European system; cultural relativism and international human rights law.

Readings: Newman and Weissbrodt (1996), chapter 4.

Module V: U.N. procedures available for violations of human rights; the case of Burma (Myanmar); the 1235 and 1503 procedures; the Freedom of Information Act; Collective and Unilateral Humanitarian Intervention; the redress and punishment of human rights violations; the Nuremberg principles; the International Tribunal for the Former Yugoslavia; Creating a Permanent International Court

Readings: Newman and Weissbrodt, (1996), chapters 5-7

In packet: Human rights ad diplomacy (1997)

Module VI: International human rights fact finding; the case of Rwanda; analysis, verification, and follow-up; the experience of the Inter-American Commission; the impact of fact-finding; incorporating human rights goals into U.S. foreign policy; defining and implementing U.S. human rights policy.

Readings: Newman and Weissbrodt, (1996), chapters 8-9.

Module VII: The problem of interpretation of human rights instruments; the case of Baby-Boy; the Inter-American Commission on Human Rights and Jurisprudence of the Inter-American Commission; other regional systems; the European system with emphasis upon homosexuality, the death penalty, and corporal punishment; The Greek case; human rights law in Europe apart from the European Convention

Readings: Newman ad Weissbrodt, (1996), chapters 10-11.

Module VIII: U.S. remedies for violations outside and within the United States; Alien-Tort litigation; international rules governing rape; the Torture Victim Protection Act; Using international law to guide interpretation of U.S. law; the doctrine of non-self execution of treaties; the current state of U.S. ratification of human rights treaties; obstacles to invoking international human rights law

Readings: Newman and Weissbrodt, (1996), chapters 12-13.

Module IX: Refugee and Asylum human rights considerations; gender-based refugee claims, such as female genital mutilation; spousal violence based asylum; women's human rights violations in general; a platform of action.

Readings: Newman and Weissbrodt, (1996), chapter 14; Tomasevski, (1993).

Module X: Political, economic, sociological, psychological, and sociocultural theories of causation of human rights violations; the theory of capitalism and overpopulation; the possible role of development; group identity and scapegoating; the European witch-case; the socialization of killing; the necessity of speaking up.

Readings: Newman and Weissbrodt, (1996), chapter 15.

Module XI: Human rights and disabled persons; children's rights

Readings: In packet: United Nations, (1989 & 1993); Cohen (1995).

Module XII: An examination of solidarity rights; the right to peace and the right to development in particular

Readings: In packet: Ferrero (1986); United Nations (1981 & 1986); Hiroaka 1996); Langley (1997)

Module XIII: Strategies for teaching human rights as "moral" education.

Readings: In packet; 'UNESCO (1968); Reardon, (1995); Wronka (1994)

Module XIV: A rigorous inquiry: What then shall we do?

There are no readings for this module.

Module XV: Student presentations on research-action human rights projects

VI. METHODS OF INSTRUCTION

Students are taught to critically reflect upon the relevance of human rights theory and praxis to promote social justice. This reflection ought to be "dragged into" one's "vital labors" as the phenomenologist Merleau-Ponty called it, in such a way that should not merely be cognitive (the mind), but that may also require changes in heart (the spirit) and conduct (the body), roughly consistent with the Humanics mission of this School of Social Work and Springfield College. To facilitate such a critical inquiry, this class will emphasize in part didactic methods of teaching, yet also rely largely on group discussion in seminar format, coupled with experiential exercises designed to foster a lived sense of the meaning of human rights.

This course, therefore, works on the assumption that "information is power," especially when people do not know that their human rights are being violated. This information, however, must be "lived" in the sense that this knowledge leads a person to social action. The instructor, furthermore, will act primarily as a resource to facilitate learning within the broad area of human rights, hoping to act as a "catalyst" to assist in igniting students' passions to pursue human rights research-action projects.

VII. ASSIGNMENT

Students are to hand in one paper on their particular area of interest in the broad field of human rights roughly between 20 and 30 pages. This paper ought to be in the form of a research-action project as discussed in class. Students also ought to do the readings and participate in class accordingly. Given the seminar nature of this class, students' participation will count equally toward the final grade.

VIII. SELECT BIBLIOGRAPHY

Alston, P. (1990). U.S. ratification of the covenant on economic, social and cultural rights: The need for an entirely new strategy. *American Journal of International Law, 84*, 365-393.

Amnesty International. (1991). *Amnesty International Report 1991.* New York: Author. In A. P. Blaustein, R. S. Clark, & J. A. Sigler, (Eds.). (1987). *Human rights sourcebook.* New York: Paragon House.

Brownlie, I. (Ed.). (1971). *Basic documents on human rights.* Oxford: Clarendon Press.

Claude, R. P., & Weston B. (Eds.). (1992). *Human rights in the   world community.* Philadelphia: University of Pennsylvania Press.

Donnelly, J. (1989). *Universal human rights in theory and practice.* Ithaca, NY: Cornell University Press.

Donnelly, J. & Howard R. (1987). *International handbook of human rights.* New York: Greenwood.

Drinan, R. (1987) *Cry of the oppressed: The history and hope of the human rights revolution.* San Francisco: Harper and Row.

Eide, A. (1987). *United Nations Commission on Human Rights. Report on the right to adequate food as a human right.* (E/CN.4/SUB.2/1987/23). New York: United Nations.

Ferrero, R. (1986). Sub-Commission on Prevention of Discrimination and Protection of Minorities. *The new international economic order and the promotion of human rights.* (E/CN.4/Sub.2/1983/24/Rev.1). New York: United Nations.

Flanz, G. & Blaustein, A. (1997). *Constitutions of the countries of the world.* Dobbs Ferry, NY: Oceana.

Friedman, J. and Wiseberg, L. (1981). *Teaching human rights.* Washington,   DC: Human Rights Internet.

Gil, D., & Gil, E. (Eds.). (1985). *The future of work.* Rochester, VT: Schenkman.

Gil, D. (in press). *Confronting social injustice.* New York: Columbia University Press.

Green, J. F. (1956). *The U.N. and human rights.* Washington: Brookings Institute.

Harvey, P. (1989). *Securing the right to employment.* Princeton: Princeton University Press.

Human rights internet. (1991). *For the record: Indigenous peoples and slavery in the United Nations.* Ontario: Author.

Laqueur, W., & Rubin, B. (Eds.). (1990). *The human rights reader* (rev. ed.). New York: New American Library.

Lauterpacht, H. (1950). *International law and human rights.* London: Stevens and Sons.

Lillich, R. (1989). The Constitution and international human rights. *American Journal of International Law, 83(4),* 851-862.

Meron, T. (1989). *Human rights and humanitarian norms as customary law.* Oxford: Clarendon.

Paust, J. J. (1983). Human dignity as a constitutional right: A jurisprudentially based inquiry into criteria and content. *Howard Law Journal, 27,* 144-225.

Rosenzweig, M. (1988). Psychology and United Nations human rights efforts. *American Psychologist, 43,* 79-86.

United States Government Printing Office. (1997). *Human Rights   Report   of Foreign Countries.* Washington, DC: Author.

Wronka, J.M. (1995). Human rights (1405-1418). In R. Edwards, (Ed.), *Encyclopedia of Social Work* 19th ed.) Washington, DC: NASW Press.

Note: An extended bibliography attached to the human rights entry in the Encyclopedia of Social Work will also be available on the first day of class. Also, please pay special attention to bibliographies with corresponding electronic data resources included in Newman and Weissbrodt (1996).

📖📖📖📖📖📖📖📖📖📖📖📖📖📖📖📖📖📖📖📖📖

TESTIMONY FOR THE

Act To Protect Universal Human Rights to Work and Live Life in Dignity*
(S. No 89, H. No 4165)
State of Massachusetts
June 1997

Humility not Arrogance to Advance Human Rights

Inscribed on the walls upon entrance to the Holocaust Museum are the words of President Clinton that humility not arrogance are necessary to advance the cause of human rights. This Act to Protect Universal Human Rights is an excellent way to heed these words by humbly acknowledging that even in this country, despite its wealth, there are among us numerous poor, homeless, and hungry. The Children's Defense Fund recently found, for example, that "one out of six children go to bed hungry each night in the United States or are at risk of being hungry."

The United States as Leader in the Field of Human Rights

Surely, the United States historically has led the world in its quest for fundamental freedoms. The Bill of Rights, a "beacon of hope" as a member of the United Nations Human Rights Committee recently called it is but one example. Also, it was President Roosevelt who called the Conference of Evian in 1938 to stop Hitler's maltreatment of Germany's citizens, primarily Jews, but also, gypsies (Roma), Poles, gays and lesbians, and people with disabilities. Though the conference was a failure, later Eleanor Roosevelt became Chairperson of the committee that eventually led to the ratification of the Universal Declaration of Human Rights in 1948. Today, that document is increasingly referred to as *customary international law*, especially since the

---

* For more information on this bill contact, the Human Rights Project, Somerville, 49 Francesca Ave., MA 02144.

298 *Human Rights and Social Policy in the 21st Century*

case precedenting Filartiga v. Pena (1980), where Federal judges Feinberg, Kearse, and Kaufmann ruled in essence that no torturer shall ever be allowed to live in this country. The United States role as leader is indisputable.

What About Economic, Social, and Cultural Rights?

The leadership role of the United States, however, appears primarily in regard to civil and political rights roughly found in the first twenty one articles of the Universal Declaration. I ask you: What is freedom of speech, or the press, or assembly to a person who is homeless, hungry, and unemployed? The rest of that document deals primarily with economic, social and cultural rights, which are the major thrusts of this Act, such as the right to rest and leisure, the rights to food, housing, medical care and just and favorable remuneration for work. Human rights are interdependent.

Toward the Creation of a Human Rights Culture

In my doctoral dissertation, which compared the Universal Declaration with United States federal and state constitutions I found that economic, social, and cultural rights are rarely mentioned. If, indeed, constitutions reflect the will of the people, also the ultimate aim of government, then this Act to Protect Universal Human Rights may serve as a "springboard" to expand popular conceptions of human rights, which the public appears to equate largely with the Bill of Rights, a beautiful, but, nevertheless, limited document. By expanding these debates we can eventually move toward a *Human Rights Culture* which is nothing more than a "lived awareness" of human rights principles, of a society committed to social justice. We have some of this, for example, in our neighboring Canada where its citizens accept the fact that a substantial sum of taxes pays for health care which is "free" for its citizens.

I know of no other similar act in this country. It appears a significant breakthrough. The Massachusetts legislature in tandem with the committed organizations sponsoring this bill appear on the cutting edge on what might lead to what scholars and activists have referred to as an "economic and social glasnost" in this country.

Only chosen values endure. I think that this Act would be an excellent way to provoke discussion and debate, so people can choose their values freely. Such discussion is the only avenue in an open society such as ours to create social policy.

Human Rights as a Predictor of Well-Being

Dr. David Gil, professor of social policy at Brandeis in his *Violence Against Children,* a nation wide study of child abuse, found that a major predictor of domestic violence was unemployment, underemployment, and lack of collective bargaining. Dr. Constance Williams, also of Brandeis, in her *Black Teenage Mothers* found that the greatest predictor of teenage pregnancy was lack of education. Both employment and education are just a couple of rights in articles 22 through 30 of the Universal Declaration. Education also is a predictor of family size, according to the annual *State of the World* (1997). This society which tolerates such high levels of unemployment and underemployment, one estimate being 33.9 million, according to the National Jobs for All Coalition out of New York City and also has "more malls than high schools" as stated in *State of the World* , (1993), is indicative surely of numerous problems.

Will Future Generations also Cry Shame?

The Conference of Evian now shames, and rightly so, many of the world's governments. At that time, the United States, despite its leadership role, was fearful that attention to Hitler's abuses would cause the world to also examine human rights abuses here, such as racism and poverty; the Soviet Union was fearful of attention to its Gulag; and Europe feared approbation from its policies in Africa.

Perhaps some of you may find it a "long haul" from the Conference of Evian to this Act to Protect Universal Human Rights, but I don't think it is. Today, when no country would dare say it is against human rights, we wonder how in 1938 the world just watched. Failure to take steps then, resulted in one of the most dreadful pogroms in history.

Surely, this Act to Protect Universal Human Rights to Work and Live Life in Dignity is a major step toward the creation of a socially just world, which we all aspire. Failure to enact it I think ,may also make future generations wonder why this state was so reluctant, given the pressing problems of the time, such as homelessness, children in poverty, and lack of health care. Will future generations also cry "shame" ? Finally, this Act it is an excellent way, in the spirit of President Clinton's call for humility to heed the ancient injunction to "examine the log in one's own eye, before plucking the spec from another's."

Thank you for your attention.

Joseph Wronka

INDEX

Author's Biographical Sketch

Joseph Wronka, Ph.D. is presently Associate Professor, School of Social Work, Springfield College where he teaches predominantly social policy, human rights, and qualitative research. He is also Research Associate, Heller Graduate School, Center for Social Change, Brandeis University where he serves as Principal Investigator OF The Universal Declaration of Human Rights Project, which aims to monitor countries' compliance with essentially the economic, social, cultural, and solidarity rights of the Declaration. He is also Vice-president of the World Citizen Foundation, serves on the editorial boards of Clarity Press and the Journal of Peace and Conflict Studies, and advisory boards of the Backman Center for Social Justice, the Economic and Social Human Rights Network, and the Human Rights Monitoring Project He received his doctorate in social policy from the Heller School, master's from Duquesne University, and bachelor's from Brooklyn College. He also did postgraduate work at the University of Nice, France.

Prior to receiving his doctorate, he lived in Alaska for six years where he directed a mental health/substance abuse center, developed a paraprofessional generalist counselor training program, practiced as a counselor and clinician, and was group coordinator for the Fairbanks chapter of Amnesty International. Before Alaska, he worked for approximately four years as clinician in the Bedford-Stuyvesant section of New York City. He also has had extensive college teaching experience in the human and social sciences.

DATE DUE

DEMCO, INC. 38-2931